Lost Palaces
of Hawai'i

Lost Palaces of Hawai'i

Royal Residences of the Kingdom Period

RALPH THOMAS KAM

McFarland & Company, Inc., Publishers
Jefferson, North Carolina

Library of Congress Cataloguing-in-Publication Data

Names: Kam, Ralph Thomas, author.
Title: Lost palaces of Hawaiʻi : royal residences of the Kingdom Period / Ralph Thomas Kam.
Description: Jefferson, North Carolina : McFarland & Company, Inc., Publishers, 2022 | Includes bibliographical references and index.
Identifiers: LCCN 2022027141 | ISBN 9781476688114 (paperback : acid free paper) ∞
ISBN 9781476646343 (ebook)
Subjects: LCSH: Hawaii—History—19th century. | Palaces—Hawaii. | Lost architecture—Hawaii. | Hawaii—Kings and rulers—Dwellings. | BISAC: HISTORY / United States / State & Local / West (AK, CA, CO, HI, ID, MT, NV, UT, WY) | ARCHITECTURE / History / General
Classification: LCC DU627 .K36 2022 | DDC 996.9/02—dc23/eng/20220629
LC record available at https://lccn.loc.gov/2022027141

British Library cataloguing data are available
ISBN (print) 978-1-4766-8811-4
ISBN (ebook) 978-1-4766-4634-3

© 2022 Ralph Thomas Kam. All rights reserved

No part of this book may be reproduced or transmitted in any form or by any means, electronic or mechanical, including photocopying or recording, or by any information storage and retrieval system, without permission in writing from the publisher.

Front cover: Keōua Hale, the former palace of Princess Ruth Keʻelikōlani in Honolulu (Hawaiʻi State Museum of Natural and Cultural History)

Printed in the United States of America

*McFarland & Company, Inc., Publishers
Box 611, Jefferson, North Carolina 28640
www.mcfarlandpub.com*

To my wife, Kathy,
and children,
Emalani and Joshua

Acknowledgments

Special thanks go to the staff of the Hawaii State Archives; Archives of the Hawaiian Historical Society; Bishop Museum Archives; Department of Accounting and General Services Land Survey Office; Department of Accounting and General Services Bureau of Conveyances; Hawaiian Mission Children's Society Library; Legislative Reference Bureau Library; Tropic Lightning Museum; and Beach Bum Café. Also David Forbes; Chloe Greer; Andie Scelsi; Catherine Robertson, Phillips Library, Peabody Essex Museum; George Miles, Yale Collection of Western Americana, Beinecke Rare Book & Manuscript Library; Lawrence B. Conyers, department of anthropology, University of Denver.

Portions of Chapter 5 have previously appeared in "Remembering the Royal Residences of Kapālama: The Homes of Princess Ruth Keʻelikōlani and Queen Liliʻuokalani," *Hawaiian Journal of History*, Vol. 47 (2013). The Hawaiian Historical Society has kindly granted permission to use the material.

Table of Contents

Acknowledgments	vi
Preface	1
Introduction	3
Chapter 1. Royal Residences of Hawaiʻi Island	11
Chapter 2. Royal Residences of Maui and Molokaʻi	32
Chapter 3. Royal Residences of Waikīkī	52
Chapter 4. Royal Residences of the Palace Yard and Vicinity	92
Chapter 5. Other Royal Residences of Oʻahu	121
Chapter 6. Royal Residences of Kauaʻi	222
Chapter 7. Preservation of Lost Palaces	231
Conclusion	243
Chapter Notes	247
Bibliography	265
Index	283

"History becomes more real when we can stand upon some spot of ground and in imagination picture the great events that happened there."
—Ralph S. Kuykendall,
Report of the Historical Commission, 1923

Preface

The construction of a science building at Honolulu Community College started the twisty trail that ended with this book. A banyan tree grew squarely in the center of the proposed site for the new campus. A newspaper had years earlier reported that a portion of the banyan tree that once stood at the corner of King and Keʻeaumoku streets had been given to the school to try and preserve. Was the tree on campus the result of the effort to keep alive part of the King Street tree? As it turns out, the portion of the banyan tree had survived at the community college but had been relocated to Magic Island years ago. The quest to find out more led to an article, titled "The Legacy of ʻĀinahau: The Genealogy of Kaʻiulani's Banyan," *Hawaiian Journal of History*. The research also revealed another banyan at Kaʻiulani Elementary and one more across King street between Kaumakapili Church and St. Elizabeth's Episcopal Church. That tree, now gone, helped identify the location of the residences of Princess Ruth Keʻelikolani and Queen Liliʻuokalani. Maps revealed another residence of Prince Albert Kunuiakea nearby.

Those identifications of royal residences became the core of another article in the *Hawaiian Journal of History*, titled "Remembering the Royal Residences of Kapālama: The Homes of Princess Ruth Keʻelikōlani and Queen Liliʻuokalani." With two lost palaces identified, who could resist finding the others?

Ralph Thomas Kam
ʻĀhuimanu, Kāneʻohe, Hawaiʻi

Introduction

Loaʻa ka hale i ke aliʻi.
The chief has a house.[1]

Guidebooks to Hawaiʻi give tourists an adequate presentation concerning the remaining royal palaces: ʻIolani Palace, Washington Place, and Hānaiakamalama (Queen Emma Summer Palace) on Oʻahu and Huliheʻe Palace on the island of Hawaiʻi. They give glimpses into the lives of members of Hawaiian royalty who lived in the residences. The four surviving structures, however, cannot adequately represent the more than seven dozen dwellings that served as residences of the Hawaiʻi royalty and high chiefs during the Kingdom of Hawaiʻi. Missing, too, are surviving examples from Maui and Kauaʻi. While the four buildings are precious reminders of the monarchy, the remaining palaces fail to do justice to the broad range of palace types and architectural styles or to show the rapid evolution of the residences following contact with the West. The first, ʻIolani Palace, shares its unique style with no other building. At the laying of the cornerstone, the *Pacific Commercial Advertiser* described the future palace as being built "in the ornate style known as the 'American composite.'"[2] The same newspaper created its own name of the style of the completed palace: "The design of the exterior of the building cannot be described in a few words or referred to any recognized order of architecture. If a name is to be coined for it we should favor 'American Florentine' as the nearest approach to a correct one."[3] The latter three Greek Revival structures were built within an eleven-year period: Huliheʻe in 1838; Hānaiakamalama, 1847; and Washington Place, 1848.

It is the *lost* palaces of Hawaiʻi—the structures that were built and disappeared during the kingdom period and the decades following the overthrow of the monarchy—that more accurately express the full range of palaces present during the reigns of first ruler of the united kingdom, King Kamehameha I, through the last monarch, Queen Liliʻuokalani.

Palaces?

Though sometimes defined as the "*official* residence of a *sovereign*"[4] [italics mine], "palace" here is meant to more broadly refer to the dwellings of any member of royalty buried at Mauna ʻAla, the royal mausoleum in Nuʻuanu, the Lunalilo Mausoleum on the Kawaiahaʻo Church grounds, the royal section of Waiola Cemetery, Lahaina, Maui, or named as a high chief by the king or privy council. Although certainly not on the scale

'Iolani Palace as it appeared soon after its completion in the 1880s. Its eclectic style defied standard classification, resulting in its designation as "American Florentine" (courtesy Hawaii State Archives, PP-10-6-007).

Hulihee Palace, built in the Greek Revival style by Gov. Kuakini in 1838, sits behind the now lost *hale pili* of Ruth Ke'elikōlani (courtesy Hawaii State Archives, PP-10-1-18).

Hānaiakamalama, shown in an 1853 sketch by Swiss artist Paul Emmert, served as the country residence of Queen Emma and Kamehameha IV. Built in 1847, Keoni Ana or John Young II, bequeathed the Greek Revival house to his niece. Detail of "View of Honolulu No. 2" (courtesy Hawaii State Archives, PP-38-1-006]).

of the palaces of Europe or Asia, members of royalty and others referred to the houses as palaces. Archibald Campbell, who visited Hawai'i from 1809 to 1810, called Kamehameha's compound in Honolulu a "palace"[5] in his account titled *A Voyage Round the World*, published in 1819. In 1824 the residence of the Kalanimoku (Chapter 5), was referred to by missionary Charles S. Stewart as a "palace," and in 1829 Ephraim Eveleth called the *hale pili* at Kamakahonu (Chapter 1) the "rude palace of Riho Riho [Liholiho]."[6] Even in the latter days of the monarchy the practice continued; in *Hawaii's Story by Hawaii's Queen*, Lili'uokalani refers to her Kapālama house as "Muolaulani Palace," (Chapter 5) the same designation as the kingdom's official residence, "'Iolani Palace." Manly Hopkins, Hawaiian "Consul-General of the Hawaiian Islands for the United Kingdom of Great Britain and Ireland,"[7] put the designation of "palace" in perspective with his comparison of Western palaces to Hale Ali'i (Chapter 4) in his 1862 work, *Hawaii: The Past, Present, and Future of Its Island-kingdom*:

Queen Liliʻuokalani seated in 1893, the year of the overthrow of the monarchy, in front of Washington Place. Built in 1848 by her father-in-law, the Greek Revival house served as her residence and that of her husband, John O. Dominis (courtesy Hawaii State Archives, PP-98-13-014).

> Suffice it to say of the palace, without tedious description, that it is appropriate, and it is in proportion to the kingdom and the capital of the islands; and in this it differs from the royal residences in some of the small German States where the palace occupies half the town and its gardens a quarter of the territory.[8]

Transition from Traditional to Western

Each of the chapters of the *Lost Palaces of Hawaii* seeks to address three historical aspects: the rapid adoption of Western building methods, the abandonment of traditional forms of construction, and the eventual adaptation of the beneficial aspects of the traditional forms into the evolved Western structures and in some cases the reintroduction of *hale pili*.

With the continual interaction with the West following the contact of Captain James Cook, Hawaiʻi experienced the rapid adoption of Western building methods and styles by the royal family and high chiefs of the kingdom. The demand for the foreign form of housing came to the kingdom early and the acquisition of knowledge of how to build Western structures required foreigners with carpentry skills. Thus the records of the voyages of John Turnbull between 1801 and 1804 included the cautionary warning to visiting mariners regarding their skilled carpenters: "it was at length discovered that our carpenter had secretly conveyed himself into one of the canoes, and had thus been carried on shore. [...] The acquisition of such a person was of inestimable value to

Tamahama [Kamehameha I] and there seemed no doubt that, conscious of the value of their prize, they would defend it with their utmost efforts." Given their inability of the crew of the *Margaret* to mount a force to recover the deserter, Turnbull expressed: "we thought it more prudent to put up with our loss; although of a person whom we could so ill spare."⁹

Turnbull recorded that the "Sandwich islanders have reached more than one gradation higher in the scale of civilization, and, understanding their own interest, consider their European visitors as the importers of new arts, and new skill and industry, into their country. The voyage of [Capt.] George Vancouver has made a most eminent and permanent change in the situation of these islanders. They have taken a leap, as it were, into civilization."¹⁰

Charles Stewart, who lived in the kingdom from 1823 to 1825 and again visited in 1829, described the complex of several *hale pili*, as the equivalent of separate rooms in Western houses. He wrote of the *kauhale* of Kekūanāoʻa, governor of Oʻahu: "Had I entered them by accident without knowing to whom they belonged I should not have thought of being in the residence of a native but from the finish of every part and from the furniture I should have supposed myself in the rooms of some foreign gentleman."¹¹

Stewart was especially impressed by the astonishing pace of change that he observed. He found change that would have taken a hundred years elsewhere compressed into a couple years in Hawaiʻi: "Contrasted with the one into which you were received in 1823 in those days considered highly respectable and elegant and with that in which Lord [George Anson] Byron and suite were ushered in 1825 the difference is equal almost to the improvements that would take place in a century in the abodes of royalty in most other countries and greater than that which now exists between the new and the old rooms in Windsor Castle."¹²

English missionary William Ellis saw the transition from traditional Hawaiian *hale pili* to Western style buildings as a mark of the civilizing effect of Christianity. He noted after a discussion of the schools that had been established by the missionaries: "Several have forsaken their grass huts," Ellis wrote, "and erected comfortable stone or wooden houses among which one built by Karaimoku the prime minister is highly creditable to his perseverance and his taste."¹³ The American missionaries had been charged to "aim at short at covering these islands with fruitful fields, and *pleasant dwellings* [italics mine], and schools and churches and of raising a whole people to an elevated state of Christian civilization."¹⁴ Théodore-Adolphe Barrot, a French diplomat who arrived in Hawaiʻi aboard the *Bonite* in September 1836, bemoaned the loss of "the originality of ancient times."¹⁵ The "Vue de Honolulu" by an artist from the *Bonite* shows just how quickly Western structures had become the dominant form. Two decades earlier, Louis Choris had recorded a "Vue de port Hanarourou" that, save the fort and buildings within it, consisted exclusively of *hale pili*.

Arranged by Island

Lost Palaces of Hawaiʻi looks at residences of the *aliʻi* by island. This arrangement allows the reader to encounter the lost palaces in a rough chronological ordering within their geographical context. The order also reflects the sequence of the integration of the islands by conquest into the united kingdom as well as the major migration of the

"Vue de Honolulu" from the 1836 voyage of Auguste Nicolas Vaillant shows the multitude of Western structures that replaced the *hale pili* on the waterfront near the harbor (courtesy Hawaii State Archives, REFVOY-3-002).

Honolulu in 1816 by Louis Choris, artist on the *Rurik* (courtesy Hawaii State Archives, REFVOY-1-042). Western structures rise above the top of the wall of the fort, while *hale pili* surround the fort outside its walls.

royal court and the capital across the island chain from Kamehameha's political base on island of Hawai'i to Maui and eventually to O'ahu.

Royal Residences of Hawai'i Island

The palaces of the island of Hawai'i in Chapter 1 include a high proportion of *hale pili*, traditional thatched structures that populated the *kauhale* or complex of residences of Kamehameha I at Kamakahonu, the residence of Chiefess Kekelaokalani and the birthplace of Kamehameha III in Keauhou. But the residences also reveal the beginnings of the evolution toward Western structures and building methods. Even the highly traditional complex at Kamakahonu included an early Western stone storage structure. The stone residence of his war counsel, Englishman John Young, built in the Western style, most likely included a roof thatched with *pili* grass. The royal residences of Hawai'i island, too, show the migration to the Western houses of Chiefess Kapi'olani and Princess Likelike.

Royal Residences of Maui and Moloka'i

Chapter 2 studies the royal residences of Maui and Moloka'i, the second group of islands conquered by Kamehameha. With the establishment of the capital in Lahaina, on Maui, the same mix of traditional and Western structures, first seen on Hawai'i, were built. The changes included not just Western structures standing side by side with traditional buildings, but the integration of Western elements into traditional *hale pili*. Halekamani featured the admixture of Western and traditional elements. Even the Western structures often took advantage of the latest in building technology. Hale Piula used pewter-colored galvanized corrugated iron for its roofing within a short period after its introduction in London.

Royal Residences of O'ahu

The island of O'ahu, the final location of the kingdom's capital, features the greatest number of the lost palaces, around two-thirds of the total. The palaces on O'ahu, therefore, are divided into three chapters. The first, Chapter 3, looks at the palaces of Waikīkī, where Kamehameha I initially established his government, and where royalty later established their retreats from the everyday commotion of government and business.

The second of the O'ahu chapters, Chapter 4, looks at the official palace, Hale Ali'i, and surveys the houses of court that grew up around it. The third O'ahu chapter, Chapter 5, examines the remaining royal residences, including Kaniakapūpū, where Kamehameha III celebrated the restoration of his kingdom with ten thousand of his subjects, and Keōua Hale, built by Princess Ruth Ke'elikōlani to rival King David Kalākaua's 'Iolani Palace.

A note on directions: Directions on O'ahu use the following terms: "mauka," meaning towards the mountains; "makai," towards the ocean; "Diamond Head," towards Diamond Head; and "'Ewa," towards 'Ewa. In Honolulu, the directions correspond roughly to mauka, northeast; makai, southwest; Diamond Head, southeast; and 'Ewa, northwest.

Royal Residences of Kauaʻi

In Chapter 6, the palaces on Kauaʻi, the last island to fall under the control of the Kingdom of Hawaiʻi, reflect the move of its king, Kaumualiʻi, and his court to Oʻahu, and the establishment of island governors to oversee the island.

Preservation Efforts

Chapter 7 examines the mostly unsuccessful efforts to preserve the royal residences.

Conclusion

The final chapter offers some concluding thoughts on the importance of preserving a memory of the lost palaces. This chapter also gives a call to action for marking the palace sites as well as a rationale.

While this volume examines more than seven dozen residences of royalty, many others have drifted out of memory. With no documented land ownership before the Great Mahele of 1848, some houses are known to exist, but their locations are impossible to determine precisely. Fortunately, native historians and foreign observers left a rich historical record for the lost palaces contained here. Although the structures and sites have been ultimately lost, this volume helps, through contemporaneous accounts, maps and illustrations to remember the lost palaces of Hawaiʻi. I sincerely hope that *Lost Palaces of Hawaiʻi* brings back to mind the places where royalty once lived, places still in our midst, and that when someone passes by the parking lot at Bethel and Beretania it calls to mind the hospitality of Rooke House and the mourning over the death of Queen Emma there.

Looking beyond the loss, however, *Lost Palaces of Hawaiʻi* celebrates the achievement of the Kingdom of Hawaiʻi in responding to the rapid change it experienced as shown through the broad variety of the residences of its royalty, palaces lost but now not forgotten.

Chapter 1

Royal Residences of Hawai'i Island

Ku ka'apā ia Hawai'i, he moku nui.
[It is well for] Hawai'i to show activity; it is the largest of the islands.[1]

With the unification of the Hawaiian Islands, achieved under Kamehameha the Great, and permanent contact with the West initiated by the expedition of Capt. James Cook in 1778, the lost palaces of the island of Hawai'i displayed a mixture of the traditional thatched structures, called *hale pili*, and brick, stone, and wooden frame buildings influenced by the West. Though today overshadowed by Oahu's population, the island of Hawai'i at first contact boasted the lion's share of inhabitants of the chain.

Residence of Kamehameha at Kealakekua, Kona, Island of Hawai'i (circa 1789)

One of the earliest descriptions of a royal residence came from George Mortimer of the brig *Mercury*. Lieutenant Mortimer visited on September 24, 1789, the house of the "king of Owhyhee [Hawai'i] Maia Maia [Kamehameha]" at "Karakakooa" [Kealakekua], which he called "very neat and commodious."[2] Mortimer's visit records the beginnings of the Kingdom of Hawai'i after Kamehameha had secured his control of the island of Hawai'i.

The first description to call the compound a palace came in the account of Urey Lisiansky, Russian captain of the *Neva*, who visited "Caracacoa" [Kealakekua] in June 1804. Lisiansky was part of an expedition commanded by Adam Johann von Krusenstern; Otto von Kotzebue served as a cadet on the voyage. The report of the palace portrayed the typical *kauhale* or group of houses present at that time. Lisiansky recorded in detail the number and uses of the *hale pili* within the compound of Kamehameha I:

> This palace [of the king] differed from the common habitations of the island in size only. It consisted of six distinct huts, erected near a tolerably large pond of stagnated water. The first hut we entered, constituted the king's dining-room, the second his drawing-room, the third and fourth the apartments of his women, while the last two served for kitchens. These huts, which were all alike, were constructed of poles, and covered with leaves. In some of them, the door was the only means of admitting light, while others had two small windows for the purpose; one near the corner, in front, and the other near the same corner, in the side of the hut. They are all erected upon a sort of pavement of stone, and are enclosed. I know not in what state the palace is kept during the king's residence in it, but when we saw it, it

was uncommonly filthy: it is, however held by the natives in such high veneration, that no one presumes to enter it with any covering on his body, except the *maro*, which is merely a piece of cloth tied round the waist.³

The descriptions of these earliest visitors capture the indigenous forms at their peak and preserve observations of a form of lost palace that has no surviving example. All *hale pili* used the same simple rectangular floor plan, differing only in size. Often the descriptions of the lost palaces contained no description of dimensions at all. Such was the case for the smaller thatched structure associated with the son of Kamehameha further up the Kona coast at Keauhou.

Kamehameha the Great (courtesy Hawaii State Archives, PP-97-5-004).

Lokomaikaʻi, Birthplace of Kamehameha III, Keauhou, Kona, Island of Hawaiʻi (1813)

While Honolulu was rapidly growing into a commercial center, the island of Hawaiʻi still served as its political base. It was there, in a *hale pili* at Keauhou, Kona, that 35-year-old Queen Keōpūolani gave birth in 1813 to Kauikeaouli, later called Kamehameha III. Her 1825 memoir makes no reference to the birth site and only scant mention to Kauikeaouli, only that he and Nāhiʻenaʻena were the remaining living children. Like Queen Kaʻahumanu, Keōpūolani was an early convert to Christianity and worked with her to break the eating *kapu*.

Although only a temporary residence for Kamehameha III at his birth, the house site was one identified as important by the island of Hawaiʻi representative on the commission on historic sites. In 1960 Violet Hanson, Hawaiʻi commissioner on the state Commission on Historic Sites, listed "Kamehameha 3rd. Birthplace" in the list of "Historical Sites on Hawaii Which Should be Preserved."⁴ The Daughters of Hawaiʻi owned the birthing location, one-third of an acre in Keauhou, bought from Bishop Estate for $50.⁵

Also at the site is a stone popularly called the Kauikeaouli Stone. Upon the stone, the seemingly lifeless body of Kauikeaouli was revived. A bronze plaque affixed to the stone on the supposed centennial of his birth reads: "Kauikeaouli Kamehameha III, Son of Kamehameha I and Keopuolani. Born March 17, 1814. Died December 15, 1854. Ka Moi Lokomaikai."[6] Queen Lili'uokalani attended the dedication ceremonies conducted by the Daughters of Hawai'i.

The site was placed on the National Register of Historic Places on July 24, 1978. The nomination notes: "Originally a pili (grass) house stood in the near vicinity of the Kauikeaouli stone. This house was where the birth actually occurred. No remains of the house or the house foundation are visible today."[7]

Today, an expanded plaque marks the birth site, which is planted with *lauae*

Kamehameha III as he appeared in 1825 (courtesy Hawaii State Archives, PP-98-16-002).

ferns. Illustrated with an image of Kamehameha III as an adult, the plaque reads:

> Birthplace of Kauikeaouli, Kamehameha III, 1814–1854. Kauikeaouli was born within this enclosure March 17, 1814 the second son of Kamehameha I and Keopuolani. His reign (1825–1854) was the longest in the history of the Kingdom. While a minor, his kingdom knew the firm regency of Queen Ka'ahumanu, briefly succeeded by his half sister Kina'u. When he assumed power in 1833 the Kingdom was beset with problems caused by immigration and foreign demands. During his reign the Kingdom of Hawai'i achieved world-wide diplomatic recognition; a constitution was developed, the tax system was reformed, and a legal basis for land ownership was instituted.

A drawing of a pair of kapu sticks in the bottom left hand corner of the plaque is joined with a verbal warning: "Kapu. Please do not enter the enclosure." Still smaller letters recognize the non-governmental organizations that maintain the site. "This monument is owned and managed by The Daughters of Hawaii. Additional care is provided by The Kamehameha Schools Bishop Estate." The symbol and logotype of the Keauhou Resort is prominently displayed in the bottom righthand corner of the plaque. The plaque is a rare example of the marking of a site of a lost palace. Further up the Kona coast sits the compound where Kauikeaouli, the future king, was raised at Kamakahonu in Kailua.

Kamakahonu (1813–1813) Kailua, Kona, Island of Hawaiʻi

Both the Kealakekua palace of Kamehameha I and the birthplace of his son pale in comparison to what has been called the most significant site of the kingdom period. The residence of Kamehameha I and Kamehameha II at Kamakahonu served as the site of the most significant events of the monarchy in Hawaiʻi, for there Kamehameha the Great died and his successor Kamehameha II, with his mothers Kaʻahumanu and Keōpūolani, broke the eating *kapu*, overturning the old religion and opening Hawaiʻi to the efforts of Christian missionaries.

John Papa ʻĪʻī, who was an attendant at the royal court, gave the names of the royal residences at Kamakahonu: "The house of Liholiho was named Hookuku; Kamehameha's house was named Papa; Keopuolani's Kualalua; and Kaahumanu's, Kapapoko."[8] It was the Western influenced building that drew the attention of John Turnbull: "His palace is built after the European style, of brick, and glazed windows, and defended by a battery of ten guns. He has European and American artificers about him of almost every description. Indeed his own subjects, from their intercourse with Europeans, have acquired a great knowledge of several of the mechanical arts."[9] Turnbull reveals in his account both the use of foreign builders by Kamehameha as well as the training of natives in the building trades.

James Jackson Jarves recounted the 1816 visit of the Russian ship *Rurik* in his 1843 account, *History of the Hawaiian or Sandwich Islands*: "[Otto von] Kotzebue visited him [Kamehameha] at his palace, and there met Liholiho and Kaahumanu; the latter made many inquiries after Vancouver."[10]

In 1819, shortly after the death of Kamehameha I, Jacques Arago, draftsman on the expedition of Captain Louis Claude de Saulces Freycinet, aboard the French ship *Uranie*, visited the town of "Kayerooa" [Kailua]. Arago made his observations in Letter CVI:

> Two or three buildings, as seen from the roads, have a good appearance, and make one regret that they are, as it were, solitary in the midst of ruins. The most considerable is a storehouse distinguished by its white front from the other huts; it belongs to the King, who uses it as a sort of repository, without venturing to confide his treasures to its keeping; these he buries in cellars. The second edifice is a *morai*, situated at the end of a jetty, projecting into the sea; the third is a house belonging to one of the principal chiefs of Riouriou [Liholiho], who had address enough, when he quitted the town, to get it consecrated *(tabooed)* in order to protect it from intruders and thieves. I was given to understand, that whoever should endeavor to enter it, would be instantly put to death, and that the owner was a very cruel and powerful man.[11]

Sheldon Dibble (1809–1845) in his 1843 *History of the Sandwich Islands* gives the most complete description of the residence of Kamehameha I at his death.[12] Dibble, an American missionary, arrived with the fourth company in 1831. Dibble's account also relates the custom of changing the location of the residence of the chief's heir following his death.

Calling the island chain by the name given by Cook five decades earlier, Ephraim Eveleth, in *History of the Sandwich Islands*, gives an account of the American missionaries on April 3, 1820, as they approached Kailua on the Kona coast of the Hawaiʻi island: "The next morning they sailed for Kairua [Kailua] bay, near which was the rude palace of king Riho Riho [Liholiho]. On reaching the place, Karaimoku [Kalaimoku

Chapter 1. Royal Residences of Hawai'i Island

Louis Choris depicted the meeting of Kamehameha and Otto von Kotzebue at Kamakahonu in *"Entrevue de l'expedition de M. Kotzebue avec le roi Tammeamea dans l'ile d'Ovayhi, Iles Sandwich"* (courtesy Hawaii State Archives, REFVOY-1-044).

or Kalanimoku] went on shore, to consult the king, previously to the landing of the missionaries."[13]

Before Kalanimoku died, he asked to be taken from his O'ahu residence (Chapter 5) to Kamakahonu on Hawai'i island. It was there, where Kamehameha I died, that Kalanimoku died on February 8, 1827.[14]

The site was at least partially standing when Jarves visited between 1837 and 1842. He wrote in his journal:

> One of Kamehameha's temples, "a house of gods," a small grass building, still exists. It is built upon a stone mole, jutting into the sea. Near it remains but one of the many wooden images of colossal size, sphinx-like head, and hideous, gaping mouth—a horrible burlesque upon the "human form divine," which formerly ranged about the exterior. [...] Nearby the temple, is the ancient house of audience of the old warrior-king—in which, after his decease, his body was dissected.[15]

Just when the house and temple fell into disrepair is not certain, but a June 1883 map of Kailua Bay gives outlines of an "Old Heiau," "Ruin of Stone House," and "Royal Boat House."[16]

Albert P. Taylor included an item from his wife in his "Historical Notes" in the 1929 *Report of the Hawaiian Historical Society* that gave an alternative definition of the site's name. The statement from Emma Ahuena D. Taylor concerning "Kamehameha's temple," in Kailua, Kona, Hawaiʻi island, gave information regarding "the names of the heiau and site thereof, of Kamehameha First's temple at Kailua, Hawaiʻi. Steps are being taken to have the Government acquire the site, now occupied by a commercial firm, for preservation." She stated:

> Temple (heiau) of Ahuena-i-Kamakahonu-i-Kai-a-Kekua, Kailua. The temple is described as follows: Ahuena (the Treasure Pile of Raging Flames)—i (at)—Kamakahonu (The Face of Death)—i—(by the)—Kai-a-Kekua (Sea of the Gods). Ahuena (heiau); Kamakahonu (the land on which it stands); Kai-a-Kekua (name of the sea.) Ahuena (The Treasure Pile of Raging Flames at the Face of Death by the Sea of the Gods). Kamakahonu, in this instance, means the land of the death penalty; women were forbidden to eat turtle flesh during the kapu days, under penalty of death.—Explanation by Mary Jane Fayerweather Montano. A long chant confirms this version, the chant on file in the Archives' Bureau.[17]
>
> The first two persons who were named after this heiau in memory of Kamehameha I, were High Chiefess Ahuena-i-Kamakahonu, the first wife of William C. Malulani Beckley, and her first cousin, the High Chief Ahuena-Kamakahonu (kane), feudal lord of Kualoa and Kaneohe (island of Oahu), the latter being the husband of Maria Kaiponuikaipoliilii Beckley. Both were called after the heiau because it was there that Kamehameha I was last seen after death, and his body prepared there for its last resting place.
>
> The next person to be named after the heiau was Kamakahonu, daughter of Judge Halali of Waialua, a descendent [*sic*] of the Kaha Luahine mahi clan that reared Kamehameha I. And also my daughter Emma Ahuenaikamakahonuikaiakekua." [The last sentence was handwritten by Mary Montano.]

Appeals for the site's preservation in the 1950s indicate the continued presence of foundations at Kamakahonu. Alice Spalding Bowen, chairman of the of the Historical Sites Commission, on February 2, 1955, pressed the land owner, American Factors, for the preservation of Kamakahonu:

> The future of Kona seems to be now in a very uncertain balance and it is the belief of this Commission and our affiliated organization, the Sites Committee of the Conservation Council for Hawaii, that due to great historical significance of your land there, your company is in the position to guide Kona's future development, beneficially, more than is any other group.[18]

The close ally of the territorial Historical Sites Commission, the Sites Committee of the Conservation Council for Hawaii, at the sixth annual meeting of the organization wrote: "Early in the year of 1955 the Sites Committee was particularly interested in the preservation of the famous heiau, Ahuena-I-Kamakahonu-I-Kai-A-Kekua, which is located near the wharf at Kailua, Kona, and where the great king, Kamehameha the First, died."[19] In the list developed by the Historic Sites Committee in 1958, "Kamakahonu (Eye of Turtle)" appeared as a site "of first importance which should be cleared, maintained, preserved and made accessible."[20] The detailed description stated: "This site is of first importance to all Hawaii as the royal residence of King Kamehameha I from 1813 until his death in 1819. The site contains foundations of the houses he built within his compound and the ruins of Ahuena Heiau which he rebuilt for his own worship."[21]

Designation of the site was not without controversy, necessitating on April 25, 1959, a letter from several prominent leaders, including Agnes C. Conrad, chairman of the Territorial Commission on Historical Sites, Violet Hanson, commissioner for the

Big Island; William Norwood, president of the Hawaiian Historical Society; Mrs. Joan Osborne, chairman of the sites committee of the Conservation Council, Iolani Luahine, Mrs. Tillie Norton, premier of the Daughters and Sons of Hawaiian Warriors; Mrs. Louise Akeo Silva, advisor of Hale O Na Alii; William C. Kea, president of the Territorial Council of Hawaiian Civic Clubs; Mrs. Pat Cooke, regent of the Daughters of Hawai'i; and Kenneth Emory, anthropologist with Bishop Museum. The letter to the editor of the *Hilo Tribune-Herald* was a careful balance between historic preservation and economic interests. [22] The National Trust for Historic Preservation also commented on the controversy. Citing Mount Vernon, President Lincoln's home and colonial Williamsburg, C. Hutton Smith concluded: "Statistics have proven that conservation of our heritage is good business."[23] Walter F. Dillingham sent a letter to Conrad, chairman of the commission on historical sites, expressing to her: "I personally regret that the plans so far do not provide a sufficient area for this memorial. I am glad, however, that general interest, financially and otherwise, has made it possible for a start which I hope will be developed into a memorial of sufficient importance to make this landmark a recognized historic site."[24]

Henry E.P. Kekahuna protested the building of a hotel at Kamakahonu that would "forever ruin the Hawaiian spirit, atmosphere and character of Ka-maka-honu!"[25] Kekahuna contrasted the treatment of Hawai'i historic sites and ones on the mainland. "Of all our historic shrines in all our Hawaiian Islands," he wrote, "the land of Ka-maka-honu, in Kai-lua, North Kona, island of Hawaii, is a very greatest. Ka-maka-honu is as sacred to Hawaii, it has been said, as is Mount Vernon to the mainland United States of America. Surely, at Mount Vernon no outrage of this kind would be possible!"[26] Kekahuna wrote in opposition to the hotel project. He also railed against the 1952 proposal that would have filled in the cove at Kamakahonu.[27]

Today the Courtyard King Kamehameha's Kona Beach Hotel, set back from its original proposed location, overlooks the sacred site. The hotel's Web site once, but no

Ahu'ena heiau at Kamakahonu (courtesy Hawaii State Archives, REFVOY-1-034).

longer, paid homage to Kamakahonu in a section titled "Capturing the Historical and Cultural Spirit of Hawaii at Our Big Island Hotel." The section benignly read:

> Our Kona, Hawaii, hotel is on one of the most historic sites in all of Hawaii. King Kamehameha the Great established his royal residence adjacent to the current site of his namesake hotel. During his reign he rebuilt Ahu'ena Heiau, a temple dedicated to Lono who was the Hawaiian God of peace, agriculture and prosperity. Here, on The Big Island, Kamehameha the Great lived and conducted matters of government, until his passing on May 8, 1819. Indeed, our Big Island hotel owes quite a debt to our island's rich history and culture.
>
> King Kamehameha's residence included all of Kamakahonu, the bay around which the hotel is focused. Besides homes, his residence also had numerous fishponds and gardens.[28]

Today, the main Web site only refers to its "historic location [and] Ahu'ena Heiau" in connection with the "award-winning Island Breeze Luau." The section titled "Extraordinary Weddings & Special Events" features Ahu'ena Heiau as a backdrop for its "ocean view venue."[29]

Within a stone's throw of the hotel, the Kamakahonu site itself is part of the Kamakahonu National Historic Landmark under the jurisdiction of the National Park Service.

Up the coast from Kamakahonu was the site of the home of a Westerner who played a key role during the accession of Kamehameha I.

John Young Residence (before 1803–1835), Kawaihae, South Kohala, Island of Hawai'i

Kamehameha's trusted advisor, John Young, who provided the knowledge of Western warfare as Kamehameha's "companion-in-arms," established his household in Kawaihae on the Kona coast.

Heiromonk Gideon on the Russian ship *Neva* visited Hawai'i in May 30, 1804, to June 8, 1804. He reported: "The position of viceroy is occupied by the Englishman Young, who formerly was an ordinary sailor aboard a merchantman. Nowadays he is very wealthy, possesses much land, laborers, *and has a stone house* [italics mine]."[30] Young married Ka'ōanā'eha, daughter of Kamehameha's brother Keli'imaika'i. It was at Kawaihae that their daughter, Fanny Kekelaokalani Young, was born on July 21, 1806. Fanny Young and High Chief George Na'ea were the parents of Queen Emma, who married Kamehameha IV.

Another early Western visitor, Adelbert von Chamisso, a botanist aboard the *Rurik*, wrote in his journal: "From out at sea, we could see the European built houses of John Young towering above the grass shacks of the natives."[31]

In 1819, Capt. Louis Isidore Duperrey drew the *Plan de la Baie de Kohai-Hai* clearly marking the residences of John Young and Kamehameha II. By 1883, the map of *Kawaihae Bay* calls the location "Ruin Young's House."[32]

Jacques Arago, in his *Narrative of a Voyage Round the World*, gives a detailed description of his visit to Young's home:

> It is difficult to say how far the opinion of Mr. Young as to the motive of Riouriou's [Liholiho's] residence at Toyai [Kawaihae] is well founded and which may be merely conjecture on his part there must however be a very powerful one. I have already described the coast on

which we are anchored the sterility of which extends far beyond the point that forms the bay. The aspect of the town and its environs is not more flattering to the view; while the tuft of cocoa-nut trees which skirt the shore, and three others which have as it were accidentally sprung up at one extremity of the town, render its barrenness still more conspicuous.

The house of Mr. Young is unquestionably the most considerable or rather the only passable one at Toyai. It is situated on an eminence, whence the prospect extends to a great distance over the sea and towards the interior of the island. On the right is seen the majestic *Mowna-Roa* [Mauna Loa], losing its head in clouds, its sides parched by the sun, and deeply furrowed with winding ravines. The greatest aridity prevails in every part; some extinguished craters appear at different points, the sea beating its base with violence. On the left the Mowna-Kaah [Mauna Kea] commands the adjacent hills; yet near its summit the eye perceives a vigorous vegetation, generally overhung by those dense clouds which give it life: at a distance, and as if to give symmetry to the picture the Mowna Laë displays its gentle declivity, majestically detaching itself in blue, from the landscape which it appears to crown.[33]

John Young from a lithograph by Jacques Arago (courtesy Hawaii State Archives, PP-82-5-009).

Besides the general scenery surrounding John Young's house, Arago also described a nearby *heiau*, still intact: "On a hill opposite to that on which the house of Mr. Young is built, there is a very large *morai* enclosed by a stone wall about four feet high. The statues seen here are colossal and regularly placed; I have counted above forty of them."[34]

A journal for the years 1809–1810 and 1821, 1825 gives a flavor of what occupied Young at his Kawaihae residence around the time of Arago's visit, including the weather, fish catches, and ship arrivals. Young also recorded news regarding other *ali'i*. On August 15, 1821, Young noted in the journal: "Keoua, John Adam's [Kuakini's] wife came to Kawaihae with all her retinue being displeased with her kane."[35]

Missionary wife, Laura Fish Judd, made a visit to Young's house in 1829. She wrote of his residence: "He lived in a dirty adobe house, adorned with old rusty muskets, swords, bayonets, and cartridge boxes. He gave us a supper of goat's meat and fried taro, served on old pewter plates, which I was unfortunate to see his servant wipe on his red flannel shirt in lieu of a napkin. […] We were sent up a rickety flight of stairs to sleep. I was afraid, and requested Dr. Judd to look around the room carefully for concealed dangers, and he was heartless enough to laugh at me."[36]

Judd's account also reveals the presence of a *hale pili* in the compound. Judd related about her stay at Young's residence: "Sleep was out of the question; I was afraid of the wind, which sometimes sweeps down the gorge of the mountain, and got up at midnight, and went down to the grass house of Mrs. Young, which was neat and comfortable. She is a noble woman. She lives in native style; one of the sons is with the king; and the daughters are in the train of the princess."[37]

Young continued to live at Kawaihae through his 93rd year of life, where legal documents place him in 1835. Captain John Kendrick, captain of the schooner *Washington* made several visits to Kawaihae and became known to John Young. On June 26, 1835, John Young signed an affidavit at "Towaihae" concerning Kendell and deeds he had for Native American lands in the Pacific Northwest: "I, the subscriber, in the year A.D. 1789, commenced a residence on the Sandwich Islands. Afterwards, in Kearakekua [Kealakekua], on the island of Hawaii, I became acquainted Captain John Kendrick, [...] from Boston Massachusetts, he having passed several winters at the above island."[38] John Young's daughter brought him to Honolulu to be treated by her physician husband, Thomas Charles Byde Rooke. He died there on December 17, 1835, at Rooke House (Chapter 5). The ahupuaʻa of East Kawaihae passed to John Young's daughter, Kamaikui, and later to his granddaughter, Queen Emma.

Following the death of Queen Emma, her Kawaihae land went into trust for the benefit of her cousin, Prince Albert Kūnuiākea. Because Kūnuiākea had no children, the land stayed in trust for Queen's Hospital.[39]

One of the addenda to the "Historical Notes" of the 1929 issue of the papers of the Hawaiian Historical Society expressed great hope for the preservation of John Young's residence in Kawaihae:

> There is a probability that John Young's house at Kawaihae, island of Hawaii, where he lived during the earlier years of his residence in Hawaii after his forcible detention from the schooner *Eleanora* by Kamehameha after 1790, will be preserved to posterity, including, of course, an area around the house to be known as "The John Young Park." At the close of the unveiling ceremonies by the Order of Kamehameha in June, 1929, of a bronze tablet marking the site of the famous temple of Puukohola, at Kawaihae, erected by Kamehameha and where the body of Keoua was taken after he was assassinated, A. P. Taylor, librarian of the Hawaii State Archives, published a plea for the restoration and preservation of the Young house, because it was there that all ship captains and many others generally consulted with Young before having an audience with Kamehameha, and it was there that much of the governmental foundation for the new Kingdom of Hawaii was studied out. Governor Judd, it is reported, favors the plan for a "John Young Park."[40]

Twenty-five years later, in 1954, the minutes of the sixty-third annual meeting of the Hawaiian Historical Society contain a similar appeal by Mrs. Ernest [Peggy] Kai "to mark and preserve the remains of John Young's house at Kawaihae, Hawaii. It is beautifully situated on a hill, has two-thirds of the walls left and, in Mrs. Kai's opinion, is the best example of an early Western type house in the Islands. The Society, while in sympathy with the idea, took no action, feeling that the organization was not in the position to undertake such a project at this time."[41]

Today, only the ruined walls of his house survive. Credit goes to the Conservation Council for Hawaii for the preservation of what remains of the site. The report of the organization's efforts noted: "The Sites Committee assisted in locating the homesite of John Young, Kamehameha I's chief advisor, so that it could be preserved from quarrying activities in the development of the harbor."[42] The key role that Young played in Hawaiʻi

Stereoscopic image of the ruins of John Young's residence at Kawaihae (courtesy Hawaii State Archives, PP-95-4-004).

history put the remains of his residence on the roster of Hawai'i buildings deserving protection. In 1960, Violet Hanson, Hawai'i commissioner on the Commission on Historic Sites listed "John Young's Home" in the list of "Historical Sites on Hawaii Which Should Be Preserved."[43] The site was owned then by Queen's Hospital.

In 2004, the Architectural Resources Group/Conservation Services conducted a stabilization and conservation of the homestead site.[44]

The Western style residence of John Young stands in stark contrast to the traditional *hale pili* of Kamehameha II.

Kamehameha II Residence at Kawaihae, South Kohala, Island of Hawai'i

Upon the death of his father, Kamehameha II moved his residence to another district as the place of the death of Kamehameha I was considered defiled. Mark Twain included an account of the relocation of the king's residence in his 1872 travel guide *Roughing It*:

> Then the high priest, Hewahewa, inquired of the chiefs, "Where shall be the residence of King Liholiho?" They replied, "Where, indeed? You, of all men, ought to know." Then the priest observed, there are two suitable places; one is Kau, the other is Kohala." The chiefs preferred the latter, as it was more thickly inhabited. The priest added, "These are proper places for the King's residence; but he must not remain in Kona, for it is polluted." This was agreed to. [...] The morning following Kamehameha's death, Liholiho and his train departed for Kohala, according to the suggestions of the priest, to avoid the defilement occasioned by the dead. At this time if a chief died the land was polluted, and the heirs sought a residence in

another part of the country until the corpse was dissected and the bones tied in a bundle, which being done, the season of defilement terminated.[45]

In a more contemporaneous depiction, Jacques Arago in 1819 described the residence of Kamehameha II during his stay at Kawaihae:

> A miserable hut, built of straw, from twenty-five to thirty feet long, and from twelve to fifteen feet broad, the entrance to which is by a low and narrow door; some mats on which several half-naked giants are reposing, and who bear the titles of ministers and generals; two chairs, on which are seated on days of ceremony, a large fat, dirty, heavy, proud man, and a stout half-naked woman, who allows herself to coquet with every stranger, without betraying her fidelity to her large-jowled husband, who is eat up with I know not how many horrible diseases; walls made of cocoa-tree leaves, well sewed together; the roof made of sea-weed much neglected, and presenting but a feeble defence against the wind and rain;—such is the palace of the monarch of the Sandwich Isles; and such are the King and Queen of Owhyhee, and such is their dignified court![46]

Kamehameha II (courtesy Hawaii State Archives, PP-97-6-011).

The impact of an account such as Arago's went beyond the readers of the book itself as portions of the details found their way into reviews in contemporaneous magazines. Magazines also produced original accounts, such as that reported in the *Atheneum* about the visit of Kamehameha to London. In giving introductory detail, the magazine described the residence of the king: "His dwelling was a poor straw-built hut, 25 or 30 feet long, and half as many wide; and the roof covered with cocoa leaves and sea-weed."[47] The latter account omitted the negative description of the royal family, written after the death of Kamehameha II and Kamāmalu.

The *Mirror of Literature, Amusement, and Instruction* published in London on July 24, 1824, just ten days after the death of Kamehameha II, gave another account of the late king's palace:

> This Palace [...] stands on a sort of terrace on the beach, which is defended by nearly thirty pieces of cannon. The Palace is a large house constructed of stakes, covered at the sides and

the sloping roof with dried grass, having at a little distance quite the appearance of a large, thatched barn. The Palace, which is spacious, has three small doors, on three different sides. A gentleman who recently visited the Sandwich Islands, and was presented to the king, in describing his reception and the interior of the Palace, where he had an audience, says, "there were a few chairs which were handed us, but the five queens, or wives of the king, sat on mats on the ground. The king was seated in a chair. Most of the king's wives, and all the other ladies who were waiting upon them had no other dress than a *pareu* (a wrapper) round the waist, which extended down to the knees. Some of them had necklaces made of whales' teeth and glass beads."[48]

The Mirror of Literature, Amusement, and Instruction, published July 24, 1824, shortly after the deaths of Liholiho and Kamāmalu, included an engraving of the Palace of the King of the Sandwich Islands.

Chiefess Kekela House Site (c. 1824–c. 1833), Ki'ilae, Kawaihae, South Kohala, Island of Hawai'i

John Young's daughter Fanny Kekela, mother of the future Queen Emma, also lived in Kawaihae at Ki'ilae. Violet Hanson, Hawaii commissioner on the Commission on Historic Sites, listed "Chiefess Kekela housesite" at Ki'ilae in the February 1960 list of "Historical Sites on Hawaii Which Should be Preserved."[49] Unlike the Kamehameha III birthplace that was owned by preservation-minded organization, the Daughters of Hawaii, the Chiefess Kekela house site was owned

Kekelaokalani, also known as Fanny Young, was the daughter of John Young and mother of Queen Emma (Library of Congress Prints and Photographs Division, LC-DIG-ds-09892).

by a private party, the McCandless family. The 1957 archeological work of Kenneth Emory of the Bishop Museum no doubt influenced her recommendation. A report of the National Park Service, which maintains a park at Ki'ilae, gave a history of the site:

> The chiefess Kekela-o-ka-lani, mother of Kamehameha IV's wife Queen Emma, lived at Ki'ilae Village in the early to mid–1800s. Her house platform [...] stood just above the well, mauka of the main road. Emory believed it to be one of the finest remaining examples of an early Hawaiian house foundation, with a paving of large, flat, waterworn stones and beach pebbles. [Emory, "Hinterland and Keamoalii," 245, 248]....
>
> An ancient legend connected with the well states that a couple found out about the water available here by watching their dog going into a certain cave and then reappearing with wet fur. Kekela directed that the cave be enlarged until water was reached, and the residents accomplished this by pounding through the rock to the spring. Emory and his party explored the Cave of the Dog ('Ilio Cave) leading from the well and found it to be a refugee cave with three entrances inland. The passage into the uppermost eastern entrance had been artificially narrowed by a stone wall. It is outside the park boundary [Emory, "Hinterland and Keamoalii," 246–248].[50]

Despite its archeological and historic importance, the land is still subject to development. In 2001, a group headed by former state representative Virginia Isbell pressed for the purchase of the Ki'ilae site as an addition to the adjacent Pu'uhonua O Hōnaunau National Historic Park. "It's jam packed with historic and cultural features."[51] Though the article notes "the grounds just outside the great wall that encloses the pu'uhonua was home to several generations of powerful chiefs," it makes no reference to the house site of Kekelaokalani.

The *hale pili* of the time coexisted with Western structures. As the court moved from Hawai'i island to Maui and finally to O'ahu, royalty built their Western style houses on the latter two islands. Thus, the residences associated with King Kamehameha I, Kamehameha II and Kamehameha III took the form of traditional thatched structures. The houses of the governors (Hulihe'e Palace) and district overseers, on the other hand, did make the transition from *hale pili* to Western buildings. Such was the case of the residence of Naihe, who administered Ka'u and South Kona, and his wife Kapi'olani.

Residences of Chiefess Kapi'olani, Ka'awaloa, South Kona, Island of Hawai'i (c. 1824)

The Chiefess Kapi'olani, not to be confused with the wife of King Kalākaua of the same name, was an early convert to Christianity best known for her defiance of Pele, the Hawaiian goddess of fire. In 1825 Kapi'olani climbed the active volcano, "neglecting every rite considered necessary to propitiate the fiery deity, she descended boldly into the domain of terror, till from the very edge of the lake of fire she cast the sacred ['ōhelo] berries upon the boiling rock! Astonished natives looked for the opening of the rocky bank on which she stood, or the lifting up of the molten fires on which she gazed, to bury her in the wrath of the insulted goddess. But lo! She stood unharmed and unterrified as before."[52] The account also indicated that the volcano was "distant one hundred miles from her house."[53] A poem, titled simply "Kapiolani," by Alfred Lord Tennyson, made the deeds of Kapi'olani famous throughout the world. Tennyson wrote:

II.
[...]
Greater and greater, and greatest of women, island heroine Kapiolani
Clomb the mountain, and flung the berries, and dared the goddess, and freed the people
Of Hah-wy-ee!⁵⁴

Charles Stewart describes the residence of Chiefess Kapiʻolani at Kaʻawaloa in 1829. He reported: "we were not surprised to find the establishment she dwells in equal, if not superior, to any we had before seen—handsomely arranged, well furnished, and neatly kept, with a sitting room, or hall, in which a nobleman, in such a climate, might be happy to lounge; and bedrooms, adjoining, where, in addition to couches which the most fastidious would unhesitatingly occupy, are found mirrors and toilettables fitted for the dressing-room of a modern belle."⁵⁵ After tea at residence of Kapiʻolani, Stewart took a short tour of the area and listened to "a rehearsal of the tragedy of Captain Cook's death on the rocks, at the edge of the water into which he fell."⁵⁶

Silhouette of Chiefess Kapiʻolani, by Persis G. Taylor, drawn in June 1839. Printed in the *Hawaiian Annual for 1926*.

Upon the death of her husband in 1831 Kapiʻolani took over the duties of magistrate of the districts of Kaʻu and South Kona. In 1836 Kapiʻolani invited Théodore-Adolphe Barrot of the *Bonite* to visit her *hale pili* in the lower village and her house under construction in the upper village that possessed "a certain European aspect." Barrot's observations regarding the houses shows the evolution of the *hale pili* as well as the room divisions noted by Stewart:

> [H]er house in the lower village, with the exception of the doors and windows, which have been enlarged, continues the same that it was before the discover of the island. [...] Formerly there was but a single room in a house, and that was used for a dining room, drawing room and bed chamber. The missionaries are now persuading the people to make divisions in their houses, and for this purpose they generally employ large curtains of *tapa* or of English calico. These separations form the sleeping apartments. [...] This place is *tabu* (prohibited to all the world).⁵⁷

Kapiʻolani died May 6, 1841, in Honolulu from complications following surgery for breast cancer.⁵⁸ Her remains were interred with those of Liholiho, Kaʻahumanu and Kīnaʻu. Timothy Dwight Hunt's description of Chiefess Kapiʻolani after her death includes a description of the house that was still under construction when Barrot visited her in 1836: "With remarkable ease she assumed civilized habits. She built a large framed house in foreign style, enclosed a yard, cultivated flowers, and in her dress, manners, and mode of living, and in the furniture and order of her house, appeared more like a Christian lady than any other high born native of her day."⁵⁹

A 1926 account about missionary John D. Paris wrote included an account of the site of his residence:

Village of Kaʻawaloa, from *A Residence of Twenty-One Years in the Sandwich Islands* (courtesy Hawaii State Archives, REFVOY-3-025).

The house was built on the foundations of Kapiolani's home, an old stone dwelling cracked by hundreds of earthquakes, but commanding a matchless view of the South Kona slope and the broad blue sea fifteen hundred feet below. The old stone house, with several acres of rocky hillside, which had been bought by Mr. Paris some years before at auction, now presented a refuge for his old age. Here Kapiolani, the Kona chiefess famed for her defiance of Pele in 1825, had entertained many a weary and appreciative traveller, refreshing them with luscious grapes and oranges after hot and dusty journeys on foot and horseback. In this old stone house Kalakaua had lived as a child, with his sisters, Liliuokalani and Likelike, their mother being a Kona chiefess. [...] Under Mr. Paris' frame house the foundations of the old Kapiolani house may still be seen, some of the rocks having been placed for the present front steps; also, a number of doors and windows from the old stone house are still doing good service at the present time, 1926.[60]

Thus knowledge of the location of the house was retained.

Residence of Governor Kuakini, Kailua, North Kona, Island of Hawaiʻi

Although Huliheʻe Palace, one of the four palaces to survive, is the best-known residence of Governor Kuakini, a *hale pili* existed before the Western structure's construction. Theodore-Adolphe Barrot of the *Bonite*, who had visited Chiefess Kapiʻolani, also visited Gov. Kuakini in 1836, prior to the construction of Huliheʻe Palace. Of his house, Barrot wrote that it "appeared very much like that of Kapiolani. Extended curtains of English calico concealed the secret apartments of the women from vulgar eyes."[61] Although no account records the disposition of the *hale pili* after the construction of Huliheʻe Palace, the structure may have continued on the site. Certainly, a prominent *hale pili* coexisted with Huliheʻe Palace—the structure favored by Princess Ruth Keʻelikōlani during her stays in Kailua, Kona.

The hali pili of Princess Ruth Keʻelikōlani stood on the grounds of Huliheʻe Palace in Kailua, Kona. The church building in the background still remains (courtesy Hawaii State Archives, PP-32-2-022).

Auanakeo, Residence of Princess Ruth Keʻelikōlani, Kailua, North Kona, Island of Hawaiʻi

As governor of Hawaii Island from January 15, 1855, through February 23, 1872, and March 30, 1872, through March 2, 1874, Princess Ruth Keʻelikōlani had Huliheʻe Palace at her disposal. The palace had passed from Kuakini to Kalanimoku to her son, Leleiohoku, and then to her. The Western structures often served as the site of formal ceremonies. Royalty often had other structures in the same enclosure in which they preferred to reside. The large *hale pili* near Huliheʻe Palace, named Auanakeo,[62] served as the everyday residence of Princess Ruth Keʻelikōlani. It was to the traditional structure that she regularly retreated and there that she died on May 24, 1883.

Residence of Princess Ruth Keʻelikōlani, Piopio, Hilo, South Hilo, Island of Hawaiʻi

Besides her residences on Oʻahu (Chapter 5) and in Kona on the island of Hawaiʻi, Princess Ruth Keʻelikōlani also maintained a residence on the Hilo side of Hawaiʻi island. The only description of her house at Piopio, Hilo, Hawaiʻi island, comes in a

1922 account by John Mortimer Lydgate, who died in the same year, at age 67. Lydgate, who arrived with his family in Hilo during the summer of 1865, when he was 10 years old, gave his recollections of Hilo town in the year 1872. Beginning at age 17, he had worked as a surveyor from 1872 to 1875, mapping the road from Hilo to Kilauea crater.[63] Of her residence Lydgate recalled: "Beyond the Waiolama on what was known as Piopio was the residence of Governess Ke-eli-ko-lani. Hers was a typical grass-house of commodious size, but with board floor, surrounded by magnificent clumps of stately bamboos and large kamani trees."[64] Lydgate highlights the integration of a Western construction element into the traditional *hale pili*—the board floor used instead of the traditional stone pebbles.

Ruth Keʻelikōlani (courtesy Hawaii State Archives, PP-97-18-011).

Piopio was an *ʻili* (a subdivision or smaller area of land) originally designated for Victoria Kamāmalu.[65] The native testimony has a number of references to her father's property in Piopio. On the Hamakua side of LCA 5157 was the garden of Kekūanāoʻa; mauka (inland or upland) of Section 2 of LCA 8854 was a road named for him.

The *Pacific Commercial Advertiser* lists the place of residence of Ruth Keʻelikōlani as Hilo, Hawaii.[66] The house, presumably, was the delivery location for Princess Ruth's request to the Ministry of the Interior on September 26, 1860, for "1 case brandy and 1 case gin."[67]

The Hilo residence would also have been the location that her husband, Isaac Young Davis, was detained while his daughter lay dying and later died in Waimea on Hawaiʻi island. He complained to the land agent, William Webster, about Keʻelikōlani in a letter dated February 15, 1861:

> Then, I appealed very strongly to the Princess R. Keelikolani to be kind, and for me to return to see the trouble that had come upon my own family, but, the Princess utterly refused to give her consent, and on the other hand strictly refused and was angry. Thereafter, I simply stayed in Hilo like a person living in Hell, and my sense of duty left me, and I was like one who was dead.

And on the 1st day of this Febry., I received letters from sundry ones informing me that "Your daughter is dead, you come back." Right then and there, I told the Princess, saying (with tears), my child is dead, and what do you think about my going to meet my family, then, the Princess did not consent properly. But, I stood up and came.[68]

Kamehameha V wrote a letter to John Owen Dominis from Piopio on November 7, 1866.[69] He told Dominis: "Please give him [servant of Kamehameha V] an order for horses to John Parker so that he can ride overland to here."[70] On October 8, 1883, Bernice Pauahi Bishop and Charles Reed Bishop signed a ten-year lease of Piopio with Joseph Nāwahī. Bernice Pauahi Bishop had inherited the lands of Ruth Keʻelikōlani's. Nāwahī later lived in Princess Ruth's Kapālama house at Mauna Kamala (Chapter 5).

A Supreme Court case in January 1886 concerning Piopio hinged on whether the ʻili was part of the ahupuaʻa of Waiakea or an "ili kupono, independent and not subservient to the ahupuaa."[71]

Residence of Kamehameha IV, Kailua, North Kona, Island of Hawaiʻi

Although the references to a Kailua residence of Kamehameha IV most likely refer to Huliheʻe Palace, the sources do not explicitly name the residence. In the days following the tragic shooting of Henry A. Neilson, Kamehameha IV retreated to Kaluaʻaha on Molokaʻi and Lahaina, Maui. While at king stayed at Lahaina, R.C. Wyllie wrote to him concerning his house on the island of Hawaiʻi: "I hope most sincerely that your Residence at Kailua will be beneficial to Your Majesty, to Her Majesty the Queen, the Prince Royal and all the Ladies and Gentlemen of Your Suite. I should like to know whether it would be agreeable to Your Majesty to receive the visits of the French Captain, or of the British Admiral, who is soon expected, if either of them expresses a wish to proceed to Kailua for that purpose."[72] The recommendation from Wyllie suggests that no suitable diplomatic venue existed at Kaluaʻaha, Molokaʻi, or Lahaina, Maui. Huliheʻe Palace certainly would have filled the bill for an appropriate location for the 1859 visits.

Emma, in a letter to her husband, whom she called Alex, wrote from Kailua on June 27, 1861: "The place is looking green, and the house very neat and nice looking. Baby [Prince Albert Edward Kauikeaouli Leiopapa A Kamehameha] enjoys this place amazingly now that he is here but he cryed [sic] bitterly on the vessel."[73] In a wish list enclosed in the same letter, Emma requested an item from another palace on the grounds of Hale Aliʻi. She asked for her "Wicker work basket in Hoikea."[74] "Hoikea" was the shortened form of the name "Hoihoikea" (Chapter 4).

In 1861 the *Friend* lists the "Marine Residence" of Kamehameha IV as the location of the proclamation of his kingdom's neutrality during the U.S. Civil War, the reference to the residence in Kailua, Kona, Hawaiʻi island may refer to Huliheʻe Palace. The proclamation, issued in August 1861, read:

Be it known, to all whom it may concern, that we, Kamehameha IV, King of the Hawaiian Islands, having been officially notified that hostilities are now unhappily pending between the Government of the United States, and certain States thereof styling themselves "The Confederate States of America," hereby proclaim Our neutrality between said contending parties. That Our neutrality is to be respected to the full extent of Our jurisdiction, and that all captures, and seizures made within the same are unlawful, and in violation of Our rights as a Sovereign. And be it further known, that We hereby strictly prohibit all Our subjects, and all who reside or may be within Our jurisdiction, from engaging either directly or indirectly in privateering against the Shipping or Commerce of either of the contending parties, or of rendering any aid to such enterprises whatever; and all persons so offending will be liable to the penalties imposed by the laws of nations, as well us by the laws of said States, and they will in no wise obtain any protection from Us as against any penal consequences which they may incur. Be it further known, that no adjudication of prizes will be entertained within Our jurisdiction, nor will the sale of goods or other property belonging to prizes be allowed. Be it further known, that the rights of asylum are not extended to the Privateers or their prizes of either if the contending parties, excepting only in case of distress or of compulsory delay by stress of weather or dangers of the sea, or in such cases as may be regulated by Treaty stipulation.

Given at Our Marine Residence of Kailua, this 26th day of August, A.D. 1861, and the Seventh of our Reign. By the King. KAMEHAMEHA. Kaahumanu. By the King and Kuhina Nui. R.C. Wyllie.

It was at his marine residence that Kamehameha IV first showed signs of being "seized with incipient paralysis,"[75] the illness from which he eventually died.

Although her 1861 letters do not explicitly mention Huliheʻe by name, letters by Emma from Kailua, Kona, in 1867 and 1868 clearly indicate Huliheʻe as the location at which they were written.[76]

Summer Residence of Princess Likelike (c. 1886), Kaʻawaloa, South Kona, Island of Hawaiʻi

Although most of the new royal residences were built in Honolulu, Princess Likelike built her summer residence at Kaʻawaloa on the island of Hawaiʻi. She had served as the governor of the island from March 29, 1879, to 1880. Likelike, more than a decade earlier, in 1874, had conveyed the site of Captain James Cook's death there to the British government through consul, James Hay Wodehouse. An account in the *Daily Honolulu Press*, highlighted the improvement in the locality, including Likelike's dwelling: "The modest monument to mark the spot where Cook fell, is naturally, the centre of attention and is a vast improvement, as is the neat appearance of the hamlet itself, compared to the general condition of the place during my [A. Johnstone?] visit in 1865. Princess Likelike's summer residence, recently erected, sheltered by cocoanut and algeroba trees has added to this improved appearance."[77]

Samuel H. Davis of South Kona, Hawaii, sent a letter to A.S. Cleghorn on September 10, 1883, regarding the availability of a house for Princess Kaʻiulani. Davis wrote:

> H.R.H. Likelike was making inquiries about land to build a house upon for the use of the Young Princess. Wm Rose, who has a lease of old Peter's house for 9 or 10 years, I think, at $60 per ann, + who has made some improvements on the house is about to leave Kona and wishes to dispose of the house and furniture (some of the latter very good). If this place would be likely to suit, kindly communicate with him, saying that I had mentioned it to you. There is considerable land but not well fenced in. Trusting that Mrs. Cleghorn and party have benefitted by the change to Kona and with kind regards from Mrs. Davis and myself to all.[78]

Captain Cook Monument near residence of Princess Likelike (courtesy Hawaii State Archives, PP-96-14-006).

Transition of the Royal Residences of Hawai'i Island

The earliest accounts of the royal residences on the island of Hawai'i describe almost solely the traditional *hale pili* at Kealakekua and Kawaihae, the residences of Kamehameha I and II and the birthplace of Kamehameha III. Soon afterward, however, the royal residences reflect the adoption of Western building techniques. The stone storehouse in the king's complex at Kamakahonu stood juxtaposed in stark contrast to the traditional thatched *hale pili*. Even royalty like Ruth Ke'elikōlani, who preferred to dwell in traditional structures like the thatched structure on the grounds of Hulihe'e, nevertheless integrated Western elements into the thatched structures. Her house at Piopio included a wooden plank floor instead of the traditional pebble platform. Eventually, the Western structures, like the houses of Chiefess Kapi'olani and Princess Likelike, supplanted the traditional altogether. This pattern would repeat itself on each of the islands.

CHAPTER 2

Royal Residences of Maui and Moloka'i

E nana mai uhi kapa 'ele'ele ia Maui, a kau ka pua'a
I ka nuku, ki'i mai i ka 'āina a lawe aku.

Watch until the black tapa cloth covers Maui, and the sacrificial hog is offered, then come and take the land.[1]
—Hawaiian proverb

Moloka'i 'āina o ka 'eha 'eha
Moloka'i, island of distress.[2]
—Hawaiian proverb

With the whaling fleets anchored off of Maui during the winters, the economic activities of the kingdom focused away from the island of Hawai'i. The political structure soon followed when Kamehameha III moved his court to Lahaina on the island of Maui. The town, originally called Lele, served as the kingdom's capital from 1820 to 1845. While most of the residences on the island of Hawai'i had been constructed using local materials, the most significant early buildings on the island of Maui used foreign materials and building techniques. Indeed, two of the residences derived their names, not from their occupants but from the bricks and corrugated iron used in their construction.

The impact of the shifting capital on the common people is revealed in the *Native Register* testimony of Kalaukumuole:

> When the *ali'i*s returned to Lahaina, Kaikioewa made a lot for his *ali'i*. Three lands were taken and a portion of the lot for the *ali'i nui*. The houses were broken at this time, and the commoners were in difficulties. Therefore, I was shamed by the reviling of the parents-in-law and I appealed to Kaikioewa for a house and he consented, therefore half of a certain land was reserved for us. [...] When Kalaikini and Kuakini returned from Oahu the houses were again broken down by Kalaimoku from Polanui to Halio. Kalaimoku ordered my house to be broken again and I appealed again to Kuakini and Kalaimoku and they consented. Therefore I again had a right to this place. Kalaimoku returned to Hawaii and died and we continued to live in this place.[3]

The testimony of Kalaukumuole displays the ease with which royalty displaced commoners from land and removed their *hale pili*. It also reveals an appeal process as well as the ability to reserve land.

Lahaina Palace or Brick Palace or Kamehameha House (c. 1809–c. 1824), Lahaina, West Maui, Maui

The naming of the residence called variously Lahaina Palace, Brick Palace, or Kamehameha House, depended on whether the observer was noting its location, construction method or resident. It served as the home of Kamehameha the Great on Maui as he consolidated his control over his newly established kingdom. Maui had been conquered after the death of Kahekili in July 1794 in Waikīkī, following the time of mourning there when "black tapa cloth"[4] covered Maui.

Archibald Campbell, who lived in Hawai'i from 1809–1810, described the Lahaina house thusly: "Tamaahmaah [Kamehameha], king of Owhyhee [Hawai'i], Mowee [Maui], Wahoo [O'ahu], and the adjoining islands, resided some years at this place. His house, which we could see from the ship, was built of brick, after the European manner. Of late he has fixed his residence at Wahoo."[5]

The royal residence in Lahaina is only referred to briefly in Jacques Arago's account and only in relation to one of the reasons for the expedition's visit on August 15, 1819: "The observatory has been fixed on a small stone elevation, close to a house built of masonry, belonging to the King; richly tufted and beautiful cocoa-nut trees create an agreeable freshness."[6]

Another early traveler to Hawai'i who visited in March 1822, William Ellis, recorded the condition of the palace more than a decade after Campbell's visit: "After breakfast on the 8th, I visited a neat strong brick house, standing on the beach, about the middle of the district. It was erected for Tamehameha; appears well built, is forty feet by twenty, has two stories, and is divided into four rooms by strong boarded partitions. It was the occasional residence of the late king but by the present is used only as a warehouse."[7]

The description of the building from the 1825 journal of James McCrae, who accompanied Lord [George Anson] Byron on the *Blonde*, gives a similar description, but calls it the residence of Ka'ahumanu. He writes: "Close to the beach nearly in front of the town, stands a brick house of two low stories, whitewashed outside, built sixteen years ago by Tamahamaah [Kamehameha] for his favorite queen Kaumanna [Ka'ahumanu], which she never inhabited, choosing rather to live, after the native fashion in a thatched hut close beside the other."[8] The 1809 date of construction agrees with other accounts.

The Brick Palace continued to serve as a landmark after the death of Kamehameha I. The description of a religious service in Lahaina, includes a reference to a temporary tent used as the dwelling of Keōpūolani: "About three hundred and fifty people had encircled the tent pitched for the temporary accommodation of the queen in a grove of kou trees near a brick building, the residence of the late king when he visited Maui."[9]

An engraving, titled "Maui from the anchorage at Lahaina" shows the Brick Palace to the right of the fort.

When the Brick Palace was destroyed is unknown, but plans for the building of a replica developed in the 1960s. The *Honolulu Advertiser* reported in 1963: "The so-called 'Brick Palace' of Kamehameha I will be reconstructed next year on the Lahaina waterfront just makai [seaward] of the present branch library building."[10] The 1963 effort included research by architect Ray Morris and a study by Community Planning, Inc., that reported the history of the structure. According to the report, the Brick Palace was constructed "some time between the years 1796 and 1802 by two foreigners living in

The two-story Brick Palace appears just right of the castellated fort in the 1843 engraving titled "Maui from the anchorage at Lahaina" (courtesy Hawaii State Archives, Paul Markham Kahn Collection 40/7).

Lahaina. It consisted of a two-story brick structure, 40 by 20-feet, divided into four rooms with strong partitions."[11]

Though most sources date the Brick Palace to 1809, the *Honolulu Advertiser* reported: "In 1802 King Kamehameha used this brick palace as his headquarters. The building, architecture and style seem vague, and the authenticity of the specifications is debatable."[12]

Morris faced the same challenges that face individuals attempting to locate the lost palaces. The "first job is to find out what kind of building the Brick Palace was and where to locate it."[13] Despite a $100,000 budget to build a replica of the palace, the royal residence never came to fruition. The precise location of the palace, on the other hand, was revealed by an archeological excavation that started on December 9, 1964, and ended February 12, 1965.[14] Among the findings of the excavation were that the bricks were "composed of locally available materials,"[15] and that the building's actual dimensions were "15 feet in width, and 41 feet in length."[16] The dig also showed the method used by the bricklayers. The archeologists noted that, "the fact that the brick were layed with their axes at right angles in each successive course (for at least the 4 courses that remained) was of interest to Mr. [Ray] Morris, who related that this was sometimes called a 'British bond'."[17] Today, the site is marked with an outline of the location of the lost palace in brick and a raised marker for "The Brick Palace of Kamehameha I."

Residence of Kaikioʻewa and Keaweamahi, Lahaina, West Maui, Maui

As the guardians of Kauikeaouli, the son of Kamehameha I and future Kamehameha III, Kaikioʻewa and his wife Keaweamahi maintained their residence at the capital of the Kingdom of Hawai'i. While many of the new building efforts in Lahaina adopted new Western construction methods and materials, some chiefs still retained their traditional houses. One of the early visitors to house of Kaikio'ewa and Keaweamahi, Charles S. Stewart, provided his usual detailed description of the residence in a journal entry for February 6, 1824, half a year before the rebellion on Kaua'i that called Kaikio'ewa away from Maui to help in its suppression:

> Yesterday afternoon our whole family walked half a mile south of the Mission House, to visit our friends Kaikioeva and Keaweamahi, who have taken possession of a new establishment in that part of the settlement; and to call on Auwae, a chief lately arrived at Lahaina from the windward part of the island. The inland walk to their plantations is the most pleasant in the district, passing, shortly after leaving the beach, through a large and beautiful grove of the cocoa-nut, and then through a succession of plantations, so thickly covered with bread-fruit trees interspersed with a great variety of luxuriant vegetables, as to appear a continued and well-planted garden.
>
> We have seen nothing in the domestic improvement of the natives, that has pleased us so much as in this visit. Both chiefs have many acres enclosed which is not common: Kaikioeva's by a high mud wall; and Auwae's by a neat and substantial fence of sticks. The entrance to each is by a painted cottage gate. Their houses are larger and better built than those of most of the chiefs; indeed we have seen none, but that of the king at Honoruru, that can compare with them, either in the excellence of the materials, or in the neatness of the construction. We were also particularly pleased with the accommodations for their servants and people. These, instead of having a part of the chief's house, which is not uncommon, or of having rude and dirty booths immediately about the doors, still more frequently the case, have neat but small houses, not more than six feet by four on the ground, and about four feet high, built regularly along the walls and fences.[18]

Residence of Keōpūolani, Kaluaokiha, Lua'ehu, Lahaina, West Maui, Maui (c. 1823)

Keōpūolani, wife of Kamehameha the Great and mother of Kamehameha III, had house at Kaluaokiha, Lua'ehu, Lahaina. She had decided in late May 1823 to take up "her permanent residence in Lahaina, in Maui, her native land."[19] Arriving May 31, Keōpūolani would live just over three months, dying on September 16, 1823. Timothy Dwight Hunt described the last day of Keōpūolani in *The Past and Present of the Sandwich Islands*: "As soon as her death was known the thousands around her house commenced their frightful wailings, which spread from village to village, from house to house, till the nation mourned."[20] William Richards in the *Memoir of Keopuolani, Late Queen of the Sandwich Islands* added a detail that helps identify the residence of Keōpūolani: "The vessels also hung their colors at half mast. A flag staff was erected in front of the house where Keopuolani died on which the national banner was displayed."[21] An illustration of the mourners in *Memoir of Keopuolani, Late Queen of the Sandwich Islands* showed a Hawaiian flag in front of her *hale pili*.

Halekamani, Lahaina, West Maui, Maui, Princess Nāhi'ena'ena (1814–1837)

The most thorough history of Halekamani comes from Kekau'ōnohi's Mahele claim for the residence called Halekamani. The foreign testimony (foreign because it

A flagpole (left) was raised in front of the *hale pili* of Keōpūolani following her death. From "A Wailing Scene," in the *Memoir of Keopuolani, Late Queen of the Sandwich Islands*, 1825 (courtesy Hawaii State Archives, Paul Markham Kahn Collection, 07/284).

was in the foreign language of English) given to support claim 6325 is dated three years after Kekauʻōnohi's death. Three individuals testified regarding the claim:

> Kuakamauna, sworn, says he knows the House Lot at Lahaina, Maui, known by the name of "Halekamani." It belonged anciently to Kalaimoku and afterwards to M. Kekauonohi, who held and occupied it up to 1845, when the Court removed to Honolulu. It was occupied anciently by the King's mother [Keōpūolani] who died and was buried there. Kalaimoku, who was a relative of the King's mother [*hoahanau* of Queen Kaʻahumanu], placed this place in charge of Kekauonohi as a Guardian of the tomb. I have heard, but do not know that

Nāhiʻenaʻena (courtesy Hawaii State Archives, PP-98-16-002).

it was so, that the King had given this lot entirely to Kekauonohi in exchange for the lot called "Pahumanamana."[22]

Abner Pākī and Charles Kanaʻina had substantially the same testimony.[23]

The presence of the burial site of Keōpūolani is corroborated in a memorandum in pencil on the back of a draft letter, written on February 16, 1854. That note places the tomb on the "SE. side of the Halekamani premises."[24]

While many missionary accounts complained about their thatched residences, at least one Western resident praised his stay in the residence of Princess Nāhiʻenaʻena. The Lahaina residence was called Halekamani, because of the *kamani* wood used in its construction.

Gorham Dummer Gilman, who lived in the house, provided the only picture of the residence as well as a written account:

> Just adjoining [the house of Kekāuluohi] was the place of the Princess Nahienaena, the only daughter of Kamehameha I, and sister of Kamehameha III. This was one of the finest straw houses in the village, erected in a plot of ground partly reclining from the beach with sea walls in front and planted with kou trees. The house was some thirty by forty feet in dimensions. [1,200 square feet in area] The interior was lined with dry banana stalks, and had hard earth floors covered with fine mats. It was very commodious and comfortable house for the climate. In later years it was occupied by the United States Consul, and through him I became a tenant of Kamehameha IV. It was here that I had the pleasure of entertaining a great number of Hawaiians and visitors from abroad, as it was almost half way between Honolulu and Hawaii. It was often a pleasure to entertain guests passing from one island to another.[25]

Although Gilman's tale also mentions by inference a residence of Kekāuluohi, he gives no further description of the structure.

One of the last contemporaneous descriptions of Halekamani came in a letter from P. Nahaolelua (Governor of Maui) to Aliiolani (Kamehameha V). He wrote to the king: "About Halekamani whether you heard it had fallen down.

It has not fallen down, but it is leaning a little, and the inside rafters have broken, and it is not proper to let this house remain this way, it should be rebuilt, because, there is no shelter inside.

I believe that a wooden building would be best, but it should be a house that you will approve, whether a Hawaiian grass house."[26]

Residence of Kekauʻōnohi, Lahaina, West Maui, Maui

Kekauōnohi, one of the wives of Kamehameha II, lived with Keliʻiahonui, son of the King Kaumualiʻi of Kauaʻi, at a residence at Lahaina, Maui. Charles Stewart describes his visit to the house, and notes "improvements" since his prior visit. Stewart was "particularly gratified in a visit to the new residence of the ex-queen Kakauonohi [sic], and her husband Keariiahonui [sic], nearly a mile inland from the beach. The approach to it is by carriage road, branching from the turnpike—which runs through Lahaina, and extends several miles along the coast on either side of it, a recent work of Gov. Hoapili—and terminating, by a circular sweep, in front of the principal building."[27] Stewart provides an extensive description of the interior of the house:

> The first room we entered was large and airy, and furnished as a parlor; and in addition to chairs, tables, and a sideboard. Had a mahogany hand-organ at one end. The whole

apartment, as well as another adjoining, into which we afterwards passed, was hung with festoons of the aromatic mairè, intertwined with other evergreens. The second room, nearly as spacious as the first, was for sleeping, and contained two large field bedsteads, of handsome, dark, cabinet wood, surmounted by canopies hung with curtains of chintz; a toilet-table—covered with white cushions, and hung with draperies of muslin, festooned with ribbon—beneath a glass, in a gilt frame, sufficiently large to reflect the whole figure; and an immense lounge, or native bed of mats, spread with silk velvet in place of sheets, with a counterpane or upper covering of satin—a couch as luxurious in material, at least, as many that afford repose to the first nobles of Christendom.[28]

Residence of Hoapili and Hoapiliwahine, Lahaina, West Maui, Maui

A chief of second rank, Hoapili lived with his wife Hoapiliwahine in a stone house bordering the church in Lahaina, built about 1832. Hoapiliwahine, also known as Kalākua and Kaheiheimālie, was a former wife of Kamehameha I and mother of Liholiho, who became Kamehameha II. Their property, known as the Hoapili premises, was the subject of a court case after their deaths.[29]

Hoapili served as governor of Maui from May 1823. In 1824, Hoapili along with Kaikioʻewa joined Kalanimoku from Oʻahu in suppressing the revolt on Kauaʻi (Chapter 6). Hoapili penned an account of the battle in a letter sent from Manowai, Waimea, to Liholiho on September 13, 1824. Unbeknownst to Hoapili, Liholiho had died July 15, 1824. "We came from Lahaina to make war in two ships with four from Oahu."[30] Hoapili returned to Lahaina after the defeat of the rebellion on Kauaʻi. As governor of Maui he issued an order on October 21, 1837, to impede alcoholic beverages from entering Maui.[31] Hoapili died in January 1840.[32]

Mokuʻula, Lahaina, West Maui, Maui, Kamehameha III (residence 1837–1845)

The location of royal complex of Kamehameha III on Maui reflected the shift of power from the stronghold of Kamehameha on the island of Hawaiʻi to the conquered island of Maui. Between 1837 and 1845, Mokuʻula was the favored site for the king's residence. The move proved transitional as Western trade later shifted the court to the sheltered harbor at Honolulu on Oʻahu.

Just when the last vestige of the royal compound at Mokuʻula disappeared is unknown. But more than a century passed before the royal past of Lahaina came back to mind with efforts to "restore" the town in the mid–1960s. By then Mokuʻula had been a public park for more than five decades. On April 25, 1918, Governor Lucius E. Pinkham had issued Executive Order No. 52, that set aside Loko o Mokuhinia Pond for "public purposes, to-wit, for a public park at Lahaina, Maui."[33] The issue brought together developers who hoped the restoration would bring about economic improvement and preservationists interested in preserving the remaining nineteenth century buildings.

The Conservation Council for Hawaii wanted to have a single voice on the increasingly controversial issue: "Agnes Conrad mentioned that anyone getting involved at the present time in the Lahaina Restoration Project would just be adding fire to the fuel. She

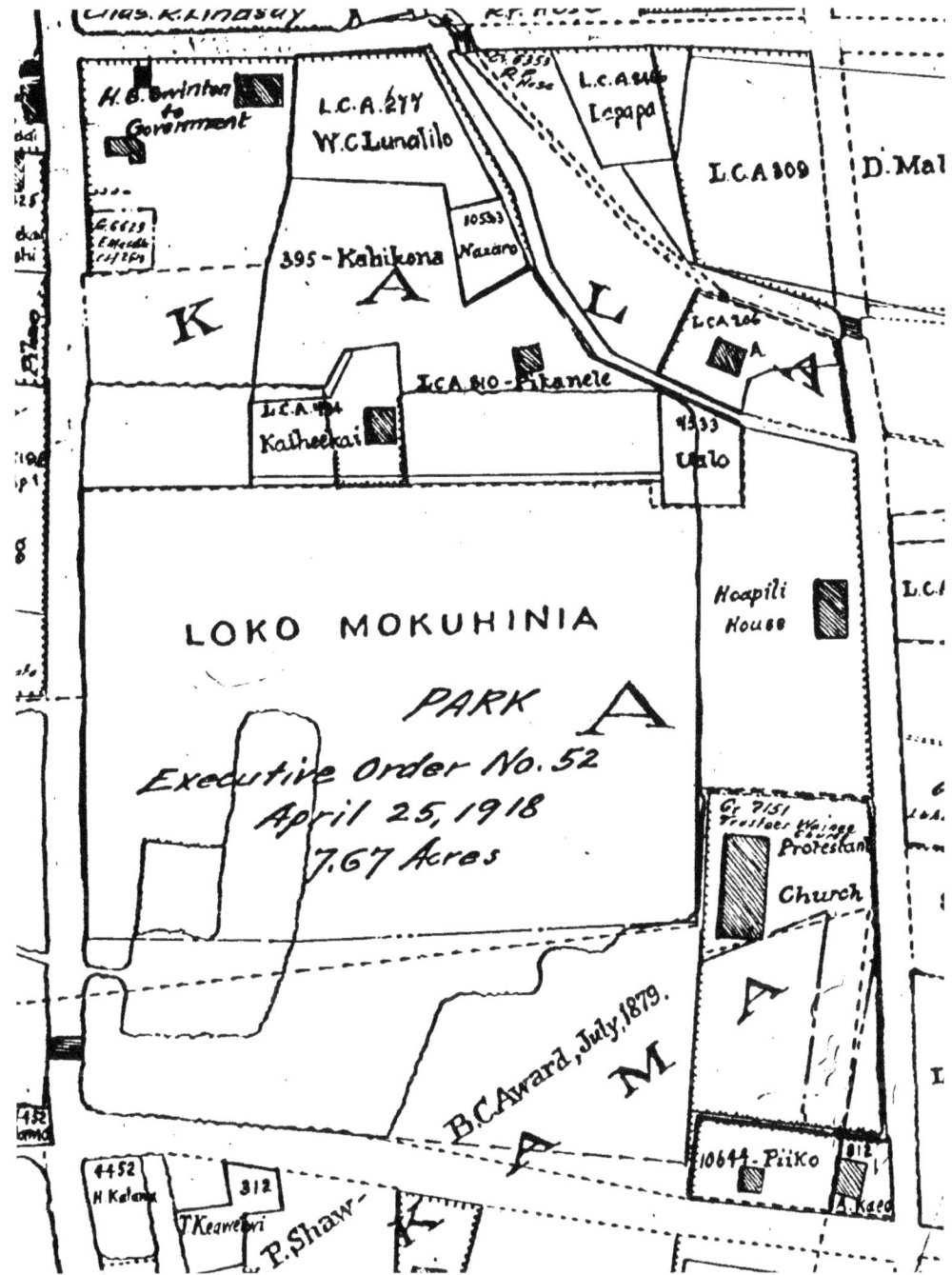

The residence of Hoapili stood next to Waine'e Church and Loko Mokuhinia. Detail of Registered Map 1262WIDE (courtesy Land Survey Division, Department of Accounting and General Services, State of Hawaii).

asked and the Board agreed that Mrs. [Beatrice] Savage [also president of the Maui Historical Society] may speak in behalf of the Sites Committee on the basis of committee agreed principles regarding this project."[34]

Buried under a baseball field the royal compound slumbered for decades until an effort to reclaim the site began in earnest in the 1990s. King Kamehameha III's Royal

Residential Complex was placed on the National Register of Historic Places on May 9, 1997.

Halehuki or Hale Piula, Lahaina, West Maui, Maui, Kamehameha III (1838–1858)

Besides the highly traditional royal compound at Mokuʻula, Lahaina, Kamehameha III erected another palace using the latest Western building technology. The edifice, named Halehuki, became known as Hale Piula after the material used in its construction. Although some disparage corrugated iron roofs today because of their industrial look, the new building material was considered innovative when it was used in the building of the new palace at Lahaina, so much so that the palace took on the name of the material itself—*piula*, Hawaiian for galvanized metal that resembled pewter.

Albert P. Taylor, in his research about ʻIolani Palace, looked into previous palaces. He noted: "At Lahaina (anciently called Lele, from the short stay of the chiefs there), was undertaken the first attempt to retain the establishment of the seat of government by the chiefs and the royal court, in consequence of which the 'Hale Puila' [sic] was erected as a palace, but which in ancient years became a court-house and continued as such up to the time of its demolition. It was erected under the direction of Kahekili (Old Thunder) who was head man under Kamehameha I."[35]

By 1843, the royal court had already shifted to Honolulu, so its use as a palace

Hale Piula is the two-story building to the far right in an engraving by Lossun-Barrett published in *Sandwich Island Notes* by George Washington Bates, 1854.

shifted to use as a courthouse. In a letter dated September 28, 1846, to P. [Peneʻamina or Benjamin] Namakeha, acting governor of Maui, John Young [II, Keoni Ana], minister of the interior wrote regarding the necessary materials for the renovation as well as their cost.[36] A couple of years later, on January 13, 1848, James Young [Kanehoa, son of John Young I] sent a letter to John Young [II, Keoni Ana], the minister of the interior, concerning the renovation of rooms of Halepiula [Hale Puila], by then being used as a court house:

> Love to you, John Young,
> The foreign judge has arrived here in Lahaina. The rooms of Halepiula are now being renovated, and are being sealed with brown cotton, and the locks are being put on, because, there are no locks; and the windows are being fixed, because, the panes were all broken. The rooms that are to be occupied by the judges are the rooms which are sealed with brown cotton.[37]

J.Y. [James Young] Kanehoa gave an update of the progress a week later in a letter dated January 20, 1848. He reported: "Here it is: Halepiula has been repaired and the rooms to be occupied by the judges are cleaner, and have been laid with brown cotton and finished, there remains only the windows which are all broken, and I have notified the Minister of Finance to send 1 case of glass so that the windows which are broken can be repaired, that is what the carpenter wants."[38] Brown cotton may refer to the bridging liner,[39] used to smooth the irregular brick surface.

Lot Kamehameha, minister of the interior, sent on February 3, 1859, a letter to R.A.S. Wood, superintendent of public works, instructing him regarding his visit to Lahaina. The future king wrote: "You will also carefully examine the Hale Piula and ascertain what materials therein will answer towards the building of the New Court house and report to his Highness the quantity thereof, and also your opinion as to what had better be done with that building."[40]

Hale Piula and its disappearance is once again mentioned at the laying of the cornerstone of ʻIolani Palace on December 31, 1879: "At Lahaina, an attempt was made to establish a permanent residence and the old palace Hale Piula was built, the ruins of which were so familiar until lately."[41]

John M. Kapena remembered the old palace in 1905: "The seat of government was first attempted to be established by the chiefs at Lahaina, and the court to be retained at that place, in consequence of which Hale Puila [sic] was erected as a palace, but which after years became a court house and continued such up to the time of its demolition."[42]

Today, Hale Piula is one of a handful of lost palaces that has been marked.

Residence of Pākī and Kōnia in Pakala, Lahaina, West Maui, Maui

Among the members of court, Pākī and Kōnia also maintained a residence in Lahaina. According to the testimony regarding the residence of Paki in Lahaina, he received the house lot at Pakala in 1837 from Kaaimalalo, the mother of Asa Kaeo. [233.3] The boundaries are given in the foreign testimony as "mauka by the fishpond of Kekuanaoa; Olowalu by Kaihe's house; makai by the seashore; Kaanapali, by A. Kaeo's lot."[43] Kekūanāoʻa wrote a letter to Kanaʻina in Lahaina informing him that: "there are two men, together with two women, coming there with Paki et al., their bodies have

been paid for here in Oahu, and they are coming, without having to pay in Lahaina for the coming year. Witness to knowing their names:
Makaena.
Kahukikolo.
Naholowaa.
Halapu."[44]

Residence of Fanny Kekelaokalani, Pakala, Lahaina, West Maui, Maui

Directly *mauka* of the Paki residence was the Lahaina houselot of Fanny Kekelaokalani. The residence sat at the northwest corner of Loko o Mokuhinia, the pond that surrounded the royal compound of Mokuʻula. The first written reference to the residence came in the testimony of Keoni Ana concerning the inherited lands of the Young and Davis descendants on February 14, 1848. After listing the ahupuaʻa on Hawaiʻi, Maui and Lanai, he adds: "and the houselot in Lahaina."[45] The lot, labeled "Fanny Young," appears in the 1884 map titled *Town of Lahaina Maui*. The map shows two structures on the property.

It was from Lahaina that Fanny sent a letter to Queen Emma on August 10, 1870.

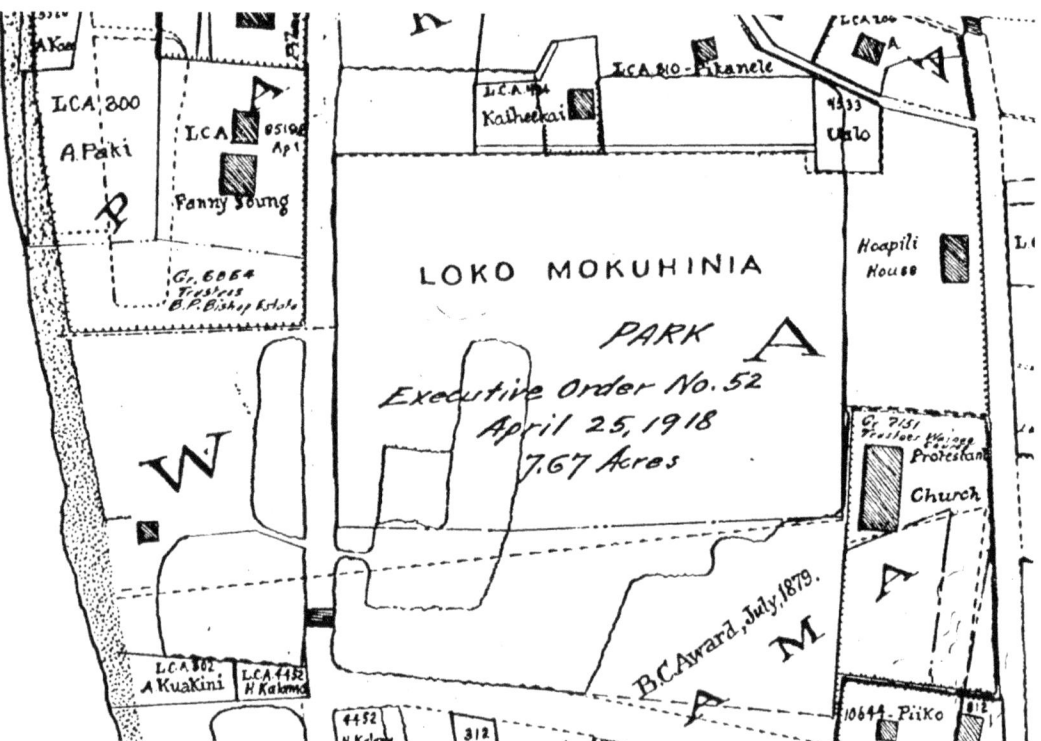

The house of Fanny Young sat between the property of Abner Paki and the northwest corner of Loko Mokuhinia, the pond that surrounded the royal complex at Mokuʻula. Detail of "Town of Lahaina Maui," Registered Map 1262WIDE (courtesy Land Survey Division, Department of Accounting and General Services, State of Hawaii).

Fanny returned to Lahaina in May 1871 and wrote another letter. She told Emma: "I arrived in Lahaina and am so cold. The waves incessantly wealed over us. There was much nausea and when I came ashore I felt ill. To this day I feel shaky, dizzy and wheezing. I am better."[46] The main news contained in her letters from Lahaina centered on a plot to shoot Kamehameha V. Her stay in Lahaina ended in July 1871. She wrote to Emma: "I am coming home. When the ship returns I will be on it, so the carriages will be there for us when we arrive."[47] Another set of letters were sent in November 1875 from Lahaina. No other surviving letters from Fanny Young are written from Lahaina after 1875. She died in Honolulu in 1880.

Residence of Peke Davis at Kapewakua, Lahaina, West Maui, Maui

Another houselot in Lahaina was occupied by Peke [Betty Davis], daughter of Isaac Davis, a war companion of Kamehameha I. In her testimony for her claim to her Lahaina property, Peke Akoni or Atoni, wrote to the Board of Commissioners to Quiet Land Title:

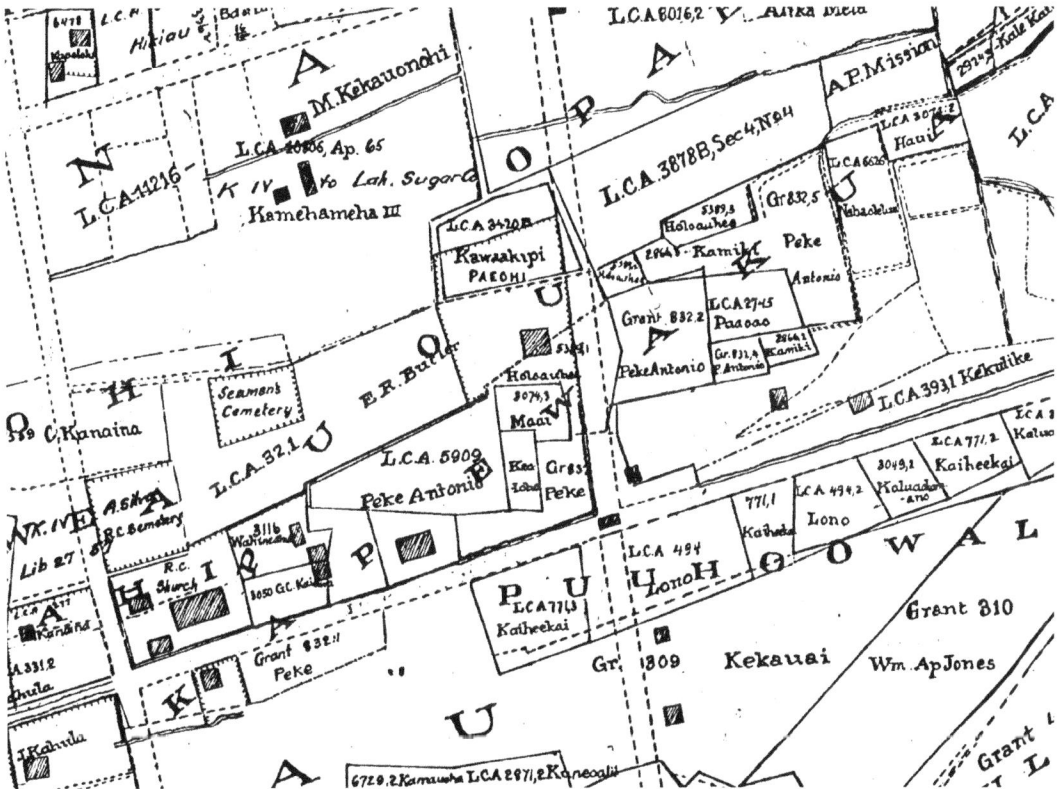

The property of Peke in Kapewakua, Lahaina, was given to her in Land Commission Award 5909. Her property is labeled "Peke Antonio" on the 1884 map "Town of Lahaina Maui," Registered Map 1262WIDE. Peke is the Hawaiianized form of "Betty," a diminutive of her English name, Elizabeth. Antonio was the first name of her husband, Antonio Sylva. Portion of Registered Map 1262 (courtesy Land Survey Division, Department of Accounting and General Services, State of Hawaii).

"I hereby petition you, publicly, for my two house lots at Kapewakua in Lahaina on the island of Maui. These are true claims, not deceitful ones, because these were enclosed completely by fence and comfortable houses were built and they have been occupied until this time."[48] The boundaries were described as having the property of Kekuanaoa on the *mauka* and Oluwalu sides, E. Butler, also called Mikapale, on the Kaanapali side, and Kimo and Kanaina on the *makai* side. Both Kekūanāo'a and Kana'ina were the fathers of kings. The Native Testimony of Z. Kaauwai said: "I have seen his [her] place in Lahaina, Maui, at Kapewakua. House-lot, 2 houses for Peke, 1 house for Kahaia. Kahaia lives there under his wife. This house-lot has been enclosed, but the entire Kapewakua land is included in this house-lot. Mauka and Olowalu, Kekuanaoa; makai, Kimo and Kanaina; Kaanapali, Mikapala. Peke received this land from his [her] father Aikake [Isaac Davis], who received it from Kamehameha I. He—Aikake—died during the time of Kamehameha I and Peke has continually lived there to this time; no one has objected."[49]

Residence of Paul Nahaolelua, Lahaina, West Maui, Maui

With the transfer of the royal court to Honolulu, the island governors constituted the primary royalty on the island of Maui. The governor of Maui from 1852 to 1874, Paul Nahaolelua, had his house in Lahaina, Maui.[50] He served under four kings, Kamehameha III, Kamehameha IV, Kamehameha V and Lunalilo.

Although the greatest share of royal residences were found on Maui at Lahaina, the more rural island of Moloka'i presented a more isolated place to escape from the hustle and bustle of Honolulu. The isolation of Moloka'i, especially the Kalaupapa peninsula, would also serve as a place set apart for individuals suffering from Hansen's disease.

Paul Nahaolelua was royal governor of Maui (courtesy Hawaii State Archives, PP-76-8-002).

Residence of Peke Davis, Kūpeke, Molokaʻi

Peke [Betty Davis] Akoni [Antonio] submitted written testimony to William L. Lee, president of the Land Commissioners on January 20, 1848. She testified: "On Molokai at Kupeke is an enclosed house lot that has been made comfortable."[51] [Also *Native Register*, vol. 3, 709]. Kaaea Hoohikiia also gave Hawaiian language testimony regarding Kūpeke.[52] A letter, dated September 9, 1853, from Samuel S. Dwight to the Minister of the Interior [Keoni Ana], included a survey of the fishpond in Kūpeke.[53] The Interior Department list dated about May 20 or 21, 1878, noted that the ahupuaʻa had been awarded to Peke in Land Claim 8524B and had a sea coast of 3,300 feet.[54] The fishpond appears on an 1897 map of Molokai.

Malama House at Kaunakakai, Molokaʻi, Kamehameha V

Kamehameha V spent much time at his quiet retreat near Kaunakakai, Molokaʻi, on the island's south shore. The daily newspapers recorded his comings and goings from Honolulu: "His majesty arrived in town last Wednesday morning from Molokai, and during the week has been residing at Iolani Palace."[55]

The residents of Honolulu were fully aware of the movements of the king from residence to residence, not only because of the journalistic coverage, but also because of the trappings of royalty. The "Court News" reported: "His Majesty embarked on the *Kamailei* on Monday [January 20, 1868] for Molokai. The usual Royal Salute from Punch Bowl was fired."[56]

The presence of Kamehameha V away from the capital was not unusual. Traveler Frank Vincent visited ʻIolani Palace in 1870, but remembered matter-of-factly: "At the time of our visit Kamehameha was absent at Molokai."[57]

A detailed description of the Molokaʻi residence is recorded by Holoholopinaau in an 1870 article in *Ke Kumu Hawaiʻi*:

> The king's own vacation house is called Malama. It is close up to the edge of the sand and if the tide is very high, the murmuring wavelet wash up and whisper to the grains of earth which were rubbed off the royal feet at the threshold of the entrance leading to the lanai.
>
> It is a grass hut, skillfully thatched, having a lanai all around, with floors covered with real Hawaiian mats. The house has two big rooms. The parlor is well furnished, with glass cases containing books in the English language... This is a very good vacation house for the king, in spite of the sun baked area.
>
> On the northwest side of the house is a large grass house, and it seems to be the largest one seen to this time. The house is divided into rooms and appears to be a place in which to receive the king's guests. There are four other fine, big houses, mostly thatched. These are surrounded by the houses of those who wait on him and some are houses used for storage.
>
> The royal residence is set apart from the rest by a wooden fence that encloses it on all sides except the sea side. The king's yard covers about three acres and is planted with trees, mostly coconuts, that are thriving nicely. Another reason we admire it so is that we saw no faucets since we left Honolulu, but when we got there we saw "the water that sleeps in the houses of men."[58]

On January 30, 1880, Mormon visitors on their way to what they called the Sandwich Islands Leper Settlement "arrived at a place called Kaunakakai, which is situated near the sea. On the south side of the island was formerly the residence of Kamehameha

V. The travelers' curiosity is aroused, on seeing the former abode of the monarch, not because of its magnificence, but on the contrary, because of its simplicity. It is a neatly built grass house, with well painted doors and windows, and surrounded by a few small but beautiful trees."[59]

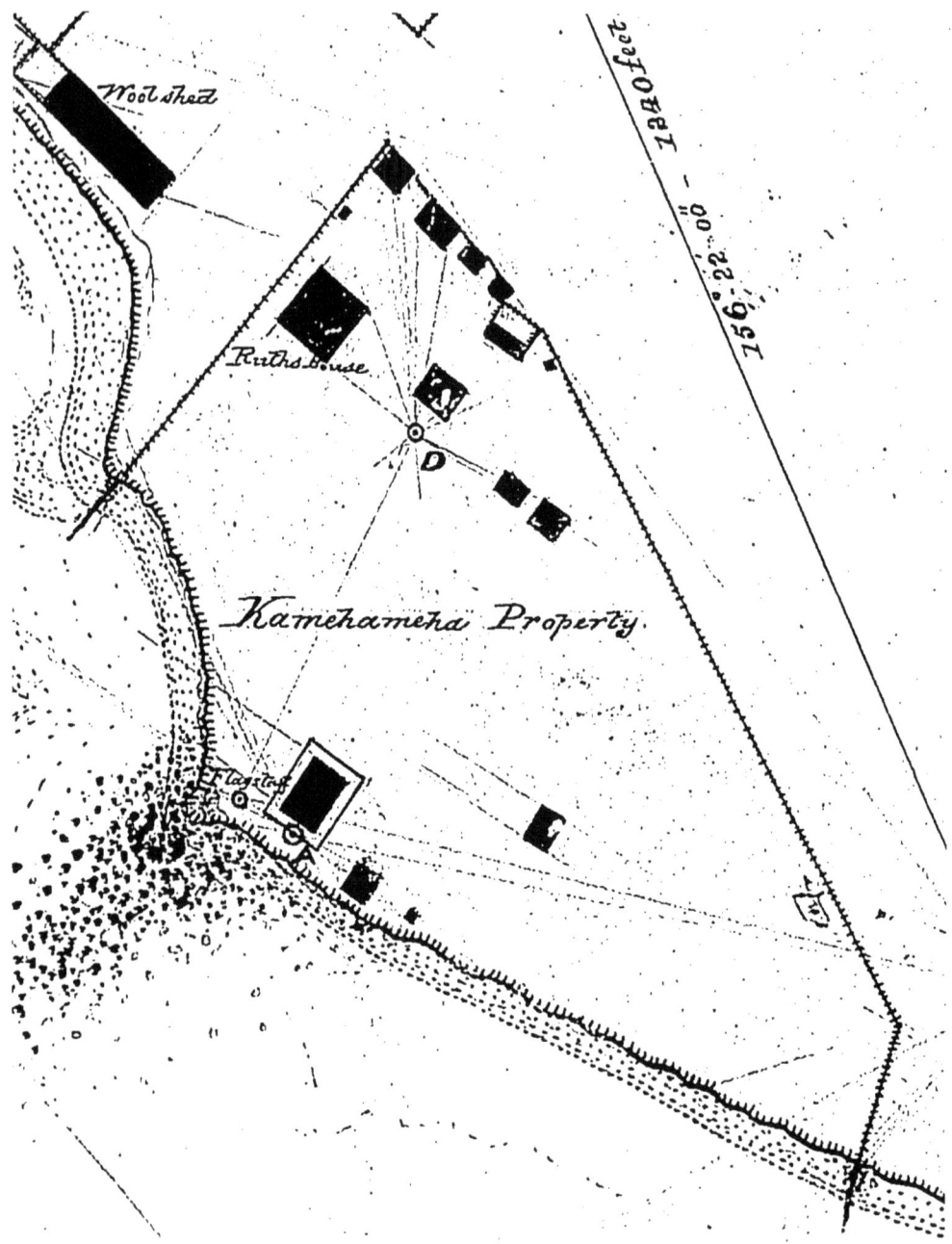

Detail of Map of Kaunakakai Harbor site with compound marked "Kamehameha Property." Registered Map 1341 (courtesy Land Survey Division, Department of Accounting and General Services, State of Hawaii).

An 1882 map of the area, titled *Kaunakakai Harbor Working Sheet* shows the enclosure of the Kamehameha property including a residence marked "Ruth's House." The unlabeled small building on the beach fits the description of the Malama residence by Holoholopinaau. A larger structure to the northwest also agrees with the 1870 account.

The debate in the Hawaiian legislative assembly reveals yet another palace at Kaunakakai that predates the one built by Kamehameha V. In supporting an appropriation for a wharf for Kaunakakai, Representative Kaunamano surmised: "It was no great wonder Kamehameha I. deserted his palace at Kaunakakai, when it had such a miserable landing."[60] The fleet of Kamehameha I had stopped at Kaunakakai on its way to the conquest of Oʻahu. Indeed, the former name for the locality, Kaunakahakai literally means "beach landing."[61]

The Commission on Historical Sites identified the specific location of the remnants of the residence and associated structures:

> On the beach at Kaunakakai where the rock foundation is. In front of the King's house was the sacred sand used exclusively by the alii when they took their sun baths. About 50 ft. mauka of this house the King [Kalākaua] built a residence for Governor Dominis and Col. Charles H. Judd. Retainers's dwellings, before burned, stood where the Standard Oil Company's buildings now stand. Canoe house on the beach stood where the present County park is. Later, small boats from schooners would come in at high tide and take the Meyers' sugar. This building was used by them as a storage shed.[62]

Today, the Malama Cultural Park, with the site of the Kamehameha residence, sits to the west of the Kaunakakai pier that features a two-lane road. Another lost residence on the island, unlike Malama House, served as a location of forced isolation.

Honolulu House, Kalawao, Molokaʻi (1873–1876)

The ailment, now called Hansen's Disease, that isolated thousands in Hawaiʻi during the nineteenth century afflicted commoner and royalty alike, so when the disease struck Peter Young Kaʻeo the location of his dwelling would shift to the lonely peninsula on the north shore of Molokaʻi. His place of residence did not immediately shift to Molokaʻi, however, as P.W. Kupa and ten others complained to F.W. Hutchinson, president of the board of health, in a letter dated November 6, 1871. The missive asked all stricken by the disease "without regard to social position or other consideration be sent to Kalaupapa immediately as it is unjust that the poor should be taken and the rich passed by." He cited, by name, "Pita [Hawaiian for Peter] Kaeo" as a prime example.[63] Kaʻeo certainly possessed "social position"; he had been a member of the Privy Council during the reign of Kamehameha IV, and served in House of Nobles starting in 1864.[64]

Ironically, as a member during the session of 1864, Kaʻeo had heard the speech of Kamehameha V at the opening of the legislature. The king stated that the increase in the disease had caused him "much anxiety, and is such as to make decisive steps imperative upon us. My Minister of the Interior will communicate to you all of the facts, and will propose measures to prevent the spread of this fearful disease."[65] More than a year and a half after Kupa's letter, Kaʻeo arrived at Kalaupapa, on July 1, 1873, six months into the reign of King Lunalilo.

Letters from Moloka'i

Three days following his arrival, in the first of a series of letters from Moloka'i to his cousin, Queen Emma, dated July 4, 1873, Ka'eo gave the status of his accommodations: "The Carpenters are putting up my Cook House and the Bath."[66] In the next letter to his cousin, who he addresses as "Dear Coz," he shared: "I thought of putting a stone wall up but was told not to as the rats and mice get into it and from there into the House."[67] He also described on July 7, 1873, the immediate surroundings: "As soon as my fence comes up I will begin to put it up and Keep the troublesome Hogs away. [...] Do not send up any of the Trees as there are no water. I think that the plants will not grow, the soil is so bad. Where my house stands it is completely surrounded with stones. Everything is finished with the exception of the article I am sending for—the picket and Trogh [sic] for the Water Cask."[68] Ka'eo depicted the geography of the wider area: "My House stands on a rise at the foot of Kauhako Hill. I am about half way from Kalawao to Kalaupapa, a distance of about Two miles. On my Left is a long line of Mountain quite perpendicular running westward into the sea. To my right the ground is rough, Hilly and volcanic in character."[69]

Although Ka'eo called the residence "my house," the phrase probably refers to possession, not ownership, for the Board of Health had voted unanimously in April 1873, three months before his arrival, to purchase of "all Lands and Houses in Kalaupapa

Map of Kalawao included in a letter to Queen Emma from Kekuaokalani (Peter Young Kaeo), dated September 30, 1873 (courtesy Hawaii State Archives). The building and enclosed yard on the road to the landing, labeled "3," indicated the residence of Peter Young Kaeo; "4," Napela's; "M," Hospital; and "K," Catholic Church. The entrance to St. Philomena Catholic Church originally faced makai down the road to the landing and is preserved today as a wing of a larger church structure expanded by Father Damien. Damien had arrived in May 1873, two months before Kaeo.

belonging to private parties, purchasing the houses on the best terms possible, and the land at about ten (10) Dollars per acre."[70]

In another letter to his cousin, dated July 23, 1873, Kaʻeo gave a detailed description of the interior of his house:

> My little cottage is very neat (the neatest and most airy, although I have to say it myself) here. My house stands on a rise facing the sea on a flat between the Pali and Kauhako hill. On the right side of my house in the corner is my Beurow back of that on the sides hangs my Hats, near the windows hang my Coats under the window is my old Koa trunk. On the mauk[a] north corner is my bed, between the front and back door hangs the curtain separating my dressing and bed room from the setting room and Parlour. On the left or East corner is my sofa by the window my Rocker makai or South corner my little table. Nearest the corner of the table my Atlas, Journal, Diary and Prayer Book. Next to that are my American Papers I got from Crabb through Wilder, and Portfolio. Next to that are my English and American papers I got from you, and also the Honolulu papers. Above the table hangs the clock. A little in front of the Atlas is my writing materials. Taking it all through it looks quite respectable. On the right side and little to the rear of the House is my Cook house with two rooms one to cook and another for to pound Poi and Keep my potatoes. My two backrooms, one is store room kept lock and the other a dining room."[71]

A September 30, 1873, letter also includes a rough map of Kalawao showing the location of his house, residence of Chiefess Kiti Richardson Napela and her husband, the hospital and the Catholic Church and other structures.[72]

In a letter to Queen Emma, dated October 11, 1873, Kaʻeo first starts to call his residence "Honolulu House."[73]

Other Accounts

Isabella Lucy Bird also shares an 1873 account of the residence of Kaʻeo in her book, *The Hawaiian Archipelago*: "Most of the victims are of the poorer classes and live in brown huts; but two of rank, Mrs. Napela and the Hon. P.Y. Kaeo, Queen Emma's cousin, have neat wooden cottages on the way from the landing, with every comfort which their means can provide for them."[74]

An eyewitness account of a visit in April 1874 by representatives of the board of health appeared in the *Pacific Commercial Advertiser*: "On the way thither [to Kalawao] we stopped for few moments at two neat wooden cottages near the road, in which reside Mrs. Napela, a former resident of Wailuku, and the Hon. Peter Young Kaeo. We found them both very comfortably situated, as suited to persons of their means and connections in life, and reasonably cheerful under their sad condition of exile."[75]

Another observer, William Knighton, focused on the lifestyles of rich on Molokaʻi. He found that those "who are well off at Molokai have wooden houses, replete with every comfort […] The Hon. P.Y. Kaeo, cousin of Queen Emma, has an excellent library in his house, chiefly of English books, and he takes an active and intelligent interest in the government of the island. An island steamer visits Molokai every month, and brings newspapers and periodicals. The *Illustrated* and the *Graphic*, the *Times* and the *New York Herald*, may be seen on the tables in Mr. Kaeo's drawing room at Molokai."[76]

The Hygienic and Medical Reports described the settlement: A mile further on [from Kalaupapa] we find another collection of houses around a pretty cottage occupied by Peter Young Kaeo, a chief and relative of Queen Emma. This receives the designation

Makanalua. Another mile brings us to Bola-bola, the residence of the superintendent, Mr. W.P. Ragsdale, and also the location of the village store and hospital."[77] The content of report, though published in 1879, most likely dates to 1876.

Although Robert Louis Stevenson arrived in Hawai'i in 1886, a dozen years after the events he recorded, he documented by interview an otherwise unreported dispute between William P. Ragsdale, by then assistant superintendent, and Ka'eo. Stevenson related the disagreement between two of the most prominent residents of the Kalawao community and the gathering of their supporters at their respective residences—Bola-bola and Honolulu House:

> That Ragsdale was arrogant is, besides, undoubted, for his arrogance came near plunging the settlement in war. Hawaiians readily obey a half-white, still more readily a man of chiefly caste. Now there lived in the settlement, in Ragsdale's day, a brother of Queen Emma, Prince Peter Kaiu [Ka'eo]. Of a sudden Mr. Meyer received (by a messenger coming breathless up the Pali) a curt, civil, menacing note from Prince Peter. If Ragsdale is going on in this way—the way not specified—Prince Peter would show him which had the most friends in the settlement, Some minutes later a second note came from Ragsdale, breathing wrath and consternation, but not more explicit than the first. Mr. Meyer put a bottle of claret in his pocket, hastened down the cliff, and came to the house of the Prince. A crowd of men surrounded it, the friends referred to, or their van: it seems not known if they were armed, but their looks were martial. Prince Peter himself, although incensed, proved malleable in debate, owned it was disgraceful for the two best-educated men in Kalawao to quarrel, and consented to leave his friends behind and go alone with Mr. Meyer to the luna's. Ragsdale lived in a grass hut on the foreland; it was garrisoned by some score of men with guns, axes, shovels, and fish spears. Ragsdale himself was on the watch but the sight of two men coming empty-handed made him ashamed of his preparations and he received them civilly. A conversation followed; some misunderstandings were explained away; an apology handsomely offered by Ragsdale was handsomely accepted by the Prince; the bottle of claret was drunk in company, and friends on either side disbanded. This ended the alarm of war, and opponents continued in a serviceable alliance until death divided them.[78]

Peter Young Kaeo does give an account of a confrontation with Ragsdale and its amicable conclusion in a private letter to his cousin, Queen Emma, dated June 26, 1874: "On the following day, I dispatched my letters and also received one from Meyer informing me that he would come down.

Yesterday he came and he, Ragsdale and I talked the Subject over, and Ragsdale said that he was misled by different rhumors [sic], and was glad to appolizize [sic] to me."[79] Thus, Honolulu House and Bola-bola almost served as sites of civil war at the settlement.

Last Description

A June 1876 *Hawaiian Gazette* account contains the last contemporaneous description of the residence of Peter Young Ka'eo, this one by a reporter who accompanied a committee appointed by the legislature to examine the condition at Kalaupapa. The former colleagues of Ka'eo arrived on the inter-island steamer *Kilauea* at Kalaupapa on June 24, 1876. The group "found Governor Ragsdale on the beach with horses for the party and immediately rode over the broad flat promontory to the village of Kalawao on its opposite side, stopping, however, on the way to call on Mr. Peter Young Kaeo, who is styled by local courtesy '*ke alii,*' the chief. He lives in a comfortable wooden cottage facing the landing, from which is distant perhaps a mile, and above which is elevated at least a hundred feet. The premises are neatly kept, and an attempt has been made to start various kinds of trees but without marked success thus far."[80]

Allowed to Return Home

Three days after the visit, on June 27, 1876, at a meeting of the board of health: "Dr. McKibbin stated that Hon. P.Y. Kaeo who had been in the Asylum for nearly three years was actually better than when sent away and under all circumstances, after a careful examination, he would recommend that he be allowed to return home under certain restrictions."[81] The board adopted the McKibbin's report, and Ka'eo soon after sailed back to Honolulu. His discharge was rare but not unique; the report of the superintendent of the Kalaupapa settlement for the period ending March 31, 1876, listed 14 as discharged out of the 1,570 "sent to the Asylum since its foundation in 1866."[82] Jack London also wrote of the misdiagnosed individuals exiled to Kalaupapa who were later sent away from Moloka'i after the bacteriological test showed no presence of the disease.[83] His three-year exile ended, Ka'eo returned to his Emma Street residence in Honolulu (Chapter 5).

The wooden structure called Honolulu House decayed, as most do in Hawai'i. The site still looks out over the stunning ocean vista from the peninsula of Kalawao. The Moloka'i settlement will eventually pass to the jurisdiction of the National Park Service, preserving other buildings on what the Hawaiian proverb that opened the chapter called the "island of distress."

Chapter 3

Royal Residences of Waikīkī

> Ke one 'ai ali'i o Kakuhihewa.
> The chief-destroying sands of Kakuhihewa.[1]
> —Hawaiian proverb

Waikīkī has long held the reputation as the playground of royalty, and justly so. The area offered royalty a peaceful alternative to the business and governmental concerns of nearby Honolulu. Even before Kamehameha landed part of his invasion fleet at Waikīkī, chiefs of O'ahu resided amidst its coconut groves, *kalo* patches and beaches. The early mentions of the residences of royalty are infrequent and brief, usually reserved to the names and locations of the houses rather than their descriptions.

Kuihelani, Helumoa, Puaaliilii, Waikīkī, Kamehameha I

Such is the case for the residence of Kamehameha I in Waikīkī. In almost a side note of his discussion of Kamehameha I and farming, John Papa 'Ī'ī wrote in *Kuakoa*: "He dwelt part of the time at Helumoa in Puaaalii, Waikiki (in a house mistakenly called Kekuaokalani; Kuihelani is the correct name) to till the famous gardens there."[2] That 'Ī'ī made special note of an erroneous reference to the name of the home of Kamehameha emphasizes the importance Hawaiians placed in the naming of dwellings. A visitor to Hawai'i in 1853, George Washington Bates, in *Sandwich Island Notes*, made reference to the residence of Kamehameha the Great in Waikīkī: "The old stone house in which the great warrior once lived still stands but it is falling into a rapid decay."[3] The stone house may actually have been the residence of Ka'ahumanu.

Queen Lili'uokalani also described sometime prior to 1895 where Kamehameha lived at Waikīkī: "Kamehameha 1st's houses stood just where Long Branch baths are and there was at that time a grove of kou trees all along that beach as far as Princess Kaiulani's bath house stands. On that account that beach was called Ulukou. Kamehameha had his court there. Chiefs of high rank of both sexes, the young and the old resided there, and there is a rock or corals in the sea of peculiar shape that was noted for the waves breaking over it. It was called Kapuni and the chiefs delighted to stand on its waves or the nalu of Kapuni. From morning till nigh they were ever in the surfs or on the sands warming themselves after a struggle with the surf."[4]

Chapter 3. Royal Residences of Waikīkī 53

Queen Kaʻahumanu (courtesy Hawaii State Archives, PP-96-6-003).

Haleopeope, Helumoa, Waikīkī, Queen Kaʻahumanu

The residence of the favorite wife of Kamehameha, Kaʻahumanu, was also located at Helumoa. The name of the house was preserved by the very entity that helped supplant the royal residence in Waikīkī. Matson Navigation Company, which ran cruise ships between the West Coast and Hawaiʻi, used its *Aloha* magazine to educate its employees about Hawaiian culture. The early tourism industry often preserved cultural references now forgotten. Such was the case of house of Kaʻahumanu at Helumoa.

The magazine shared the account about the site where the Royal Hawaiian Hotel was being constructed in 1926: "Kaahumanu, favorite wife of Kamehameha I, built a house of coral on the very grounds where the Royal Hawaiian hotel is now building. Haleopeope, she called it, which might be liberally translated 'house of trinkets,' and here she kept her valued possessions, such as feathered capes, feather tufted kahilis or royal standards, tapa cloth of rare design, hand carved calabashes and surf boards for the use of her guests."[5] The literal translation is less romantic; the name of Kaʻahumanu's Waikīkī residence, Haleopeope comes from: "*Hale* and *opeope*, to fold up, as clothes. The name of the house where the chief's wardrobe is kept."[6] David Malo makes these comments regarding the name: "The keeper of the king's apparel (master of the king's robes), or the place where they were stored, was called Hale opeope, the folding house."[7] Other accounts have Kamehameha I building the coral house at Puaʻaliʻiliʻi.

The missionary accounts often described places away from the trading areas frequented by visiting commercial ships. Thus, the account on September 1, 1824, preserved the presence of Kaʻahumanu and Kaumualiʻi at Waikīkī as well as their motivation.

Constructed in 1926, the Royal Hawaiian Hotel supplanted the sites of Haleopeope and Hale Lama at Helumoa, Waikīkī (courtesy Hawaii State Archives, PP-42-10-009).

"Preached at Waititi, the favorite spot of retreat for Kaahumanu and Taumuarii, when they wished to retire from the noise and bustle of Honoruru when they used to get into their top wagon drawn by natives and removed to this beautiful spot."[8] The service drew few participants, however, because of the revolt on Kauaʻi (Chapter 6).

Residence of Kamehameha III, Helumoa, Waikīkī

Although no written account of the Waikīkī residence of Kamehameha III exists, a photograph from the Hawaiian Historical Society identifies a structure different from the *hale pili* of Kamehameha V. The structure most likely was part of the compound at Helumoa. Mary Kawena Pukui ties Kamehameha III and Waikīkī to the Hawaiian saying: "Ke one ʻai aliʻi o Kakuhihewa."[9] Originally a curse, the saying applied to the conquered king of Oʻahu. When Kamehameha III planned to change the capital from Lahaina to Honolulu, a kahuna counseled against move, citing the curse. Just as his father had come over the seas to conquer Oʻahu, the kingdom of Kamehameha III was eventually overtaken by a conqueror from far across the sea.

The residence of Kamehameha III at Helumoa, Waikīkī (courtesy Hawaii State Archives, PP-115-6-004).

Hale Lama, Helumoa, Waikīkī, Honolulu, Kamehameha V, Princess Ruth Keʻelikōlani, and Princess Bernice Pauahi Bishop

The image of Hale Lama at Waikīkī presented an idyllic scene to the world. Illustrations of Hale Lama pictured the *hale pili* of Kamehameha V amidst a towering grove of coconut trees. The *hale pili* itself maintained a simple structure with four corners. The roof has a dual pitch, one angle to cover the house itself and another angle to cover the verandah that wraps around the house. Though built using traditional materials, the railing of the lanai does feature a Western adoption—diagonal bracing not present in pre-contact buildings.

The idyllic setting, however, did have its dangerous side, as Kamehameha V discovered in April 1869. As told in a *Hawaiian Gazette* article, titled "Narrow Escape for His Majesty," the Kamehameha dynasty almost came to an earlier end: "On Saturday last [April 10, 1869], about the hour of noon, His Majesty the King, accompanied by the Hon. W. P. Kamakau, Circuit Judge of Oahu, was walking in the cocoanut grove at Waikiki, adjacent to his seaside cottage, when three paces past a cocoanut tree, which stood in the path of the pedestrians, suddenly fell, with a crash, right in the place that half a minute before had been occupied by the King."[10]

Even after his brush with death, he chose the same location to celebrate another

Hale Lama (courtesy Hawaii State Archives, PP-115-6-005).

year of life. To celebrate his birthday on December 11, 1869: "His majesty gave an Ahaaina to his household at his seaside residence at Waikiki."[11] The Honolulu Rifles, resplendent in their new uniforms, honored the king with a parade.[12]

After the death of Kamehameha V on December 11, 1872, the property passed to his half-sister, Princess Ruth Keʻelikōlani. Ruth, in turn, bequeathed the land to Princess Bernice Pauahi Bishop. The Bishops built their home on the ʻEwa bank of the mouth of Apuakehau Stream. Then the lands fell under the stewardship of the Bernice Pauahi Bishop Estate following her death.

The development of the Royal Hawaiian Hotel at the Helumoa site required the relocation of Hale Lama. The *Friend* noted the role of the Daughters of Hawaiʻi in preserving the royal *hale pili*: "In 1921 the grass house, 'Halelama,' formerly the retiring house of King Kamehameha the Fifth at his Waikiki residence, 'Helumoa,' was brought to Nuuanu, a gift from the Bishop Estate. It was repaired, rethatched, and furnished in the mode of ancient days. Extensive repairs at various intervals make it a great responsibility, but it retains a special interest for visitors."[13] The change from sunny Waikīkī to the rainy Nuʻuanu grounds of Hānaiakamalama turned a gift into a burden during the nearly two decades following the move. So when Kamehameha School for Girls offered in 1938 to relocate the costly, high-maintenance house to their Kapālama campus (then located where Farrington High School sits today), the Daughters of Hawaiʻi agreed to pass on the historic preservation responsibility. The eventual fate of Hale Lama is shrouded in the fog of war. Taken over during World War II by the U.S. Army, the Kamehameha campus was occupied by people unfamiliar with the significance of the structure. According

Kamehameha V (courtesy Hawaii State Archives, PP-97-9-008).

Bernice Pauahi Bishop Waikīkī Residence (courtesy Hawaii State Archives, PP-89-7-003).

Hale Lama sat on a stone platform next to the driveway leading to Hānaiakamalama (courtesy Hawaii State Archives, PP-32-4-023).

to Barbara Jane Del Piano, when the students returned to their campus, the house of Kamehameha V was gone.[14]

'Āinahau, 'Au'aukai, Waikīkī (1872–1955), Princess Likelike and Princess Ka'iulani

Built at Waikīkī, Honolulu, during the last year of the reign of Kamehameha V, 'Āinahau at 'Au'aukai (literally, "bathing in the sea"), served as

Hale Lama was relocated to the grounds of Hānaiakamalama by the Daughters of Hawai'i (courtesy Hawaii State Archives, PP-32-2-034).

the home Princess Likelike and Princess Victoria Kawekiu Kaʻiulani Lunalilo Kalaninuiahilapalapa. Archibald Scott Cleghorn bought a portion of ʻĀinahau on April 25, 1872, just two years after his marriage to then chiefess Likelike on September 22, 1870. They were wed at Washington Place, the residence of Likelike's sister, Liliʻuokalani. Maaua and Koihala sold Apana 1 and a portion of Apana 2 of Land Commission Award 7597 to Cleghorn for $300. The land had originally been given to Anederea Kamaukoli "by Kaahumanu I in the year in which Poki [Boki] sailed to Nanapua [Erromanga island in the New Hebrides, now Vanuatu] and disappeared. That was when I acquired this ʻili and from that time I have occupied this land as konohiki." Queen Liliʻuokalani recounted the association of the property with Kaʻahumanu in a handwritten account:

> It was during his [Kamehameha's] residence here [Hamohamo] that Kaahumanu moved away from the party with her ladies and Kahus and made her residence just where Governor Cleghorn's houses are. Just mauka of where she lived were the streams and patches filled with taro belonging to Aikanaka. They were chiefs who were never in want of food for they never permitted their kahus to be idle, so that from these patches were furnished food for Kamehameha and all his people. Kaahumanu was quite pleased with the situation and from there went down to meet Kamehameha and his party and all joined in the pleasure of surf riding. From that circumstance Mr. C's place was called Auaukai. After Kamehameha and his party went away some of his kahus remained his name was Kamaukoli and he felt he had the right but really he had none.

It was Kamaukoli who received the Land Commission Award for Auaukai. On December 25, 1875, Kaʻiulani's godmother, Ruth Keʻelikōlani, deeded Royal Patents 4492 and 4493 to Victoria K. Cleghorn. The lands had originally been awarded as fort lands to Kekūanāoʻa, father of Keʻelikōlani.

In the deed, "Kamalii Wahine Victoria Kaiulani Cleghorn" received the property for $1.[15] Cleghorn and Likelike still lived at their Emma Street residence until 1879, so

Princess Likelike married Archibald Scott Cleghorn. Her sister, Queen Liliʻuokalani, named their daughter, Princess Kaʻiulani, heir apparent (courtesy Hawaii State Archives, PP-98-9-019).

'Āinahau sits behind the great banyan tree (courtesy Hawaii State Archives, PP-90-5-008).

'Āinahau was considered their "country" residence. Prior to the purchase of the Waikīkī site, "the grounds were occupied by many grass houses. In the first half of the last [nineteenth] century and many years prior it was the abode of certain Oahu chiefs. It has historical associations."[16] One of the earliest Western visitors, Captain George Vancouver, "anchored his ships directly in front of Ainahau on March 20th 1793, and coming ashore, walked through these grounds to meet the men who were high in authority at the time."[17] Despite the rich "historical associations" of the property, no vestige of the lost palace, nor of its pleasure grounds would exist thirty-five years after the publication of the 1904 article.

Although the name "'Āinahau" is well known, the word's meaning is disputed. Hawaiian language authority Mary Kawena Pukui gives the most straightforward interpretation claiming the simple definition, "*hau* tree land."[18] *Paradise of the Pacific* in a 1904 article focused on the house and grounds claimed a meaning of "cold land." The author explained: "By singular circumstance it is sometimes visited by draughts of cold air from Manoa Valley when the temperature of other localities is warm. However, there are no discomforting effects of this phenomenon."[19]

Although better known for the Indian banyan tree planted on the grounds in 1873, 'Āinahau also boasted 500 Washingtonia palms that commemorated the birth of Princess Ka'iulani in 1875.[20] A year after the planting, the first anniversary of the birth of Ka'iulani was feted with "a grand luau or native feast, given at Waikiki by the parents of

Chapter 3. Royal Residences of Waikīkī

the youthful princess."[21] A visitor in June 1877 described the house and grounds during a tour of Waikiki:

> Our party drove to the handsome marine residence of H.R.H. the Princess Miriam Likelike, married to the Hon. A. Scott Cleghorn. It is situated further inland from the beach, beyond the King's villa. The pleasure-grounds are handsomely laid out, with flower-beds filled with rare and fragrant plants, conspicuous amidst which are the deep red flowers of the *hibiscus*, contrasting pleasantly with the vivid green of the acacia, the old familiar Indian banyan, the Hawaiian *Hau*, and other arborescents. The villa, into which our party entered awhile, contains interesting portraits of departed and living members of Hawaii nei.[22]

The account also gives a description of the *hale pili* that was part of the compound: "A grass house adjoining [...] me a most unequivocal surprise, as, judging from the name, I had taken such a place to somewhat an Australian 'umpie'; but was astonished to meet instead with such a charming and elegantly furnished *budoir*, whose walls were constructed entirely of plaited grass—hence the name—and the roof of thatch."[23]

The celebration in 1877 for her second birthday "was honored by the presence of His Majesty the King and a large proportion of the persons most distinguished in official and social life in Honolulu."[24]

Besides Kaʻiulani, Cleghorn had three daughters from his first wife: Rose, Helen and Annie. A three-year-old princess appears with her half-sister, Helen, in a photograph dated 1878. A trellis appears on the front lanai of the house in the background, called the "Princess Likelike's house" in a later photograph. The dual-pitch hipped roof with a broad lanai is a prominent feature of the house of Kaʻiulani's mother. Two stairways provided access to the residence, each with a short set of steps. The corner of the residence includes a trellis with vines growing to around halfway to the roofline, and a

Kaʻiulani, aged 3 years old, in the garden of her home with her half-sister Helen Cleghorn (courtesy Hawaii State Archives, PP-90-5-007).

palm tree. Photographs show the vines grown to the roofline and later partially covering part of the roof. The royal palm trees frame the house on the two front corners.

By 1882 the Waikīkī gardens and residence had become an entertainment location for the monarchy, both internationally and locally. On March 30, 1882, the Japanese Envoy paid a visit to ʻĀinahau, where he visited "the little Princess Kaiulani."[25] When Kalākaua had visited Japan in 1880, he had proposed an alliance sealed by the betrothal of Princess Kaʻiulani to a Japanese prince. The visit of the HBMS *Champion*, in June 1882, provided sufficient cause for a "very pleasant entertainment" in honor of the ship's captain and officers. Attended by the royal family and H.B.M Commissioner Major Wodehouse and his family, the event featured: "Croquet on the lawn, promenades in the beautiful grounds and dancing on the spacious lanai."[26] In August 1882, Governor Cleghorn and Princess Likelike played host to party attended by the royal family, members of the legislature and government ministers. The event gave the "assembly present an opportunity of becoming acquainted with the pretty little Princess [Kaʻiulani, then seven years old]."[27]

Like Lunalilo's house in Waikiki, ʻĀinahau sometimes was simply referred to as the "marine residence." In January 1883 a celebration took place at ʻĀinahau: "Her Royal Highness, Princess Likelike received a number of friends at her marine residence at Waikiki, on Saturday afternoon, to celebrate her 32d birthday. The day was fine and a stroll about the well arranged grounds around the house, was a pleasant treat to the many who enjoy, and appreciate the flowers and well ordered gardens. Amongst the guests we noticed a number of well dressed ladies, who all wished Her Highness many happy returns of the day. The Hawaiian band, under the brilliant leadership of Mr. Berger played a number of pleasant selections from operas."[28]

The birthday of Princess Kaʻiulani, her eighth, would take place later that same year. The grounds of ʻĀinahau "never looked better than yesterday [October 16, 1883] when their lovely shades and pretty openings were filled with ladies and children, gaily and most handsomely attired. [...] The lanai had been fitted up as a dancing room for the little folk, and presented a very pretty scene when they gathered there for a quadrille or a waltz."[29] In 1886 another luau in honor of her birthday took place at ʻĀinahau, where, following the receiving of guests, "all repaired to the spacious lanai, where a magnificent luau awaited the distinguished company. The members of the Royal Family were seated at a table extending along the upper end, His Majesty the King occupying the central position in the recess over which were gracefully disposed on a background of ferns the Royal Arms."[30] Thus, the decoration recalled the embellishment of the *hale pili* called Haleuluhe (Chapter 5).

Like her sister, Queen Liliʻuokalani, who wrote songs about her residences, Muʻolaulani and Paoakalani, Princess Likelike would compose a song about her beloved ʻĀinahau that would outlive the house and its storied grounds.

ʻĀinahau
by Princess Miriam Likelike

Na ka wai lūkini
Wai anuhea o ka rose
E hoʻopē nei i ka liko o nā pua
Na ka manu pīkake
Manu hulu melemele

Nā kāhiko ia o kuʻu home
Hui:
Nani wale kuʻu home
ʻO ʻĀinahau i ka ʻiu
I ka holunape

Chapter 3. Royal Residences of Waikīkī

A ka lau o ka niu	Are the adornments of my home
I ka uluwehiwehi	Chorus:
I ke ʻala o nā pua	Beautiful is my home
Kuʻu home, kuʻu home i ka ʻiuʻiu	ʻĀinahau so regal
Na ka makani	Where the fronds
Aheahe i pā mai makai	Of the coco palms sway
I lawe mai i ke	The beautiful grove
Onaona līpoa	The fragrance of flowers
E hoʻoipo hoʻonipo me ke ʻala	At my home, my home so regal
O kuʻu home kuʻu home	It is the gentle breeze
Kuʻu home i ka ʻiuʻiu	From the sea
It is the perfume and the lovely	That brings the sweet
Fragrance of roses that sweeten	Odor of līpoa sea weed
The leaf buds of the flowering plants	Mingling with the fragrance of my love
The peacocks	Of my home, my home
And the yellow feathered birds	My home so regal[31]

ʻĀinahau would not serve exclusively as a site of mirth and song; the *Hawaiian Gazette* reported in its February 1, 1887, issue that Princess Likelike "had felt well enough to come into town the early part of last week. Unfortunately the exertion has been followed by a serious relapse. Drs. McKibbin and Trousseau in attendance."[32] She would not recover from the relapse and died February 2, 1887. The *Daily Herald* lamented: "With yesterday's setting sun sank out of earthly existence Her Royal Highness Princess Miriam Likelike. She passed away at her Waikiki residence at a quarter past 5 o'clock, after an illness of several weeks."[33]

The celebration of the twelfth birthday of Kaʻiulani would not take place because of the death of her mother. Her thirteenth birthday reception on October 16, 1888, therefore, was the first in two years.[34] Her birthday had been preceded two months earlier at ʻĀinahau by the wedding of her half-sister, Helen Cleghorn, to Col. James H. Boyd.[35] Helen was the second of the three daughters that Archibald Cleghorn had with his first wife. The oldest, Rose Cleghorn, had married James William Robertson in July 1876.[36]

It was not the royal residents who would secure the memory of estate. Poet Robert Louis Stevenson secured the immortality for the banyan at ʻĀinahau with a poem he wrote 1889 for the thirteen-year-old Kaʻiulani. The poignancy of Stevenson's words comes as much from the poem as from the note that precedes it: "Written in April to Kaiulani in the April of her age; and at Waikiki, within easy walk of Kaiulani's banyan! When she comes to my land and her father's, and the rain beats upon the window (as I fear it will), let her look at this page; it will be like a weed gathered and pressed at home; and she will remember her own islands, and the shadow of the mighty tree; and she will hear the peacocks screaming in the dusk and the wind blowing in the palms; and she will think of her father sitting there alone.—R. L. S."

The poem, titled simply "To Kaiulani," captures the sacrifice that the move would entail:

Forth from her land to mine she goes,	And I, in her dear banyan shade,
The island maid, the island rose,	Look vainly for my little maid.
Light of heart and bright of face:	
The daughter of a double race.	But our Scots islands far away
	Shall glitter with unwonted day,
Her islands here, in Southern sun,	And cast for once their tempests by
Shall mourn their Kaiulani gone,	To smile in Kaiulani's eye.

On May 10, 1889, Kaʻiulani left Hawaiʻi for schooling in England, under the guardianship of businessman Theo H. Davies. There she attended Harrowden Hall School, an Anglican school for girls. The Bishop of Leicester reported on the progress in May 1890: "A letter from the head of the private school the Princess is attending states that she is applying herself to her studies, stands at the head of the German class and is very near the top of the class in English."[37]

Another of the half-sisters of Kaʻiulani, Annie Pauai Cleghorn, married J. Hay Wodehouse in December 1890.[38] The account of the reception gives a short description of ʻĀinahau including the presence of a "glazed alcove at the head of the dining hall."[39] The wedding report also referred to a cottage, possibly Princess Likelike's house, on the grounds where the couple displayed their wedding presents. A photograph of the house of Likelike shows the vines covering part of the roof. On the nearest stairway a woman reclines on the steps. A couple stand on the same set of stairs. On the stairs to the rear of the photograph another couple stand on the steps.

While Kaʻiulani was still away in England, King Kalākaua died and the throne passed to Liliʻuokalani. Ever aware of the dangers of a lack of succession, on March 9, 1891, Queen Liliʻuokalani named Princess Kaʻiulani as heir presumptive or future queen. Archibald Cleghorn would serve as governor of Oʻahu from November 11, 1891, to February 28, 1893, more than a month after the overthrow of his sister-in-law, Queen Liliʻuokalani, on January 17, 1893.

Kaʻiulani left England, arriving in the United States on March 1, 1893. She met President Grover Cleveland at a special reception on March 13, 1893. In a speech to 1,000 persons gathered at Palace Square, Bush said, "I believe it was due to Kaiulani's influence that the [annexation] treaty was withdrawn."[40] Kaʻiulani returned to England on March 22, 1893.[41] The celebration of the eighteenth birthday of Kaʻiulani at Washington Place on October 17, 1893, was a bittersweet event. The *Pacific Commercial Advertiser* called her the "ex-princess Kaiulani."[42] By 1895, the Helen Boyd and her family moved to ʻĀinahau.[43]

New House

Kaʻiulani would not return until November 9, 1897. She would come back to a new house, built especially for her return. Even before her return the news of the new house had pleased her. In a letter to her aunt Liliʻuokalani she had written: "I am so glad that Father is putting up a proper house at Ainahau. It has always been my ambition to have a house at Waikiki worthy of the beautiful garden."[44]

The new house would feature a grand hall containing the treasures of the Cleghorn family. Princess Kaiulani would host a birthday gathering at ʻĀinahau for her cousin Prince David Kawānanakoa in February 1898:

> Princess Kaiulani very gracefully entertained a hundred or more of her friends in a luau at Ainahau, Saturday afternoon. The Princess was seated in the head table with the Princes Kawananakoa and Kalanianaole at either side while at the two longer tables connected therewith and arranged so as to allow of comfort in being seated on the floor were the guests of the afternoon, most of whom were Hawaiians.
>
> The luau was altogether a very charming affair and distinctively Hawaiian. Hardly a native dish was overlooked in the make-up of the repast, and young ladies stood ever ready to attend even the smallest wants of the guests.

The 1897 'Āinahau featured the same broad lanais as the previous house but included rich ornamentation popular at the time (courtesy Hawaii State Archives, PP-92-8-012).

For some time before the beginning of the luau, the Hawaiian National band played under the banyan tree immediately in front of the main house. When the feast began, the music was transferred to a position near the large dining hall.

When appetites had about been satiated, Prince David Kawananakoa arose and proposed the health of Princess Kaiulani. This was drunk standing by the men as was the health of Prince David proposed a little later on by Hon. A. S. Cleghorn. It turned out that Kawananakoa was 30 years old and the luau was given in his honor.

A number of people were invited to continue the festivities during the evening."[45]

The interior of the residence of Archibald Scott Cleghorn displayed the royal standards, called *kahili*, and other objects collected from his decades in Hawaii (courtesy Hawaii State Archives, #23,224).

The day after her twenty-third birthday, Ka'iulani fulfilled the duty of royalty and received "the Hawaiian people at Ainahau from 2 to 5" on Monday, October 16, 1898.[46] The next day she met with "other than Hawaiian visitors from 3 to 6 p.m. The occasion [was] her birthday."[47] What was scheduled as the "last reception"[48] of year, on November 1, 1898, would end up being her last reception ever.

Princess Ka'iulani would not celebrate another birthday; she died at 'Āinahau on March 6, 1899. Unlike her mother, Princess Likelike, whose body was removed from 'Āinahau to lie in state at 'Iolani Palace, Ka'iulani remained at her beloved residence. The former Royal Hawaiian Band, under the Republic of Hawaii called the Hawaiian Band, that used to play music for her birthdays under the banyan tree, gathered one last time to play dirges while Ka'iulani remained at 'Āinahau.[49] Ethelinda Shaefer Castle shared a description of the mourners at 'Āinahau on the Authors' Evening of the Kilohana Art League:

> The silence remained undisturbed until the night had far advanced. Then from the forest came a hushed murmur, as of approaching throngs, and the soft sound of many naked feet on heavy dust. The body of the Princess was not yet cold, but already the frenzied grief at her loss had summoned her people together.
>
> A sudden wailing cry, sharp, prolonged, broke out upon the night. It was such a cry as brought those pale-faced watchers to their feet beside the bier. Louder and louder it rang throughout the darkness, seeming to carry in its single strength the anguish of an entire

Princess Kaʻiulani stands on the steps of the 1897 residence at ʻĀinahau (courtesy Hawaii State Archives, PP-96-8-018).

people. Others followed it—fierce, distinct—until the great forest surged with the blended grief of mourning. The piercing screams of peacocks, who lift their voices when the dead is near, joined in the tumult.[50]

A service was conducted by the Bishop of Honolulu there with her immediate family and close friends in attendance.[51]

On the evening of March 10, the remains of Kaʻiulani were taken directly to

The peacocks on the ʻĀinahau grounds "joined in the tumult" of mourning the death of Kaʻiulani (courtesy Hawaii State Archives, PPBER-2-9-011).

Kawaiahaʻo to lie in state.[52] After the body of Kaʻiulani left her Waikīkī residence, Elsie Mae Robertson, the daughter of her half-sister, Rose, reported sensing the spirit of the late princess at ʻĀinahau:

> Miss Robertson (left behind at Ainahau on account of illness), together with a number of native and Japanese servants, were the only ones remaining in the house after the departure of the body for the church. This young lady had just taken a reclining position on one of the "hikieis" or divans that are to be found all over the house, when, it is asserted, she heard noises that made her blood run cold. Transfixed to the spot, she listened for their recurrence, and in a very short time they were repeated. The room on the upper floor that had been occupied by the Princess seemed to be in an awful state of unrest. The sound of a myriad of bodies passing through the room and tossing furniture about, it is said was what met the ears of the frightened people. Then came a rush of wind. The door of the room leading out into the hall opened with a burst and something came down the stairs with a rumbling sound. Then the door leading to the walk that connects the main house with the lanai opened in the same mysterious way and closed again with a slam. The chairs and tables on the walk were overturned, and a voice which was, according to the people in the house, unmistakably that of the dead Princess, was heard to cry, "Kauka! Kauka!" [Doctor! Doctor!][53]

A major reception once again took place at ʻĀinahau on October 23, 1900, when Cleghorn invited 190 visiting "Nobles of Islam Temple Ancient Arabic Order of the Mystic Shriners" to his storied Waikīkī residence: "The guests were escorted across a wide lawn and into the house, where each in turn was presented to Liliuokalani. The presentations were made by Mrs. James W. Robertson, Mr. Cleghorn's daughter. Mr. Cleghorn, owing to illness, did not appear."[54] A luau for 500 guests, hosted by Prince David Kawānanakoa on the lawn of his house, followed the reception.[55]

In February 1901 ʻĀinahau served as the honeymoon location for Cleghorn's grandson, Archibald Scott Pauli Robertson, and Eliza Crowningberg.[56] His sister, Elsie Mae Robertson and James F. Jaeger had their wedding at the Cleghorn residence in September 1901. The *Hawaiian Star* reported: "The luxuriant grounds were enhanced by brilliant effects of artificial lighting and the house and lanais profusely decorated with ferns and island flowers."[57]

The beauty of ʻĀinahau, captured by Theodore Wores, won over critics of his San Francisco exhibition: "Unquestionably one of the best paintings shown by Mr. Wores is a moonlight of the bay of Honolulu, looking toward Diamond Head from Ainahau. This was given the easel of honor."[58]

Even after the demise of the monarchy, issues related to the rights of kings still found their way to the courts of law. In January 1902, the case of *Kapiolani Estate v. A.S. Cleghorn* reached the Supreme Court. The dispute centered on a small portion of the ʻĀinahau property that had been sold to Kalākaua by Ruth Keʻelikōlani, but had been possessed by Cleghorn and Kaʻiulani. The property was later bequeathed to Kapiʻolani and upon her death became part of her estate. At question was whether King Kalākaua, as reigning monarch, was under the same limitations as ordinary citizens regarding adverse possession. Chief Justice Walter F. Frear (later Territorial Governor), for the majority, ruled in July 1902 that the constitutional provision did not apply in the case of the king's private actions or regarding his private lands. The decision allowed the disputed property to remain part of ʻĀinahau.

ʻĀinahau continued to be a gathering place for social gatherings. Cleghorn hosted a reception in October 1904 for Liliʻuokalani a couple weeks before her voyage on her way to Washington, D.C. Cleghorn's hospitality, however, was not limited to royalty. The great and the small found welcome at ʻĀinahau. The society page of the *Evening Bulletin* noted in January 1906: "Ex-Governor Cleghorn, who often gives delightful teas, entertained at Ainahau on Thursday afternoon for Miss O'Meara."[59] His hospitality elicited a warm response in the same newspaper a few weeks later: "Ex-Governor Cleghorn's little teas at Ainahau are very popular. Mr. Cleghorn has a charming way with him and his guests much appreciate his hospitality."[60] Similar hospitality was extended to the visiting Southern California Editorial Association in September 1906: "On the lawn before the famous home Mr. Cleghorn received guests with the courtly grace which has always been one of the pleasures and memories of Ainahau. The guests were given the freedom of the home and they reveled in the art treasures in the lanai. [...] For nearly an hour the home was invaded by the Californians, and after a peep into the old native grass house, the visitors were whisked away."[61] In March 1907, Cleghorn opened ʻĀinahau to the wives of visiting businessmen from Los Angeles. "Fair Guests Royally Received at Ainahau" the *Hawaiian Star* headline proclaimed. The report concluded: "The beauties of the place supplemented by the gracious courtesy of their host captivated all of the fair visitors."[62]

Despite the demise of the monarchy and his lack of an official position, Cleghorn gave a picnic at ʻĀinahau on June 26, 1909, for the visiting Japanese naval squadron.[63] His brother-in-law, King Kalākaua, had attempted to arrange a marriage between Kaʻiulani and a Japanese prince during the monarch's voyage around the world.

Private citizen Cleghorn also faced indignities unheard of during the monarchy. Despite the size of ʻĀinahau grounds, Cleghorn found the silence of his estate disturbed by individuals shooting birds on Sundays. He wrote in a letter dated July 27, 1909, to Governor Walter R. [sic] Frear: "It seems remarkable that having lived at Ainahau since the year 1872 and during the period under the Monarchy I was never subject to this annoyance. [...] It may be a matter of little importance to you and your Attorney—General, but it is most annoying to persons living at Ainahau."[64]

The letter would be one of the last complaints from Cleghorn. He had brought up the same issue four years earlier to the Board of County Supervisors. He brought to their attention: "a shooting last Sunday in the neighborhood of Ainahau. Several pigeons had been killed, and other birds which he had desired to keep near Ainahau were being driven away."[65]

Frear responded promptly to the former Governor of Oahu: "I have your letter of yesterday, and regret very much that you are still annoyed by persons shooting birds on Sundays in your neighborhood.

"There seems to be no special law governing the case at present."[66]

Of one late night visitor, Cleghorn had no complaint. He reported in 1909: "I wonder if I have a leper living on or near my estate? On moonlight [sic] nights, about two a.m., a veiled woman appears near the grass house and sits there on a bench. Towards morning she disappears. I have never seen her, but my people have. They are afraid to speak to her." When asked if he would have her captured and taken to the settlement on Molokaʻi, Cleghorn replied: "By no means. [...] The poor creature is doing no harm and if it pleases her to live there I shall not interfere as long as she keeps her distance. In fact, I see that food is left her on the bench."[67]

Open to the Public

Cleghorn would open ʻĀinahau to the general public for the first time with a May Day festival on Saturday, April 30, 1910. Although open to the public, tickets for the event cost 50 cents for adults and 25 cents for children. The publicity noted: "Ainahau is peculiarly free from rain and even though it is raining in town it is very unlikely to be raining there."[68] The prediction rang true as the *Evening Bulletin* reported blue skies and balmy air. The society page writer effused: "Nature has lavishly endowed with beauty Ainahau the gem of Waikiki, whose owner threw open its gates for the first time to the public, giving the world of Honolulu the privilege of seeing the home where royalty dwelt and whence genius gathered inspiration. This day has marked a new era in this ideal spot and many hearts will find happiness in viewing the beautiful May Day festival."[69] Sadly, Cleghorn opened ʻĀinahau to the general public for the last time.

Cleghorn Dies

Cleghorn died in Honolulu at ʻĀinahau on November 1, 1910. One report focused on the impact on ʻĀinahau itself: "One of the most beautiful places in the Islands, a home where all have been received alike; where in the past, joy has been unconfined is today shrouded in gloom, for the master is dead."[70] Like his daughter Cleghorn lay in state at ʻĀinahau, but his funeral rites took place at St. Andrew's Cathedral. The procession lined up at Emma Square, the park that he had tended decades earlier, and went to the burial place at the Royal Mausoleum.

Ka'iulani Park

To create a lasting memorial for his late daughter, Cleghorn willed 'Āinahau to the territory for a park. Ironically, Cleghorn's son-in-law, J.H. Boyd, had published a public notice in July 1897 that 'Āinahau was not "a thoroughfare, a public park or public recreation ground."[71] Sixteen out of twenty-eight members of the legislature, however, "spurned" Cleghorn's gracious gift, some because of a restriction in the will that required the park to be closed at night, others that the land might revert to the heirs after improvements had been made.[72] Not voting, but opposed to turning 'Āinahau into a park was "Archie Robertson, one of the heirs who has been opposed to the gift of this property to the government."[73] By 1914, the deadline was fast approaching to accept the gift. J.M. McChesney, in a last-ditch effort, wrote to Gov. Lucius E. Pinkham: "It has been stated to me by an attorney that the acceptance of the offer by the Governor by proclamation would be sufficient."[74] The governor replied to McChesney five days later:

> I have taken under consideration your communication of January 30, 1914, relative to Ainahau Park, and herewith hand you Opinion 358 of the Deputy Attorney General, Hon. Arthur G. Smith.
> You will understand therefrom that I have no authority to act in the premises.
> The limit of time specified in the will of the late A.S. Cleghorn will prevent any action in view of its immediate expiration.[75]

Opinion No. 368 underscored the pertinent sentence from the will: "The acceptance of such deed upon such terms and conditions to be authorized by act of the legislature within two years after the offer of the trustees hereunder to execute such deed."[76] Smith concluded his opinion: "Such a condition was in his power to impose; and having imposed it, no other method of acceptance will be effective."[77] The legislature and governor both set into motion the destruction of the botanical wonder.

'Āinahau Hotel at Waikīkī

For a brief time the 'Āinahau estate remained intact. In 1915 'Āinahau was leased to Mr. and Mrs. E.H. Lewis. A July 1916 announcement reported the expected arrival of Ira Davis of California "to take up his manager's work at the popular beach resort."[78] Mr. Lewis also detailed improvements to 'Āinahau: "several hundred dollars has recently been spent at the Ainahau and with the addition of a new dining room and new kitchen, also two cottages and entire renovation of the quarters, Ainahau will make a bid for its share of the local and transient trade. Eight more cottages are ordered."[79] Despite the positive outlook, the hotel's days were numbered.

For Sale

Within three months of the announcement, came news of a potential sale to "a big Eastern hotel company [...] one of the largest on the Atlantic Coast."[80] The Cleghorn trustees set the price at $65,000, and "if the hotel company will meet this figure the deal will undoubtedly go through. The land comprises 11 1-3 acres and would make an ideal

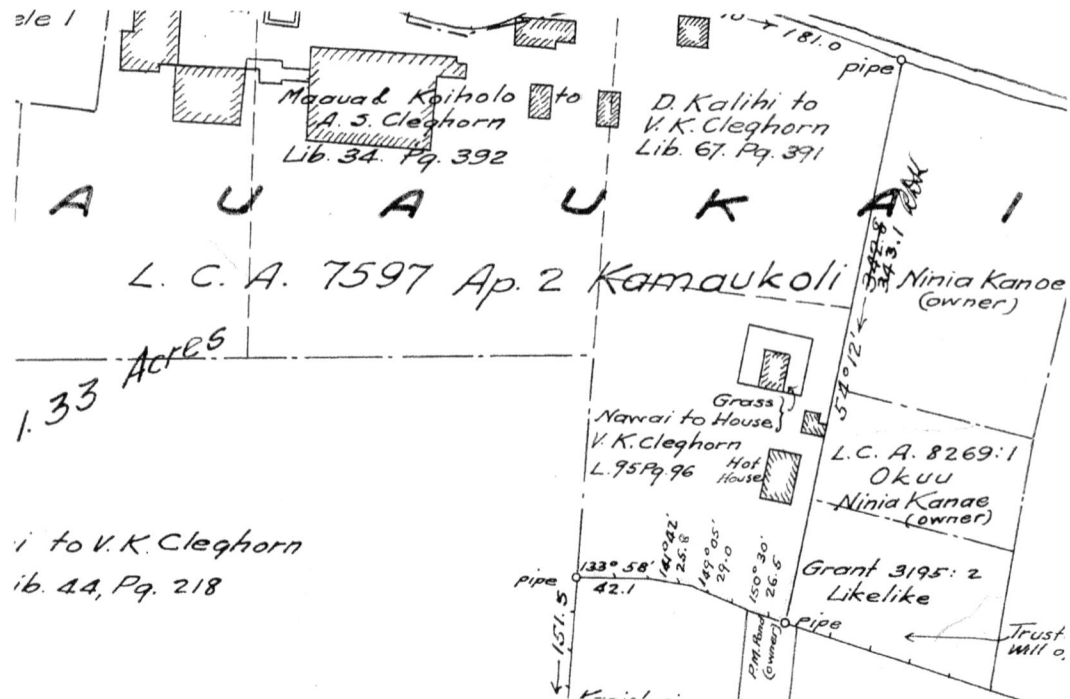

The first Land Court Application for subdividing the property, numbered 350, showed the various building on the ʻĀinahau property including the location of the Grass House (courtesy Land Survey Division, Department of Accounting and General Services, State of Hawaii).

place for such a big hotel as it is understood is planned by the company."[81] The metamorphosis from kamaʻāina estate to Eastern hotel company property caused the local newspaper to lament: "The passing of Ainahau to outside interests marks another step in the rapid dissolution of the old Hawaiian homes and customs, for it is one of the last of the old homesteads around which centered the old Hawaiian life."[82] The trustees also had an alternative plan for ʻĀinahau: "If, however, in the meantime for some reason the deal falls through [James W.] Pratt is planning to subdivide the property and sell the lots for homes. He has already drawn up tentative plans and is only waiting for the hotel company to decide whether it wants it before going ahead with subdivision."[83] The company's decision sealed the fate of ʻĀinahau.

By January 1917, ʻĀinahau lots were being readied for sale: "The romantic spot is to be cut up into lots and will become the home to many future Honolulans."[84] In the end, neither its links with royalty, nor its botanical beauty were enough save ʻĀinahau from destruction by Percy M. Pond and the Guardian Trust Company. The obituary for ʻĀinahau read: "So at last it has been subdivided into building lots. Smooth concrete streets now cut through its labyrinths of tropic wilderness, between the drowsy palms and across the winding paths that Stevenson and the Princess trod. The great house still stands, and Kaiulani's banyan, more huge and gnarled than in the days gone by, still spreads its sheltering arms over yard and veranda."[85] The Cleghorn mansion stood in the midst of one-story cottages on its own oversized lot, numbered 26, with 20,820 square feet of land, the hale pili on yet another lot and the banyan tree part of another lot. The property was bought by a Hollywood filmmaker, W.F. Aldrich, and his wife Peggy.

'Āinahau Destroyed

Even with the grand house on its own lot, the historic royal residence would not survive, destroyed by fire in the evening of August 2, 1921. The *Honolulu Advertiser* reported: "Ainahau's a total loss. Not a stick of the old house remains standing."[86] The loss did elicit memories of the house's royal past: "The old house, in the days of the Cleghorns, had a spacious drawing room, once a ballroom, which was a veritable museum filled with a collection of mementoes of the old Hawaiian days, and upon the walls, then, were the portraits of kings and queens, princes and princesses."[87] Although the Cleghorn treasures had long before been transferred from 'Āinahau, the fire destroyed the motion pictures of Aldrich stored there: "For two or three years the house had been used for the development of films depicting life in the islands. Some films which can never be replaced, including those taken at the funeral of Queen Liliuokalani, the big eruption of Kilauea, and other pictures of historic and scientific value were destroyed."[88] The banyan tree may have prevented the fire from spreading to nearby recently built bungalows. Sparks from the fire reached all the way to the Moana Hotel. In the end the banyan tree was all that remained to bring to mind the lost palace that once stood there. In 1925 the idea of marking the banyan got underway. "The particular spot chosen by the press for their memorial is one of the most romantic spots in Waikiki connected not only with the life of Stevenson but also with the lives of King Kalakaua, Princess Likelike, Princess Kaiulani and other members of the royal families."[89] With the large mansion gone, the owner of the property, Paul Ernst Richard Strauch, in 1925 subdivided the large lot into two smaller ones. The boundaries also took advantage of the new land that filling of the adjacent Apuakehau Stream created. The completion of the Ala Wai Canal would further expand the size of the property.

'Āinahau Hale Pili

Unlike the Western-style mansion, the 'Āinahau *hale pili*, on nearby Lot 67,[90] escaped harm and was eventually relocated to the Salvation Army site in Mānoa. The name of the thoroughfare next to the property was Kapili Street, referring to the one of the names of Princess Miriam Kapili Kekāuluohi Likelike. That house, built by Princess Likelike, was "used as a sleeping chamber and as a spot to while away the hours of the day."[91] The owners, James and Muriel Bergstrom, subdivided the property into two lots in 1925, a lot fronting Kapili Street (67-A) and the other (67-B) containing the *hale pili* accessible via a 4-foot-wide alley. The development forced the relocation of the house to the "grounds of the Salvation Army in Manoa Valley."[92] The *hale pili* almost didn't make it to its new location:

> When the Bergstrom property at Ainahau was sold, the owner advertised for some individual or institution to take charge of the relic and preserve it.
> Miss R. Payne, Salvation Army commandant in charge of the industrial activities in Manoa, heeded the call. Going to Waikiki to claim her property she found laborers had already dismantled the hut. So rudely in fact, that it lay a ruin on the ground. Others, she was told, had expected to salvage what was left and to re-erect it as a chicken coop.
> Miss Payne moved the remnants and restored them, adding a few touches of modernism such as windows to admit light and wood treatment to forestall the activities of the termite.
> [...]
> Inside are a number of relics, loaned by Mrs. Lily Auld, an intimate of island royalty. You

may see a cane once worn by a king—a present from another king. A warriors [sic] spear, long dark, sharp, reposes in the rafters. There is a tapa board—of great historic value.[93]

Thus, the last memorable structure left the site of the lost palace. Only the great banyan tree remained. The Daughters of Hawai'i were deeded the portion of the property on which the tree grew, in Lot 61-B. The organization dedicated the plaque marking the banyan tree in 1931. Development would eventually lead to the loss of the banyan tree in 1955, the last vestige of the grand gardens of 'Āinahau. The site today sits under the parking structure of the Waikiki Townhouse on Tusitala Street.

The relocated *hale pili* would be torn down in 1983. Explained Bette Stillwell, manager of the Salvation Army's Waioli Tea Room, "it became dangerous for elderly people. Salvation Army officials decided to tear the rickety old building down."[94] A larger reconstruction of the 'Āinahau *hale pili*, designed by architect Ray Morris, was opened with a luau on May 21, 1983.[95] That structure, too, has been replaced, so no trace of the original *hale pili* remains. The Ainahau Gardens condominium, on a street named for Stevenson (Tusitala [Samoan for storyteller]), today occupies the site of the Cleghorn mansion.

Marine Residence (1863–), Kaluakau, Waikīkī, Honolulu, King Lunalilo and Queen Emma

As with other royalty, Lunalilo also maintained a residence in Waikīkī called the Marine Residence. His house sat on roughly 30 acres at Kaluakau. The residence consisted of an L-shaped main building with steeply pitched gables at either end, one facing the front of the structure and the other facing left. A wing with lower-pitched roof stretched from the main part of the house with its gable perpendicular to front facing gable. A veranda wrapped around the inside of the L-shaped footprint of the main building and across the front face beneath the gable. Another lanai ran along the front of the wing that stretched to the right.

Mutiny

Lunalilo was recuperating at his Waikīkī residence on Sunday, September 7, 1873, when word came to him of the mutiny of members of the Household Guard stationed at the Barracks mauka of 'Iolani Palace. The king's other O'ahu residence, Ha'imoeipo (Chapter 4) also sat adjacent to the Barracks. With the king living at Waikīkī, official acts took longer to complete, allowing informal attempts to end the mutiny: "While the signature of His Majesty, who was at Waikiki, was being obtained to this order, an informal 'Court of Enquiry' was being convened at the barracks to examine the grievances of the men. This court consisted of Col. D. Kalakaua, Col. J.M. Kapena and Capt. Mahuka."[96] The government also tried to take advantage of distance to Waikīkī to remove the leaders of the mutineers from the barracks: "It was hoped that they [the mutineers] would listen to the King in person, and be persuaded to go to his residence at Waikiki for an interview, meanwhile possession could be taken of the barracks, and this course was next resorted to. On Wednesday morning, the 10th inst. [September 10, 1873], His Majesty sent a message to the soldiers that he would be pleased to receive delegation from them, and hear their disobedience of his order, and also their grievances."[97] Ultimately the mutiny ended without bloodshed.

Marine Residence

Though it was not called the Marine Residence in any accounts of the mutiny, the Waikīkī house already had picked up the name by 1872.[98] The name "Marine Residence" is similar to the one Kamehameha IV applied to his Kailua residence on the island of Hawai'i. Just as the reference to Hulihe'e Palace as the Marine Residence was rare, so, too, was use of the same appellation for Lunalilo's Waikīkī house. It was, nevertheless, how Lunalilo referred to his Waikīkī residence in the codicil to his June 7, 1871, will.

Queen Emma, in a letter to Peter Young Ka'eo, simply used the location "Waikiki" to signify the

King William Charles Lunalilo called his Waikīkī house the Marine Residence. Photograph by Menzies Dickson (courtesy Hawaii State Archives, PP-98-15-018).

residence when she told him of the latest decline in the king's condition. On September 2, 1873, she wrote: "One night he slept out on the grass in front of his house [at] Waikiki where he is now and took cold in his injured lungs."[99] As King Lunalilo's health continued to decline, people in Honolulu wondered who would inherit his properties, including the Marine Residence. Queen Emma, in a letter to Paul Nahaolelua on January 23, 1874, eleven days before Lunalilo's death, reported: "The big talk about town these days is the King bequeathing his own entire properties to me. This was heard from Alapaki as the King asked him to come and see him. He talked with the King and the King decided all his properties would be for me. However, I haven't heard whether this is true or not."[100]

The talk was partly true; Lunalilo did make a change to his will eight days after Queen Emma's letter. In a codicil to his will, dated January 31, 1874, King Lunalilo made the following bequest: "After the decease of my father, I devise the premises at Waikiki, Oahu, known as my Marine Residence, to Queen Emma, her heirs and assigns forever." Lunalilo's father, Charles Kana'ina, died on March 13, 1877, triggering the transfer of the property to Queen Emma. The trustees of the Lunalilo estate then deeded the four acre site comprising the Marine Residence to Queen Emma. She contended, however, that the bequest referred to the entire ʻili, not just the house site since the water source and kalo lands to support the residence were outside the house site. She brought suit during October 1877 term of the Supreme Court against the trust "to recover the remaining twenty-five acres."[101] Emma prevailed with the "verdict rendered for the plaintiff."[102] Only two members of the court, Charles Coffin Harris and Lawrence McCully, wrote the decision. The third, Albert Francis Judd, Sr., had written the codicil in question.

Queen Emma had a visit from a nearby royal neighbor in October 1883. In a letter to her friend Flora Jones she wrote: "Mrs. Cleghorn's little girl [Princess Kaʻiulani] has just been in to ask me to a garden party she intends keeping her birthday with." The party took place on October 16, 1883, at ʻĀinahau.[103]

When Queen Emma died in 1885, her will specified that a portion of her lands, including Kaluakau, be placed in trust to benefit persons named to receive lifetime annuities and provide scholarships at St. Andrew's Priory and eventually, upon the deaths of those receiving the annuities, for the benefit of Queen's Hospital and Prince Albert Kūnuiākea and his descendants. Kūnuiākea, one of the few living relatives of Queen Emma, contested the will contending that she was not of sound mind when she made the will:

> The will of her late Majesty, Emma, was duly propounded for probate by the executor and trustee therein named, Mr. Alex. J. Cartwright. Hearing was had, and the will was admitted to probate. Thereupon, Mr. Albert K. Kunuiakea cousin and next of kin of deceased, who had contested the will in the Probate Court, appealed to the jury on the principal issue as to whether the will was made while the testatrix was of sound mind.[104] The contestant moved that a Hawaiian jury be empanelled to try the case. This was refused by the Chief Justice who presided and the case was tried by a mixed jury of six Hawaiians and six foreigners. To this exception was taken and the question before the Court is whether such refusal was correct.[105]

Kūnuiākea did not prevail in his challenge of the will nor in his appeal based on the composition of the jury.

The trustee for Estate of Emma Kaleleonalani, Alexander Joy Cartwright, outlined to the court on October 19, 1886, his future plans for the Kaluakau and other properties: "Mr. Cartwright said he would probably apply to the Court for sale of lands that are unproductive to the estate. That the Government would likely purchase 300 square feet of the Hanaiakamalama premises for the use of the Honolulu Water Works, where it intends to put up a Reservoir. [He was authorized on August 5, 1890, to sell all of Hānaiakamalama at public auction. The property was sold on August 27, 1890, to the government for $8,000.] And that he expects to lease the Queen's Waikiki Residence to the Proprietor of the Hawaiian Hotel who will use it as a summer resort for hotel arrivals in connection with the Sea Baths."[106]

After an examination of the trustee's annual account in 1892, the court asked that, "a note be made of this item of $439.39 which is for repairs on premises at Waikiki known as The Lunalilo Waikiki Residence."[107] The *Tourist Guide Through the Hawaiian Islands* included the residence as a place of interest in 1895: "A little beyond, on the left hand side of the road is the marine residence of the late queen. It is a simple, unpretending, wooden structure standing in a large lot planted with coconut trees."[108]

Despite his challenges to the validity of Queen Emma's will, Kūnuiākea received payments from the trust. Cartwright also got Kūnuiākea's consent to allow the transfer of "articles enumerated in the late queen's unfinished codicil to the Trustees of the Museum for the reception of ancient Hawaiian relics."[109]

Kūnuiākea continued to receive half the income from the properties specified for his support until his death on March 10, 1903. Even after his death, his estate continued to receive payments "from the residue of $2633.96 in 1903 ordered by a decree of Judge J.T. DeBolt dated October 9, 1905, to be paid by the Emma Estate to the Estate of A.K. Kunuiakea."[110]

The Queen Emma Estate also sold on January 5, 1903, a "Strip of land Kalao Kou (LCA 85590), Waikīkī, conveyed to the Territory re condemnation for street widening purposes."[111] Approximately 22.18 acres remained.

The last annuitant, Grace Kamaikui Wahineikaili Kahoalii, died January 6, 1916. Today, the lands under the International Marketplace and the surrounding area continue to benefit the Queen's Medical Center. In 2014 the Queen Emma Foundation embarked on a redevelopment effort for the site.

Pualeilani (bef. 1882, demolished after 1922)

King Kalākaua and Queen Kapiʻolani also maintained a residence in Waikīkī called ʻUluniu, and later Pualeilani. It was to his beachside home that Kalākaua

Detail of the M.D. Monsarrat map of Honolulu (1897) shows Bishop at Helumoa, Queen Emma at Kaluaokau, Kapiolani at Uluniu and Liliuokalani at Hamohamo. The box above the first "m" in Hamohamo is the location of the unlabeled ʻĀinahau. Registered Map 1910 (courtesy Land Survey Division, Department of Accounting and General Services, State of Hawaii).

brought the sacred threshold of Liloa. On May 8, 1880, Keʻelikōlani sold to "Kalākaua the King" 4-51/100 acres of land at ʻUluniu in Waikīkī-kai "makai o ke Alanui" next to the property of Makale Paty.[112]

In 1884 Kalākaua sold rights to the Pualeilani artesian well, reserving a portion of the water supply for his property. The Finance Committee's Report to the Legislative Assembly of 1884 called the $5,500 appropriation "a price considerably above the cost."[113]

Following the death of King Kalākaua on January 20, 1891, Pualeilani became the main residence of Queen Kapiʻolani, though a room was assigned for the Queen Dowager at ʻIolani Palace. The *Sacramento Daily Record-Union* reported on Liliʻuokalani's ascent to the throne and the kingdom's future succession plans: "Queen Kapiolani had two of her nephews created princes, but they are not in the line of succession, and will probably be passed over by Lilioukalani [sic] in naming her successor, according to the constitution, as she is not partial to the young men, or indeed to any of Queen Kapiolani's blood. Her sister's child is almost certain to be proclaimed heir apparent."[114]

The treasures of Kapiʻolani on display at her Waikīkī retreat called Pualeilani (courtesy Hawaii State Archives, PP-96-18-022).

Following the overthrow of the monarchy, the home of Dowager Queen Kapiʻolani became a *de facto* meeting location. The Hooulu and Hoola Lahui society held its annual meeting at her Waikīkī home in February 1896.[115]

Queen Kapiolani deeded her properties to David Kawānanakoa and Jonah Kūhiō Kalanianaʻole in exchange for assuming up to $50,000 of her debts and providing monthly payments to her of $1,000.[116]

Queen Kapiʻolani died at Pualeilani on June 24, 1899. The funeral opened the private residence to the eyes of the curious public as the *Independent* noted in the subhead "A Large Concourse of People Paid Their Respects to the Late Queen":

The room in which the remains of Queen Dowager Kapiolani at her residence at Waikiki was thrown open to the public yesterday and many of her old time friends, foreigners and Hawaiians passed by the bier and took a last glance of the noble woman. Curiosity broght [sic] numerous strangers to Pualeilani, and all admired the wonderful display of kahilis, feather leis and costly laces and jewels which were placed around the royal bier.

Colonel Soper and Major Potter were present, representing the Government. Among those who paid their respects were President and Mrs. Dole, Mr. and Mrs. Sewall, and many other high officials. This evening the remains will be transferred to Kawaiahao Church, which will be thrown open to the public from Friday noon to Saturday at midnight. The princes received the people calling at Pualeilani with the graceful courtesy inherent in their race and family.[117]

An account from the *Advertiser*, reprinted in the *Hawaiian Gazette*, gives the most complete description of Pualeilani:

The home where the alii breathed her last is one of great picturesque beauty. The entrance is through a long driveway, over grass and under shady trees. The foliage is luxuriant, being scattered with lavish and throughout the grounds that encircle the little home. The latter is plain and unadorned. No one would have thought, upon looking at it, that it was the home of one whose head had worn the crown. It is unpretentious, but it is comfortable and that was what the late dowager most wanted. A large cocoanut palm in front of a little two-story, latticed cottage, aged and weather beaten. This cottage was the home of Kapiolani.[118]

Queen Kapiʻolani (courtesy Hawaii State Archives, PP-97-15-001).

The vestiges of the monarchy continued at Pualeilani even after the annexation of Hawaiʻi. A notice in *The Independent* in 1902 announced: "Princess Kawananakoa will receive on the first and third Tuesdays of each month at Pualeilani, Waikiki from 3 to 6 pm."[119] A duplicate front-page notice in the same paper followed the next day. The "Local and General News" column of *The Independent* noted the following week: "Princess Kawananakoa holds her

Pualeilani sat in the midst of lush foliage (courtesy Hawaii State Archives, PP-92-9-001).

first reception tomorrow afternoon [March 4, 1902] at Pualeilani, Waikiki, the former home of the late Queen Dowager Kapiolani."[120]

> St. Patrick's Day 1902 featured an event highlighting two of the Campbell scions. A week before the event, in a story titled "Shadows of Coming Events," *The Independent* announced of the two Campbell sisters:
> Miss Alice Campbell, second daughter of the late James Campbell, will come out and enter society on that day it being also her natal day and coming of age. Great times are in store at the Campbell mansion on Emma street where festal preparations are being made for the happy celebration of the day It is also reported that on that day and at the same place Prince and Princess Kawananakoa will give their first public reception making the coming out of their sister a very auspicious event long to be remembered by the fortunate participants.[121]

The same story also reported another planned reception unrelated to the Emma Street events on St. Patrick's Day. The reception at one of the royal residences asserted the continuance of the monarchy, especially for Hawaiians, and fittingly would take place at Pualeilani. The newspaper announced:

> Prince and Princess Kawananakoa will, on Friday afternoon from 3 to 6 o'clock, give a reception to all Hawaiians, at their residence at Pualeilani, Waikiki. They will be assisted by Prince and Princess Kalanianaole, Col. and Mrs. S. Parker will also be present. Hawaiians will no doubt turn out to do homage and pay their respects to their young aliis. These happenings are looked forward to with interest and pleasure by all of those most interested.[122]

Prince Jonah Kūhiō Kalaniana'ole would later that year vie with Robert Wilcox, a former resident of Mu'olaulani (Chapter 5), to serve as Hawai'i's delegate to the United States Congress.

An announcement a couple of days later made clear the intended audience for the event: "A reception will be given by Prince and Princess Kawananakoa tomorrow afternoon at Pualeilani, Waikiki, *for the Hawaiian people only* [italics mine], from 3 to 6 o'clock."[123] According to the first two words of the news coverage following the event, the reception drew all in the city, "Tout Honolulu." The reporting in *The Independent* gives the flavor of the event:

> Tout Honolulu was present at Pualeilani yesterday afternoon when Prince and Princess Kawananakoa were "at home" to hundreds of friends. The reception was held in the large lanai, which was filled with the precious and costly gifts which King Kalakaua and Queen Kapiolani received from their numerous friends. The Princess received her guests at the entrance to the reception hall where she stood surrounded by Miss Rosie Cunha, Miss Alice Campbell, Miss Chrystal and Miss Irene Dickson. After greetings were over the guests wandered from the hall down to the beautiful conservatory with flowers and ferns and to the handsome marble bath near by filled with crystal like water. Refreshments were served in the dining room under the direction of Mrs. George E. Smithies. An attempt to enumerate the guests present would be to print a copy of the Honolulu blue book. Many were there and voted the Princess a "prince" of entertainers.[124]

The *Hawaiian Star* reported that the reception "was made one of the most important social functions of the season by the hundreds who received greeting and welcome from the princess between the hours of three thirty and six o'clock." The account also gives an extended description of Pualeilani and leaders of Hawaiian society:

> The drawing room of the late Dowager Queen Kapiolani was constantly filled with the leaders of Honolulu society in dainty afternoon toilettes or conventional frock coats. Assisting the hostess to receive were three of her intimate friends, Miss Rosie Cunha, Miss Irene Dickson and Miss Chrystal, while Miss Alice Campbell, the latest debutante, stood by her sister's side. Edward Lilikalani acted as a courtly chamberlain while Hawaiian musicians played native airs behind bowers of palms and ferns and dainty refreshments were served. Decorations of potted plants and a profusion of blossoms were plentifully placed as a background to the modish costumes of the guests.[125]

The Princess Kalanianaole also held receptions at Pualeilani, on alternating Tuesdays from Princess Kawānanakoa. The first, on March 28, 1902, was announced in *The Independent*: "Princess Kalanianaole will be 'at home' at Pualeilani next Tuesday."[126] Another announcement a couple of years later had her reception scheduled for July 19, 1904.[127] The two women were married to two of the sons of Princess Victoria Kūhiō Kinoiki Kekaulike: Jonah Kūhiō Kalanianaʻole and David Kawānanakoa. Kekaulike was the sister of Dowager Queen Kapiʻolani.

In 1910 the future of the Uluniu site was tied closely to the neighboring ʻĀinahau property. The government had the choice to create a large park from the grounds of the former royal residences. The alternative would be the subdivision and sale of the properties.

> In the event of the territorial government not taking the whole block and adding it to Ainahau park, it is probable that the Kapiolani Estate managers will do as the late owner desired and add the six acres to the domain. The balance of the block, with the exception of three acres, which will be reserved for Prince Kuhio's home, will then be cut up into lots and sold. Should the government decide to take the property for a park, the Prince would give up his reserved portion of three acres.
>
> The tract that will either be turned into a park or else cut up and sold is known as Uluniu and comprised the estate and residence of the late King Kalakaua and Queen Kapiolani.[128]

Unfortunately, the government did not decide to preserve the open space of the former royal estates: The Uluniu Tract subdivision surrounded the 3.595 acres of Pualeilani in the 1912 offering of lots for sale. P.M. Pond submitted, on February 16, 1915, a file plan for a portion of Uluniu to the territory of Hawaii bureau of conveyances. The 8.5 acre tract included all of the queen's estate 'Ewa of Uluniu Avenue. Less than two weeks later, a revised file plan, called Royal Grove Tract, increased the size of the subdivision to 12.753 acres, including portion *mauka* and *makai* of the queen's residence.

On March 8, 1913, a story in the *Honolulu Star-Bulletin* reported "one or two offers for the whole of Pualeilani at Waikiki"[129] were being considered.

The house, by then known as the Prince Kuhio Kalanianaole home, was the site of a "tableau" titled "Night in Hawaii," staged for the U.S. secretary of the interior, Franklin Lane, in June 1918.[130] By June 1919 the last part of the Kapi'olani estate in Waikīkī had been subdivided into 30 lots known as Pualeilani Lots.

Bounded by Kuhio Avenue on the northeast, Lili'uokalani Avenue on the southeast, Koa Avenue on the southwest, and Uluniu Avenue on the northwest, Pualeilani is today bisected by Prince Edward Street, named for brother of Princes Kalaniana'ole and Kawānanakoa, Prince Edward Abnel Keli'iahonui. Pualeilani sat on land originally awarded to Mataio Kekūanāo'a. With the subdivision of Ainahau in 1917 and Uluniu and Pualeilani by 1919, the land of Hamohamo remained as one of the last unbroken estates in Waikīkī.

Residences of Lili'uokalani at Hamohamo, Waikīkī

Just Diamond Head of the Uluniu site, Lili'uokalani, under the name Lydia Kamakaeha, received the deed for "all that tract of Land situated at Waikiki, Island of Oahu, known by the name of Hamohamo including all the Taro patches, fish ponds and Cocoa Nut Groves" on July 8, 1859, from Ane Keohokālole, Kapa'akea and David Kalākaua for one dollar.[131] Of the "Lands with the King," number 12 in the list, Hamohamo, went to Keohokālole.[132] On August 28, 1867, Mrs. L. Kamakaeha Dominis received from the estate of C. Kapa'akea the deed for land in Kamookahi, Waikiki, consisting of interest in Apana 2 of Royal Patent 4449 [LCA 10535]. Kamehameha V was deeded Apana 1 and Apana 3 of the same royal patent. In 1883, Lili'uokalani made an exchange with the Roman Catholic Church for a site assigned for a Roman Catholic school in 1854 under the 1850 school act. [Department of Instruction]. When Lili'uokalani established her Deed in Trust in 1909 it contained a list of the ten properties that comprised her holding in Hamohamo.

Lili'uokalani wrote of the area: "This ili or land is called Hamohamo. Commencing from the Long branch and following up the stream past the bridge at Apuakehau still running up along Hon. A.S. Cleghorns, then from there turning mauka to a grass hut stream turns in an easterly direction and following that course it suddenly turns makai a little ways then turns easterly again and turns makai into the sea. Before the last easterly turn the boundary line continues straight to the sea and all the land within the boundaries described is called Hamohamo. Kamehameha sought this place after the celebrated battle at Nuuanu. It belonged to Aikanaka the grandson of Keaweheulu one of his generals and chief counsellors [sic]."[133]

Kealohilani, Hamohamo, Waikīkī, Queen Liliʻuokalani and Prince Jonah Kūhiō Kalanianaole

In Waikīkī, at Hamohamo, Queen Liliʻuokalani maintained a beachfront residence, called Kealohilani, later occupied by Prince Jonah Kūhiō Kalanianaʻole. The residence sat just *makai* of the where today Kalakaua Avenue intersects Liliuokalani Avenue. She inherited the house and land from her father Caesar Kapaʻakea on August 28, 1867.[134]

On March 30, 1882, Liliʻuokalani invited the students of Kawaiahaʻo Female Seminary, its faculty and parents of the pupils, to a picnic where a "ramble on the beach and sea bathing were enjoyed, and a bountiful lunch partaken of."[135]

With the advent of city rail line January 1, 1889, Liliʻuokalani's chamberlain soon ordered her own tramcars "to convey her and suite to her seaside residence at Waikiki. Two cars were coupled and festooned with ferns and flowers. The finest span in the stables was hitched in and with festive song and twanging banjo the company of sable dignitaries was gaily conducted to their sea-side home."[136]

In 1890, when Liliʻuokalani invited more than 100 teachers and students from Kawaiahaʻo Seminary, she accommodated the larger numbers by erecting a canvas lanai over a 50-foot long table."[137]

After the overthrow, Liliʻuokalani reflected in *Hawaii's Story by Hawaii's Queen* about her Waikiki home, especially the ability of individuals to set aside their political differences while enjoying the beautiful grounds of Kealohilani:

> Political events have brought me leisure, and from the view through the porticos of my pretty seaside cottage, called Kealohilani, I have derived much amusement, well as pleasure: for as

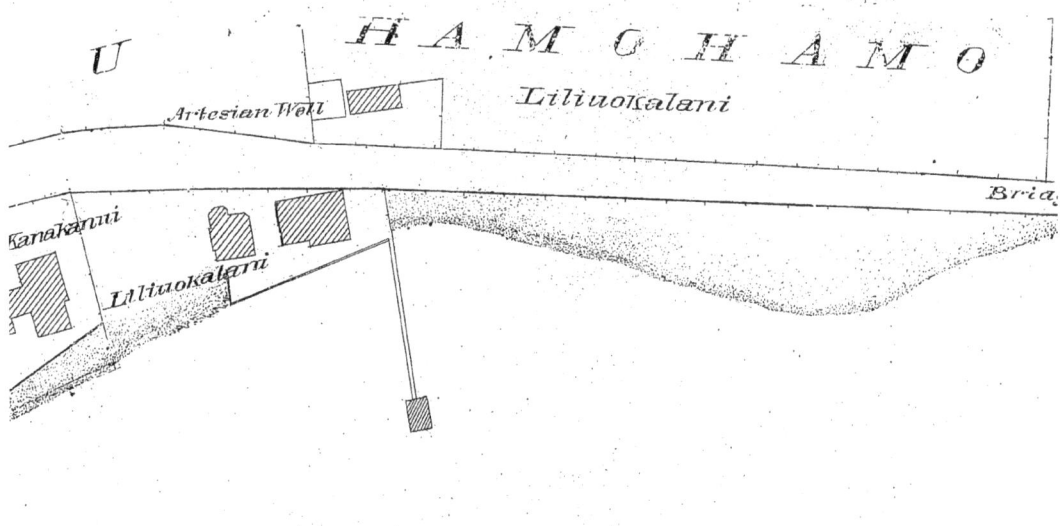

The beachfront property marked "Liliuokalani" included her residence Kealohilani and a long pier. Today the pier would be located roughly *makai* of the intersection of Kalākaua and Liliʻuokalani avenues. Detail of Registered Map 1793 based on surveys taken in 1895 and 1897 (courtesy Land Survey Division, Department of Accounting and General Services, State of Hawaii).

the sun shines on the evil the good, and the rain falls on the just and the unjust. I have not felt called upon to limit the enjoyment my beach and shade trees to any party in politics; and my observation convinces me that those who are opposed to my system of government have not least diffidence about passing happy hours on which are certainly my private property. To watch families of the Royalist and the Provisionalist mingling together, sharing each the other's lunch-baskets, and spending the day in social pleasures at the "Queen's Retreat," one would never suspect that racial or political jealousy had any place in the breasts of the participants.[138]

In 1905, Liliʻuokalani wrote a letter from Kealohilani complaining about one of the tenants at Hamohamo. Regarding those living on the lots at Hamohamo, Liliʻuokalani recounted, "it had always been customary to call on them to do some work, say, three or six times a year as often as I needed their assistance as payment."[139] Later she implemented the alternative of paying a dollar instead of required service. Liliʻuokalani asked that the tenant who neither paid the dollar nor provided service be charged rent of $5 per month.[140]

When Liliʻuokalani created her trust in 1909 she reserved for herself only two properties: Washington Place on Beretania and Kealohilani in Waīkīkī.[141] In celebration of her seventy-fourth birthday, in 1912, Liliʻuokalani held events at both of her houses. At Washington Place a formal visitation by members of her organizations took place in the morning, and then later in the afternoon a less formal event occurred at Kealohilani. The Hawaiian-language newspaper, *Kuokoa Home Rula*, reported: "A ma ka auina la hora 3 oia ahiahi, a ia he luau nui mawaho iha o Kealohilani Home, malaila i noho ai he anaina nui e paina a hoomaikai i ka mea mana loa, e hooloihi I ke ana o ka Moiwahine a piha he hookahi huneri makahiki."[142] ["And in the afternoon at 3 o'clock, there was a great luau outside of Kealohilani Home, and there sat a large group who ate and gave thanks to the almighty, so that the Queen could live longer, reaching a hundred."][143]

The 1909 Deed of Trust made the provision for a *hānai* son of Liliʻuokalani: "For Joseph Kaiponohea Aea, the premises at Waikiki known as 'Kealohilani', with the appurtenances and the Fishery of Hamohamo, for his lifetime, and on his death for the lawful heirs of his body for their lifetime (or so long after the death of said Joseph Kaiponohea Aea as the law will permit, with reversion then to the Trustees)." With the death of Aea on November 14, 1914, Kealohilani would remain in the trust.

In 1915 Prince Jonah Kūhiō Kalanianaʻole would mount an effort to have the trust voided. In an attempt to end the suit by Kalanianaʻole against the Liliuokalani Trust, trustees made an agreement that deeded Kealohilani in fee simple to him.

Residence of Prince Jonah Kūhiō Kalanianaole

Soon after his possession of Kealohilani, Prince Kūhiō Kalanianaole demolished Liliʻuokalani's cottage, building in its place his residence that he called Pualeilani after the subdivided estate of Kapiʻolani. The prince mounted cannon from Punchbowl, no longer used to announce the comings and goings of monarchs, on the seawall of his house. The cannon were named Kalola and Kalahikiola.

Prince Kalanianaole and his wife Elizabeth Kahanu celebrated their silver wedding anniversary at Pualeilani in 1921. They had married October 8, 1896, at the Anglican Cathedral, "the wedding being strictly private."[144]

After the death of Prince Jonah Kūhiō Kalanianaʻole on January 7, 1922, Princess

Chapter 3. Royal Residences of Waikīkī

Prince Jonah Kūhiō Kalaniana'ole and Princess Elizabeth Kahanu celebrated their 25th wedding anniversary at Pualeilani (courtesy Hawaii State Archives, PP-97-2-015).

Kalaniana'ole played host to a farewell luau in April for her late husband's replacement in Congress, Henry Alexander Baldwin.[145] Princess Kalaniana'ole married James Frank Woods in 1923.

In 1930, a follow-up event to the commemoration of sesquicentennial of the 1778 visit by Captain James Cook, the Liloa stone was moved from Pualeilani to the grounds of 'Iolani Palace: "The sacred stone Liloa, placed in front of the Cook tablet, is the original *paepae Kapu o Liloa*, the forbidden threshold of the great King Liloa of ancient

Patricia Hunt plays in 1935 on one of two cannons mounted on the seawall of Pualeilani. The cannons, from the saluting battery at Punchbowl, were all that remained of the residence. They had been loaned to Prince Jonah Kūhiō Kalanianaʻole (courtesy Hawaii State Archives, PP-37-2-011).

Hawaii. It was brought to Honolulu by King Kalakaua, and retained by him at 'Honuakaha' and 'Pualeilani.' Presented to the Hawaii State Archives by Mrs. J.F. Woods, the former Princess Kalanianaole, as a guard stone to the Cook memorial."[146]

She died February 20, 1932. In 1935 the house was offered for sale for $30,000. "The Kuhio home, owned by the Elizabeth K. Woods estate, but with title invested in the Kapiolani estate, Ltd. stands on the makai side of Kalakaua avenue facing Liliuokalani."[147] Mayor Wright had made Waikiki beach improvement a campaign promise.[148] A member of the city board of supervisors, Philip N. Sing, said he would push for the purchase "if arrangements can be made to buy the land for $30,000 in two yearly installments of $15,000 each."[149] Opinion was divided on Honolulu Board of Supervisors, who could not decide on the purchase. Some felt city and county finances to be too shaky to make such a purchase. Others bemoaned the loss of a taxable property.[150] "And what will we do with that beautiful building?" Supervisor Manuel C. Pacheco asked.[151] The indecision caused James G. Needles, who had an option to lease the Kalanianaʻole house, to consider opening a restaurant there. His application for a liquor license caused neighbors to urge the city to "rush action on the proposal to purchase."[152] Sing's resolution for purchase of the Kalanianaʻole property passed on a vote of 4–4 with Pacheco voting in favor.[153] The court condemned the property the following month.[154] As to Pacheco's question: "It is understood that the city will eventually demolish the building which now occupies most of the property."¹⁵⁵ The park board decided the fate of the mansion. "A bit of the past glory of old Hawaii will go beginning Monday [June 17, 1935] when FERA [Federal Emergency Relief Administration] workers start work on the razing of the home of the late Prince and delegate in congress, Jonah Kuhio Kalanianaole, recently purchased by the city-county. [...] With the demolishing of the old *palace* [italics mine] the beach will be enlarged by 220 feet."¹⁵⁶ The day before the destruction of Kūhiō's palace, three Japanese princes visiting Hawai'i were guests at a program of "Royal Entertainment." The caption under the photograph of the princes and officers of the Japanese training cruisers *Asama* and *Yakumo*, provides an ironic juxtaposition to the destruction of the lost palace: "A program of the type which once were given before the royalty of the Hawaiian monarchy was presented last night at

Hula dancers at Lalani Hawaiian Village (courtesy Hawaii State Archives, PP-32-10-007).

Lalani Hawaiian Village for the visiting Japanese princes, cadets and naval officers."¹⁵⁷ Lalani Hawaiian Village stood on land at Paoakalani Street and Kalakaua Avenue.

Paoakalani, Hamohamo, Waikīkī, Queen Lili'uokalani

Like Kealohilani (royal brightness), Paoakalani (royal perfume) came to Lili'uokalani through her mother, Ane Keohokālole, as part of the deed of Hamohamo.

Lili'uokalani fondly remembered Paoakalani during her imprisonment at 'Iolani

Palace. During June 1895, she composed "Ku'u Pua I Paoakalani—My Flower at Paoakalani." The Hawaiian lyrics and their English translation are both by Lili'uokalani.

Ku'u Pua I Paoakalani
—My Flower at Paoakalani

1.
E ka gentle breeze a pa mai nei,
Hoohali'ali'a mai ana ia'u,
E ku'u sweet never fading flower,
I pua i ka uka o Paoakalani.

Chorus.
I ke mau i ka nani o na pua,
O ka uka o Uluhaimalama,
Aole na'e hoi e like,
Me ku'u pua i ka la'i o Paoakalani.

2.
Lahilahi kona ma hiona,
With softest eyes as black as jet,
Pink cheeks so delicate of hue,
I ulu i ka uka o Paoakalani.

Chorus.
I ke mau i ka nani, etc.

3.
Nane ia mai ana ku'u aloha,
E ka gentle breeze e waft mai nei,
O come to me ka'u mea e li'a nei,
I ulu ika uka o Paoakalani.

Chorus.
I ke mau i ka nani, etc.
Liliu.

1.
O ye gentle breeze that waft to me,
Sweet, cherished memories of thee,
Of that sweet never fading flower,
That bloom in the fields of Paoakalani.

Chorus.
Tho' I've often seen those beauteous flow'rs,
That grew at Uluhaimalama,
But none of these could be compared,
To the flowers that bloom in the fields of Paoakalani.

2.
Her face is fair to behold,
With softest eyes as black as jet,
Pink cheeks so delicate of hue,
That grew in the field of Paoakalani.

Chorus.
Tho' I've often seen, etc.

3.
Now name to me the one I love,
Ye gentle breezes passing by,
And bring to me that blossom fair,
That bloometh in the fields of Paoakalani.

Chorus.
Tho' I've often seen, etc.[158]

Jennie K. Wilson recounted in her "Notes on Music Collection of Queen Lili'uokalani": "This song was composed while the Queen was imprisoned. [...] The song Paoa-ka-lani was composed in 1895." The song became popular, no doubt, because of the circumstances of its composition. In 1897 "My Flower at Paoakalani" was one of the selections chosen by the Kamehameha Alumni Club at a fundraiser for a Kamoiliili Native Church.[159] Another concert to raise funds for new hymnals at St. Andrew's again featured "Ku'u Pua I Paoakalani," this time sung by the Emerald Glee Club.[160]

The Uluhaimālama compared to Paoakalani may be another residence of Lili'uokalani. Jennie K. Wilson recounted in her "Notes on Music Collection of Queen Lili'uokalani":

> Ulu-hai-mālama, Where Lili'u'o-ka-lani had a house of this name, where there is a graveyard mauka of where Kawananakoa School is now. She told John Wilson that this song was composed in his honor, but he did have this put on the copy with the Queen's picture on the outside. When the Queen spoke to him about it he said that he thought she had made a mistake.
>
> The Queen had her home Paoa-ka-lani, a very nice grass-house at Wai-kīkī, for which a street in the locality is named.
>
> John's mother, Mrs. Eveline Townsend Wilson, was a friend of the Queen from childhood. [...] When baby John's mother went out to Paoa-ka-lani or Washington Place she took the baby with her.

Copy of "Kuu Pua i Paoakalani" sheet music found in the cornerstone of Lili'uokalani Elementary School (courtesy Hawaii State Archives, Manuscript Collection, M-494, Box 3-3).

Although Jennie K. Wilson mentions a residence at Uluhaimalama, a survey on June 23, 1891, shows no structure though it lists the circumference of the fence, 581 feet, the necessary boards and 35 pounds of nails needed to complete the job. A rectangle is drawn on the map but outside the fenced area.[161]

Cook Sesquicentennial

Even after the death of Liliʻuokalani, Hamohamo continued to serve as a gathering place. Act 256 that created the Cook sesquicentennial commission provided it no direction other than the dates "for the ceremonies during the week of August 15th to 19th, 1928, commemorating the 150th anniversary of the discovery of the Hawaiian Islands by Captain James Cook."[162] The Senate Bill 257 had been introduced by the grandson of missionary Dr. Gerrit P. Judd, Lawrence McCully Judd, who had been appointed to fill a vacancy in the territorial senate. The legislature left the details for the ceremonies to the five-member commission with its budget of $20,000. Although Cook had first sighted Kauaʻi on January 18, 1778, and landed two days later, the approval of the Act on May 2, 1927, did not give sufficient time to plan for the commemoration of first contact. Two years earlier, in 1925, commission member Albert Pierce Taylor at a meeting of the Hawaiian Historical Society had proposed the celebration of the anniversary. Other members included Col. Curtis Piehu Iaukea; Delegate Victor Stewart Kaleoaloha Houston; Bruce Cartwright, Bishop H.B. Restarick and J. Frank Woods. Edgar Henriques served as executive secretary. H.E. Gregory of the Bishop Museum joined the group in September 1927.

Albert Pierce Taylor was secretary to Lorrin A. Thurston, annexation commissioner in Washington, D.C., from 1897 to 1898 before coming to Hawaiʻi in August 1898. He was also secretary to Walter Francis Frear, territorial chief justice of the supreme court (1898–1907) and later governor (1907–1913). Taylor later served as secretary to Hawaiian commission charged with developing the Organic Act.[163] The commission elected as chairman Curtis Piehu Iaukea, who had served as chamberlain of the royal household for Queen Liliʻuokalani and later trustee for the Liliʻuokalani Trust.[164] The 1930 *Men of Hawaii* noted of Houston: "Although born in California, Mr. Houston, through his mother [Caroline Poor Kahikiola Brickwood Houston], is a member of an old Hawaiian family." Bruce Cartwright was grandson of Alexander Joy Cartwright and former president of the Hawaiian Historical Society. Restarick was then president of the Hawaiian Historical Society and bishop emeritus of the missionary diocese of Honolulu. Woods was the husband of the widow of Prince Jonah Kūhiō Kalanianaʻole, who had died in 1922.

The play "Hawaii 150 Years Ago," by James "Kimo" A. Wilder, was presented August 20, 1928, at Hamohamo. Rehearsals for the play started in early July under the direction of the author and the wife of member A.P. Taylor. Emma Ahuena Davison Taylor (d. 1937) was a member of the Historical Commission in 1922, 1925 and 1933. Mrs. Taylor preserved in her name, Ahuena, the memory of Kamehameha's heiau at Kamakahonu.

Cook commemorative coins, designed by Juliette May Fraser, reflected the Americanism of the time, included the phrases "E Pluribus Unum," "In God We Trust" and "United States of America." Captain James Cook is described as "Discoverer of Hawaii." The sesquicentennial is reflected in the dates 1778–1928.

The movies of the Cook celebration included footage of Hamohamo (Captain Cook Collection #156).

The Liliʻuokalani Trust continues to fund the Queen Liliʻuokalani Children's Center that perpetuates the vision of Liliʻuokalani for the "benefit of orphan and other destitute children in the Hawaiian Islands, the preference given to Hawaiian children of pure or part-aboriginal blood."[165]

Today the swimming pool of Liliʻuokalani Gardens sits roughly where the Paoakalani residence once stood. Kūhiō Beach Park has replaced the Kealohilani cottage. Divided and developed lost palaces of Waikīkī still serve as places of leisure but for millions of visitors and residents.

CHAPTER 4

Royal Residences of the Palace Yard and Vicinity

*Ka lonolau no i ka lonolau.
Chiefs seek the society of chiefs.[1]
—Hawaiian proverb*

When Kamehameha I established his compound on the beach of Kou, now called Honolulu, his court established their residences nearby, strung along the beach near the harbor. The same practice took place on Oʻahu once again when the capital of the kingdom transferred from Lahaina, Maui, to Honolulu in 1845. With the official seat of the monarch established at Hale Aliʻi, the members of court once again clustered their residences around the palace. Unlike the *hale pili* built on the shore at the beginning of the century, the members of court built Western structures to rival one another.

Hale Aliʻi (November 1845–1876), Pohukaina, Honolulu, Renamed ʻIolani Palace in 1863

The focus of the royal residences in the palace yard and vicinity was the palace called Hale Aliʻi and later, after the death of Kamehameha IV, ʻIolani Palace. Of all the royal residences built during the reign of Kamehameha III, it stood as the grandest, serving as the home of Kamehameha III, Kamehameha IV, Kamehameha V, Lunalilo, and Kalākaua, their queens and children. The structure destined as the residence of five monarchs, however, was not originally slated for that purpose. With the kingdom's capital in Lahaina on the island of Maui, the Greek Revival house was initially built in July 1844 for the five-year-old Princess Victoria Kamāmalu by her father, Matiao Kekūanāoʻa, the governor of Oʻahu.[2] A letter dated May 15, 1844, from J.S. Hart to Kekūanāoʻa, gives the builder's proposal for completing the governor's residence. Hart promised to complete the house in three months for $800.[3] With the transition of the court to Honolulu, King Kamehameha III quickly claimed the structure as his own when he arrived in August 1844. As noted in a speech by Charles Coffin Harris at the laying of the cornerstone of ʻIolani Palace: "but inasmuch as it was the only spacious building in town, the King established his residence in it."[4]

Gerrit P. Judd reported on May 21, 1845: "During the present year the Palace in Honolulu has been completed, and much progress has been made with that at Lahaina."[5] The *Polynesian* on September 6, 1845, reported "a cargo of royal household furniture has

Chapter 4. Royal Residences of the Palace Yard and Vicinity

Photograph of Hale Aliʻi taken from the south-east (courtesy Hawaii State Archives, PP-10-5-002).

arrived at Honolulu for the new palace for the residence of the King, which was expected to be completed by the 1st. of November."[6] The palace was indeed completed by November 1, as a musical soiree was conducted on October 29, 1845, at the king's residence. Musicians from H.B.M.'s ship *America* sent "twenty well trained musicians of an excellence in their art far beyond any thing that had ever before been heard in Honolulu."[7] Following a musical program, and after "the missionary families had retired, dancing commenced."[8]

Despite the loss of his newly built house to the king, Kekūanāoʻa would not suffer financial loss. In the Privy Council meeting September 7, 1846, Kekūanāoʻa "remarked that the King take over the Palace and the King …] pay Kekuanaoa's debts." The offer was accepted.[9]

Missionary Levi Chamberlain recorded at least one event at what he called the "King's Palace." His journal entry for August 10, 1848, gave no description of the palace itself but noted: "All the missionaries were invited to be present. None went from our house. Some of our neighbors went. Understand there was not a very large company."[10]

Paul Emmert's 1853 lithographs captured an early image of Hale Aliʻi, referred to in Plate No. 1, View of Honolulu From the Harbor, as the "Palace of King Kamehameha III."[11] The centerpiece, titled "A View of Honolulu from the Catholic Church" shows the northwestern face of Hale Aliʻi.

George Washington Bates gave the most thorough written description of Hale Aliʻi during the last year of the reign of Kamehameha III. He first reflected on the use of the word "palace" to describe the residence: "It is denominated the 'palace.' To a person who has ever visited any of the abodes of European sovereigns, such a term would at once convey an idea of regal magnificence; but the residence of the Hawaiian monarch produces nothing that is superfluous, or even splendid. On the contrary every thing about

Hale Aliʻi appears to the left of the flag in a detail of an 1854 lithograph titled "No. 2. View of Honolulu. From the Catholic church/sketched from nature by Paul Emmert" (courtesy Library of Congress Prints and Photographs Division, LC-DIG-pga-00316).

it is plain even to plebeianism, and induces a visitor to think that he may be treading the apartments of a chief rather than the palace of a sovereign."[12] The Greek Revival style, with its sparse lines and minimal decoration, no doubt lead Bates to his perspective on the "palace."

Bates then walked his reader on a tour from the gates of Hale Aliʻi and gave a detailed description of the exterior:

> The grounds on which it stands cover between two and three acres, and are inclosed with a heavy wall of rough coral. A visitor enters on the south side between lodges occupied by sleepy sentinels. A small but beautiful grove of trees wave their stately foliage on either side of the path leading up to the royal apartments, and their cool shade reminds one of the groves of the Academy and the Lyceum, where so many of the old masters read, studied, and rambled. A few steps bring you in front of the palace proper. It has a very simple, rustic appearance. The walls are composed of coral procured from the reefs along the shore of the harbor. The ground plan covers an area of seventy-four feet by forty-four. The building is a story and a half high. A noble piazza eight or ten feet wide and raised a few feet above the ground entirely surrounds the building.[13]

Sandwich Island Notes also contained a detailed depiction of the interior of the palace: "The chief apartment is the one in which the king holds his *levees*. In the centre of the eastern wall of the apartment stood the chair of state. Its unpretending aspect led me to invest it rather with republican simplicity than monarchical aristocracy. Several well-executed paintings hung on the walls. They represented the then ruling monarch Kamehameha III.; Liholiho, or Kamehameha II.; Kekauluhoi [sic], the late Premier; and a full length portrait of Louis Philippe, King of the French. On a large centre-table were arranged several diminutive but exceedingly fine pieces of statuary presents from the King of Denmark."[14]

After the death of Kamehameha III, his successor Kamehameha IV took up residence in Hale Aliʻi. Gorham D. Gilman remembered Hale Aliʻi during the reign of Kamehameha IV:

> This building was built of coral with a high basement and one story, high studded and sloping roof with a large lookout room on top. It was divided into a large hall through the centre, a large reception or throne room on the right, with two rooms on the left. It was mainly used for public purposes, the king preferring the quiet quarters of the cottages in the yard, where he lived according to his chosen Hawaiian style. Some very brilliant receptions were held there to which the public was generally invited with all the official and distinguished guests who happened in town.[15]

Gilman also shared an account that reflected the ceremonial nature of Hale Aliʻi versus the informality of other residences on the palace grounds:

> A little incident may not be out of place here. Having received an invitation to attend one of the receptions of King Kamehameha IV., a friend and myself entered the grounds at the mauka gate, intending to pass around and enter at the front of the building. As we were passing the bungalow a friendly voice, somewhat familiar, hailed us and asked us to come up on the veranda. We accepted the invitation and were welcomed by the king himself, who invited us to seats and cigars. While chatting upon social events the king, suddenly, looking at his watch, said hastily, "Excuse me, gentlemen, I am due in the throne room in five minutes," and disappeared within. Passing to the front entrance of the palace, up the broad steps, and across the wide veranda to the brilliantly lighted rooms, we found a large company gathered. In a short time the band announced the arrival of His Majesty and presentations began. These were made by the officers of the court, dressed in full uniform, and with great formality. When our turn came, my friend Mr. Bartow, and myself were escorted by two of the officers to the presence of the king. We were announced with much formality by the stereotyped expression, "Your Majesty, permit me to present to you Mr. Gilman." With a formal bow on the part of both, we passed on, as if it were the first time we had ever been in the royal presence, while really it was only a few minutes since we had been smoking together.[16]

Despite being considered the king's permanent residence seventeen years earlier in 1845, calls for a new palace were already circulating during the reign of Kamehameha IV. An editorial in the March 20, 1862, *Pacific Commercial Advertiser* proposed a new royal palace. "A Palace for the Royal family is needed," the newspaper opined, "and if any mode can be devised by which it can be erected during the coming biennial term, the necessary funds should be voted. It becomes every nation to seek the personal comfort of its sovereign and his family, and to provide for them a residence suited to the dignity of their position, that they may command the respect due to them as rulers. The bare fact that His Majesty has signified his wish that an appropriation be voted for this object, ought to be sufficient reason why it should be voted at the earliest moment practicable."[17]

The royal family would not see a new palace during the reign of Kamehameha IV. The four-year-old Prince of Hawaiʻi took ill, so much so that on August 19, 1862, his parents had him baptized using the Anglican rite. Since no Anglican clergy had yet arrived, a Congregational minister conducted the service.[18] Sadly, Prince Albert Edward Kauikeaouli Leiopapa A Kamehameha died at Hale Aliʻi at 8 a.m. on Wednesday, August 27, 1862. His body lay in state at the palace, the viewing taking three hours to complete. "It was a sorrowful but not a dreadful sight; for the young face wore a calm, sweet smile, and round the bier were vases filled with fragrant flowers, and at the head, a table bearing Queen Victoria's christening present—a large silver vase of beautiful workmanship."[19]

Mary Evarts Anderson recorded a visit to the palace shortly after the prince's death: "When we arrived at the palace gates, the guard opened them wide for us, and we passed on to the rear of the palace where was the queen's own suite of rooms. On the steps we were met by the minister of foreign affairs, who escorted us to a reception-room, and a few minutes later to the drawing-room."[20]

On the October 21, 1862, the Bishop of Honolulu baptized Queen Emma at Hale Aliʻi. "At one end of the chamber was the altar at which the king and queen had been married, covered with a gilded crimson cloth. The font stood in front of the altar, placed on the table. It was the small one of alabaster given by Lady Franklin. At one end [of the room] was the Queen of England's present for the baptism of the prince, as if to is remind all of his untimely death without possessing the same privileges as his royal mother."[21]

Despite his desire to build a new royal residence, Kamehameha IV would die at the old palace on November 30, 1863, before entertaining any plans for a new palace. As a sign of respect, the gates of Hale Aliʻi were draped in black.[22]

The succession of Kamehameha V occurred immediately upon the death of his brother with no interregnum or gap between the reigns.

At the next meeting of the Privy Council after the death of Kamehameha IV, on December 7, 1863, Kamehameha V requested that the name of Hale Aliʻi be changed to "St. Alexander Palace" to honor his recently deceased brother. The council took action on the king's request by resolution:

> Resolved that this Council thank His Majesty for consulting them in regard to the name of his own Palace—that after duly considering the Question, they would prefer the "Iolani Palace" to the "Alexander Palace" but that they respectfully defer to His Majesty right to give to his own Palace what ever name may best please himself.[23]

The choice of names was recorded in the minutes by the secretary of the privy council, David Kalākaua, from a communication from the king's acting chamberlain, John O. Dominis, that informed the council that the king had "styled His residence 'Iolani Palace.'"[24]

The funeral of Kamehameha IV took place just shy of two months later, on Wednesday, February 3, 1864. The procession went from the newly named ʻIolani Palace to the Episcopal Chapel on Kukui Street, where the service was conducted in Hawaiian using the *Prayer Book* that had been translated by the late king. Following the service the procession continued to the yet unfinished mausoleum at Mauna Ala.[25]

Kamehameha V did not remain exclusively in the palace enclosure. The newspapers of the day recorded various meetings at Hale Aliʻi. For instance, after a discussion there with Queen Emma in the morning, their first since her return from England, "Towards evening the King went to Waikiki where he has taken up his residence."[26]

An account in 1867 reflects the diplomatic role played by ʻIolani Palace: "On Wednesday the 16th inst. [January 16, 1867], at 12, m., His Majesty the King received at Iolani Palace W.L. Green, Esq., Acting Commissioner and Consul-General of Her Britannic Majesty, who introduced to the Sovereign James Hay Wodehouse, Esq., the newly accredited Commissioner and Consul-General of Her Majesty the Queen of Great Britain."

At that meeting Wodehouse addressed the King, saying "[I] beg to assure you that Her Majesty's government will ever feel a lively interest in the welfare and prosperity of the islands under your sway, and that they cherish the hope that the same friendly relations which have for so many years happily subsisted between the Sandwich Islands and Great Britain will continue between the two countries."[27]

The King, in turn, thanked Wodehouse, especially noting that "The kind invitation extended by your illustrious Sovereign to a member of my family and the numerous marks of sympathy and attention received by Queen Emma, on her recent visit to England, have impressed my people and myself with a deep feeling of gratitude. I am happy to have this opportunity of returning publically, through you, my thanks to Her most gracious Majesty Queen Victoria."[28]

Such a detailed account of an event at the palace was the exception rather than the rule. Most accounts of events at the palace, recorded simply as "Court News" in the "Local News" column of the *Hawaiian Gazette*, described little more than how long the king had resided at the palace, and when the Cabinet Council meetings had taken place.

It would be visitors to the islands who provided details of what ʻIolani Palace looked like. The most thorough description of the interior, for instance, comes from Frank Vincent, who visited Hawaiʻi from April 10, 1870 through May 24, 1870, during the reign of Kamehameha V:

> We found the royal palace at the eastern extremity of the city, surrounded by gardens and lawns three or four acres in extent, and inclosed [sic] by a high wall of rough-hewn coral. A sleepy, barefooted sentinel admitted us by a wicket. To the left were the barracks, with a few soldiers lolling around some light iron cannon. Before us a broad, hard avenue, shaded by beautiful trees, led to a simple one-story edifice, built of coral from the reef in the harbor, encompassed by a noble piazza, and surmounted with a huge square cupola. Iolani Palace, as it is called is about seventy-five feet in length and fifty in width. After looking over the grounds (which were not kept in very good order—possibly because a new palace was in contemplation) [The proposed palace of 1871 is described in Chapter 5], we mounted a flight of stone steps, and entered the royal mansion through a wooden doorway which opened into an immense hall. A long table, covered with green leather, occupied the centre of this room and, upon it was a rack of law books. Some admirably executed paintings adorned the walls, among them a full-length portrait of Louis Philippe, one of the Emperor of Russia, and half-a-dozen of other European sovereigns and statesmen. These paintings had been presented to the different Kamehamehas by the celebrities whom they portrayed.
>
> A door opened from the hall into the library, a lofty room with green upholstery. The walls were hung with fine paintings of Kamehameha I, surnamed the Great; Kamehameha III; Kamehameha IV., when a young boy; and Kaahumanu, the female premier, who was one of the first of royal blood to embrace Christianity. On one side of the room stood a secretary and an iron safe; another side contained handsome cases, two filled with French and two with English books about one thousand volumes in all. Among them were several very valuable illustrated and scientific works "Audubon's Birds of America," Wilkes's "United States Exploring Expedition," and others. On the centre-table stood an elegant set of Lord Macaulay's works. Adjoining the library was the Crown Room, so called because the king places his crown here in state upon a magnificent table of native woods. This apartment is furnished in brighter colors than the library, and contains several very fine steel-plate engravings—two of the British House of Lords and Commons in session, one of Prince Albert of England, and another of the Duke of Wellington. Crossing the hall brought us to the grand reception-room, which occupies one half the building and bears the same relation to Iolani Palace that the East Room does to the White House at Washington. The walls and furniture are richly gilded, and two large chandeliers, each containing ten kerosene lamps, depend from the lofty ceiling. At the centre of one side of the room stands the royal chair of state used by the king on reception days. On the wall behind it hangs a splendid painting of Kamehameha IV in full uniform.[29]

Lot Kamehameha Kapuaiwa, Kamehameha V, died at 'Iolani Palace on December 11, 1872: "At 20 minutes after 10 o'clock he breathed his last, without suffering," reported F.W. Hutchison, minister of the interior, Stephen Phillips, attorney general, and Robert Sterling, minister of finance.[30]

During the reign of the next resident of 'Iolani Palace, King William Charles Lunalilo, another visitor, Isabella Lucy Bird, arrived in Honolulu. She recorded her visit to Hawai'i, from January 24, 1873, to August 7, 1873, in her book *The Hawaiian Archipelago*, a compilation of letters she sent to her sister in England. In her discussion of "notable edifices" in Honolulu, she wrote of 'Iolani Palace: "It stands in pleasure grounds of about an acre in extent with a fine avenue running through them and is approached by a flight of steps which leads to a tolerably spacious hall decorated in the European style. Portraits of Louis Philippe and his queen presented by themselves and of the late Admiral [Richard Darton] Thomas adorn the walls. [...] There are also some ornamental vases and miniature copies of some of [Danish sculptor Bertel] Thorwaldsen's works. The throne room takes up the left wing of the palace. This unfortunately resembles a rather dreary drawing room in London or New York and has no distinctive features except a decorated chair which is the Hawaiian throne."[31]

By 1874 the *Hawaiian Gazette* was pushing to have the already completed Ali'iolani Hale designated as the palace and the palace grounds turned into a central, public park. The newspaper based its proposal on the cost to build a new palace. Of course, the old palace was still available, but the *Hawaiian Gazette* noted: "it is well known that the present palace buildings are all going to ruin, and are unentantable, compelling His Majesty to rent premises elsewhere to live in."[32]

With the election of David Kalākaua as king, 'Iolani Palace and the other residences in the palace yard would soon disappear. Peter Young Ka'eo, in exile on Moloka'i, wrote of the changes in the Palace yard in a letter to Queen Emma, dated October 26, 1874: "I can well fancy how the Palace premices [*sic*] now looks, as D.K. [David Kalākaua] has had all the buildings moved away, His time will I have no doubt come when he himself will also be removed."[33]

Ka'eo wrote to Emma in March 23, 1875: "By your description, the old Palace grounds is one large open Space. Does D.K. think of improving it? Or what?"[34]

Despite the formal name change to 'Iolani Palace, some continued to refer to the palace by its old name. Lili'uokalani, in her diary entry of January 21, 1875, referred to "ka Pa o ka Hale Alii nei."[35]

By the spring of 1876, an assessment of the palace had been conducted. "On the examination of the old Palace," the department of the interior reported, "it was found to be in such a condition, that any expenditure of money upon it for extensive repairs would be wholly unadvisable, it was therefore decided to tear it down"[36]

On June 5, 1876, William L. Moehonua submitted "statement of the 'items of the expenditure classed' in the Biennial report under the heading of Improvements 'of present Palace and Grounds.'"[37]

The *Hawaiian Gazette* wryly dissected the report of the minister of finance regarding the "improvements to the present palace and grounds." Commenting on the cost overruns and interpretation of "improvement," the newspaper observed: "The 'present palace' was improved by being razed to the ground, and the sum of $36,911.31 was expended on the grounds."[38] The newspaper also noted that the original appropriation had totaled only $15,000 and that the balance had been transferred from other appropriations.

Chapter 4. Royal Residences of the Palace Yard and Vicinity 99

When Walter Coote visited Honolulu in 1879 he gave an account of the palace grounds just before the construction of the new 'Iolani Palace in *Wanderings, South and East*. He also described his impression of the other residences within the palace enclosure, houses that would be demolished with the completion of the new palace. Coote records of his tour and interview of King Kalākaua:

> His palace is at present not imposing, but a new one is to be built and the bricks are already piled in a formidable heap within the gardens. The amount of royal pomp and state is very small. A seedy sentinel there is at either gate who flings open wide the portal with melodramatic air, and presents arms as though his snider were a warclub; within the walls, however, there are merely a dozen wooden shanties which do not deserve even the name of bungalows. In the garden are some tamarind trees and clumps of bamboo and an old fountain and some flowers. The king receives us in one of the wooden shanties and his room is pleasant; there are bookshelves, photographs and a table covered with papers. He sits at his table in a gilt Frenchified chair with a large crown on the back. and we are given similar chairs only without crowns. […] We discuss various topics, the islands, the volcanoes, his new palace, his late visit to America. When are we in Europe to receive a visit? In 1880 or 1881, he hopes; it is the ambition of his life; England he holds to be the land of foremost interest.[39]

On December 31, 1879, the birthday anniversary of his queen, King Kalākaua dedicated the more lavish 'Iolani Palace that still stands.

The king's residence and ones nearby just above Palace Walk formed the nucleus of court life in Honolulu. Included close to the palace of the king was the house of the Kuhina Nui, Keoni Ana.

Kīnaʻu Hale, 'Iolani Palace Yard, Honolulu

The house, called Kīnaʻu Hale, located in the 'Iolani Palace yard, is most likely named in the honor of the daughter of Kamehameha I and sister of Kaʻahumanu. Albert Pierce Taylor, librarian of the Hawaii State Archives, recorded the following about Kīnaʻu Hale: "When John Young [Keoni Ana], son of the Englishman who was detained ashore on Hawaii in 1790 from the schooner Eleanora, and afterwards became a principal advisor to Kamehameha I, was Premier, he built and lived in 'Kinau Hale', on the northern boundary."[40] If Taylor is accurate, Keoni Ana built the house between June 10, 1845, and January 16, 1855, when he was Kuhina Nui or Premier. Since Kīnaʻu died in 1839, she could not have lived in the house called Kīnaʻu Hale. The name of the home, instead, may have reflected the close ties with Kīnaʻu. Keoni Ana was named by Kamehameha III as Kuhina Nui, or premier, in 1845, because, Victoria Kamāmalu, the daughter of Kīnaʻu, was still a minor.

After the death of Kamehameha III, his queen, Kalama, and her husband's son, Albert Kūnuiākea, lived in Kīnaʻu Hale.[41] Keoni Ana died on July 18, 1857, leaving a will that gave his "home (pahale noho) next to the Hale Alii to H. Kalama."[42]

Honokaʻupu, Pohukaina, Honolulu

Thomas Thrum, whose *Hawaiian Almanac and Annual* helped preserve many recollections about nineteenth century Hawaiʻi, recorded a brief description of Honokaʻupu: "A short distance from the palace was a two-story coral house, occupied by

Kinau Hale is most likely the building, just below the flag, with the hipped roof and three windows, that blocks the view of Hale Ali'i in an 1854 lithograph titled "No. 2. View of Honolulu. From the Catholic church / sketched from nature by Paul Emmert" (courtesy Library of Congress Prints and Photographs Division, LC-DIG-pga-00316).

Kekauluohi and her husband Kanaina, who were the parents of Lunalilo, who afterwards came to the throne as William, the First."[43] On September 13, 1829, Chiefess Lydia Nāmāhana lay in state at the residence of Kekauluohi before being taken to her funeral at Kawaiaha'o Church.[44]

The furnishings of the residence is described by Francis Warriner in July 1832: "Kekau-lu-ohe had a handsome looking-glass, a mahogany table, a few Canton chairs, and a high post bedstead with appropriate curtains."[45] The date of the construction of the house differs by a year according the testimony of Charles Kana'ina regarding "Honokaupu," on September 13, 1847: "This is claimant's [Charles Kana'ina's] dwelling place. Kaahumanu gave it to Kekauluohi, who built a stone house upon it in 1833. Claimant has held it many years. It was given to them on account of their taking care of the Royal cemetery. There are seven houses on this piece. Two persons claim houses there. This claim is on behalf of Kanaina's son [Lunalilo]."[46] Kekuanaoa testified to the same date: "that stone house was built in the year 1833. That is a corpse house which was the purpose that house had been built there and Kanaina had lived there as a watchman."[47]

Besides funerals, the residence was also the site of more joyous occasions. On February 2, 1837, Kamehameha III and Kalama, daughter of Naihekukui, were married "by the Rev. H. Bingham at the stone residence of Kekauluohi and Kanaina, who were uncle and aunt of the bride. It was there that the marriage ceremony was held and also a wedding party as prepared by the Chiefs where singing and wedding songs were sung."[48]

Chapter 4. Royal Residences of the Palace Yard and Vicinity

John Papa ʻĪʻī also recorded details about the residence at the time of Kinau's death: "On the first day of January 1839, the guns were to be fired at the Fort at noon; Kinau with the child [Victoria] Kamamalu, Ii and his wife [Sarah], and the rest of the household arose early and went to stay at Honokaupu, Kekāuluohi's coral stone house at Pohukaina. They did not return to the Fort until after Kinau's death [on April 4, 1839]."[49]

With the house empty, Charles Wilkes stayed in the home of Kekāuluohi in 1840 at the behest of the governor of Oʻahu, Mataio Kekūanāoʻa. Kekāuluohi at the time served as Kuhina Nui and styled herself Kaʻahumanu III. Wilkes recorded:

> The governor, Kekuanaoa, kindly placed at my disposal the large stone house belonging to Kekauluohi, in the square where the tomb in which the royal family are interred, is situated. The tomb was at that time undergoing some repairs. The state coffins, which are richly ornamented with scarlet and gold cloth, and in two of which the bodies of the late king Liho-liho, and his wife were brought from England, in the frigate Blonde, were deposited in the house I was to occupy. The governor had them at once removed to the tomb, and in two days I was comfortably established, and engaged in putting up my instruments, and getting ready to carry on our shore duties.[50]

Wilkes added architectural detail later in his account: "The house which the kindness of Governor Kekuanaoa had placed at my disposal, was a double one, of two stories with piazzas in front, and a wing on one side."[51] The stay of Wilkes in the house owned by Kekāuluohi is easily explained by a practice common at the time. Wilkes recounted: "The house though convenient was seldom occupied by its owner; they invariably prefer the grass-houses, which are more convenient for their mode of life, and better adapted to the climate; and if they could be preserved in the state they are when first built, they would be exceedingly pleasant residences."[52] Wilkes also commented on the transition from the *hale pili* to the Western stone structures: "The chiefs have much ambition to own an European house which are built of coral blocks taken from the reefs to the westward of the town of this there appears to be an inexhaustible supply. It is found in layers of from one to two feet in thickness and by cutting through them a block of almost any dimensions may be obtained."[53] Though not referring specifically to Kekūanāoa, the chief and governor of Oʻahu, he would embark in 1845 on building for his daughter Victoria Kamāmalu a Greek Revival structure at Pohukaina just north of the residence of Kekāuluohi.

James Jackson Jarves, recounting his stay in Honolulu from 1837 to 1842 in *Scenes and Scenery in the Sandwich Islands*, also describes the royal residence: "Kekauluohi owns a large two-story stone house in the upper part of town, well furnished, though the grounds about it are not in the best order."[54] Jarves also describes the location of the royal tomb as "near the house of Kekauluohi"[55] The memory of the location was reported four decades later at the laying of the cornerstone for ʻIolani Palace: "Kekauluohi, the Premier, mother of the late King Lunalilo built her home within what now constitutes the palace yard, a few rods eastward of this spot."[56]

Laura Fish Judd, wife of missionary physician, Gerrit P. Judd, gave the best description of the interior of Honokaʻupu. She remembered her stay in the house in October 1843:

> The die is cast—we have left our pleasant home in the Mission premises and moved into a furnished stone house of the premier [Kekāluohi], adjoining the palace. The old lady [39 years old] has not occupied it since the death of her sister, Kinau [April 4, 1839], who was laid in state in this drawing-room for six weeks. Prince David, the eldest of Kinau's sons, died here

also [December 15, 1835]. The pupils in the royal school near us assure our children that the house is haunted, and wonder how we can bring our minds to live in it, affirming we shall surely see ghosts.

The high ceiling, large windows, and papered walls afford such a contrast to our little cottage, that I feel like a traveler at a hotel, or on board a finely-furnished steamer—a mere lodger for the night. The situation is cooler than at the Mission, and commands the sweet breeze from the valley. The upper room is a fine place for school, where I spend an hour and a half each morning with the children. They are allowed to attend the royal school in the afternoon, which is quite agreeable to Mr. and Mrs. Cooke, as well as their royal pupils. It is so near that I can over-look the play-ground from the window where I am writing.[57]

Kekāuluohi served as Kuhina Nui, co-ruler with the king, following the deaths of her sisters Kaʻauhumanu and Kīnaʻu (courtesy Hawaii State Archives, PP-98-1-001).

Kekāuluohi died at 6:30 a.m. on June 7, 1845. The funeral procession traveled one of the shortest distances possible, "from her House to the Church [Kawaiahaʻo] and back to the Royal Cemetery."[58]

Albert Pierce Taylor recorded: "In the premises known as Pohukaina, in the southeast (Waikiki-makai) corner, at King and Likelike streets, the High Chiefess Kekauluohi, the Premier, mother of Prince Lunalilo, who became King in 1873, erected her house."[59]

The name of the residence was also used for a bathing pool and the area around it. The map titled *Plan of Honolulu* applies the name "Honokaupu" to two parcels just *mauka* of Queen Street between Fort and Richards Streets.[60] John Papa ʻĪʻī also places the "bathing pool of Honokaupu, above Queen Street, north of a pier at the corner where Queen and Alakea Streets now meet."[61]

Hāliʻimaile, ʻIolani Palace Yard, Honolulu, Victoria Kamāmalu (1825–bef. death of Kamehameha V)

Displaced by Kamehameha III from the house that he had built for his daughter, Victoria Kamāmalu, Matiao Kekūanāoʻa lived in a nearby house called Hāliʻimaile, a

Chapter 4. Royal Residences of the Palace Yard and Vicinity

name literally meaning a covering of maile, a vine noted for its fragrance.

Abner Paki testified about Hāli'imaile in October 18, 1848: "This lot is on Corner of Broadway [King Street] Richards St. in Honolulu. Mauka is J. Youngs [Keoni Ana's] house lot, Waikiki Palace Yard, Makai, Broadway. Ewa Richards Street. Claimants title to this lot is from Kinau, who took it up and improved it about 1825, and it has been held by her and claimant [Kekūanāo'a] ever since in peace. It is Victoria's land."[62] In the *Native Testimony* Paki testified that Kekuanoa had "received it as idle land in the year 1826."[63]

When Emmert published his "View of Honolulu from the Catholic Church, No. 2." in 1853, he titled the vignette for Hāli'imaile: "Prince Alexander and Lot." The two princes were the sons of Kekūanāo'a and Kīna'u.

Chief Justice Charles Coffin Harris gave his recollections of Hāli'imaile at the laying of the cornerstone of the present 'Iolani Palace in December 1879: "Kekuanaoa's

Kekūanāo'a and his daughter, Victoria Kamāmalu, both served as Kuhina Nui (courtesy Hawaii State Archives, PP-98-2-006).

Emmert view of Hali'imaile (Plate 2, Cut 5). Princes Alexander and Lot would reign as Kamehameha IV and Kamehameha V respectively (courtesy Hawaii State Archives, PP-92-8-015).

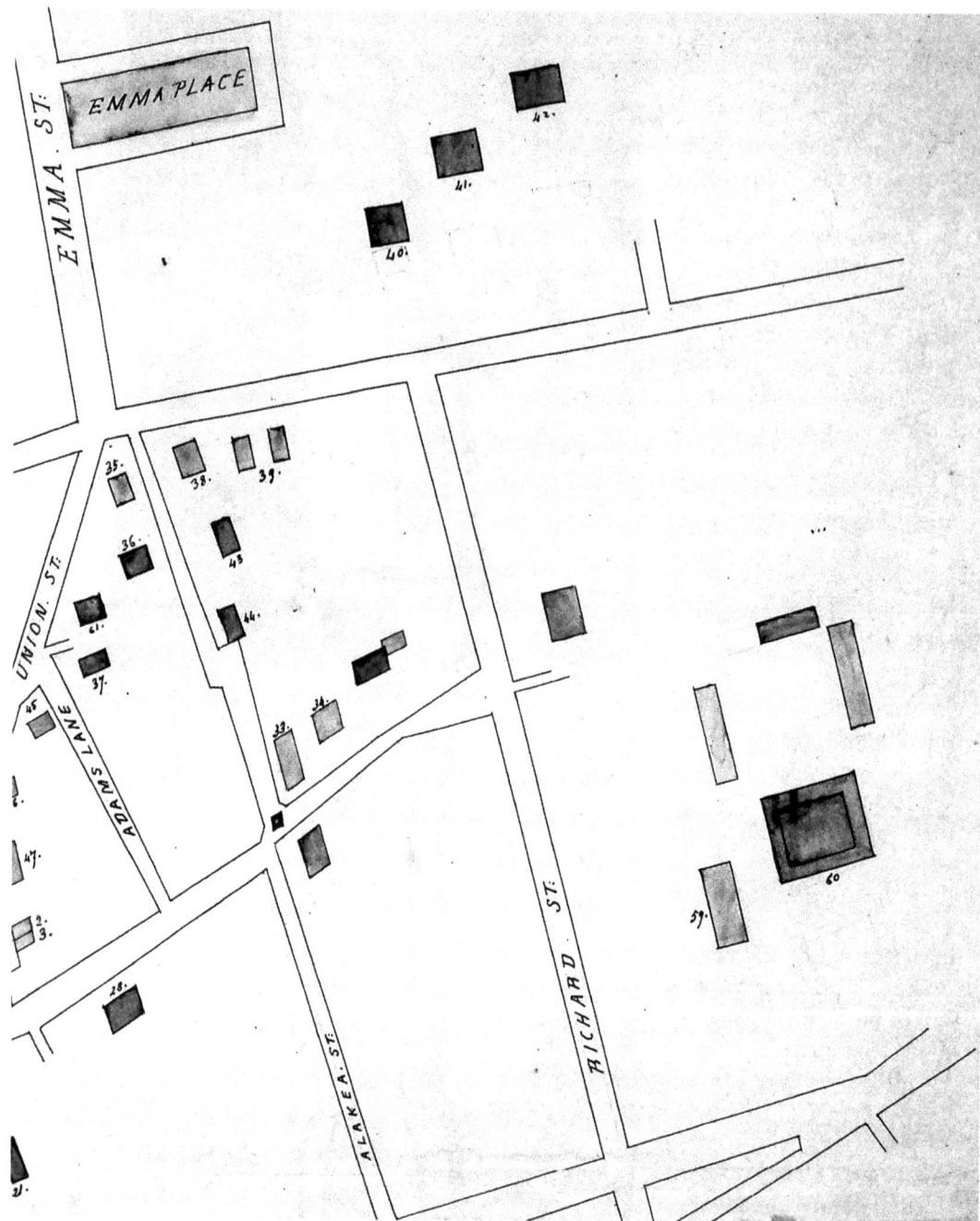

Detail of the 1862 Plan of Honolulu shows several buildings surrounding Hale Aliʻi (labeled 60). Hāliʻimaile (labeled 59) is listed in the key as the residence of Prince Lot. The unnumbered building off of the upper right-hand corner of the palace is most likely Ihikapulani. To the left, at a right angle, is Hoihoikea. Off the upper left hand corner of the palace sits Kinau Hale. At the *mauka*–Diamond Head corner of Richards Street and Palace Walk is the Hōlani, residence of Kekauonohi (courtesy Hawaii State Archives M-61 Oversize N2-1).

house, which he called Haliimaile, occupied the west corner of this enclosure. This was a humble stone cottage, and the Governor Kekuanaoa took a sudden idea of building a much more ambitious house, gathered a vast quantity of coral stones, and raised the lofty walls of what he intended to be a magnificent structure, which remained for a long time as a monument of the building enterprise of His Excellency, and were removed and the stones sold by his son Kamehameha V.; and thus that palace vanished into thin air."[64]

The *Plan of Honolulu* map records the location of a site, marked Prince Lot and its relation to the palace. Though the map has no date, it is usually dated as 1862 because it marks the properties in the estate of Louis H. Anthon, Danish consul, who died in Copenhagen, Denmark, on August 13, 1862. By 1862 Alexander was already reigning as Kamehameha IV, so Lot's name alone was attached to the residence.

Hoihoikea, 'Iolani Palace Yard, Honolulu (–1901)

Albert Pierce Taylor, in his research about 'Iolani Palace, identified several other nearby structures, including Hoihoikea, residence of King Kamehameha III, King Kamehameha IV, and King Kamehameha V. Taylor, who conducted his research at the Archives Building on the 'Iolani Palace grounds, wrote: ""Hoihoikea" was the name given to a large, old-fashioned, livable cottage erected in the grounds a little to ewa and mauka of the old palace, in which Kamehameha III, Kamehameha IV and V resided, the palace being used principally for state purposes, It was a dwelling place, provided with simpler comforts of a citizen, and greatly enjoyed by sovereigns. The "Bungalow," built later and used largely as a family residence by King Kalakaua, occupied a site ewa of "Hoihoikea," or between the Palace and Richards street."[65]

At the groundbreaking of the new 'Iolani Palace, speaker Judge Charles Coffin Harris, an eyewitness to events in the Palace Yard, gave a brief history of what he called "Hoikea." On the birthday of Queen Kapi'olani, December 31, 1879, Harris gave an aural tour of the grounds: "Hoikea which is now standing, and within your sight, has been the scene of some of the most interesting incidents in Hawaiian history. It was the personal home of Kamehameha III, and here he who has the honor to address you, argued before the King himself, since regular courts were established. This court, which was soon after abolished, was called the Supreme Court, and the King sat as judge. […] Here Kamehameha III, died, and in that house many of the most important councils to decide the destiny of this nation. The name itself 'Hoikea' (the life returns) is in commemoration of the restoration of the flag by Admiral Thomas."[66] Harris skips over Kamehameha IV, who probably used Ihikapukalani/Kauluhinano instead.

Harris remarked on important occurrences that took place at Hoihoikea: "During the reign of Kamehameha V. the Ministerial councils were held there more often than in the house that stood upon this spot ['Iolani Palace]. There was held the council which summoned the Constitutional Convention, the eventual result of which was the abrogation of the Constitution of 1852, and the establishment of the present one by proclamation. Here Kamehameha V.—he of the firm will—succumbed to his fate, and the dynasty of the Kamehameha Kings became extinct."[67]

The final destruction of Hoihoikea, the residence named for the restoration of sovereignty, came at the hands of the government that supplanted the monarchy: "the palace of King Kamehameha, has been torn down [in 1901] to make way for a more modern building."[68]

Ihikapukalani/Kauluhinano (erected by King Kamehameha IV), 'Iolani Palace Yard, Honolulu, Queen Emma (1856–1879)

Located on the southeast side of Hale Ali'i, Kamehameha IV erected a residence for his wife, Queen Emma, called variously Ihikapukalani or Kauluhinano. A February 1856 contract for the building gives "Particulars and Specifications of Carpenters and Joiners Work to be done in making certain additions and alterations for a private residence in the Palace Yard Honolulu for His Majesty King Kamehameha IV."[69] Albert Pierce Taylor noted in 1930: "This is probably the house afterwards called Ihikapulani [sic], and was placed about where Banyan Tree now stands."[70] The contract called for carpenters to "move the house to about 7 feet nearer to the Palace." The only drawing of the carpentry is in the margins of the contract and specifies the dimensions of the moldings. Like the work done on Hale Piula (Chapter 2), the contract also specifies the use of "brown cotton" here included to prepare the walls to "receive the paper."

Since the contract refers to "certain alterations and additions" and specifies that the workers "move the house" at least part of the residence may have already existed prior to the reign of Kamehameha IV. George Washington Bates, in his *Sandwich Island Notes*, wrote during the last year of the reign of Kamehameha III: "On the right of the main building, in a detached form stood the private apartments of the monarch; on the left those of his queen. They were framed buildings, sustained on basements, having walls of coral, and looking very much like rural cottages erected for the mere object of

Line drawing of Hale Ali'i, with Ihikapukalani/Kauluhinano to its right (courtesy Hawaii State Archives, PP-10-5-001).

economy."[71] The "addition" may have been the portion devoted to the residence for the queen. Regardless of who built the structure, the contract called for a massive overhaul, down to the moldings and wall treatments. The changes, no doubt, were designed to make the residence suitable for his queen.

Unlike the arrangement of Kamehameha III that had the residences of the king and queen on opposite sides of Hale Aliʻi, Kamehameha IV and Emma had their dwelling spaces adjacent to one other on the Waikīkī side of the palace. Though having separate sides and names, the residence, nevertheless, was considered as one structure and referred to in the singular: "The dwelling occupied by their Majesties, which is a separate building from the Palace, has been recently erected, and is also elegantly furnished and in keeping with the latter."[72]

The relative locations of the residences were detailed by John M. Kapena, from his 1879 speech at the groundbreaking for Kalakaua's ʻIolani Palace. He shared:

> The last house that was recently demolished was known on the makai side as Kauluhinano and as Ihikapukalani on the mauka side, erected by Kamehameha IV for his queen, where they spent most of their time during his reign. Those who had the good fortune to be invited to partake of the gracious hospitalities of the king and queen will not soon forget the refined and courteous manners of those royal personages. In Ihikapukalani was born their child, the Prince of Hawaii.[73]

The son of King Kamehameha IV and Queen Emma, Prince Albert, Ka Haku o Hawaiʻi, was born at on May 20, 1858. The necessity of building a new place for the queen to live may have been related to the presence of the widow of Kamehameha III, Dowager Queen Kalama, in Kīnaʻu Hale prior to her move to Pihanakalani at Haʻimoeipo.

An editorial in the March 20, 1862, *Pacific Commercial Advertiser* proposed a new royal palace. "A Palace for the Royal family is needed," the newspaper expressed, "and if any mode can be devised by which it can be erected during the coming biennial term, the necessary funds should be voted. It becomes every nation to seek the personal comfort of its sovereign and his family, and to provide for them a residence suited to the dignity of their position, that they may command the respect due to them as rulers. The bare fact that His Majesty has signified his wish that an appropriation be voted for this object, ought to be sufficient reason why it should be voted at the earliest moment practicable."[74] The royal family would lose its first member, Prince Albert Ka Haku O Hawaiʻi, on August 27, 1862; he died at Hale Aliʻi. Sadly, Kamehameha IV would also die at the palace on November 30, 1863, before entertaining any plans for a new palace.

No records indicate how the residence of the queen was used during the reigns of the bachelor kings Kamehameha V and Lunalilo; the former lived in Hoihoikea and the latter in Pihanakalani at Haʻimoeipo. Mention of Ihikapukalani again takes place at the end of the latter's reign. With King Lunalilo on the verge of death, the supporters of Kalākaua jockeyed for living arrangements. Queen Emma in a letter to her cousin Peter Young Kaʻeo on Molokaʻi (Chapter 2) reported the disposition for several of the lost palaces: "[William] Ka asked and got the promise of living at Ihikapu, Kahananui takes Kanaina's house near it at Pohukaina, if David should become King. Mrs. Dominis was to have Kinau Hale. This you can judge high disloyal speculations were going on, and the man not dead."[75] After the razing of ʻIolani Palace in 1876, other buildings in the palace enclosure took on official roles. In another letter to Kaeo, dated January 22, 1876, Emma wrote of the baptism of Kaiulani and "reception and breakfast at Ihikapukalani, on the week after. Piolani gave a public reception at Ihikapukalani to the ladies of town."[76]

Later Ihikapukalani came close to being destroyed. Queen Emma described the circumstances in a letter to Kaeo: "There was a fire in Ihikapukalani on election day [1876]. A soldier laid his cigar down on a matrass [sic] in drawing-room and burnt a matrass up, nearly burning the house down, but [it was] put out in time."[77] Fortunately the house survived, for in the absence of 'Iolani Palace, it continued to serve as the site for official functions. When the heir apparent to King Kalākaua's throne, William Pitt Leleiohoku II died on April 10, 1877, the "remains lay in State [...] in the house at Iolani Palace known as Ihekapukalani [sic]."[78] The funeral took place in the same place, in the "large audience-room of *Ihikapukalani* House."[79]

Ironically, a fire chant for King Kalākaua mentions the residence: "So lives my land heated everywhere by the sacred kapu-fire of 'Ihi-kapu-lani."[80] Mary Kawena Pukui explains the reference to the house:

> King Ka-lā-kaua and Queen Ka-piʻo-lani took up residence, somewhat ostentatiously in the eyes of their critics, in the house after their election. The name of the house, "hallowed royal kapu," associates the house with the fire burning kapu, as does the mention in Kuokoa, April 18, of its appearance on the night of the royal party's arrival by carriage after landing from the tour: "Before the doors of 'Ihi-kapu-lani house were lights in the form of a crown and above that were decorations used in ancient times. Upon a roof was a fire container kept burning by a handsome youth."[81]

Mauka of the 'Iolani Palace Yard

John Papa ʻĪʻī recorded the name for the group of residences just mauka of the ʻIolani Palace Yard. "New houses were built on the north side of the Pohukaina enclosure, and Kalanimoku called them Halehanaimoa. (This is the place where Kapakuhaili [Queen Kalama], widow of Kamehameha III was living at the time of her death."[82] The prominent houses included Hōlani, owned by Kekauōnohi; Pihanakalani at Haʻimoe-ipo, residence of Queen Kalama; and Kuaihelani, the property of Jane Lahilahi Young Kaʻeo.

Hōlani, Richards and Palace Walk, Honolulu
(before February 1848–after 1898)

The residence of High Chiefess Mikahela Kekauʻōnohi, called Hōlani (the name of a mythical place), was located on the mauka-Diamond Head corner of Richards Street and Palace Walk. Kekauōnohi was the granddaughter of Kamehameha I and a wife of Kamehameha II. It most likely dates to before 1848. She and her husband signed Mahele claim, No. 11216, at "Holani House."[83] Though the claim has no date, it is placed with other claims dated during February 1848. She also refers in the *Native Register* for Mahele claim 6194 to her "stone-walled house lot named Holani"[84] in a verification of conveyance of the lot north of hers to Iosua Kaʻeo, which was called Kuaihelani. The verification was signed on February 9, 1848. It was a fitting pairing, for the house immediately *mauka* of Hōlani, Kuaihelani, was also named for a mythical island.[85]

The stone house most likely dates to after the request by Kekauōnohi for building materials for Hōlani. The Privy Council approved, on May 27, 1850, the cutting of the coral used to build the residence of Kekauōnohi. "Mr. Armstrong read an application from Kekauonohi to cut 6000 coral stones for building her own house."⁸⁶ Resolution 5 read: "Resolved; That Kekauonohi be permitted to cut six thousand Reef stones for her own use."⁸⁷

Gorham D. Gilman included the residence of Kekauōnohi in his recollection of houses of the early 1840s, although it might refer to an earlier residence closer to the waterfront. After a discussion of Halekauwila on Queen Street, Gilman went on to describe other prominent residences in the area: "Beyond this [Halekauwila] towards Waikiki were the premises occupied by Governor Kekuanoa [sic] and beyond these the residence of the high chiefess Kekauonohi and her husband, Kealiiahonui, son of the former king of Kauai, who was brought as a hostage from that island and married to his royal companion."⁸⁸

An account by H.L. Sheldon, explains the references to the property later as "Haalelea Lawn: "June 2d, died in Honolulu the high chiefess Kekauonohi, grand-daughter of Kamehameha I., aged 46 years. She was one of the wives of Liholiho, before the introduction of Christianity. After his death in London in 1824, she was married to Keliiahonui, son of Kaumualii, the last King of Kaua'i. She acted as Governess of Kaua'i for several years, removing to O'ahu in 1844, and acted, up to her last sickness, as one of the King's principal advisers in all matters of state. After Keliiahonui's death in 1849, she married Levi Ha'alelea [November 6, 1849], to whom she devised her large landed possessions by will. There was a large attendance of natives and foreigners at her funeral [Kekauōnohi died June 21, 1851] from the old homestead on the corner of Richard street and Palace Walk."⁸⁹ The *Polynesian* gave the particulars of the funeral: "The funeral of the late Kekauonohi, grand-daughter of Kamehameha I, will take place on Monday, the 30th instant, from the house of the deceased, in Richards Street, at 10 o'clock."⁹⁰ The Chamberlain's Notice in the next issue of the *Polynesian* added that: "The procession will move from her residence in Richard [sic] Street, to the large native church, and from thence to the Royal Cemetery."⁹¹

Hōlani passed to Levi Ha'alelea with the rest of Kekau'ōnohi's estate which her will described as "from Hawaii to Kauai, the lands, houselots, including real properties, personal properties, immovable and movable properties, those items of my person including clothes and food, those items great and small, everything that is known or heard of as belonging to me, all these things shall belong to my heir."⁹²

Following Kekau'ōnohi's death, Ha'alelea married Amoe Ena, daughter of a chiefess and a Chinese businessman, on January 19, 1858, in Hilo.⁹³ Titus Coan officiated.

Even after Kekau'ōnohi's death, the residence continued to be called Hōlani. That name is listed as the site of Ha'alelea's death on October 3, 1864,⁹⁴ and in the inventory of the personal property of the estate of Levi Ha'alelea, the various items are recorded as "In Holani."⁹⁵ The inventory indicates the internal divisions of the house. It lists on the upper story a mauka room, middle room and a small room (makai), on the lower floor, a large room and small room, and a dining room and pantry and a kitchen.⁹⁶

An 1874 map of the neighboring property of Charles Kana'ina shows the boundaries of the Ha'alelea grounds. On October 16, 1875, Amoe A. Ha'alelea sold Hōlani and her other properties to John Harvey Coney for $25,000. Coney was the husband of Laura Ena Coney, sister of Amoe Ena Ha'alelea. John and Laura Coney named their son John Haalelea Coney. John H. Coney died on October 9, 1880. The 1888 city directory lists Mrs. J.H. [John Harvey] Coney, widow, as living at "44 Richard."⁹⁷

Albert Pierce Taylor, who arrived in Honolulu in August 1898 as secretary to Lorrin

The residence Kekauʻōnohi and Haʻalelea (courtesy Hawaii State Archives, PPO-31).

A. Thurston, Hawaiian Annexation Commissioner, gave the most detailed description of the residence: "At the time of annexation in 1898 Haalelea Lawn as the place was known was under a lease and used as a boarding place. [...] Haalelea was a fine old two-story coral-stone house, surrounded by wide verandahs, or lanais, a mansion harking back to old colonial or Southern architecture."[98] The premises must have been under lease before annexation, for the *Hawaiian Gazette* reported in February 1896: "A card party was given at Holani Pa Wednesday evening by Mrs. Graham to the members of the cast of 'Meridith's Old Coat' and a few others."[99] "A tea to meet Mrs. Rudolph Spreckels and Miss Joliffe of San Francisco was given by Mrs. Graham at her home, Holani Pa, Saturday afternoon."[100] A twelve-year-old Harvey Graham. He wrote to *St. Nicholas: An Illustrated Magazine for Young Folks* from Holani Pa. He wrote: "I live far away in the Hawaiian Islands in a beautiful place by the name of Holani Pa. I have been here for some time and I expect to stay for some time to come but for all that I enjoy myself very much but never more than when I can sit under the trees and read my St. Nicholas. I have been taking the magazine ever since I was three years old that is for nine years and it has become the most precious book I have. I must close now as I will go crazy if I don't read my November number. Hoping to see this printed in the January number I remain Your devoted reader Harvey Graham."[101]

The Vos family invited many guests to their residence at Hōlani. On June 2, 1898, Hubert Vos invited journalists covering the Spanish-American war to a dinner at his residence.[102] A month later the *Evening Bulletin* reported that a farewell poi supper "for Mr. and Mrs. Julian Monsarrat who leave for the States on the Gaelic today, and Mr.

and Mrs. Hubert Vos, who leave for the Orient in a few days, was given at the studio of Mr. Vos, at Holani Pa."[103] Among the attendees were A.S. Cleghorn and his daughter Princess Kaʻiulani. A year later Mr. and Mrs. Hubert Vos "entertained a number of passengers going through in the Doric at a poi luncheon in Holani Pa today [August 15, 1899]."[104] Ululani Haalelea continued to live there and "gave a poi luncheon for Mrs. Henry W. Howard at Holani Pa [on February 1, 1899]."[105] Another family member also lived at Hōlani Pa; Mrs. L.A. Coney had a visit by her daughter Mrs. Frank Ashton of Berkeley, California.[106]

By 1902 "the stone walled lot" of Kekauōnohi presented enough of a safety hazard to have a portion of the coral wall torn down. Streetcar conductors going in the Diamond Head direction on Hotel Street would have to yell, "Look out for the stone wall on the left,"[107] as they passed the grand estate. The coral wall of Haʻalelea Lawn was not set back the usual distance from the streetcar track, thus occasioning the warning. When built more than a half-century earlier, the offending wall fronted a much narrower Palace Walk; after the wall's demise the road width was standard from Fort Street to Punchbowl Street with a safe distance between the streetcar and the road's edge.

Though not affecting the ownership of Hōlani, the second Mrs. Haalelea, Amoe Ena Haʻalelea, fought the efforts of Kaae to overturn the probate of Keliʻiahonui, the first husband of Kekauōnohi.[108] Amoe Ena Haʻalelea died in 1904. A marble plaque above the royal pew of Kawaiahaʻo honors Amoe Ena Haalelea, her husband, Levi Haʻalelea and his brother Haʻalilio. The dedication of the plaque in 1907 provided an opportunity to reminisce about the marriage of Ululani Ena and Levi Haalelea:

> The honeymoon was spent at the old palace in Kailua, and from there Haalelea brought his bride to his home in Honolulu—the place known in those days as Holani Pa is now called Haalelea Lawn. The house was an especially fine one for the time, and to the young bride coming from Hawaii to Honolulu for the first time everything was as beautiful as a dream. The Queen Dowager [Kalama, wife of Kamehameha III], cousin of Haalelea, had her residence adjoining Holani Pa, and it was with her that Mrs. Haalelea spent much of her time. [...] Her happy marriage lasted but seven years. She had a love for books and poetry and many beautiful verses in Hawaiian are from her pen. It was one of her dreams to translate Ben Hur, a book which she greatly admired, into Hawaiian, and the work was partially done at the time of her death.[109]

In 1905, William H. Coney, city editor of the *Evening Bulletin*, which recorded many of the social events at the compound, died at "Holani Pa, the family residence near Central Union Church."[110]

The University Club entered into a lease with the Coney estate for the use of Hōlani as a clubhouse. The University Club started in 1897 with graduates of "Harvard, Williams, Cornell, Yale, Oberlin, Amherst, Columbia, Wesleyan, Dartmouth, Brown and other American colleges." In 1928, the beneficiaries of the John H. Coney Trust Estate petitioned the court to sell the property on which the University Club was located because the trust was actually losing money on the lease. The club had a long-term lease through 1935, but the income derived from it did not cover the expenses needed to maintain the property. Judge E.K. Massee ordered on July 9, 1928, the sale with an upset price of $109,000.[111] The University Club bought the property for the upset price and recorded the deed on February 12, 1929.[112] The following year the University Club merged with the Pacific Club, owners of the former Cleghorn residence on Emma Street (Chapter 5). The combined club met there for the first time on October 10, 1930. The University Club sold

Hōlani to the new Pacific Club entity. By 1937 Hōlani was part a portion of the Pacific Club properties sold at a foreclosure auction to Hugh Howell, Jr. for $35,000.

Taylor described the site after the residence had been razed: "Only the high stone wall, said to have been erected three quarters of a century ago, still remains of the old estate, and remains practically the only landmark of the olden days of Honolulu, except for Washington Place, former home of Liliuokalani, and its adjoining neighbor the Stone House, occupied in bygone days by the missionary Armstrong family, and these old houses are on Beretania street."[113] Today, only Washington Place remains of the three landmarks: Parke Chapel supplanted Stone House and the Korean and Vietnam War Memorial sits on the State Capitol grounds where a portion of the wall once stood.

Kuaihelani (early 1840s–before 1891) Beretania Street, Honolulu, Jane Lahilahi Young Ka'eo and Prince Albert Kūnuiākea

Just *mauka* of Hōlani and across the street from Washington Place stood the house of one of the daughters of John Young. Gorham Gilman mentions the residence of Jane Lahilahi Young Ka'eo as one of the houses standing when he arrived in the early 1840s: "And mauka of this [the Ha'alelea residence on Palace Walk and Richards Street] coming up Beretania street, was the residence of Kaeo, and Lahilahi, the parents of the late Prince Albert [Kūnuiākea] recently deceased."[114]

The testimony to the Board of Commissioners to Quiet Land Titles for Land Court Award 6194 includes a Verification of Conveyance for the Kuaihelani site:

> I, by the Grace which God has given to the people of means, therefore do hereby graciously give a house lot of mine, and it is conveyed absolutely to Iosua Kaeo, for him and his heirs; I shall have no rights to this place. This enclosure is on the east side of Waialeale Road [Richards Street] of Beretane [Beretania], on the west of my lot which was transferred to the Government and on the north of my stone-walled house lot named Holani.
>
> The ones with the rights therein are my subject who was given it, and the Ali'i. In Witness whereof, I set my name on this 9th day of February, 1848, at Honolulu, Oahu.
> M. Kekauonohi
> Aarona Keliiahonui[115]

Albert Kūnuiākea, son of Kamehameha III and Jane Lahilahi, was born on June 18, 1851, at Kuaihelani. In May 24, 1858, Jane Lahilahi and her husband, Joshua Ka'eo, mortgaged their property, which was paid off November 10, 1859, following his death on June 27, 1858.[116]

Jane Lahilahi Young Kaeo died at "her residence at Kuaehelani [sic], Beretania Street," on January 12, 1862.[117] Her obituary delineated the nature of the long illness preceding her death: "Mrs. Kaeo suffered for over eight years from a stroke of paralysis, yet bore her lot with exemplary fortitude and a contented, cheerful temper."[118] She was the mother Peter Young Ka'eo and Albert Kūnuiākea, and sister of Keoni Ana, Grace Kama'iku'i Rooke and Fanny Kekelaokalani Naea. Her son, also known as Peter Young Kekuaokalani, would serve as administrator of her estate.[119] Before their deaths, Joshua Ka'eo and Jane Lahilahi petitioned the probate court, on June 18, 1858, to appoint a guardian for their almost seven-year-old son, Albert Kūnuiākea "to manage the entire estate, and to educate him, and assist him with all his needs."[120] Accordingly, on June 30, 1858, three days after the death of Joshua Ka'eo, the court appointed "Hazaleleponi K.

Kapakuhaili the Queen Dowager and T.C.B. Rooke" as guardians.[121] On March 6, 1863, a division deed gave Royal Patent 2647 to Peter Young Kaeo.[122] Later, to settle the debts of Kaeo, the marshal, William Cooper Parke, held an auction of the property. Peter Young Kaeo's aunt, Fanny Kekelaokalani, put in the highest bid.

By 1872 an inventory of the property listed: "Kuaihelani—House lot in Honolulu with an old house not tenantable."[123] When Kūnuiākea reached the age of twenty-one, he no longer needed a guardian, but on November 11, 1872, Fanny Kekelaokalani petitioned for the "appointment of a guardian for the said Kunuiakea Ka'eo, whereas he is not managing his estate, and his entire estate will be gone without him receiving further benefit. If a guardian is not appointed, then his entire estate will be gone permanently."[124] The request was witnessed by his cousin, Queen Emma. Kūnuiākea stated and signed: "I hereby agree to the appointment of a guardian, knowing it is in my best interest to do so." Governor Paul Nahaolelua of Maui was appointed the same day.[125] After Nahaolelua's death, Queen Emma petitioned on January 11, 1876, for a guardian for Kūnuiākea claiming that "the habits of said Albert Kuniakea [sic] are such that if he should have control of his own property, he will be reduced to poverty—and in fact that the said Albert is a spendthrift,—And, your petitioner further represents that she is the nearest surviving relative of said Albert except his brother Peter Young Kaeo who is now resident at Kalaupapa on the island of Molokai."[126] Peter Young Kaeo had his residence (Chapter 2) at Kalawao, Molokai, starting in 1874.

The court in the 1876 petition "said it would hear evidence of the reformed state of the adult, Kunuiakea."[127] On January 13, 1876, Palua, Kunuiakea's nurse, testified "Kunuiakea's mode of living is now very quiet and not as it was before. Now, if he has any money he does not squander it as before. I am his nurse. I live at his house—opposite John Dominis."[128] Another witness, Keawe gave sworn testimony: "I know Kunuikea. I think he had changed from what he was. My wife was one of Kunuiakea's mothers."[129]

Alexander Joy Cartwright said, "that her Majesty the Queen would cheerfully give it [the guardianship] up at the end of the year if she found that he reformed."[130] The court, in spite of the testimony, appointed Queen Emma as the guardian of Kūnuiākea, a guardianship that lasted until April 1880.[131]

Kūnuiākea's half-brother Peter Young Ka'eo died on November 26, 1880. The Hawaiian *Kingdom Statistical and Commercial Directory and Tourists Guide, 1880–1880*, has a listing for "Kanueakea, A landowner, p r 46 and 48 Richard street, Honolulu."[132] Kūnuiākea sold the property in March 1883 to Alexander Joy Cartwright. Even after the sale Kūnuiākea continued living at Kuaihelani. He wrote a letter to Queen Emma from "Kuaihelani June 16th 1883,"[133] and is listed in the 1884 city directory as living at "46 Richard."[134]

By 1886 a news account places the Kūnuiākea residence in Kapālama (Chapter 5). Cartwright conveyed the property in January 4, 1886, to John Adams Cummins.

On June 3, 1891, the church laid the cornerstone for Central Union Church directly across the street from Washington Place. Edward Griffin Beckwith gave an invitation to Lili'uokalani, whom he called "Dear Friend and Most Gracious Sovereign" to attend the cornerstone ceremony "at the junction of Beretania and Richards Sts." He closed his invitation with "Wishing you long life and prosperity." She wrote on the envelope that had enclosed the invitation: "Did not go because I was at Hilo—on my Tour to the people."[135] On May 17, 1892, it purchased the property at the corner of Beretania and Richard Streets (R.P. 2647 & pc. Land) from Charles R. Bishop and other trustees. The first

A view of Central Union Church built on the grounds of Kuaihelani at the corner of Beretania and Richards streets. The photograph looks *mauka* up Richards Street towards Stonehouse. The stone wall in the foreground surrounds the neighboring Haalelea Lawn. The photograph was taken March 29, 1912 (courtesy Hawaii State Archives, PP-15-5-010).

service was conducted on December 4, 1892. The congregation used the grounds of Stone House, across Beretania Street and adjacent to Washington Place, to park its carriages.

Pihanakalani at Haʻimoeipo, Honolulu, Queen Kalama, Lunalilo (before 1869–August 1881)

When Queen Kalama, also known as Hakaleleponi, lived at Haʻimoeipo, literally "fascination," is unknown, but the *mauka* entrance to the palace grounds between her residence and Hale Aliʻi was named in her honor and called Hakaleleponi gate. She called her house there "Pihanakalani,"[136] though most references to the site call it Haʻimoeipo. Pihana could refer to the birthplace of Keōpūolani.

She moved with her son, Albert Kūnuiākea, from Kīnaʻu Hale to Haʻimoeipo:[137] "Even after the death of his reputed father [Kamehameha III], he remained with Queen Kalama up to the time of her death, with the exception of the days he attended school at Ahuimanu, under the tuition of the Roman Catholic Mission with Father Walsh as tutor."[138]

Victoria Kamāmalu stayed at Pihanakalani shortly before her death at Papakanene

(Chapter 5) in 1866. Queen Kalama, who died Tuesday, September 20, 1870, left her properties to her uncle and hānai father, Charles Kanaʻina. Kalama was the daughter of I-Kapeʻekukai, sister of Kanaʻina's mother, Kauwe. Precisely when Lunalilo started living at Haʻimoeipo is also unknown, but the 1869 Bennett's lists the address for Prince W.C. Lunalilo as Palace Walk.[139] When Isabella L. Bird visited Hawaiʻi during the reign of King William Lunalilo, she described a common practice among the royals: "At present the palace is only used for state receptions and entertainments for the king is living at his private residence of Haemoeipio [sic] not far off."[140]

Haʻimoeipo would also be the site of King Lunalilo's death. On January 19, 1874, Queen Emma wrote a letter from Haʻimoeipo to Lucy Peabody: "Come down quick as you can, the King is in danger." In a lengthy postscript she added: "There is a great move to get Kalakaua appointed successor and it is represented that it is the wish of the people but it is not the truth, only his party thinks so and talk to steer the people up in favor of it. The king is firm to have me appointed, this is a secret he told me so himself just now, never breathe it to any one but send word to Kewiki and Simon for me, to work openly in my favor they need fear nobody. I shall be chosen, the King says come what may no one but me shall sit on the throne."[141]

On February 3, 1874, King Lunalilo died, failing to name a successor. His house soon became a locus for mourning: "The news of the King's death flew over the town like a flash of electricity, and by 10 o'clock many hundreds of people had collected in the grounds of Haimoeipo, the King's private town residence where the body lay."[142] The official mourning, however, took place next door: "At 1 o'clock, preparations having been completed in the Palace near by, the body was placed on a bier and conveyed thither, to be laid in state on the ensuing day."[143] A month and a half later, on Tuesday, March 18, 1874, crowds brought *hookupu*, gifts, to "H.R. Highness Charles Kanaina, at Haimoipu [sic] the residence of the late King Lunalilo."[144] An 1874 map, titled *Plan of Land Owned by H.H. C. Kanaina*, shows the outline of Haʻimoeipo.

A little over three years after the death of his son, Kanaʻina died on March 13, 1877, without leaving a will. The probate court, in a decision dated January 6, 1880, ordered the sale of his property. Listed as Lot 9, the "well known lot of Haimoeipo, situated on Palace Walk, and containing an area of 78/100 acres" was sold on April 3, 1880.[145] Later, the physical structure called Haʻimoeipo was sold. On Saturday, July 30, 1881, by order of the Minister of the Interior, "the House 'Haimoeipo,' Lately Occupied by Kanaina"[146] was sold. The structure was sold in two parts. The advertisement announcing the sale noted: "The lower portion of the house, being composed of Coral Stones, will be sold in a separate lot."[147] The sale required the house "to be removed within 14 days from day [of] sale."[148]

Haʻimoeipo continued to be the subject of litigation long after the sales. In 1894 "Kahakuakui (w), who with her husband receives $30 per month under the will of Bernice P. Bishop, has sued the Hawaiian Government, in ejectment, for the valuable land situated in Haimoeipo, Honolulu, next to the Barracks. A.S. Hartwell, who defends on behalf of the Government, now has two claimants to contend with. The other claimant, Thomas R. Mossman, is awaiting a decision in respect to the plea in bar set up by the Government."[149] As late as 1905 the last case making a claim on Haʻimoeipo, that of Lucy Peabody, was adjudicated.

Despite the absence of a physical structure, the area still retained the name of the lost palace. At the turn of the century, on April 24, 1901, a political rally supporting the establishment of county governments took place at "Haimoeipo square near the drill shed."[150] The Home Rule party held another mass meeting April 27, 1901, "at Haimoeipo outside of the drillshed"[151] that featured delegate Robert Wilcox as one of the speakers.

Today, the lost palaces of Kekauōnohi (Hōlani), Queen Kalama (Pihanakalani at Haʻimoeipo), and Jane Lahilahi Young Kaeo (Kuaihelani) form portions of the State Capitol grounds.

Mililani, Honolulu, Namauu, John and Sarah ʻĪʻī (1848–1871)

Although most of the court residences clustered on the *mauka* side of Hale Aliʻi, one residence was built on the *makai* side of King Street. High chief Nueku Namauu lived directly *makai* of ʻIolani Palace. The land was an *aliʻi* award to him in the Great Mahele. Namauu was one of eight chiefs who were "advanced a degree higher in the ranks of chiefs" during the legislative session of 1845. He was appointed to the Privy Council on October 9, 1846, and to the Board of Commissioners to Quiet Title Land Titles on August 18, 1847, where he served with John Papa Ῑʻī. Namauu died on December 9, 1848. In his will Namauu gave one-third of his property to his wife, Kapoli, and two-thirds to Kekūanāoʻa. The testimony of Pahao about R.P. 4490: "I knew Namauu; he lived there, close by, in a place now called Mililani. After Namauu's death [October 6, 1848 according to Kekūanāoʻa] I built a house there by order of Kekuanaoa, as I understood for Kapoli [Namauu's widow]. When the house was finished, John Ii lived there with Kamamalu ['Mililani House']."[152] ʻĪʻī and Kamāmalu had been living at Mililani for

The house of John ʻĪʻī appears as one of the vignettes in Paul Emmert's 1853/1854 "View of Honolulu from the Catholic Church, No. 6" (courtesy Hawaii State Archives, PP-38-1-005).

a little more than a year when the smallpox epidemic of 1853 hit Honolulu. ʻĪʻī recounted: "On June 1, after all of the members of Ii's household had been vaccinated, they left Mililani house, where they had been living since November 1, 1852, to sail to Hawaii."[153]

John ʻĪʻī died in May 1870. The house was demolished about 1871 when Aliʻiolani Hale was constructed.[154]

New Palace Grounds

Besides the building of Aliʻiolani Hale, Kamehameha V made plans for a new palace, and during the fifth year of his reign, a site for a new royal palace was obtained: "After considerable difficulty, a convenient and eligible site for the erection of a Palace, of 100 acres in extent, was finally secured at Makiki. The work would have been commenced but for the untoward accident that a gentleman, whose signature is necessary to secure legal title to a part of the land, is absent from the country. Twenty thousand two hundred and forty-five dollars and fifty cents of the appropriation for this purpose have been expended. $5,981 in payment for the land, and $309 for furniture, $10,000 has been sent to Europe for the same purpose, and the remainder has been used in procuring stones and other material."[155]

Included in the expenses for the two years ending March 31, 1870, was a line item under the Department of the Interior for Royal Palace for $60,000.[156] The optimism of the 1868 report did not continue. Four years later the Appendix to the Report of the Minister of Finance from the Interior Department in 1872 noted: "I has been impossible to proceed with this work,—the necessity of which becomes more apparent from year to year,—owing to the want of a proper site. All that has been done is the purchase of two lots of land, and a written agreement made for the prospective purchase of another."[157]

The official palace never moved from Pohukaina. By 1892 the C.N.

Kamehameha V started the purchase of a hundred-acre site in Makiki for the new palace grounds (courtesy Hawaii State Archives, PP-97-9-009).

Spencer, Minister of the Interior, asked Archibald Cleghorn, governor of Oʻahu, to "take charge of the government piece of land situate at Makiki and known as the Parade Ground" and that the site "be used for parading soldiers instead of the Palace Square."[158]

Proposed Palace of 1871

Although not a physical structure that was lost, the proposal for a replacement for the 1845 ʻIolani Palace, the plans for a new structure present a vision of what a new ʻIolani Palace would have looked like if it had been built by Kamehameha V instead of Kalākaua. In September 1871, during the reign of Kamehameha V, plans were started to replace the old palace. A letter from Ferdinand William Hutchison, Minister of the Interior, to A.S. Webster, Hawaiian Consul at Sydney, Australia, outlined the requirements: "It is the intention of this Gov't to build a Royal Palace here and to commence operations as soon as they can procure suitable plans."[159] The reason for sending the letter to Sydney showed the importance placed on making the royal residence fit the climate of the islands: "but, as we have no architect here capable of designing such a building, and as architects in Northern Countries would not be likely to have a proper appreciation of the nature of the climate of these islands ... it has appeared to his Excellency probable, that in Sydney, where the summer climate is very similar to ours an architect might be found more likely to design an appropriate building."[160]

The proposed palace shared an architectural style later used in the 1879 ʻIolani Palace: "The style of the building considered most suitable is the Italian, of one storey in height, which may however be departed from to a certain extent to give variety to the outline. All of the principal rooms must be on the ground floor, but some of the bedrooms, and perhaps the Ladies and gentlemens retiring rooms might be in the second storey. The main entrance should have a spacious portico, semicircular or semielliptical in form, in front, flanked by wide verandahs with columns of the Ionic Order; in fact it is desirable that the entire front and at least two sides of the building should be protected."[161]

Reiterating the importance placed on climate, Hutchison reported: "The doors and windows must all be large and lofty with ample means of free ventilation. The prevailing wind is North west, and the front of the building will be South west."[162]

After mentioning the availability of materials and the cost of labor, Hutchinson continues: "I mention these things to enable the architect to form an approximate estimate of the cost of executing his design, as it must not exceed £16,000."[163] In contrast, Kalākaua's ʻIolani Palace cost $349,163.29 to build.[164] The cost would be $8,476,398 in 2012 dollars.[165]

G. Allen Mansfield, Architect, Sydney, New South Wales, sent on October 26, 1871, a memorandum to accompany his design for "a Royal Palace at Honolulu for His Majesty the King of the Hawaiian Islands." He made special note that: "It has been prepared with especial reference to the requirements of a tropical climate, and presents the greatest facilities of ensuring coolness and most ample ventilation."[166] The proposed design varied radically from the ʻIolani Palace that followed: "The general outline of the plan is that of a quadrangle surrounding an inner court."[167] Mansfield was paid £125 for "preparing the design of proposed Royal Palace at Honolulu, for His Majesty the King of the Hawaiian Islands."[168] Another design came from Sydney architect Thomas Rowe.[169]

Chapter 4. Royal Residences of the Palace Yard and Vicinity

Neither of the designs was used for the new 'Iolani Place that King Kalākaua started building in 1879. Even with the new palace, the king still needed personal quarters, so he built Hale 'Ākala or The Bungalow in the *mauka*-'Ewa corner of the expanded Palace Yard.

Hale 'Ākala or The Bungalow (1879–1919)

Built in the northeast corner of 'Iolani Palace yard, Hale 'Ākala, or The Bungalow, provided King David Kalākaua with a respite from the formal activities. Other names for the structure include the King's House, the Queen's House and Healani.[170]

The expansion of the palace grounds was completed in the first year of his reign, on May 10, 1875 [CSF 6141]. It was in this corner of the newly expanded grounds that the Bungalow arose. The exterior of the Bungalow is fairly well documented in black-and-white photographs, but even the color of the building is hinted at by its name; 'ākala means, "pink." The interior of the Bungalow is described in detail by an Australian reporter in 1885: "His Majesty does not habitually reside at the Royal Palace. He usually inhabits a commodious wooden bungalow in the palace grounds. [...] The ground floor of the interior of the bungalow was very dark, but ... I contrived to grope my way up a steep and tortuous staircase, and passing through an antechamber,

King Kalākaua and Queen Kapi'olani on path to Hale 'Ākala, also known as the Bungalow. The name of the structure indicates that it was painted pink. In the accompanying group is Col. C.H. Judd, his partner in Leilehua Ranch (courtesy Hawaii State Archives, PP-96-13-016).

I was ushered into the presence of His Majesty, a David Laamea Kalakaua, King of Hawaii."[171]

The Bungalow received extensive damage during the Wilcox Revolution of 1889.

An inventory of "Healani House" appears in an undated journal of William Owen Smith. Though no date is recorded for the inventory, the entries for "Queen's Room" and "Queen Dowager's Room" suggest the book records the property following the overthrow of Queen Liliʻuokalani in 1893. Smith was Attorney General and Commissioner of Crown Lands following the overthrow. The furnishings included two koa tables, four sofas, two "horse hair" lounges, and more than six dozen chairs.[172] With the plethora of chairs in the rooms of "Healani House," including twenty-six of one type, the house provided a space for informal meetings and entertainment. Although the boathouse shared the name "Healani," the other residence most likely would not have contained the same degree of furnishings.

Today, only ʻIolani Palace remains of the dozen royal residences built in the Palace Yard and vicinity.

Chapter 5

Other Royal Residences of Oʻahu

> Oʻahu, ka ʻōnohi o na kai.
> Oʻahu, gem of the seas.[1]
> —Hawaiian proverb

Even before the transfer of the capital of the Kingdom of Hawaiʻi to Honolulu in 1845, the economic growth of Honolulu combined with the desire of Kamehameha the Great to secure his latest conquest, had already attracted royalty to Oʻahu. As on the other islands, the residences reflected a mix of traditional and Western forms, with the foreign styles eventually achieving dominance. The initial grouping of residences clustered around the *kauhale* of Kamehameha I near the waterfront next to the fort defending the harbor.

Residence of Kamehameha I (c. 1810–), Honolulu

The premier *hale* of the complex, the residence of Kamehameha I displayed the rapid adoption of Western modes of building. When King Kaumualiʻi ceded Kauaʻi in 1810, Kamehameha I no longer needed to build an armada to complete his plans to unify the archipelago. Archibald Campbell's 1810 account, *Voyage Round the World*, recorded: "During my stay the building of the navy was suspended, the king's workmen being employed in erecting a house in the European style, for his residence in Hanaroora [Honolulu]. When I came away, the walls were as high as the top of the first story."[2] Campbell detailed the mix of traditional Hawaiian structures and Western ones in his description of the king's compound:

> The king's residence, built close upon the shore, and surrounded by a palisade upon the land side, was distinguished by the British colors and a battery of sixteen carriage guns, belonging to his ship, the Lilly Bird, which at this time lay unrigged in the harbor. This palace consisted merely of a range of huts, viz.: the king's eating-house, his sleeping-house, the queen's house, a store, powder-magazine, and guard-house, with a few huts for the attendants, all constructed after the fashion of the country.[3]

Another visitor, Adelbert von Chamisso, a botanist on the Russian ship *Rurik*, described Honolulu upon entering the port of Honolulu on November 27, 1816: "Over the breakers we could see the pleasant looking city, shaded by slender coconut trees, consisting of O-Waihian grass houses, and European ones with white walls and red roofs."[4] The king's house described by Campbell as being built "in the European style" in 1809 would presumably be included in the description of European houses recorded by Chamisso five years later.

Another Westerner, Jacques Arago, draftsman on the French expedition of Captain Louis de Freycinet, makes no mention of the Honolulu house in 1820.

Residence of Isaac Davis, Honolulu

While John Young kept his residence on the island of Hawai'i, the other Western advisor of Kamehameha I, Isaac Davis, moved to O'ahu and maintained his residence near to the king in Honolulu. Archibald Campbell, who described the Honolulu residence of Kamehameha I, stayed with Isaac Davis. Campbell described the house of Davis: "His house was distinguished from those of the natives only by the addition of a shed in front to keep off the sun; within, it was spread with mats, but had no furniture, except two benches to sit upon."⁵

Kamehameha the Great (courtesy Hawaii State Archives, PP-97-5-006).

It was at the residence of Davis that Campbell manufactured a loom for the king. This act was opposed by other Westerners because they wanted to provide cloth for trade.⁶

On the map *Honolulu in 1810* Paul Rockwood and Dorothy Barrere place the residence of Davis just 'Ewa (west) of the intersection of Nuuanu and Merchant streets.⁷

Residence of Hoapili at Punahou, Mānoa, Honolulu

Another of the most trusted advisors of Kamehameha I, Ulumāheihei,⁸ known better by his nickname, Hoapili (close friend) also resided where his king lived. Thus when Kamehameha lived on O'ahu in preparation of his invasion of Kaua'i, Hoapili stayed on land in Mānoa that he had inherited from his father, Kameeiamoku, one of the twins who appear on the royal crest. At the fiftieth anniversary of its founding Punahou School proudly related its history: "Hoapili resided several years at Punahou near the spring and during the Conqueror's second residence on Oahu from 1804 to 1811 he also and his wives frequently visited this charming retreat. Hoapili gave Punahou to his daughter Liliha who married Governor Boki, and after their return from England in the

Blonde in 1825 they frequently resided here."[9] In 1829 Boki conveyed Punahou to missionaries who established, in 1841, Oʻahu College, now known as Punahou School after the name of the water source (the translation of Punahou is new spring).

Closer to the complex of Kamehameha I were the houses of his son Kamehameha II, called Hookuku, and that of his favorite wife, Kaʻahumanu, called Halehui.

Hoʻokuku, Honolulu, Kamehameha II

As seen with Kamakahonu (Chapter 1) and Mokuʻula (Chapter 2) the court maintained close proximity to their sovereign. So it was that his son and heir to the throne, Kamehameha II, lived near the Honolulu house of his father. In 1957 Dorothy Barrere and Paul C. Rockwood constructed a map titled *Honolulu in 1810* based on the written description by John Papa ʻĪʻī in *Kuakoa* in 1869. "Liholiho, then heir apparent, lived nearby [at Honuakaha] at his residence Hookuku, where he was attended by chiefs under the supervision of Papa, medical kahuna and *kahu* to Kamehameha."[10] At the time Kamehameha II would have been roughly 13 years old.

Halehui, Honolulu (1809–1812), Kaʻahumanu

While the residence of the king is more often mentioned by early visitors, one observer who caught the attention of the favorite wife of Kamehameha I, Queen Kaʻahumanu, recorded the presence of her residence and the hospitality of royalty in Hawaiʻi. Archibald Campbell, who had had his legs amputated after a shipwreck in the frigid waters of the Pacific Northwest, noted that he "attracted the notice, and excited the compassion of the queen; and finding it was my intention to remain upon the islands, she invited me to take up my residence in her house. I gladly availed myself of this offer, at which she expressed much pleasure; it being a great object of ambition amongst the higher ranks to have white people to reside with them."[11] Halehui was

Queen Kaʻahumanu (courtesy Hawaii State Archives, 96-6-001).

located in the compound of Kamehameha I 'Ewa (west) of the intersection of Fort and Queen streets.[12]

Residence of Lydia Nāmāhana Piʻia, Honolulu

Lydia Nāmāhana Piʻia, the sister of Kaʻahumanu and also wife of Kamehameha I, also maintained her residence near the fort in Honolulu. Otto von Kotzebue described her house in December 1824 in *A New Voyage Round the World*: "it was a pretty little wooden house of two stories, built in the European style, with handsome large windows, and a balcony very neatly painted."[13]

Paul Rockwood and Dorothy Barrere in their *Honolulu in 1810* placed the residence of Nāmāhana on the beach of Kuloloi on the Diamond Head-*makai* side of the intersection of Fort and Queen streets.[14]

Pākākā (1821–1821), Honolulu

The residence named Pākākā was built on a stone pier at Honolulu harbor. A *heiau* of the same name formerly occupied the site. John Papa 'Ī'ī shared an account of Pākākā as the place where Kaumualiʻi landed when he came of Oʻahu in 1810 to meet with Kamehameha I. Though the wharf was there, 'Ī'ī makes no mention of residences at Pākākā, only of "houses close to Pakaka."[15]

Gilbert Farquhar Mathison, who arrived in Honolulu on June 25, 1822, described his visit to Pākākā: "I went with the Consul to the palace of the King, if such a term can be applied to a grass hut, floored with mats, and only distinguished from the rest by a few cannon placed about it *in terrorem*."[16] Mathison also described the Queen's residence, which combined traditional and Western furnishings: "The ground part of the apartment was matted, and the walls hung round with mats, with a large and handsome mirror on one side, and upon the whole had a comfortable appearance; though the furniture, comprising several Chinese chests, a mahogany table, and three matted bedsteads."[17]

The presence of the royal residence on a wharf at Honolulu made landing at the port problematic, as the related by Charles Stewart, who arrived in 1823 with the second company of missionaries from the American Board of Commissioners for Foreign Missions. The palace's location made the landing area *kapu*. Stewart wrote: "Perceiving a low stone quay on a point under the fort, and near a cluster of native buildings, we were about to land on it, when a party of islanders exclaimed 'Tabu! Tabu!' and informed our interpreters, William and Richard, that the largest of the houses was the residence of the king; and he prohibited any one from landing at that place."[18]

Stewart later provides the most detailed description of the palace, which he puts in italics, no doubt to indicate the ironic sense with which he uses the word to describe the *hale pili*. He also locates the structure on the pier itself:

> The *palace* stands on a stone quay within a few feet of the water. It is a large and fine house for one of the kind; perhaps fifty feet long, thirty broad, eight feet high at the sides, and thirty at the peak of the roof. The exterior is entirely composed of a thatch of grass; and in appearance it is strikingly like the Dutch barns seen in many parts of our country. There are two large

Chapter 5. Other Royal Residences of Oʻahu

Port of Honolulu, from the book *Voyage Pittoresque Autour Du Monde*, printed in Paris in 1822, plate XVIII. Drawn by Louis Choris from the 1813 voyage of the *Rurik* (courtesy Hawaii State Archives, VOY1-036).

doors, one at each end, and several windows without glass, but furnished with Venetian shutters on each side of the house.[19]

Stewart notes the early adoption of Western building features within the traditionally built *hale pili*: "This is the only native building in which I have observed windows."[20] Stewart also describes the interior of the palace in detail:

> The interior, making one apartment only, is neat, well finished, and elegant, for the Sandwich Islands. All the timbers, the side posts, a row of pillars supporting the ridgepole through the whole length of the house, the rafters, &c. &c. are straight and substantial, and all beautifully hewn. The cinet [sennit] or braid formed from the shreds of the husk of the cocoa-nut, by which the whole are fastened together, exhibits both skill and taste in its manufacture and arrangements.[21]

Besides the integration of Western architectural features into the structure of residences, the highly portable Western furnishings made an early impact on the interior architecture. After reporting the construction, Stewart shared the furnishings of the palace: "The furniture is rich, consisting, besides handsome mats with which the ground is everywhere covered, of three or four large chandeliers of cut glass suspended between pillars running through the center of the building; of mahogany dining and pier tables; crimson Chinese sofas and chairs; several large pier glasses [tall mirrors set between windows] and mirrors."[22]

A map titled *South Coast of Oahou*, surveyed by Lt. C.R. Malden of the H.M.S. *Blonde*, shows the use of a structure at Pākākā in 1825 as a navigational landmark. The line passing by the *hale pili* has the notation: "The South end of a dark coloured hut on the wharf in one with E. Chimney of Grimes House N. by E. (Magc.) leads clew of E. Bank."[23]

Kaʻahumanu gave Pākākā to Kalanimoku, who, in turn, made an agreement in

January 11, 1827, with James Robinson for "one half of the wharf commonly called the King's Wharf, situated near the Southwest angle of the Fort in Honolulu, extending in front one hundred yards or thereabout, and running back one hundred yards thereabout."[24] In return, Robinson agreed to "pay to Karaimoku, his heirs, executors, administrators and assigns, one half of all monies received."[25] In 1847 James Robinson & Co. charged $3 to $5 for wharfage.[26] In the 1862 Hawaiian Supreme Court case of *L.* [Luka, Hawaiian for Ruth] *Keelikolani v. James Robinson*, Princess Ruth asked the court to compel Robinson to give an accounting of the monies due the heirs of Kalanimoku. The issues involved in the case revolved around land ownership before the Great Mahele of 1848, and inheritance of property in 1827 before laws were written. When Kalanimoku died in 1827 the interest in the wharf went to his son Leleiohoku, and in 1848 upon the death of Leleiohoku to his son by Ruth Keʻelikōlani, John Pitt Kīnaʻu. The presence of Robinson at the pier was in dispute, but the transfer document quieted complainants.

On March 9, 1850, Kaauwai, a witness for James Robinson, swore: "Kekuanaoa, who at one time had protested James' place which is at Pakaka, makai of Queen street, and at the sign C as indicated in Metcalf's surveying of the land, has come to withdraw his complaint for that place, for he has seen Kalanimoku's deed to James and on this date, it has been conveyed to James."[27] After the death of Kīnaʻu in 1859 the interest went to his mother, Ruth. The court sided with Keʻelikōlani and required Robinson to provide an accounting of the monies due the heirs of Kalanimoku.

Residence of Kalanimoku, Honolulu (1821)

John Young's journal entry for March 10, 1821, recorded "This day we heard that Try Mookoos [Kalaimoku's] wife and child are both dead at Oahu; the wife died in childbirth."[28] "Likelike, wife of Kalanimoku died in Honolulu March 4, 1821."[29]

Residence of Kamehameha II (1823), Honolulu

William Ellis also gave an account of the funding for the king's house shortly before November 1823: "A short time before his embarkation for England, a large native house was built for Rihoriho [Liholiho], at Honoruru [Honolulu], in the island of Oahu. During the three days after the king went into it, the people came with their gifts. No individual, not even the queens, entered the house without presenting the king a sum of money; several gave upwards of fifty dollars; and we saw more than two thousand dollars received in one day."[30] The account does not indicate where the residence was built other than "at Honoruru." The new house, built in 1824, would have been different from the "palace of the king" visited by Mathison in June 1822.

Palace of Kalanimoku (1824), Honolulu

The willingness of Kalanimoku to lease Pākākā was due, no doubt, to the presence of his own residence in Honolulu, a house called the palace of Kalanimoku. The first use of "palace" as an appellation for a home other than the king's came in Charles S.

Stewart's *Journal of a Residence in the Sandwich Islands*. He records: "This building will bear the name of *palace*."[31] Stewart continues with a detailed description:

> It is of stone, plastered and whitened, two and a half stories high, sixty-four feet in front and forty in depth; and externally except in the roof, is not unlike Mr. J. Fenimore Cooper's house at Fenimore. The second story, the front doors and windows of which open on a covered piazza or verandah, is that in which the regent will live. It consists of one very large apartment in front, upwards of fifty feet long, and proportionally wide, designed for a saloon in which to entertain strangers—commanding, from its elevation, a fine view of the island and ocean—and a small neat room at one end for a cabinet, to be furnished with an escritoire, &c. The rest of the floor is divided into sleeping rooms for himself and one or two confidential attendants.
>
> The expense of the building exclusive of the stone is estimated at six thousand dollars. It stands in an enclosure of several acres, which is to be planted, and kept in a state of cultivation: and the whole establishment will give quite a new aspect to Honoruru, from whatever point it is viewed.[32]

Hawaiian observer John Papa ʻĪʻī also described the house of Kalanimoku: "He [William Ellis] built his house at the corner of King and Punchbowl Streets, on the right side, and Kalanimoku greatly desired to build his stone house nearby. Thus it that Pohukaina house was built on the north side of Ellis' house, adjoining his yard. It also adjoined the houses of the king, of Kaahumanu, and of other members of royalty. These houses, built in 1824, were surrounded by a very large wooden fence, and the enclosure was called Pohukaina."[33]

According to missionary Hiram Bingham, the palace of Kalanimoku was finished on July 21, 1824. Bingham wrote:

> Kalanimoku while contemplating a visit to Kauai to regulate its affairs hastened to make his own stone dwelling house habitable in which he sought not only to provide for the comfort of his family and friends but to aid in elevating the nation. He desired to be conveniently near the missionaries who had already secured his confidence. In attempting to imitate a foreign style of building he caused a deep excavation to be made for a cellar and laid the foundation of his house on a bed of conglomerated coral shells and sand in which he sank a well. In reference to this part of his house in his somewhat usual strain of pleasantry he said to some whose distrust had been obvious "My cellar is larger than Binamu's." By this he shrewdly satirized the puerile jealousy of those who had said that the cellar of the missionaries was made for purposes of war. On the floor of the second story, he had a commodious and pleasant saloon, or hall, with a verandah, four lodging rooms, and a school-room for the accommodation of the young prince and his friend Haalilio, whom he wished to be under my [Hiram Bingham's] particular instruction. These six rooms were ceiled, painted, lighted with good glass windows, and comfortably furnished. About the 20th of July, he entered it, with the voice of prayer and praise. The superiority of this house or palace, as to its cost, dimensions, height, and finish, and my subsequent familiarity there as a teacher, procured for me the compliment of living "like a *nabob*." The workmen, however, it was found, had widened the building and greatly increased the thickness of the walls, just at the surface of the ground, which marred their strength, forbade their permanency, and in the end, occasioned material loss and disappointment.[34]

Another missionary, Ephraim Eveleth, also gives a detailed description of the compound in his account of funeral services for Kamehameha II and Kamāmalu at Kalanimoku's palace in May 1825: "The procession then entered Karaimoku's large enclosure, and moved to his thatched house, fitted up for the temporary reception of the bodies, by being arched overhead, and completely lined with black *tapa*, and having a firm platform erected at one end covered with mats."³⁵

"Mr. Pitt [Kalanimoku] chose to receive the company in his grass house, rather than in the fine stone building lately erected by him."³⁶ Stewart provided a detailed description of the audience with Lord Byron with the new king, Kamehameha III. Although Stewart was impressed by the Western structure, he still expressed awe for the traditional building Stewart noted that the *hale pili* of Kalanimoku:

Kalanimoku, also called Kalaimoku, is written here as Taymotou before the orthography of the Hawaiian language was settled (courtesy Hawaii State Archives, PP-97-4-004).

is one of the largest and best built native houses on the island and being new, was as pleasant, and perhaps more appropriate than the other would have been. The whole apartment was floored with new and handsome mats, and made a pleasant and spacious room of audience. There are four doors, one on each side, and one at each end; that at the south was appointed for the entrance on this occasion. Every thing was in readiness when we arrived. At the upper or north end of the house on an elevation or platform of mats the top one of which was of very fine texture, and beautifully spotted and striped with stained grass, stood a Chinese sofa, on which the young king and the princess his sister, who came from Lahaina in the Blonde, were seated, both in plain suits of black. Between them and partly round the princess lay splendid garment of yellow feathers, edged with the van dyke pattern, points alternate black and red, and lined with crimson satin.³⁷

The *hale pili*, mats and the feather skirt of Nāhiʻenaʻena represented the peak of traditional native Hawaiian craftsmanship. But the Western influence can already be seen in the number of doors and the use of furniture. In this instance the furnishings showed Eastern influence no doubt influenced by the trade of sandalwood with China.

The *hale pili* of Kalanimoku were depicted by A. Pellion during the visit by Louis de Freycinet and his ships *Uranie* and *Physicienne*.

A description in *Missionary Records, Sandwich Islands* of missionary Charles Stewart and Captain Finch watching a royal procession reveals two aspect of the palace. The two men "took their stand in the upper verandah of the palace built by Kairamoku [sic] commanding a fine view of the whole street from the chapel to the house where they were to be set down."³⁸ The use of the verandah on the palace of Kalanimoku stands in

Chapter 5. Other Royal Residences of Oʻahu 129

The *kauhale* of Kalanimoku (courtesy Hawaii State Archives, REFVOY-2-018-5).

contrast to the early missionary Saltbox structure; the two stories also stand in contrast to the single floor, single room, *hale pili*. The integration of the lanai into his Western style residence exemplifies the Hawaiian practice of adapting the styles to the local climate.

"Palace of Karaimoku [Kalanimoku], Native Chapel, Cottage of Mr. Ellis." From Charles S. Stewart, *Journal of a Residence in the Sandwich Islands, During the Years 1823, 1824 and 1825.*

The prominent Western structure also served as a navigational landmark. A *Map of Oahou* surveyed in 1825 by Lt. C.R. Malden of the H.M.S. *Blonde*, marks the location of "Pitts House." A line to aid navigation bears the notation "E. of the East end Pitts White House."

Pohukaina became part of the 'Iolani Palace grounds during the reign of King David Kalākaua. The king named the street that marked the boundary after his sister Likelike and the gate that opened onto the street took on the same name.

Residence of Kamanele, Honolulu

Kaʻuaʻumokuokamanele, daughter of Kuakini, governor of Hawaiʻi island, lived with her *hānai* parents in Honolulu on Oʻahu. She was more commonly called by the abbreviated form of her name, Kamanele. The residence of Kamanele [LCA 247 (6)] was located at the intersection of Printers Lane and Punchbowl, ʻEwa of a parcel owned by Gideon Laanui [LCA 278 (2)]. Built about 1823 by her *hānai* parents, the property was originally fenced to prevent the children under their care from wandering into the gardens of Kalanimoku. Kamanele, who was born in 1814, would have been nine or ten years old at the time. Gideon Laʻanui disputed the claim of Charles Kanaʻina to the house lot.[39]

John ʻĪʻī explained: "Laanui had authorized Kamanele's guardians to live there and they had enclosed the property with a fence. During her lifetime, Lydia was Laanui's wife. Since that time, Kekauonohi took all of this place for Kekauonohi without Laanui's approval."[40]

Also built near Kalanimoku's Palace, on King Street, was the residence of another key advisor to Kamehameha II, Haʻalilio, who had accompanied the sovereign on his ill-fated visit to London.

Residence of Timoteo Haʻalilio at Punchbowl and King Streets (1820–1820), Honolulu

On the Waikīkī side of Punchbowl Street, *mauka* of Kawaiahaʻo Church, stood the residence of Timoteo Haʻalilio, brother of Levi Haʻalelea, who inherited Hōlani. Haʻalilio had occupied the property from 1820 when American missionaries had first arrived. He married Hana Hooper on June 7, 1826.[41] From April 8, 1842, Haʻalilio served as ambassador to the United States, England and France.

James Jackson Jarves described the house of Haʻalilio in *Scenes and Scenery in the Sandwich Islands*, published in 1843. Leading the reader on a tour, Jarves begs:

> Stop gentle sir open this gate which stands so conspicuously in this neat white wall. Within a well laid out garden meets the view arbors of grape vines, a fish pond, many kinds of forest trees, flowers in full bloom, a well brushed greensward. This is very pretty. Here is a neat office. Enter, books table secretary and writing apparatus all fit for a gentleman's study. Look there a kitchen neat and in good order, here a bath room, all in separate buildings as is the fashion in these islands. Now we will peep into the drawing room. It is a thatched building but how very pretty and airy. The posts are all painted the thatch laid on as smooth as can be. Paintings adorn the walls, the best China matting is on the floor, the furniture is abundant comfortable and handsome. Look into the bed room that bed stead is made from a cabinet wood grown on the island than which no other country can produce a more beautiful. The

counterpane is as white as snow. Examine every thing cupboards and all Yankee house keepers would say that every thing was as neat as wax. And it is indeed so crack and corner all alike clean. This is certainly a model for any one.⁴²

The fate of his *hale pili* would be revealed in a letter from Kekūanāoʻa to Haʻalilio on February 28, 1844. After telling about him about the departure of Admiral Thomas and the arrival of British Consul William Miller and the illness of W.P. Leleiohoku, Kekūanāoʻa abruptly gave Haʻalilio the news: "Your grass house at Kanaana has been destroyed by fire. It is not certain who did it but it is suspected [Francis J.] Greenway set fire to it and he is being held at the Fort." Kekūanāoʻa attempted to soften the news by telling him: "We are building you a stone house on the same site, stones are being hauled."⁴³ Haʻalilio through Gerrit P. Judd withdrew the charge in May, however, believing that it was not possible "to identify said Greenway as the person who in fact set fire to the late residence of Haʻalilio," though a large amount circumstantial evidence pointed to him as the culprit. Haʻalilio, nevertheless, charged that Greenway was "of unsound mind and by reason of confirmed inebriety unfit to be suffered to go at-large [...] because he has made repeated threats to burn the town of Honolulu. And is when at-liberty boisterous and uncontrollable and there is great danger that he will commit some act detrimental to the public and private interests of this community."⁴⁴ Haʻalilio asked that a jury be convened to determine whether Greenway was insane. Haʻalilio died December 3, 1844, aboard the *Montreal*, while returning from Boston, Massachusetts, after concluding diplomatic work in the United States.

Timoteo Haʻalilio served as a diplomat from the Kingdom of Hawaiʻi (courtesy Hawaii State Archives, PP-96-5-001).

His widow, Hana Haʻalilio, made a claim for the King Street property to the Land Commissioners on October 15, 1846, giving the history of the ownership: "Kinau gave us (we two, including Haalilio) this place, to fence this place which was left by the road, along side the church. When Binamu [Bingham] heard that we had taken that place he went to Kinau to say that this place was his for the church. Kinau told Binamu that it had become Haalilio's. Kinau said to us: 'Binamu told me that place was his. I told him it was Haalilio's.'" Afterwards, Kinau died, and preparations began for the roads, and Binamu again came and spoke to Haalilio about this place. Haalilio said to him, 'That place is not for me, it has been given to Hana. The lepo [adobe] is ready to fence that place for her."⁴⁵

The property was given to Hana Haʻalilio as Land Court Award 238. The property is now part of the grounds of Honolulu's city hall, Honolulu Hale.

The *hale pili* were rapidly giving way to the wooden framed houses favored by the missionaries.

Frame House of Kaʻahumanu (1824), Honolulu

In his journal entry for May 26, 1824, Stewart mentions the death of Kaumualiʻi, husband of Kaʻahumanu, and his passage from "a small frame house in which he was taken ill, to a larger one, which had just been completed for Kaahumanu."⁴⁶ The house would have been one of "only three frame houses"⁴⁷ in Honolulu in 1824. On June 20, 1824, Charles Stewart gave a more detailed description of the house and its origin: "Kaahumanu has also had a new house built during the year; it is of wood, and was prepared in all its parts for erection, before it was bought from America. It is well papered and painted, and, in its dimensions and general appearance, similar to some of our best wooden houses at Cooper's-town."⁴⁸ The prefabricated house had already been introduced three years earlier when the first company of missionaries built Hale Lāʻau (wood house), a structure that still stands. Stewart also gives the home's location: "The chiefs, all well dressed in full black, arranged themselves in front of Kaahumanu's frame house, within a few yards of the water's edge."⁴⁹

Andrew Bloxam, a naturalist aboard the *Blonde*, the ship that returned the bodies of Kamehameha II and Kamāmalu to Hawaiʻi from London, described Kaʻahumanu's residence, including the internal divisions, in his diary entry for May 5, 1825: "I slept in a house close to the landing place, belonging to Queen Kaahumanu, built in the European fashion but without any chimney. It had been built by the Americans, was two stories high with a garret above, and a balcony opening from the second story, and being within half a dozen yards of the sea we enjoyed bathing very much. It had four very good rooms, two on the ground floor and two above, the latter sleeping rooms."⁵⁰

When Stewart returned to Hawaiʻi five years later, he once again described her house (120–122). During the visit Captain W.B. Finch of the U.S.S. *Vincennes*, who carried communication from the president of the United States, sent a letter to Kaʻahumanu, diplomatically declining an offer from her:

> I would accept the house which you offer, as a residence during my short stay here, but it had not been my custom to live outside the walls of my vessel.
> Mr. Jones has already offered me a suitable apartment but I declined occupying it.
> I value this proof of your desire to extend hospitality to me, quite as much as if I actually enjoyed it.
> I feel a great wish for your welfare and am happy in having been the herald of advice which you esteem good for you.
> Let what my government has said to you engage your deepest attention: honest motives have dictated the language.⁵¹

Another Frame House?

After Kaʻahumanu died at Pukaōmaʻomaʻo in Mānoa on June 5, 1832, "her body was immediately removed to her home in Honolulu. [...] On June 8 [1832], Kaahumanu's body was moved from her house to the church, accompanied by a long procession of residents, missionaries, member [sic] of the church and commoners."⁵²

John Papa 'Ī'ī reported a similar account of the activities after the death of Ka'ahumanu: "When her body was brought from Manoa to her frame house in the enclosure of Pohukaina, it was accompanied by a great procession. Finally, on the last day of June she was laid in the royal mausoleum there."⁵³

A map titled *A Plan of the Harbour of Honoruru, In the Island of Oahu*, dated 1825, by Lt. C.R. Malden, marks the location of "Kaahumanu's hut" at Pohukaina.⁵⁴

The house may be another frame house of Ka'ahumanu, because according to John Papa 'Ī'ī it was located "in the enclosure of Pohukaina" and not "a few yards from water's edge" as described by Stewart, or "within a half dozen yards of the sea" as reported by Bloxam. Since the frame house was prefabricated, the original frame house located near the sea may have simply been relocated to Pohukaina. It is more likely, though, another house. Otto von Kotzebue described the house of Ka'ahumanu as "Near [...] the abode of the missionary Bengham [Bingham]."⁵⁵ Kotzebue compared the house with that of Nāmāhana: "Her [Ka'ahamanu's] house, built partly of wood and partly of stone, is larger than the one I have described as the habitation of the other Queen [Nāmāhana]; like that, it has two stories and a balcony, and it is similarly furnished."⁵⁶

The residence of Ka'ahumanu at Pohukaina may have been the site of the Chiefs' Children's School. Abner Paki testified: "The houses in the lot formerly belonged to Kaahumanu but were built by Kalaimoku."⁵⁷ Kekūanāo'a, too, testified that the lot belonged to Ka'ahumanu.

Beretania, Pelekane, Honolulu (–1829)

A rival of Ka'ahumanu, the governor of O'ahu, Kamā'ule'ule, usually called Boki or Poki, maintained his residence in an area named Pelekane, named for Great Britain, the respected international power in the Pacific. John Papa 'Ī'ī recounted that after the return of the

Boki and Liliha (courtesy Hawaii State Archives, PP-96-2-002). Boki, the brother of Kalanimoku, was governor of O'ahu. Following the death of Boki, Liliha took over as governor. Liliha was the daughter of Hoapili.

bodies of Kamehameha II and Kamāmalu from London, "Kalanimoku stayed at Pohukaina with all the chiefs except Boki, who lived in the house he built on Beretania Street which he named Beretania."[58] Boki had been one of the Hawaiian chiefs who had journeyed with the king and queen on their ill-fated voyage. The death of Kamehameha II had resulted in the accession of Kamehameha III to the throne and necessitated a suitable residence on Oʻahu. In the account of the building of Haleuluhe, ʻĪʻī refers to the palace being built at "Beretania, where Boki's dwelling was."[59] Aside from these references, no further description of Boki's residence exists.

Country Residence of Boki and Liliha, Nuʻuanu, Honolulu

A more detailed description exists for the country residence of Boki. Charles Stewart made a visit the country residence of Boki and Liliha in Nuʻuanu during a visit on Tuesday, November 3, 1829. The narrative also documents the construction by Boki of the road up to the Pali. The extended account, as with many of Stewart's, gives detailed descriptions of the surroundings:

> Less than two miles from the [Nuʻuanu Pali] battle ground, brought us, by a fine stretch of turnpike, down a gentle hill, to a grove of acacia, surrounding the temporary abode of Boki—a rural and refreshing spot, on a slight elevation near the road side, beneath the shade of some beautiful trees, and within hearing of the rumbling of numerous mountain torrents, and the dashing of a distant cascade. The governor designs to build a country house at this place, but the present establishment is merely an encampment in booths, for himself and household, while he is superintending the construction of the road. The principal building, a little cottage, or rather tent of poles, scarce twelve feet square, thatched with the green and shining leaves of the dracæna [more likely the leaves of the *Cordyline fruticosa* or ti plant, which looks similar to the *dracaena*], stands on a terrace of sward, some feet above the level of the ground in front. It is chiefly intended as a shelter in sleeping; the terrace itself, in the shade of the grove presenting a more inviting place for all other purposes. This, just strewn with fresh fern leaves, and spread with mats, was the reception room to which Madam Boki, in a handsome dress, and head tastefully crowned with flowers, gave us a most cordial welcome, followed by a presentation of boquets. Every thing around was admirably suited to refresh and delight us: and two or three hours past rapidly after our ride, in lounging and in conversation, while we were served with fruit and wine.[60]

Less than a month after the trip with Stewart, Boki and Kamehameha III signed an agreement with Capt. Thomas Blakesley to sail to the South Pacific in search of sandalwood. Boki sailed for the New Hebrides on December 4, 1829, never to return to Hawaiʻi.

In another account of the country house, Franz Julius Ferdinand Meyen referred to it as the "winter palace for Madame Boki." After meeting with the royal court, in June 1831, Meyen explored the countryside with Dr. T.C.B. Rooke:

> We had already been long wandering about in the dark, when the continued rain, which began after sunset, incommoded us extremely, and we at length reached the large building which had been assigned for our night's quarters. The house belonged to Madame Boki, who offered us the use it. It served as a sort of winter palace for Madame Boki, as well as for the royal family, into which they could retreat, when it was too hot in the plains. The temperature here was extremely agreeable, although the house was not above 600 or 700 feet above the level of the sea. During our stay there, the thermometer never rose above 17° R [Réaumier scale, 70 degrees Fahrenheit]. There is an uncommonly interesting prospect from this spot.

The whole valley at the opening of which the town Honoruru lies, and which is clothed with the most luxuriant vegetation, and the loveliest tints of verdure gradually slopes towards the sea, the shores of which are covered on the one side with plantations of cocoa and palms, and, on the other, with many hundred scattered huts and houses of the town, and the inclosures of the royal fish-ponds On either hand the valley rise steep walls of rock, often from 800 to 1000 feet high, clothed with beautiful plants and having here and there a small cascade.

Madame Boki had given orders to the inhabitants of the smaller huts, in the vicinity, to pay every attention to our people; in consequence of which we received in the evening, soon after our arrival, a very large calabash filled with poë [poi], which the people devoured with great avidity.[61]

Their host, Liliha, died August 24, 1839. The first mention of building Kaniakapupu, the country residence, takes place in 1840, and Mayen's account does call Boki's country residence the "winter palace for Madame Boki, as well as for the royal family." One could easily speculate that the two Nuʻuanu country residences were indeed at the same site.

Haleuluhe (c. 1829), Honolulu, King Kamehameha III

At the laying of the cornerstone of ʻIolani Palace on December 31, 1879, Chief Justice and Chancellor of the Kingdom of Hawaiʻi, Charles Coffin Harris, delivered an address that identified the numerous places in which royalty had lived. Harris identified Haleuluhe as the first residence following the decision to abandon Lahaina as capital of the kingdom: "The young King Kauikeaouli, whose royal style and title was Kamehameha III, under the advice and influence of his great chiefs and counsellors [*sic*], moved to Oʻahu in 1843, and established his residence in the Haleuluhe, a large grass house at Pelekane, where now stands St. Andrew's Church."[62]

Thrum's *Almanac and Annual for 1906* captured the memory regarding Haleuluhe by John M. Kapena, minister of foreign affairs and commissioner of crown lands under King Kalākaua: "The advice and persuasions of the principal chiefs and councilors induced King Kauikeaouli, styled Kamehameha III, to remove the government to Oahu in the year 1843, and he took up residence in the Haleuluhe, at Pelekane, in the vicinity where now stands the Episcopal Church."[63] The similarity of the two accounts, no doubt, is related to Kapena delivering the Hawaiian language version of the speech that Harris delivered at the laying of the cornerstone of ʻIolani Palace.

Although both Harris and Kapena give 1843 as the year that Kamehameha III started living at Haleuluhe, the date most likely refers to its establishment as the official palace. Since two Hawaiian historians, John Papa Ïʻī and Samuel Kamakau, record that Boki built Haleuluhe for the king, and Boki disappeared after his ill-fated voyage to the New Hebrides in December 1829, a much earlier date is indicated. In 1829, Kamehameha III, who began his reign four years earlier, would have been the "young King" that Harris alluded to; by 1843 Kamehameha III was 30 years old.

The two Hawaiian historians also give a much richer description of the residence, including the source of the name of the structure. John Papa ʻĪʻī relates: "After the ruler and all the chiefs returned to Honolulu with Boki, a house was built for the king at Beretania, where Boki's dwelling was. The house was lined with the stems of the *uluhe* fern laid horizontally."[64] Kamakau gives a similar reason for the name of the residence and identifies the geographical source of the building materials: "Boki set the whole district

The *kauhale* of Kamehameha III at Pelekane (courtesy University of Hawaii Digital Collection).

of 'Ewa, headed by Kane-pa-iki, hauling posts and rafters for a new king's house, afterwards called 'The-fern-house' (Ka-hale-uluhe) because it was first covered from the top of the roof to the posts with uluhe ferns tied down neatly inside."

Charles Stewart, in a special article in advance of his book describing his October 1829 visit, wrote in detail of the *kauhale*, or group of houses, that formed the royal compound: "Within the king's grounds (from intrusion into which a high fence kept off the populace,) every thing was in a high degree, neat and orderly.

There were separate houses for the king's household, and for the offices and sleeping room of the king."[65] The "high fence" described by Stewart agrees with the watercolor painted during the visit of Capt. F.W. Beechey of the H.M.S. *Blossom* in May 1826. The painting also shows the several thatched structure within the enclosed grounds.

Stewart estimated that the "palace of thatch [was] more than one hundred feet long, fifty or sixty broad, and more than forty high."[66] To put the dimensions in perspective, the *hale pili* was approximately two-thirds the size of Kawaiaha'o Church and half the height of its current clock tower. Stewart also describes the exterior treatment that gave the structure its name. The palace was "beautifully finished and ornamented with fern leaves, and furnished with a pebbled area."[67]

> The royal guard was composed of two hundred men, forming a double file, and wearing a white uniform with scarlet cuffs and collars, and black caps; their commander Kahuhu, was dressed in scarlet with gold lacings and an expensive sword. As Capt. Finch and party passed the gate, they presented arms in exact military style, and the commander of the kings' forces, Kekuanoa [sic], receiving them in the full and rich suit of a major general, and with the gracefulness of a polished gentleman, ushered them through the glass folding doors into the interior of the palace. It is in one vast apartment the timbers being in sight, and the wood beautifully hewn and contrasted with braided lashings of the bleached fibre of the cocoa, wrought into tasteful patterns and applied at close and regular intervals, so that the posts and rafters have the appearance of natural sections. The thatch of the building is also concealed

from view by an elegant native tapestry, made of a brown mountain vine tied together like the bamboo window blinds; one continued tissue of this fabric is extended from the floor to the peak of the roof through the whole apartment between the timbers and the thatch, and thus imparts a very rich appearance. The floor, instead of rushes or grass which were formerly the foundation for the mats, was made of stone and mortar as hard and smooth as marble.[68]

Stewart described in detail the early integration of Western architectural elements into the one of the last grand *hale pili*. The stone floor, especially, differed from the traditional use of fine pebbles. The "glass folding doors" protected the interior from the outside elements, allowing for larger entrances and for large windows. These doors stand in contrast to the low doors of the Kealakekua *hale pili* of Kamehameha II (Chapter 1).

The interior also reflected the change from the traditional to a hybrid form. Stewart, after recording the increased use of Western elements in the building itself, nevertheless, paid respect to the native elements:

Upon this [the Western style floor], beautifully variegated mats of Tauai [Kaua'i] were spread—forming a carpet as delightful, and appropriate to the climate, as possible. Large windows on either side, and the folding doors of glass at each end, are hung with draperies of crimson damask; there were also handsome pier tables, and large mirrors; a line of glass chandeliers suspended through the centre, with lustres and candelabra of bronze, ornamented *or molu* [gilded with powdered gold], were affixed to the pillars lining the sides and ends of the apartment; and portraits in oil, of the late king and queen, taken in London, were placed at the upper end, in carved frames richly gilt. In the middle of the room about sixty feet in front, or two thirds the length of the apartment, the young monarch was seated in an arm chair spread with a splendid cloak of yellow feathers.[69]

What Stewart called "appropriate to the climate" would continue as a concern to the inhabitants of the royal residences in Hawai'i. Even though the king's house featured the trappings of Western royal residences—gilded candelabra, crystal chandeliers and mirrors—they retained the best of the native handiwork, interior elements that dwarfed the Western furnishings in the hours needed to produce them. The intricate Ni'ihau mats with its delicate patterns and weaving, and feather cloak composed of nearly a million tiny feathers, are representatives of the pinnacle of the native culture. The royal family also adopted one of the highest forms of art in the Western world; the oil paintings of Kamehameha II and Kamāmalu had no cognate in traditional Hawaiian culture.

The descriptions by Stewart, especially in an American scientific journal helped spread word of the progression of what Westerners considered civilization in Hawai'i across the Atlantic to Europe. The detailed description of the palace in the *London Illustrated News* commented on the rapid change the palaces experienced: "In 1829 domestic comforts had been so multiplied, that in the royal residence there were carpets, crimson draperies, handsome pier tables, and large mirrors, glass chandeliers, lusters and bronze candelabra."[70] Although the "carpet" to which Stewart referred were Ni'ihau mats, the British publication otherwise accurately drew from Stewart's account, down to the order of the items.

When Franz Julius Ferdinand Meyen, a botanist aboard the Prussian ship *Princess Louise*, arrived in Honolulu on June 22, 1831, he joined the ship's captain, W. Wendt, to present gifts from the King of Prussia to Kamehameha III. Meyen described the palace of Kamehameha III:

The residence of the king is built in the fashion of the Indian huts, but is quite a palace compared with them in point of size; though, placed by the side of the houses of the merchants and particularly of the missionaries at Honoruru [Honolulu], it is a mere barn. It is about 140 feet long, of which the first 120 feet form one entire apartment, down the centre of which are placed the pillars that support the beams of the roof. These pillars, as well as those along the walls, are made of trunks of the cocoa-nut tree, covered with long reeds, which are interwoven with grasses and particularly with the stalks of various beautiful ferns the space at the end of the house is partitioned off by colored curtains. It has on each side two small chambers, and a large one in the centre. These small apartments serve as sleeping and dressing rooms they are furnished with large heaps of fine mats from fifteen to twenty piled upon one another the upper one being always finer than the one below it and they form a very soft couch. The centre apartment contains two portraits in broad gold frames, one of the present king [more likely an image of Kamehameha II cited by Stewart] and the other of the queen who died in London. There is also a picture representing the Meeting of the Congress at Washington. The saloon in which the court was held was without any ornament; the floor was covered with fine mats, and the furniture consisted of a large oval table of polished wood, two japanned benches with backs a side table with water standing on it, and a few wooden chairs.[71]

The use of the vertical beams to support the ridge of Haleuluhe displays a different construction method from other *hale pili*, even large ones, which featured interior space without obstructions.

John N. Reynolds of the United States Frigate *Potomac* described his visit to the "king's palace" in August 1832. After an excursion to the Pali, an invitation was extended for dinner. As noted by Mayen, the *hale pili* featured a traditional structure with Western furnishings, including the Prussian gifts given by the earlier visit:

The palace was certainly the finest native building we had seen; and though its interior was not void of elegance, we saw no "glass folding doors" [Stewart's "folding doors of glass"]. The frame, or wicker-work lining of the inner house was very neat. The floor was covered with mats, of the finest texture and beautifully figured, brought from some neighboring island, and sent as *taxes*. The supper-table was also covered with a mat, and extended from one end of the room to the other. The usual curtain ran across the apartment, and enclosed the bed, forming a sitting-room. The walls were lined with paintings of the different soldiers and officers of the Prussian army, sent by the King of Prussia. The portraits of the king, *Riho Riho*, of the former queen, and also of George IV., were set in rich gilt frames, giving a handsome finish to the apartment. The Declaration of Independence, at the head of the room, was a glorious sight to look upon. […] After looking around the palace and grounds we retired much pleased indeed highly gratified with the entertainment.[72]

The account by Reynolds agrees with those of Stewart and Meyen and demonstrates that the accounts of previous visits were sufficiently studied in detail to note the absence of items.

Théodore-Adolphe Barrot, a French diplomat who arrived in Hawai'i aboard the *Bonite* in September 1836, also gave a detailed description of the Haleuluhe, including its location, interior divisions, furnishings, paintings and books. As to its location within the enclosure of Pelekane, Barrot wrote: "This house is situated at the extremity of an extensive court, surrounded, as are all of the houses of this country, by a wall of bricks dried in the sun. In this enclosure are nearly fifty huts, which serve for kitchens, store-houses, lodging for he King's servants, and barracks for the soldiers."[73]

A portion of the wall surrounding Pelekane still exists behind St. Peter's Episcopal Church and St. Andrew's Priory School.

Haleuluhe continued to serve as the residence of Kamehameha III as evidenced by a meeting there in 1840. Kekāuluohi, Kuhina Nui from June 8, 1839, to June 7, 1845, wrote in her journal: "On this day [February 5, 1840], the Chiefs held a meeting at Pelekane, with Kekauluohi, for the purpose of first settling the problems among themselves, in accordance with section 7, and section 8 of the Fundamental Laws regarding Taxes of the Government, upon the Chiefs, as follows: 'I have sent for you so that we, together, may discuss the law that was promulgated by Our Child.'"

Besides serving as the palace for Kamehameha III, the residence also served as the site of significance for a future king. According to Joseph Poepoe in *Ka Moolelo O Ka Moi Kalakaua*, King David Kalākaua was born at Haleuluhe, although the reference might be to any of the buildings in the complex.

Queen Liliʻuokalani, too, born two years after her brother, David, may have born at Haleuluhe. Liliʻuokalani wrote of her birthplace: "The extinct crater or mountain which forms the background to the city of Honolulu is known as the Punch-Bowl; at its base is situated the Queen's Hospital [....] Very near to its site, on Sept. 2, 1838, I was born."[74] Though she does not explicitly name Haleuluhe, the royal compound of Pelekane was within a block of the hospital.

Today, Pa Pelekane, site of Haleuluhe, hosts a number of institutions with British roots: The Cathedral Church of St. Andrew, started by Kamehameha IV and Queen Emma; St. Andrew's Priory School and St. Peter's Episcopal Church.

Residence of Kekūanāoʻa, Honolulu

Stewart also gave an extended description of another *kauhale*, that of Kekūanāoʻa, which displayed a continuation of the practice of devoting each house to a purpose. The sleeping and eating houses still existed, but Stewart noted the presence of Western furniture, the "spread table and sideboard" in the "dining hall." Replacing the men's and women's eating and sleeping houses, eliminated by the breaking of the *ʻai kapu*, the *kauhale* of Kekūanāoʻa now featured a "sitting room." Stewart again made a comparison of the Hawaiian and Western forms of the room. The ventilation of the house, a key consideration in the traditional form, led Stewart to call the room "a delight." Stewart's journal account once again showed the mixing of native and Western elements:

> A large door at each end opens a fine draft for the air the floor was beautifully carpeted with mats while in the centre stood a rich couch of yellow damask with armed chairs placed on either side so that those occupying them enjoyed all the benefit of the breeze sweeping through. On one side a native lounge or divan extended the whole length of the apartment spread with a succession of the finest mats beautifully variegated [...] with stained grass and furnished with round pillars of damask and silk velvet it looked more tempting to us on entering from the noontide heat of a tropical day than the Ottomans of more polished drawing rooms would under circumstances of less lassitude. A pier table covered with a rich cloth a large mirror and a portrait of Manuia completed the furniture on that side on the opposite a curtain or screen of handsome chintz looped up a foot or two at the bottom partially discovered a boudoir.

It was from this house, that Kekūanāoʻa, husband of Kīnaʻu, would make his journey to oversee the agricultural lands in Mānoa.

Kilauea, Makiki, Honolulu, Kalanimoku

John Papa 'Ī'ī described a house that Kalanimoku built solely to be able to better handle the intrigues of court. In order to communicate with his friend, Matiao Kekūanāo'a, about the actions of Boki, Kalanimoku built a residence along the road that Kekūanāo'a frequented. "As Kekuanaoa was frequently seen riding horseback to his work at Puu Pueo [in Mānoa], Kalanimoku decided to build a comfortable dwelling near the road so he could see him personally. [...] Kalanimoku [...] lived in his 'watching house' at Makiki which he named Kilauea."[75] Besides the extensive agricultural estates in Mānoa, the valley also served as the site of the country residence of Queen Ka'ahumanu.

Kahoiwai, Puka'ōma'o (February 22, 1825–), Mānoa, Honolulu, Queen Ka'ahumanu

At the same time that Kamehameha III was living at Haleuluhe, and Boki left on his ill-fated voyage, Queen Ka'ahumanu, Kuhina Nui, lived at her residence, called Puka'ōma'o or Puka'ōma'oma'o. The name comes from the words "puka" meaning door and "'ōma'o" meaning green.

Also known as Kahoiwai, Ka'ahumanu's home was literally a place of legend. The house's location was the setting of the tale of the maiden Kahalaopuna, a story of her jealous betrothed, her murder by him, and her rebirth.

Ka'ahumanu, the favorite wife of Kamehameha I and Kuhina Nui, had built a house in Honolulu near the fort, but her health caused her to retreat to her Mānoa home in 1825, seven years before her death. In the 1828, second edition, of his *Journal of a Residence in the Sandwich Islands*, missionary Charles S. Stewart referred to the ill health of Ka'ahumanu in his journal entry of February 24, 1825:

> Kaahumanu does not enjoy very good health, and by the advice of Dr. Law, her private physician, has retired three or four miles up one of the valleys, east of Honoruru, for the benefit of the mountain air.
>
> [...]
>
> The road leading to the retreat of the queen, has been almost constantly marked by the *equipages* (two or three single horse waggons [*sic*]) of the *nobility*, and by crowds of more humble gentry on foot, with hundreds of attendants and servants bearing furniture and provisions and a variety of luggage.
>
> Karaimoku and his family have since the absence of Riho Riho, has included the young queens. Kekauruohi, Pauahi, Kinau, and at present Kekaunohi, are the only *grandees* that remain at Honoruru. The etiquette of the Court seems to demand their presence, at least occasionally; and though Kaahumanu left on the morning of the 22d, they have just returned this evening from spending the day with her.[76]

Charles Stewart would again visited Hawai'i in 1829 and 1830, this time as a Navy chaplain on board the U.S.S. *Vincennes*. He wrote then of Puka'ōma'oma'o:

> There is now a good carriage road, in that direction, as far as the country house of Kaahumanu, nearly five miles from Honolulu. Her residence is beautifully situated; and the selection of the spot quite in taste. The house is an inferior building, but stands on the height of a gently swelling knoll, commanding, in front, an open and extensive view of all the rich

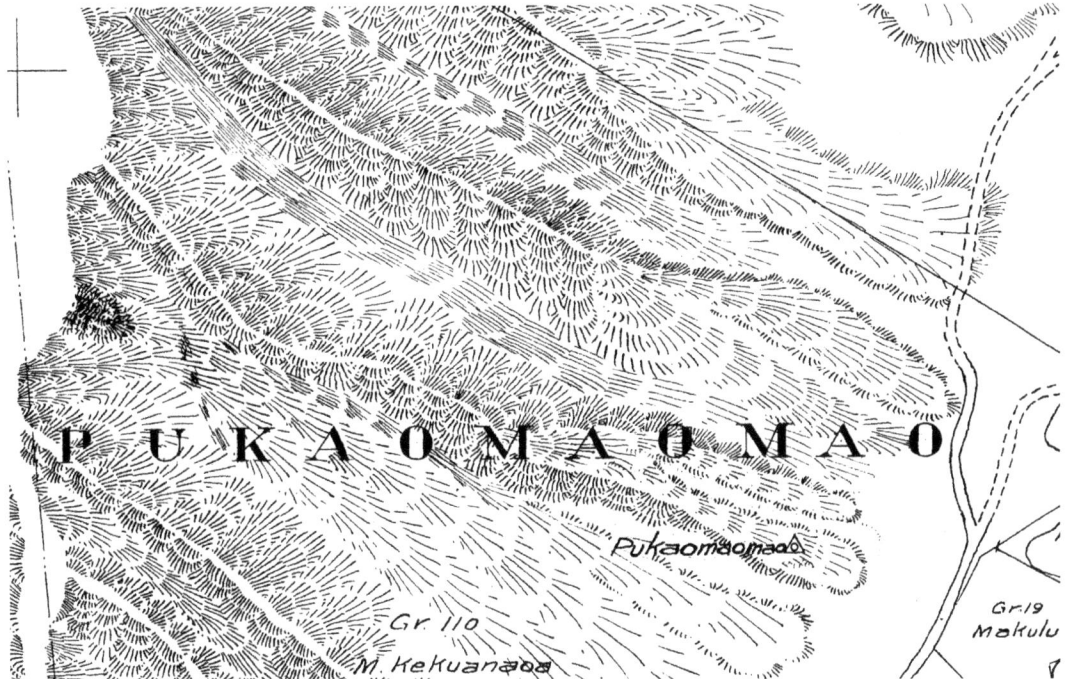

A portion of Mānoa, shown in an 1882 map, takes its name from the residence of Queen Ka'ahumanu. Detail of Registered Map 1068WIDE (courtesy Land Survey Division, Department of Accounting and General Services, State of Hawaii).

> plantations of the valley; of the mountain streams meandering through them, and the humble habitations of the farmer sprinkled around; of the district of Waititi; and of Diamond Hill, and a considerable part of the plain, with the ocean beyond. On the right, the ground rises rapidly for a few rods, to a thicket of hibiscus and Eugenia, at the foot of a magnificent mountain, exhibiting from the base to its summit—a perpendicular height of a thousand feet—as rich a variety of projecting cliff and wild recess, of dripping rocks and mantling foliage, of graceful creeper, pendant shrub, and splendid flower, as Arcadia itself can boast.[77]

Ka'ahumanu would live for seven years after her move to her Mānoa home. John Papa 'Ī'ī wrote of Ka'ahumanu: "Kaahumanu died on June 5, 1832, at her house with the green shutters in Manoa valley close to Kawaihoolana. Because of her love for Manoa she went there during her last illness after having been sickly for four or five years. The doctors said she had intestinal trouble, her intestines having been punctured by a bone. This might have been so. Before her departure from this world, she said to her chief, to her 'children,' to the friends who came to talk to her, and to her teacher, Bingham, 'Hele au la (I am going.)'"[78]

Laura Fish Judd, too, described Ka'ahumanu's last days after her return from a tour of the islands:

> Kaahumanu wished to go to her favorite retreat in the secluded valley of Manoa, and requested Dr. Judd and myself to accompany her. Here a bed of sweet scented *maile* and leaves of ginger was prepared, over which was spread a covering of velvet, and on this she laid herself down to die. Her strength failed daily. [...]
>
> Mr. Bingham who was hurrying the New Testament through the press, had a copy finished

and bound in red morocco, with her name in gilt letters embossed on the cover. When it was handed to her she looked it through carefully from Matthew to Revelation, to satisfy herself that it was all there, then she wrapped it in her handkerchief, and laid it upon her bosom, clasped both hands over it, and closed her eyes in a sweet slumber, as though every wish of her heart was gratified.

Just at evening she awoke and inquired for her teachers Mr. and Mrs. Bingham, who had just arrived and who had come to her bedside. "I am going," said she, "where the mansions are ready." Mr. Bingham replied, "Lean on the Beloved through the waters of Jordan." "Yes," she answered, faintly. "I shall go to Him and be comforted." The swift-winged messenger hasted on his errand and with a faint "aloha," a gentle pressure of the hand, the eyelids closed, and the throbbings of that affectionate heart were stilled forever.[79]

She died at 3 a.m., June 5, 1832, at Pukaʻōmaʻomaʻo. Laura Fish Judd shared an account of the actions of missionary Hiram Bingham immediately following the death of Kaʻahumanu: "Mr. Bingham stood in the cottage door. With uplifted hands and a distinct voice he commended the infant nation, bereaved of its most valuable chieftain and ruler, to Israel's God. He prayed that her fallen mantle might rest on the shoulders of some Elisha, and that the lonely band, deprived of the support and encouragement of her on whom they were accustomed to lean with so much confidence, might turn with stronger purpose, and take hold of the everlasting strength in this hour of darkness and trial."[80]

Alexander Stevenson Twombly, nearly seven decades after her death, reported that when Kaʻahumanu neared the time of her death, she "retired to her house, a few miles away, in Manoa Valley. It was a beautifully situated residence, commanding a fine view. Streams of clear water flowed through the grounds. Behind the house was a delightful grove, dark and filled with birds. She had built a little cottage at the edge of this wood for the accommodation of the American teachers who came to see her."[81]

Twombly also gives one of the best descriptions of the interior: "The rooms of the regent's house were handsomely fitted up with mahogany tables, carved bedsteads, glass lamps and other comforts of civilized life."[82]

The structure had already started to deteriorate roughly two months after Kaʻahumanu's death, when visited by Francis Warriner of the United States Frigate *Potomac*. He recounted: "We visited the residence of the late regent Kaahumanu which was in bad repair, where we were presented with a peculiar species of apple, full of juice, from trees on the premises."[83]

The Rev. Samuel Parker, during a visit in the summer of 1836, described the further decline of Pukaʻōmaʻomaʻo: "At the upper end, Kaahumanu, the late queen regent, who died in 1832, had a house built for retirement from the bustle of Honolulu, and for devotion, near a beautiful grove of ohia and kukui trees, on an eminence commanding a view of the valley below. [...] When I visited this spot of remembrance, the buildings were far gone to decay; but not the cherished regard of her piety and philanthropy. The spot presented a very pleasing view of the high and presipitous [sic] mountains around on every side; excepting the south, which is open and exhibits the grandeur of the rolling ocean."[84]

In 1848 the land was sold to Edmund H. Rogers, recorded as Land Patent Grant 111. The adjoining property, sold to Rogers in 1850 and recorded as Land Patent Grant 473, makes reference to the "road leading to Puka Omaomao" as one of the its boundaries.[85] The Privy Council Report of Committee on Missionary Lands and on the course to be pursued in regard to them, given August 19, 1850, listed E.H. Rogers who arrived in 1832 and for the American Protestant Mission. [On the same day, the Report on house lots belonging to chiefs in Honolulu was given]. The committee reported that 81 acres had been granted to him.[86] "Mr. Wyllie brought forward and read a report of a committee appointed on the 29th April and powers enlarged on the 24th June to report respecting lands applied for by Missionaries. (See Resolutions on the days mentioned.)"[87]

In 1890 Thomas Thrum commented about the Mānoa home:

> The locality where the good queen passed away shows little evidence now of ancient royal residence. It is situated well in the valley at a place known as Komoawaa; the residence called Pukaomaomao, from its green painted doors and blinds. Puulena, the old Chinese burial ground, from the year 1845, situate at the head of the central road of the valley, is said to have been part of Kaahumanu's estate.[88]

Komoawaa, an 'ili of Waikīkī, is listed as a property of Victoria Kamamalu agreed upon in the Privy Council on August 27, 1850.[89] A list is attached in a letter from her father, Matiao Kekūanāo'a to the Minister of the Interior, Keoni Ana, John Young II. Victoria Kamāmalu was the daughter of Kīna'u and sister of Kamehameha IV and Kamehameha V.

When introducing the legends of Mānoa, Albert Pierce Taylor chose the summer home of Queen Ka'ahumanu to introduce the legends of the valley. The setting is where "Queen Kaahumanu ended her days in peace at Kapuka-o-maomao (the green gateway to the valley)."[90]

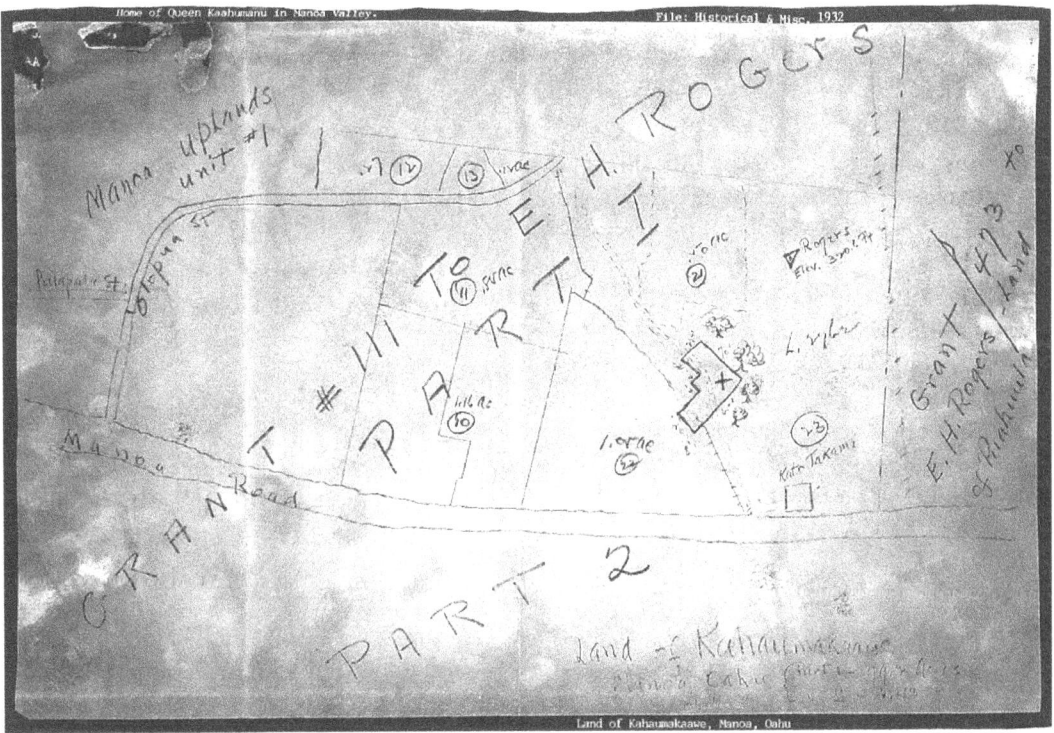

Outline of Pukaoma'oma'o on 1932 Kahaumakaawe map (courtesy Hawaii State Archives, U-178, Historical and Miscellaneous File, 1932). **The Daughters of Hawai'i visited the site in 1932 and observed the foundation of the building.**

In June 1932, a century after Kaʻahumanu's death, the Daughters of Hawaiʻi, whose mission was to "search out and mark interesting historic spots in the islands" visited the site of her residence: The *Honolulu Star-Bulletin* recorded:

> Just past the junction of Manoa Rd. and Oahu Ave. in upper Manoa valley, surrounded by market gardens and where automobiles whiz past, a green overgrown path leads off the highway to a tiny clearing, shaded by fine old hau trees and bushes in which there is a stone foundation of a former house. The stones are moss covered and the structure which once covered them has long since disappeared. Yet this is historic ground, the homesite of one of the islands' greatest queens.
>
> Kaahumanu, queen of Kamehameha the Great, had her summer house on this cool spot. It was doubtless the same sort of grass house which was in general use, although probably more spacious and elaborate as befitted a queen. The dimension in one direction is 60 feet. The place was known as Kahoiwai, or "Returning Water."[91]

The June 1934 issue of *The Friend* recorded the efforts of the Daughters of Hawaiʻi to mark the site. "The Daughters hope in the future to mark with a suitable tablet, 'Pukaomao-mao,' former site of the country home, 'Kahoiwai,' of Queen Kaahumanu in Manoa Valley." The Daughters' desires for a suitable marker never came to reality, though, they did glimpse at the foundation of the house site during their visit in 1932. Barbara Ann Del Piano records the result of their visit in *Nā Lani Kaumaka, Daughters of Hawaiʻi, A Century of Historic Preservation*:

> Early in 1932 a group of fifty-six Daughters went to Mānoa to locate the site. After meeting at the junction of Mānoa Road and Oʻahu Avenue, they followed a land office map a short distance into the valley and located the spot. A narrow path overhung with branches led from the street to the house site, where they found only a small, moss-covered portion of the stone foundation, all that remained of the Queen's former home.[92]

The only visual record of the house, a 1932 photostat copy, shows an outline of the home, marked with an "×" in the land of Kahaumakaawe, Manoa, Oʻahu. George Awai of the territorial land office created the map on January 12, 1932. It is possible that the map is the very one used by the Daughters of Hawaiʻi to locate Pukaʻōmaʻomaʻo in that same year. The map indicates that the land was part of Grant 111 to E.H. Rogers, Part I, and adjacent to Grant 473 to E.H. Rogers, land of Puahuula. The map also gives the elevation of the knoll behind the house, sometimes referred to as Rogers, as 340.6 feet.[93] *Place Names of Hawaii* identifies Pūʻahuʻula as the "site of Queen Kaʻahumanu's home, Pukaʻōmaʻo (green apertures) [...] Kaʻahumanu died here on 1832."[94] Mary Kawena Pukui, in *Sites of Oahu*, gave the meaning of Pūʻahuʻula as "(Pu here is short for Puna) 'Spring-of-the-Feather-Cape.' There was a moʻo who lived there. Somewhere mauka of Pukaomao."[95]

Mary Montano wrote about "Kapukaomaomao (The Green Gateway): Known as 'the Mermaids spring' (Kai lua o ka moʻo) Kihanuilanilulumoku (The great heavenly mermaid who soothes the land). [...] On the boundary of Puahuula and Kapukaomaomao (the Green Gateway) is to be found the spring Pukaomaomao's. The verdant entrance to the mountains of the goddess. It is situated at the foot of the knoll called Kalehua" at Puahuula and near the present roadway—in the background are beautiful mountains

Despite the inability of the Daughters of Hawaiʻi to persuade Bishop Estate to donate the site as a park, the marking of the site, nevertheless, remained a high priority in the minds of many. The *Forty-Ninth Annual Report of the Hawaiian Historical for the Year 1940*, though, seems to imply a change in access to Pukaʻōmaʻomaʻo: "*Until very recently* [italics mine] one could clamber up to the foundation stones of Pukaomaomao, in the little Japanese flower garden above Olopua Street, a short mile mauka of the Waioli Tea Room, and today a thicket of *hau* trees still twists itself protectingly about some of these stones."[96] When Hawaiian Historical Society member Henry P. Judd (1880–1955) recommended "places for designation as Territorial Monuments" in an August 1942 report for the territorial commission on historical sites, he recommended the marking of only one of the lost palaces. The third-highest ranked site on his Oʻahu list was "Pukaomaomao—Kaahumanu's home, Manoa valley. In this spot, the last residence of the famed Queen Kaahumanu, situated not far from the Waioli Tea Rooms, the favorite wife of Kamehameha passed away."[97] The proposed marking of Kaʻahumanu's home reflects her preeminent standing in the memory of missionary families. A tablet was unveiled at Kawaiahaʻo Church on August 30, 1903, remembering Kaʻahumanu's role in overthrowing the *kapu* system and her support of Christianity. The Bishop of Oxford, too, in his preface to Manly Hopkins' *Hawaii: The Past, Present, and Future of Its Island-kingdom*, paid homage to the role of Kaʻahumanu: "It is not a little remarkable, too, that in this sudden and entire deliverance of the people from the meshes of their old superstition, the leading instrument should be a woman—a Queen-mother, strengthening the halting hands of the young and trembling king, to break the bondage under which he groaned, but before the threats of which he quailed."[98] The site where she died, therefore, was invested with importance to the religious history of Hawaiʻi and its transition from the *kapu* system to Christianity.

Huelani Place, named for the water source for Pukaʻōmaʻomaʻo, affords a view of Diamond Head, or Diamond Hill as Charles Stewart called it in his account of the residence of Queen Kaʻahumanu (photograph by the author).

Between 1946 and 1949 Bishop Estate subdivided the land surrounding her home as Manoa Uplands. The developers recognized the royal heritage of the area. They announced in February 1950: "Manoa Uplands, in olden times the home of the alii, today is the scene of a large-scale real estate development which will eventually put nearly three million dollars worth of fine homes on the market. [...] Many years ago Manoa Uplands was more or less reserved for the alii of Oahu."[99] The first home even bore a name hinting at the area's royal past: "The model home, at 3319 Halelani Drive is called "Hale Lani" ... heavenly home."[100] Hale Lani may also be translated as royal house.

By the time the Commission on Historical Sites developed lists of historical sites in 1959, Pukaʻōmaʻomaʻo, which at one time ranked as the third most important site on Oʻahu, was no longer included. Only the name of a road near the location of Kaʻahumanu's house—Halelani Drive—preserves, however obtusely, a memory of the lost palace site. *Place Names of Hawaii* also identifies Huelani Drive as another street name pointing to Kaʻahumanu's royal home; Huelani literally means "royal gourd (referring to the well for Kaahumanu's home)."[101] Huelani Place has a view of Diamond Head (or Diamond Hill[102] as Stewart called the crater).

Residence of Timiteo Haʻalilio, Mānoa, Honolulu

Below Pukaʻōmaʻomaʻo, an advisor of Kamehameha II and envoy to the United States maintained a residence. The *Polynesian* makes reference to a Mānoa residence of Haʻalilio in regards to a celebration of Independence Day on July 4, 1840. American residents "gave a dinner at the house of Haalilio in the valley of Manoa. The King and his suite, with many other invited guests were present."[103] Although celebrating an American event, the dinner "was cooked in native style and the manner of partaking nearly so."[104] Less than two years later Haʻalilio would be serving as envoy to the United States. Reynolds reflected the informality of the Independence Day event in his journal entry for July 3, 1840: "Some trying to get up a dinner for tomorrow up at Manoa Valley—they put me to ask the King & Strangers—I asked Capt Chiene; Capt. Metcalf & Mr Wood—Evening I heard I had omitted many others—which I never Knew anything about."[105] Despite gaps in the invitation list, Stephen Reynolds recorded a successful gathering: "About forty persons, among whom the King and several of his suite—Capt Chiene, Locy Metcalf-Humphreys, English masters—Sergmore Francisco Delano—with a pretty general turn out of Yankees—went up to Haalilio's house in Manoa Valley—where there was a very good Luow [*luau*] & other eatables—with a plenty of good Drinkables got down about sundown."[106]

The heiau called Kawapopo, destroyed sometime before 1850, was situated on the property. Hana Haʻalilio received Royal Patent Grant 639, consisting of 2.1 acres, in 1851. The neighboring properties were owned by Matiao Kekūanāoʻa (Grant 644), Charles Kanaʻina (Grant 643) and E. Rogers (Grant 111), who also owned land adjacent to Pukaʻōmaʻomaʻo. Thomas Thrum, in his survey of Mānoa residences mentioned Haʻalilio: "The site of the various houses that once sheltered Haʻalilio and his retinue is pointed out just above the old Ehu homestead, known later as the 'Charley Long' premises and till very recently, part and parcel of Montana's Kaipu Dairy. The Rev. H. Bingham of early Hawaiian Mission fame, is also referred to by old timers as having had a

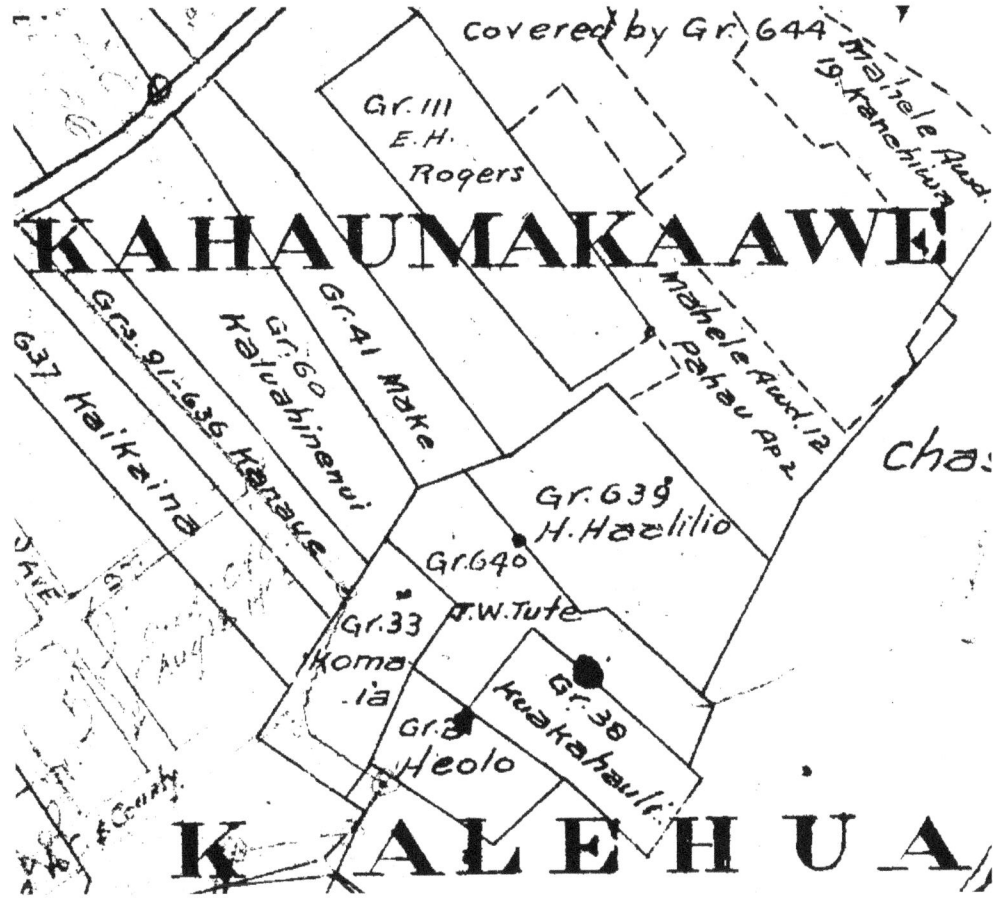

The property of Hana Haʻalilio, labeled "Gr. 639 H Haalilio" in an 1882 map of Manoa by H.D. Alexander. Her husband, Timoteo Haʻalilio, the first diplomat, died in 1844. Detail of Registered Map 1068WIDE (courtesy Land Survey Division, Department of Accounting and General Services, State of Hawaii).

residence adjoining the Haalilio premises, though his history makes no mention thereof."[107] The land is now part of Mānoa District Park.

Residence of Kīnaʻu, Honolulu (–1839)

The residence of Kīnaʻu in Honolulu is depicted in the manuscript diary of Richard Brinsley Hinds found in the collections of the Museum of Natural History in London. Hinds served on the H.M.S. *Sulphur* during its around-the-world voyage from 1836 to 1842.[108] The drawing of the house has the handwritten caption "Queen Regent Kinau" beneath an L-shaped building with a gable at the end of one wing and a gable over hipped roof on the other wing. "Queen Regent" most likely refers to her role as Kuhina Nui from July 1832 to her death on April 4, 1839. The building shows the Western influence despite its thatched composition, with a shift from a simple plan of most *hale pili* with its four corners to a complex plan with six corners. The July 1832 account of

Jeremiah N. Reynolds, in *Voyage of the United States Frigate Potomac*, calls the residence of the Kuhina Nui: "the palace of the Queen Regent Kinau."[109]

Kīna'u also occupied a Western style residence: "We found her [Kīna'u] at her house near the fort with her husband and several of the chiefs. The house has 'adobe' walls, and a native roof lined with mats. One side of the apartment in which we were received, was occupied by a pile of mats, which served as a divan or a bed according to circumstances. A board partition, neatly painted separated it from the sleeping-apartment of Kinau. The furniture consisted of a table, a China desk, Windsor chairs, and arm-chairs for the king, governess, and commodore."[110]

Also in the vicinity of the fort stood the residence of Kamehameha III, Halekauwila, the last of the great *hale pili*.

Halekauwila or Hale Kauila (1836–184?), Honolulu

As with many of the palaces constructed in the traditional manner, the name of Halekauwila was derived from natural material from which it was constructed. The wood of the kauwila tree was prized by builders for its durability. Hawaiian historian Samuel Kamakau revealed the origins of the structure: "When she [Nahi'ena'ena] became pregnant the Oahu chiefs bades her come there to give birth, and Kina'u built her a house called Ka-hale-kauila where she awaited the arrival of the child whose birth was the cause of her last illness."[111] Both the baby and mother would die shortly thereafter. Halekauwila would eventually serve as the house of the grieving king. In

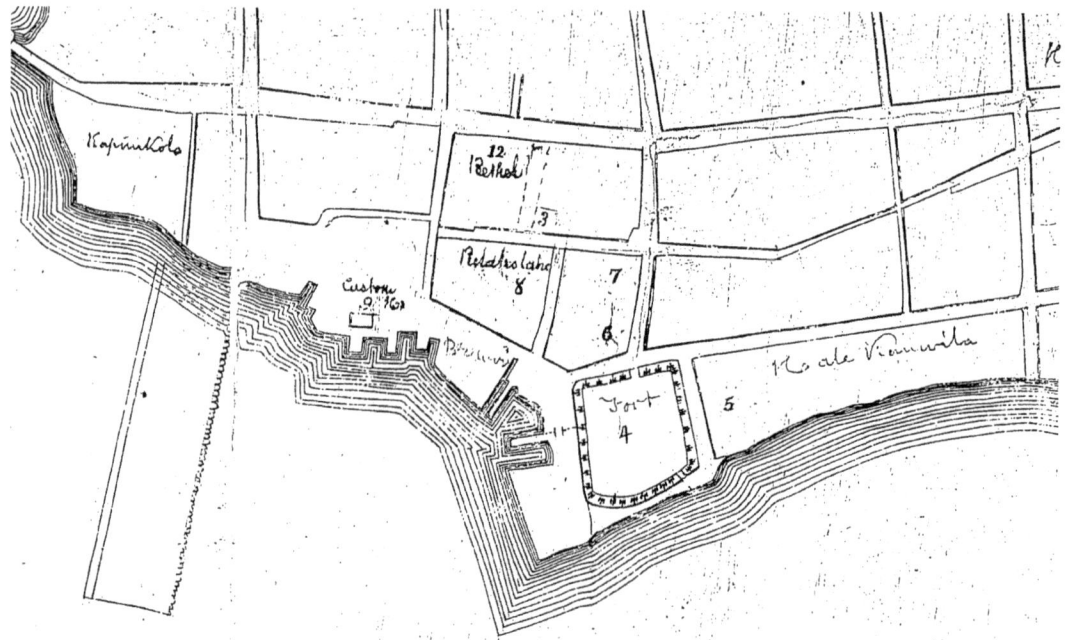

The location of Hale Kauwila, next to the fort, is marked with the number "5." Detail of Registered Map 241 (courtesy Land Survey Division, Department of Accounting and General Services, State of Hawaii).

The interior of Halekauwila is depicted in *Assemblée des Chefs des Iles Sandwich en conférence avec Commandant de la Vénus* by Louis-Jules Masselot (courtesy Hawaii State Archives, REF-VOY 3-10-009).

his communication with the United American consul, Kamehameha III addressed the influence of American missionaries from "Kauwila House, present Residence of the King of Hawaii, October 28, 1839."[112]

James Jackson Jarves, in *Scenes and Scenery in the Sandwich Islands*, gave the location and use of Halekauwila: "To the east of the fort are the barracks and royal enclosure. Within it, is the Kauila house, a neat and handsome edifice, containing the hall of audience and the room where the supreme court sits when in session. Both are well furnished."[113] Like many of the palaces, Halekauwila served a ceremonial and residential purpose. Gorham Gilman, who arrived in Honolulu in 1841, also gave his recollection of Halekauwila in a 1904 account: "On the Waikiki side of the fort was a short street running from Queen street to the water. Near Queen street was Halekauwila, one of the largest and finest thatched houses on the island, the town residence of the king and queen and also at times the place of meeting of the council."[114] Kamehameha III had married his queen, Kalama, on February 14, 1837. Kalama was the *hānai* daughter of Charles Kana'ina, father of Lunalilo, a future king. Kamehameha III had previously been engaged to Kamanele, daughter of Kuakini, governor of Hawai'i.

As with Haleuluhe, Halekauwila served a dual role as residence and meeting place. Halekauwila was the site of a meeting between the French captain of the *Venus* and Kamehameha III. The drawing of the meeting recorded the only known image of Francisco de Paula Marin.

The use of Halekauwila as a royal residence was short-lived, when the royal couple moved to Hale Ali'i in 1845 (Chapter 4). "Hale Kauwila" is listed as a public building in 1847 "containing the offices of the land commissioners and of the native judges."[115] Registered Map 241, which was probably drawn in 1847, has the site of "Hale Kauwila" marked by the number "5," just southeast of the "Papu" or "Fort."

Residence of Thomas Charles Byde Rooke on Union Street (1830–1830), Honolulu

Thomas Charles Byde Rooke arrived in Honolulu in 1827, a ship's doctor on board the whaler *Ophelia*.[116] He asked the ship's captain to allow him to remain in Hawai'i. Rooke married high chiefess Grace Kamaikui Young, daughter of John Young, the war companion of Kamehameha I and Kaoanaeha, daughter of Keli'imaika'i, brother of Kamehameha I. Rooke bought in 1830 for $200 the lot on Union Street and lived in a coral building at "the angle made by Hotel and Union streets."[117] A receipt signed by Na Mele Alina, dated August 19, 1830, reads: "Received of Mr. Rooke the sum of two Hundred Dollars on consideration my giving the house and premises belonging to me and situated in Honolulu up to him forever." The land there was owned [Land Court Award 118-B] by Kamaikui, and was adjacent to property [Land Court Award 924] owned by Thomas Charles Byde Rooke, the *hānai* parents of Queen Emma. The Privy Council authorized the Royal Patent for claim No. 924 on March 8, 1852.[118]

The 1891 Dakin Fire Map No. 6 shows the building as a carriage factory with a dwelling on the second floor. The area is labeled "Honolulu Carriage Factory."

Elizabeth K. Pratt recounted the residents of the building in an 1912 interview with a *Hawaiian Star* reporter: "The first person that I can remember who lived in the building was Doctor Rooke, the foster-father of Queen Emma. During her girlhood, prior to her marriage to Kamehameha IV, she resided in a cottage at the rear of the structure and her cousin, Peter Young Kaeo, lived in the larger building."[119]

Pratt also recalled the subsequent uses for the building: "Later the building was used for government offices. The financial department and the department of the interior were situated here for several years until all the offices were moved into the Government building, later called the Judiciary, now being remodeled."[120] An indenture was dated July 7, 1862, between the Estate of the late T.C.B. Rooke and H.R.H. L. Kamehameha, Minister of the Interior, leased the buildings on Union Street for the government for five years. The building subsequently housed government finance and interior offices. The 1869 *Honolulu Directory* lists "Government House 4 Union and 75 Fort."[121]

The listing for Kaeo in the *Hawaiian Kingdom Statistical and Commercial Directory and Tourists Guide, 1880–1880*, records his address as "5 and 7 Union Street."[122]

Birth Site of Queen Emma

The property may also have been the birth site of Queen Emma. The residence in which Emma was born was described as a "house *makai* of the premises now occupied by the Catholic Sisters."[123]

The Union Street lot sits *makai* of property labeled "Sisters of the Sacred Heart (owners)" on Land Court Application 917. Chauncey Bennet's *Honolulu Directory* includes a listing for "Sisters of the Sacred Heart 2 Garden lane."[124] Grace Kamaikui

Chapter 5. Other Royal Residences of Oʻahu 151

The residence of Thomas Charles Byde Rooke and later Peter Young Kaeo, a two-story building with a hipped roof, sits across the street from the tower of the Central Fire Station (courtesy Hawaii State Archives, Paul Markham Kahn Collection 38/001).

was sister of Fanny Kekelaokalani, Queen Emma's birth mother. Kekelaokalani had no house lots in Honolulu.

On March 16, 1901, James F. Morgan held an auction to sell the Union Street property under "instructions from the attorneys of Colonel C.K.C. Rooke,"[125] nephew of Thomas Charles Byde Rooke, from whom he had inherited the property. The sale sold the two adjacent Union Street properties, identified as Lot A and Lot B. According to the advertisement, the 28,621 square foot lot was "occupied by the Wright Carriage Co. and several stores."[126] Lot A adjoined "King Bros. on Hotel Street."[127] At the auction, Lot A was sold to W. Wolters for $81,000.[128] The smaller Lot B went to Bruce Cartwright for $22,400.[129]

Rooke House (before 1836–1912), Kaopuana, Honolulu, Queen Emma

Thomas Charles Byde Rooke subsequently took up residence above his practice in a Greek Revival house at the corner of Beretania and Nuʻuanu streets. Levi Chamberlain recorded the earliest mention of Rooke House. His entry for December 18, 1835, recorded: "The funeral of Mr. Young was attended this afternoon from the house of Dr. Rooke."[130] At the probate hearing for the will of John Young, Rooke testified: "I knew John Young while living and he is now dead. He died during the month of December at my house in Honolulu. This was in the year 1835.[131] The house was the site of a more joyous occasion less than a month after John Young's death. Queen Emma was born on January 2, 1836, and immediately after her birth the little chiefess was carried to the residence of Dr. Rooke, which then became her home until her marriage."[132]

One of the earliest images of the Rooke House appears in a pencil drawing that includes a Western building labeled "Doct Rook's" and a large thatched structure labeled "Native Church." The sketch, by Mrs. Lydia Rider Nye, captures the view looking down Beretania Street at Rooke House between Bethel and Nuuanu streets on the left, and Kaumakapili Church, the second native Hawaiian church, on the right. In the depiction a small *hale pili* appears on the Nuʻuanu and Beretania corner of the property. While the sketch is undated, Nye lived in Hawaiʻi from 1842 to 1844. So prominent and well known was the house that the Commercial Hotel gave its location in an 1846 advertisement in the *Polynesian* as: "Just past the residence of Dr. Rooke."

In a letter to John Young [Keoni Ana], dated February 11, 1848, T.C.B. Rooke applied to secure his interest in the Beretania house lot. He wrote to the Kuhina Nui: "Previous to the death of the late Premier [Kekāuluohi, who died June 7, 1845] I made divers applications for an extension of the lease of the premises. I now occupy, called Kaopuana. I now take the liberty of applying through your Highness to know on what terms I may be allowed to commute my leasehold for an Allodial Title; or if it should so please his Majesty in preference, for the extension of the period of my lease. I beg leave to add that with the hopes of such indulgence, which was promised me verbally by his majesty I have already expended between eight and nine thousand Dollars on the Premises."[133] He followed the application with a survey of the property, completed by himself, dated April 25, 1848.

Besides serving as the family residence, the house also served as the physician's office and clinic for T.C.B. Rooke. Many of his royal relatives would spend their last days at Rooke House. Such was the case when, on January 22, 1850 "at the residence of Dr. Rooke, Melie Kuamoo [Kaoanaeha], relict of John Young, and mother of His Excellency, Keoni Ana, Min. of the Interior, in the 62d year of her age."[134] Less than a year later, on October 1, 1851, at 5:30 a.m., James Young Kanehoa, her son and cousin of Queen Emma, who served then as governor of Maui, died in Honolulu. The funeral took place on Saturday, October 4, 1851. The *Polynesian* announced: "The public are invited to attend at the house of Dr. Rooke."[135] R.C. Wyllie communicated to the foreign ministers: "The procession will start at 10 A.M. precisely, on that day, from the House of Dr. Rooke, whence it will proceed to the Royal Cemetery, in the same order, as that which was observed in the case of the late Governor of Hawaii [William Pitt Leleiohoku]."[136]

On June 19, 1856, Emma Rooke married King Kamehameha IV, who had ascended to the throne two years earlier. She was dressed in her bridal gown at Rooke House.[137] After the wedding, she moved to nearby Hale Aliʻi and Ihikapukalani (Chapter 4).

Queen Emma's *hānai* father died on November 28, 1858, bequeathing a life estate in Rooke House to his wife, Grace Kamaikui Rooke, and upon her death to Queen Emma. Even while living at Ihikapukalani (Chapter 4) in the palace yard, Queen Emma still frequented her childhood home, visiting her *hanai* mother. It was the house of Mrs. Rooke that Sophia Cracroft visited on May 25, 1861: "Mrs. Rooke has a very good house, furnished in European fashion, and we were interested in seeing the external marks of civilization in which the Queen had passed her early life. She took us into the drawing-room then left us to find her mother, explaining that she was exceedingly shy and nervous and never went out anywhere."[138]

Thomas Charles Byde Rooke, Emma Rooke and Grace Kamaikui Rooke (courtesy Hawaii State Archives, PP-96-3-018).

With the death of her son on August 27, 1862, and husband on November 30, 1863, Queen Emma, who called herself Kaleleonalani (flight of the heavenly chiefs) in remembrance of her great loss, returned to her childhood residence located about four blocks from Hale Aliʻi.

When Queen Emma's *hanai* mother, Grace Kamaikui Rooke, died July 25, 1866, Rooke House passed on to Queen Emma. The queen opened her house to the sisters building nearby St. Andrew's Priory School.[139]

Though not written by Queen Emma, a *mele* praised Rooke House and its beloved inhabitant:

Nani wale kō lei e ʻEmalani ē	Beautiful is your lei, dear Emmalani
I moani I ke ʻala o Luka Home	Which carries with it the fragrance of Rooke Home
Hoʻohihi mai ana ke ʻala onaona	The sweet scent is very entrancing
Ika lei momi nani a ka lāhui	Of the beautiful gem garland of the people[140]

Another Western visitor, Isabella Lucy Bird, recounted her visit to Queen Emma in a series of letters to her sister in 1873. She published her description of Rooke House in her 1875 book, *The Hawaiian Archipelago*:

> The winter palace as her town house is called, is a large shady abode, like an old-fashioned New England house externally, but with two deep verandahs, and the entrance is on the upper one. The lower floor seemed given up to attendants and offices, and a native woman was ironing clothes under a tree. Upstairs, the house is like a tasteful, English country house, with a pleasant English look, as if its furniture and ornaments had been gradually accumulating during a series of years, and possessed individual histories and reminiscences, rather than as if they had been ordered together as "plenishings" from stores. Indeed, it was the most English-looking house I have seen since I left home, except Bishopscourt at Melbourne.[141]

The reference in 1873 to the "*old-fashioned* [italics mine] New England house" illustrates how quickly architectural styles shift. The popularity of the Greek Revival style lasted from about 1820 to 1860. By the 1870s the sparse style seemed outdated.

So many factors contributed to the few remaining royal residences in Hawai'i. Rooke House nearly burned on the evening of August 25, 1873. Queen Emma wrote the next day to her cousin, Peter Young Kaeo: "Rooke House escaped total destruction by fire last night. The lamp in [the] aiuupuu ['ā'īpu'upu'u, steward or butler] room burst and the flames instantly spread where oil ran, licking it up and burning the sides of the room. There was no one in save Laweoki, a little boy 7 year old. Lucy and I were sewing in the room above when I heard him utter a subdued, surprised exclamation, 'Auwe,' and call for Mamaina. I detected at the moment also strong smell of lamp smoke. We both ran down and found the room in flames, dark with smoke. Lucy shouted for help. Hiram ran in and smothered it with a towel, as well [as] he could. By that time a crowd was outside and Laanui's bed quilt extinguished the fire, so no harm was done, but it was quite an escape. Everyone was terribly excited and noisy after the accident."[142]

Fanny Young Kekelaokalani, birth mother of Queen Emma, died at Rooke House on September 4, 1880. Queen Emma, Peter Young Ka'eo and Albert Kūnuiākea were in the funeral procession. Ka'eo would die two months later at his Emma Street residence.

Queen Emma's Funeral

Queen Emma herself would die less than five years later. A description of the funeral at Queen Emma's residence appears in *The Banner of Faith* from a letter from St. Andrew's Priory, a school founded by the Queen. The account reveals the location of the Queen's death and the presence of a telephone at the house:

> It was on S. Mark's Day, April 25 [1885], about 2.30 p.m., when Mrs. Wodehouse, the Consul's wife, came in and told Sister Phoebe that she had heard by telephone that Queen Emma was dead. Sister Phoebe went off with her at once to Rooke House, and in a short time returned to tell us the sad news was only too true. The Queen had been seized with an apoplectic attack at 12.50 p.m. Her maid at once telephoned for the doctor, who hastened with all speed to her side. She rallied so far from the first stroke as to be able to walk round the room, but a second attack came on, followed soon after by a third, in which she passed away. Sister Phoebe then took Stella [Keomailani, later Cockett] and Fanny (the Queen's cousins who are pupils at S. Andrew's Priory) back to Rooke House with her, and stayed there till between 10 and 11, when Sister B [Beatrice] took her place for the first part of the night, Sister A [Albertina] relieving her at 3 a.m. so that some one besides natives might be there to see that everything was properly done. Preparations were at once made for the removal of the body from the room in which she died to the drawing-room, where it was to lie in state. At 8 p.m. a requiem service was said by the Rev. A. Macintosh.[143]

The account also gave a description of house itself, especially the verandah and outside staircase: "Most of her native people grouped about the yard, *i.e.* garden and were wailing, of course. The room in which she was laid, the same in which she was dressed for a bride, is upstairs, surrounded by a verandah reached by an outside staircase. In the verandah we waited for some time, for the preparations were not quite completed; there we were in the midst of the wailing inside and outside. It is the most piteous, heart-rending sound, especially when one knows it, as in this case, to be genuine; children lamenting for their mother."[144]

Chapter 5. Other Royal Residences of O'ahu

With her ties with Queen Victoria and her English grandfather, news of Queen Emma's death was reported extensively in Great Britain, including the *London Illustrated News*.

Queen Emma and Rooke House were remembered in 1904 by Gorman D. Gilman, former resident of Nahienena's *hale pili*, Hale Kamani (Chapter 2), who had arrived in Honolulu in 1841. He recollected: "On the Waikiki side of this corner stood the residence of Dr. and Mrs. Rooke, who were the foster parents of Queen Emma. This residence was one of the most hospitable in town and the doctor's genial disposition made him many friends. Emma, as she was usually called before the title of Queen was added to her name, was an exceedingly pleasant and agreeable young girl. She was an attendant at the Royal School where the children of the high chiefs were being educated for the positions which they were likely to assume in later life."[145]

The *London Illustrated News* included a drawing of the interior of Queen Emma's house where her body lay in state in 1885. The drawing titled "The Coffin Lying in State" shows in the background the tall double-hung twelve over twelve windows featured in some Greek Revival structures.

Queen Emma Hall

After Queen Emma's death the Trustees of the Queen Emma Estate made repairs to Rooke House, now calling it Queen Emma Hall. The *Daily Bulletin* reported on the new use for the residence: "The committee in charge are now fitting it up for a Reading Room, Social Hall, and Classrooms for Hawaiians."[146] Donors to Queen Emma Hall included the Hon. A.F. Judd, J.B. Atherton and the Hon. C.R. Bishop.[147] Religious services "in the English language, for English speaking Hawaiians"[148] took place in the hall starting in May 1887. A report in January 1888 by A.F. Judd called the effort the "Queen Emma Hall, Hawaiian Branch of the Young Men's Christian Association." Although listing the numerous groups using the hall, Judd concluded in his report: "your committee think it would not be wise to assume the responsibility of a long lease of the premises, and advise the Association agree to take them for the term ending July 31, 1888, with the expectation of continuing, if it shall be deemed advisable."[149]

T.C.B. Rooke's Will

Despite the efforts of the trustees, believing that the residence had passed to Queen Emma's estate, the will of her father, T.C.B. Rooke, governed fate of Queen Emma's residence after her death. At question was whether the property passed on to Queen Emma and her son, or passed on to T.C.B. Rooke's nephew, Charles Keane Creswell Rooke. Rooke was represented in the case by Reuben D. Silliman, who had been appointed as circuit court judge by President McKinley just prior to the decision.[150] The Supreme Court decision in the case of *C.K.C Rooke v. Queen's Hospital* referenced the crucial part of the will of T.C.B. Rooke:

> *I give and bequeath* all my real and personal estate, of what nature or kind soever, to my wife Grace Kamaikui Rooke to be used and enjoyed by her during the term of her natural life, and from and immediately after her decease, *I give and devise* the same to my adopted daughter Emma Rooke, and her children for ever, *but* should the aforesaid Emma Rooke, decease before me, the said testator, or decease without leaving any issue, then *I hereby give and bequeath* the same unto my Nephew and Godson Creswell Charles Keane Rooke […] and his heirs for ever.

The Supreme Court in its decision in *Rooke v. Queen's Hospital* laid out the chronology crucial to deciding the case:

> The will is dated February 28, 1852. Emma married King Kamehameha IV June 2, 1856 and gave birth to the Prince of Hawaii May 20, 1858. The testator executed a codicil to his will May 29, 1858 substituting another person for one of the executors named in the will and died November 28, 1858. The will was probated January 26, 1859. There was only one subscribing witness to the codicil but the law (Civ. Code, Sec 1465) requiring two was not approved until May 17, 1859 and did not take effect until August 1, 1859. The testator's wife Grace Kamaikui died soon after. The Prince died in 1862. The King died in 1863. Queen Emma died in 1885.[151]

The Supreme Court ruled on May 11, 1900: "Colonel [Charles Keane Creswell] Rooke [...] upon her [Queen Emma's] death without leaving any issue surviving her became entitled by way of executory devise or remainder as the case might be to the lands in question in fee simple in possession."[152] This ruling affected only the lands bequeathed to Queen Emma from her father.

The same auction that had sold the Union Street properties of T.C.B. Rooke also tried to sell the Queen Emma Hall property, labeled as Lot C. The advertisement called the lot: "the finest store and business property offered for sale in the city."[153] Despite the attractiveness of the property, the Queen Emma Hall lot remained unsold: "Lot C, being the Queen Emma Hall premises did not find any bidder, the upset price being $95,000, and was therefore not sold.[154] The owners turned to renting the property for income. An advertisement appeared in the *Evening Bulletin*: To Let—Furnished rooms. Queen Emma Hall."[155] Another offered the hall at $2 per night for "socials, luaus, club or lodge."[156] The owner, Cresswell P. Rooke, son of Col. C.K.C. Rooke, also started to remove valuable portions of the house, in particular "two fine koa posts," that a janitor later reported stolen.[157]

C.K.C. Rooke died August 17, 1903, and the property passed to Mary Rooke. With an absentee landlord half a world away in England, the property quickly deteriorated. A 1904 account of the property lamented the condition of "Queen Emma's former palace."[158] The writer envisioned the return of the residence's former royal occupant:

> Could Queen Emma return to earth she would find what once was her magnificent mansion at the corner of Beretania and Nuuanu streets and the large grounds put to strange uses.
> There is no evidence of royalty there now. Instead there are large piles of wood, lumber, many drays, rock ballast and in fact a varied assortment of belongings of a small Japanese village. The former halls of royalty are occupied by a Japanese doctor, a Japanese boarding establishment and are the headquarters of several small Japanese enterprises. Most of the koa finishings in the interior have been removed. The whole place presents the air of a haunted house.
> Years ago, when Queen Emma lived as consort of King Kamehameha IV, Queen Emma Hall was one of the showplaces of the city and the center of the social activity of the town. Queen Emma was a member of the Rooke family and a descendant of John Young. The Queen Emma Hall is still the property of that family [Mary Rooke, widow of C.K.C Rooke] but they long since ceased to take an active interest in maintaining the Hall in the splendor of former days. [...]
> As one of the most famous landmarks of the city Queen Emma Hall will probably not exist long.[159]

The rock ballast most likely was the property of S. Yokomizo, who advertised a "Great Reduction in Price of Crushed Rock." His office was at "Queen Emma Hall, corner of Nuuanu and Beretania; Tel. Blue 1211."¹⁶⁰ S. Yokomizo also offered "Firewood for Sale at Great Reductions" in a 1905 advertisement in the *Pacific Commercial Advertiser*.¹⁶¹

A 1907 account of a fire at the property, agreeing with the earlier depiction, called Queen Emma Hall: "that ancient and historic frame pile set far back from the road and surrounded by rubbish."¹⁶²

In 1908 the tax appeal court set the value of the Queen Emma Hall property at $30,000,¹⁶³ for what seven years earlier had been offered for sale with an upset price of $95,000.

Ye Liberty Theatre opened on the site of Rooke House on the evening of February 22, 1912, with a performance of the Mortimers, a vaudeville act. The *Hawaiian Star* described the new venue as "fireproof, with perfect ventilation and spacious and numerous exits."¹⁶⁴ The Liberty Theater was a site listed in a 1930 guide to Hawai'i, but not for its own importance. Townsend Griffiss remembered the lost palace less than two decades after its destruction: "The first thing of interest that comes our way is the Liberty Theater, where the most spectacular Chinese performances are presented. To us, however, it has deeper significance. This was the site of 'Rooke House,' the old home of Dr. and Mrs. Rooke, where Queen Emma spent the greater part of her younger days."¹⁶⁵ A parking lot replaced the theater, which closed its doors in 1980. A century after the razing of Rooke House, without a marker to recount its historic associations, few recall the importance of the site. Further up Nu'uanu Valley, beyond the still extant Hānaiakamalama, Queen Emma's summer palace, sits another summer palace and place of remembrance of the Kamehameha dynasty.

Kaniakapupu (1845–before 1875), Luakaha, Nu'uanu, King Kamehameha III

The heat of summer in Honolulu caused many ali'i to retreat to the cooler climate at higher elevations. It was in Nu'uanu, literally "cool heights," that Kamehameha III built his "summer palace." Perhaps Kamehameha III was following the example of Boki who had planned a Nu'uanu home. The preparation for the building began even before the shift of the capital to Honolulu. A letter from Kekāuluohi, Kuhina Nui, then in Lahaina, to Kekūanāo'a on March 13, 1840, told the governor: "This again I wish to remind you in accordance to your information concerning a plan which you had consulted to the building of the King's house; together with the stones and other materials to the building."

Kamehameha invited Théodore-Adolphe Barrot and the officers of the *Bonite* to visit the Pali and later to dine and enjoy entertainment. Barrot wrote: "After dinner we all mounted our horses again and started for the King's country house, where we were to hear Hawaiian songs and see Hawaiian dancing. On the way to the Pali we had left this house on the right."¹⁶⁶ He described the *hale pili* that existed prior to the construction of Kaniakapupu as "a cottage built in the aboriginal style of architecture."¹⁶⁷ Though native workers no doubt had constructed the *hale pili*, the construction of the Western-style Kaniakapupu required foreign workers. Interior department records detail the builders and how the building was financed: "I wish to let you know that according to the King's reference to me, the white men carpenters and the masons [*na haole kamenā a me ka poe*

Sketch of "King's Summer Palace," Kaniakapupu, later printed as a vignette of Paul Emmert's "View of Honolulu" (courtesy Hawaii State Archives, Theodor Heuck Collection).

hahau] will be paid from the money that derives from the King's cultivated lands to the Tax assessor. This money will be expended to the wages of the white men carpenters and the masons; and all other materials, such as boards and window panes."[168]

Despite the plans for a new stone house, the presence of the *hale pili* there still required constant maintenance. On May 7, 1842, Kekūanāoʻa asks Puapua: "Please carve some ilima battens [thatch purlins], say about 3000 in all. This is the number of battens which you are to make for the King's house at Luakaha."[169] Mrs. Nye wrote in her Journal on November 24, 1842, "Tomorrow a picnic is to be given at the King's cottage (about five miles in the valley of Nuana [Nuʻuanu]."[170] The next day Nye visited the Pali and proceeded to the king's residence. "The house was tastefully decorated—the rafters and posts were prettily festooned with shrubbery, the vines of which drooped gracefully, forming rustic arches over the viands. The dinner was cooked in native style, and the manner of partaking nearly so."[171]

Although the site of smaller entertainments, Kaniakapupu is better known for the Restoration Day events that took place there. Ten months after Nye's visit Gorman

Gilman described the Hawaiian feast—the *pāʻina* on August 2, 1843, celebrating the restoration of Hawaiian sovereignty by Admiral Richard Darton Thomas. "After riding about three miles or half an hour we came in sight of the place. It is a pleasant spot in the valley on a gentle assent [sic] and among a fine grove of trees (Said to be the pleasantest place in the whole valley.)"[172]

After the feast participants sang the "Restoration Anthem" to the tune of "God Save the King":

> Hail to the worthy name! Still, in our every heart
> Worthy his country's fame— Thy worth shall live!
> Thomas the brave! Live! in a nation's praise—
> Long shall thy virtues be Live! in these grateful lays—
> Shrined in our memory Live! while our numbered days
> Who came to set us free! A memory give!
> Quick o'er the wave! [...][173]
> We meet, but meet to part;

Laura Fish Judd identifies the author of the song as E.O. Hall and adds an initial stanza not included in the *Friend* account:

> Hail to our rightful King! Long reign this dynasty;
> We joyful honors bring And for posterity
> This day to thee. The scepter be.[174]
> Long live your majesty;

In an undated letter from Matiao Kekūanāoʻa to Kuhina Nui, Miriam Kekāuluohi, addressed as M. Auhea, the Oʻahu governor told the Kuhina Nui: "His Majesty said it would be alright for the men to return to Nuuanu to complete his stone house. That's what His Majesty said to me and I am informing you."[175]

On May 21, 1845, the minister of the interior, Gerrit P. Judd, reported that: "During the present year 'The King's villa' at Nuuanu has also been finished."[176] More than just a residence, the king also conducted business from Kaniakapupu. His public reply to E.S. Kamakau concerning the employment of foreigners as ministers was made from "Nuuanu, Oahu, August, 1845."[177]

On July 31, 1847, two years after the completion of the stone palace at Nuʻuanu, a second feast celebrating the "Restoration of the Hawaiian Flag by Rear Admiral Thomas" took place. The *Polynesian* reported: "The morning unfortunately was lowery, much rain fell in the valley, and some showers reached the town. Notwithstanding this and the muddy roads, by early dawn, parties on foot and horseback were thronging the road to the King's residence at Nuuanu, where the appointed feast was to come of."[178] The festivities took place on the grounds of the summer palace of King Kamehameha III. "Outside the house, extending 600 feet towards the Pali, a rustic table spread over with fern leaves, and raised a foot from the ground, had been prepared for the poi eaters."[179]

The food for the estimated 12,000 attendees included: "271 hogs, 482 large calabashes of poi, 602 chickens, 3 oxen, 2 barrels salt pork, 2 of bread, 3,125 salt fish, 1320 fresh do."[180]

The day's entertainment, though lacking any hula, did feature another ancient art. The *Polynesian* reported: "There was considerable excitement among the people while the *Lua*—the old process of disjointing bones and strangling—was being displayed, as it no doubt for the moment revived many old associations of heathenism, which had been long forgotten."[181]

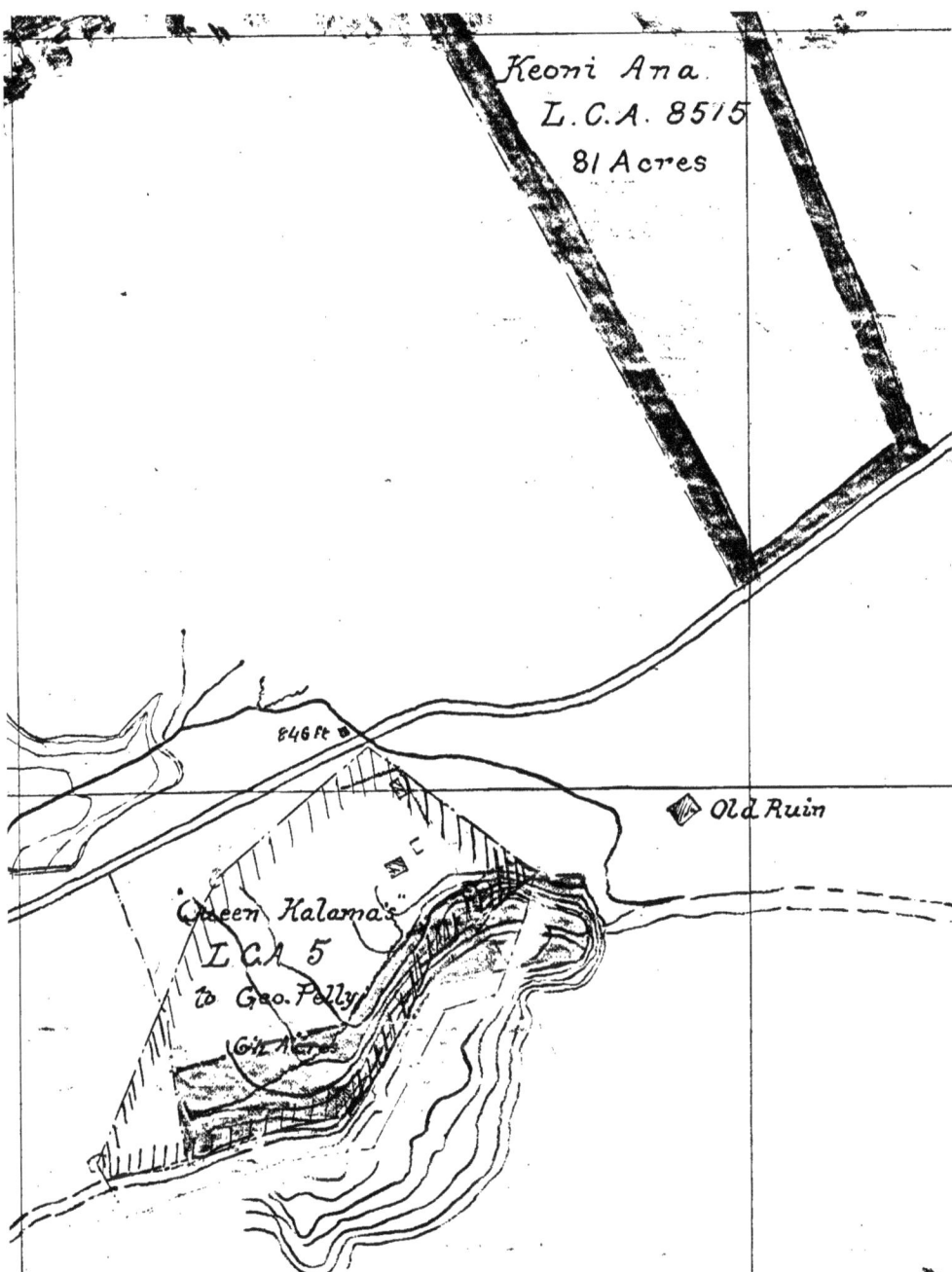

Kaniakapūpū is labeled as "Old Ruin" on Registered Map 133 (courtesy Land Survey Division, Department of Accounting and General Services, State of Hawaii).

Gorham Gilman wrote a 1909 article titled "Honolulu and Its Suburbs in the Latter Forties," in which he recounted his impressions from the late 1840s. Of Kaniakapūpū he recalled: "The last building in the valley after the foreign style is His Majesty's county seat, at which he spends considerable time during the summer. It is about five miles from town and a pleasant ride. It is in a fine situation and is surrounded by many of the original forest trees. It is a plain stone building with one large room and two sleeping rooms, the whole surrounded by a neat paling fence. It was here that the great meal fete was given by His Majesty to Admiral Thomas at the time of the restoration."[182]

The first image of Kaniakapūpū appears as part of a series of lithographs printed in 1853 or 1854 by Paul Emmert. Kaniakapūpū is included in Plate No. 2, View of Honolulu from the Catholic Church, as "King's Summer House."[183] A pencil drawing of Kaniakapūpū was used as the basis for the Emmert lithograph.

When precisely Kaniakapūpū was abandoned is unknown, but thirty years after the completion of its construction, an 1875 map of Luakaha, Nuuanu Valley, Kona, Oʻahu, calls the Kaniakapūpū site an "Old Ruin." An 1884 map also labels the site as "Old Ruin." Charles Warren Stoddard recounted his tour of Nuʻuanu in his 1885 book, *A Trip to Hawaii*, contrasting the "stately white columns" of Hānaiakamalama with the "grimy walls of a forgotten palace of an almost forgotten King."[184] Similarly, a December 1903 article in *Paradise of the Pacific* describes: "four crumbling stone walls that once were a part of Kamehameha III's country palace. The structure had only one story, forty feet long by 20 feet wide. There are also remnants of a paved walk around the walls."[185] The author contrasted Kaniakapūpū in its heyday to its condition at the beginning of the twentieth century: "There were merry doings and regal ceremonials on this spot, where wild vegetation now holds sway."[186]

One of the least accessible sites of the more than sixty lost palaces, Kaniakapupu is also one of the few sites marked. Cleared by volunteers George Arnemann and Walter Bayer in the early 1950s, the structure came to the attention of the sites committee of the Conservation Council for Hawaii. Under the category Works in Progress, the sites committee reported in January 1954:

> King's Summer Home. Kania-ka-pupu, the Nuuanu Valley summer home built by Kamehameha III and the site of the famous feast which celebrated Restoration Day, is the latest concern of the Sites Committee. The coral walls of the old home are still standing within the forest reserve of Nuuanu. Several trips were made to the site in September and October. Two volunteers, Mr. George Arnemann and Walter Bayer, cleared the interior of the house and the terrace on which it is located of trees. The Sites Committee believes the site should be preserved and possibly opened to sightseers as a Historic Site. A resolution to that effect will be proposed at next meeting. Interest in the site is due to the fact that there are few remains of buildings or memorials to Kamehameha III.[187]

The close relationship between the Conservation Council for Hawaii and the Honolulu water board provided a ready source of funding for the marking of the Nuʻuanu royal residence:

> Kaniakapupu: Kamehameha III's summer home ruins in the forest reserve at Luakaha in Nuuanu Valley will be appropriately marked with a large bronze plaque by the City and County Water Works Department. Interest in saving these ruins was roused by Bryant Cooper and two laymen, George Arnemann and Walter Bayer. These two men cleared the site and found interesting walls standing which show the type of construction used during the time of Kamehameha III. Edward Morgan, Water Works Department head, has assured the committee that he will do all in his power to preserve any sites on property under his control and that he will erect markers to be paid out of Water Work funds.[188]

The following year, in February 1956, the committee reported: "Our Committee unearthed the Kamehameha Third Country Palace at Luakaha a couple of years ago and made it known to the public, which unfortunately cannot be made available to the

Chapter 5. Other Royal Residences of Oʻahu

public, as it is in the watershed area, the Board of Water Supply has marked this historic spot with a bronze plaque during the last year."[189]

The Conservation Council for Hawaii in a 1957 report of the accomplishments of its sites committee noted the marking of Kaniakapūpū: "Kamehameha III's Summer Palace, one of the oldest buildings in Hawaii, has been marked by a plaque through the efforts of the Territorial Historical Sites Commission."[190] The credit for marking the site was not misappropriated by the sites committee, for the commission was for the most part made up of Conservation Council sites committee members and the Honolulu Board of Water Supply which paid for the marker was an organizational member of the council.

The bronze plaque reads:

<blockquote>
Kaniakapupu
Summer Palace of King Kamehameha III
and His Queen Kalama

Completed in 1845 it was the scene of
entertainment of foreign celebrities
and the feasting of chiefs and commoners.
The greatest of these occasions was
a luau attended by an estimated ten
thousand people celebrating
Hawaiian Restoration Day in 1847
Commission on Historical Sites
</blockquote>

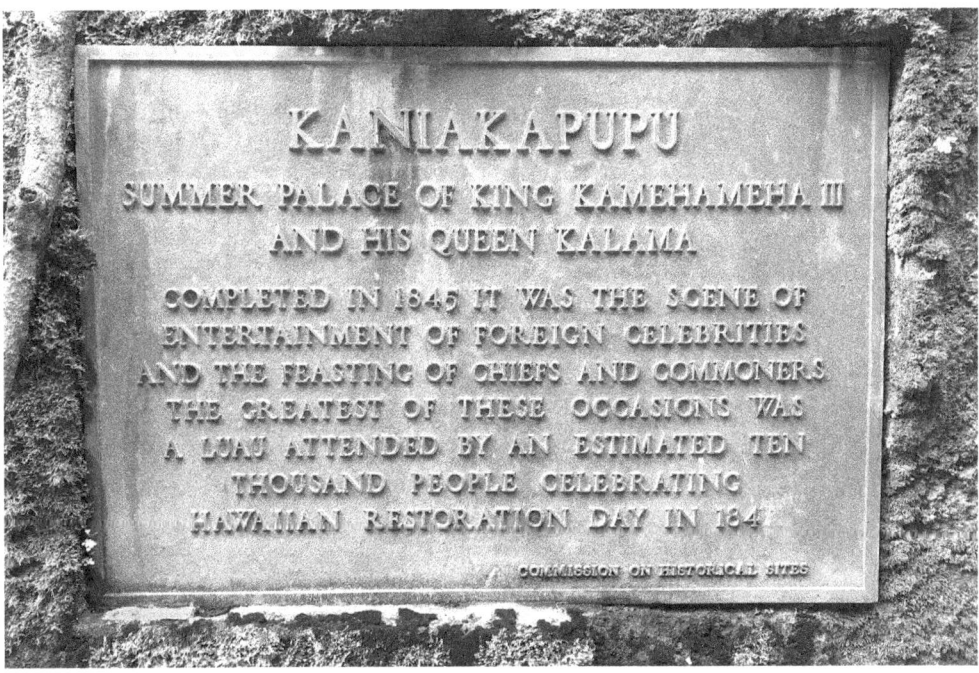

The Conservation Council for Hawaii and the Board of Water Supply installed a marker at Kaniakapūpū to mark the site of the lost palace of Kamehameha III (photograph by the author).

The ruins of Kaniakapūpū today (photograph by the author).

Despite the marking of the site in 1957, Hawaiiana researcher Henry E.P. Kekahuna, in his 1959 essay, "Our Ignored Gold Mine of Hawaiiana," listed Kaniakapūpū among the "unmarked, little known, and little visited places of cultural interest and scenic beauty."[191] He wrote: "Right in little-known historic Nuu-anu Valley, for instance, lies Pu'pu'-kani-oe, homesite of King Ka-mehameha III, of which few of us have even heard. It was there in honor of Rear-Admiral Thomas, following his restoration of the independence of the Hawaiian Kingdom in 1843, the most lavish native feast in our recorded history was held."[192] Kamakahonu and Kaniakapūpū are the only lost palaces listed by Kekahuna, although he does record royal residences that predate Kamehameha's unification of the Hawaiian islands: the royal residence of Pakiha where Queen Kekea-lani-wahine lived, and the residence of Lono-i-ka-makahiki in Kaha-luu.[193]

Kaniakapūpū was the only lost palace to appear on the list of Mayor's Historic Building Task Force in 1966. The site was placed on the National Register of Historic Places on October 15, 1986, one of only four lost palaces so designated.

Haleakalā or 'Aikupika (1847–1900), Honolulu

The residence of Abner Pākī served as the childhood residence of Princess Bernice Pauahi Bishop and Queen Lili'uokalani. Gorham D. Gilman, who arrived in Honolulu before Pākī erected his Greek Revival structure gave his recollections of the 1840s in 1904: "There was a fine large straw house with wide veranda, ample grounds, and a long row of servant's houses. One of the beautiful ornaments of the place was a fine large tamarind tree, planted the day of Mrs. Bishop's birth."[194]

In 1847 the *hale pili* gave way to a Greek Revival style residence. The earliest account of the new structure is recorded on May 22, 1847, in the *Polynesian*: "The prospect for mechanics and for the rapid improvement of the town this season. […] *Private Buildings.*—the [house] of Mr. Paki […], in preparedness."[195] The childhood home of Queen Lili'uokalani and Princess Bernice Pauahi Bishop, the residence named Haleakalā, would reflect the changes during the period that started with the relocation of the monarchial court to Honolulu to its overthrow. Shortly after the death of its owner, Pākī, in June 1855, the *Friend* wrote of Haleakalā: "The residence occupied by Paki, situated at the very heart of our city, is admired by all for the taste and beauty with which it is laid out and ornamented. It would do credit to a gentleman of the most cultivated predilections."[196]

Princess Bernice Pauahi Bishop inherited the house following the death of Abner Pākī on June 13, 1855, and Kōnia on July 2, 1857. She and her husband, Charles Reed Bishop, lived there. An announcement of the baptism at Haleakalā of their *hānai* son, Keolaokalani Pākī Bishop, appeared in *Hoku o ka Pakipika* on February 12, 1863. It is most likely that their son, who Ruth Ke'elikōlani gave birth to, also died at Haleakalā on August 29, 1863.

Later Mrs. Dudoit, wife of the former French consul, and then Mr. Hamilton Johnson, who later managed the Royal Hawaiian Hotel,[197] turned the residence into a boarding house. Johnson called the place Hamilton House. In 1893 Haleakalā became the Arlington Hotel.[198]

Upon Bernice Pauahi Bishop's death the downtown residence went to her estate, to the long lasting regret of *hānai* sister, Lili'uokalani:

Bernice Pauahi Bishop, daughter of Abner Pākī and Laura Kōnia, was raised at Haleakalā (courtesy Hawaii State Archives, PP-96-1-007).

> But nevertheless I must own to one great disappointment. The estate which had been so dear to us both in my childhood, the house built by my father, Paki, where I had lived as a girl, which was connected with many happy memories of my early life, from whence I

had been married to Governor Dominis, when he took me to Washington Place, I could not help feeling ought to have been left to me. The estate was called Haleakala, or House of the Sun, and the residence received the name of Aikupika; but both these are forgotten now in that of the Arlington Hotel. This wish of my heart was not gratified, and at the present day strangers stroll through the grounds or lounge on the piazzas of that home once so dear to me. Yet memories of my adopted parents still cling to that homestead, and rise before me not only when I pass its walls, but as I recall in a foreign land the days of my youth.[199]

Two years after her published expression of disappointment in *Hawaii's Story by Hawaii's Queen*, in 1900, the object of her desire no longer existed. The *Pacific Commercial Advertiser* highlighted Liliʻuokalani's connection to the property in its headline: "Liliuokalani's Childhood Home to Go Under the Hammer Today" and its commentary that "Liliuokalani will pass a lonely quarter of an hour as the time approaches for the sale of what she holds so dear."[200] It also emphasized the finality of the loss: "Before the echoes of the auctioneer's mallet have died away the wreckers will have begun the work of tearing to pieces the building and dismantling the beautiful grounds so long the home of charming hospitality and in which so many comers to Hawaiian shores have looked their first on the foliage and exquisite growth of the Islands."[201] The newspaper also made the historical connection between the overthrow and the Queen: "But the Arlington has known other and sterner scenes. Once it held the soldiers of a nation upholding the hands of a new-born government."[202]

Troops from the U.S.S. *Boston* occupied Hamilton House, once known as Haleakalā, the childhood home of Queen Liliʻuokalani (courtesy Hawaii State Archives, PP-36-3-002).

Chapter 5. Other Royal Residences of Oʻahu 167

Haleakalā once stood in the grass lot in the foreground, at the corner of Bishop Street and King Street (courtesy Hawaii State Archives, PP-41-6-010).

The *Friend*, a missionary publication, lamented the passing of yet another landmark when the Arlington Hotel was torn down in October 1900: "The past month has witnessed the destruction of two residences in the business part of the city, which have been over 50 years conspicuous as social centers. One was the noted Paki House, built by the high chief Abner Paki on King street in the forties. It was for thirty years the beautiful home of the distinguished Princess, Mrs. Bernice Pauahi Bishop. For some years past it has been occupied as the 'Arlington Hotel.' [...] Mr. [Alexander] Young is about to build a grand hotel on part of both premises, extending from King to Hotel street. Both houses have just been demolished, and the splendid old shade trees are being destroyed. A new street is to be opened through, parallel with Fort street. It will be extended seaward to Queen Street, and probably inland to Beretania. [...] Very few edifices now remain in Honolulu which date back more than fifty years."[203] The article fails to remember the Hawaiian name for the home, Haleakalā, and that the recently deposed Queen Liliʻuokalani lived there as a child, nor that the men from the U.S.S. *Boston* used the residence, then called Hamilton House, as a staging area in their support of the Committee of Safety's overthrow of the monarchy.

The Alexander Young Hotel remained on the site until it, too, was demolished to make way for a commercial complex that remembered the former resident of Haleakalā in the name of the development, Bishop Square, and one of the towers, Pauahi, and in the landscaping of the open space that reintroduced the Tamarind tree that had once graced the grounds of Abner Pākī's residence. Across Bishop Street from Bishop Square, under the Cades Schutte Building at 1000 Bishop, about 50 feet *mauka* of King Street, sits the original location of Haleakalā.

Papakanene, Mokuaikaua, Honolulu (1853–1853), Kekūanāoʻa and Victoria Kamāmalu

Although he gave up the house that he had built for his daughter to Kamehameha III for the king's palace, Kekūanāoʻa still had several other residences from which to choose, as did his daughter, Victoria Kamāmalu. Samuel Clemens, writing as Mark Twain for the *Sacramento Daily Union*, referred broadly to all the properties of Victoria Kamāmalu in his report of her death: "The Princess was possessed of immense landed estates, and formerly kept up considerable state. She rode in a fine carriage, and had her guards and sentries about her several residences, in European fashion."[204]

An advertisement in the January 12, 1860, *Pacific Commercial Advertiser* listed the address for each of the island governors. For Kekūanāoʻa, the announcement listed his location as: "Honolulu, near the Court House."[205]

Princess Victoria Kamāmalu died at Papakanene on May 29, 1866. Kekūanāoʻa died two years later at the same location on November 29, 1868. John Papa ʻĪʻī, the guardian of Kamāmalu at the Chiefs' Children's School recorded: "Kamamalu died [...] at Papakanene, Waialae. She was first taken ill in February, at a party for visitors at Haleakala House, the home of Pauahi. She was permitted to leave and went to Pihanakalani [Pihanakalani, Haʻimoeipo (Chapter 4)] house. From then on, the illness weighed upon her. It was thought that she would feel better at Pihanakalani, but she wanted to return to Papakanene. When she arrived there paralysis set in, and she was in bed for three weeks before she was taken. On Sunday evenings the members of her two churches

King Kamehameha V prepared Papakanene, the residence of the late Matiao Kekūanāoʻa, for the use of the Duke of Edinburgh during his visit in 1869. Photograph circa 1880 (courtesy Library of Congress Prints and Photographs Division, 2016651978).

pleaded with the Lord, but the trouble was too grave for their petition. The doctors, too, were unable to make her well. The length of her life was twenty-seven years and seven months."[206]

Despite being the residence of Victoria Kamāmalu, Kuhina Nui, and Kekūanāoʻa, the governor of Oʻahu and father of two kings, Papakanene would have another royal name popularly attached to it—that of the Prince Alfred, Duke of Edinburgh, then fourth in line for the British throne, behind his brother's son and eventual king, Prince George. Among his many foreign honors was Knight of the Order of Kamehameha I, given by Kamehameha V in 1865.

Kekūanāoʻa built the structure about 1853.[207] John Papa ʻĪʻī reported a much earlier use of the name Papakanene: "At the time Liholiho left for England, the chiefs were living along the beach of the harbor of Kou. Kalanimoku lived at the fort part of the time, but on this occasion he was at his place on the south side of the Fort in his first houses, Papakanene and Mokuaikaua."[208] Kalanimoku had died more than twenty-five years earlier in February 1827. So it was at the house that Kekūanāoʻa built in which the Duke of Edinburgh resided.

Liliʻuokalani tells of the visit of a member of British royalty to Hawaiʻi and his accommodations in one of the lost palaces: "In the year 1869 the Duke of Edinburgh, Prince Alfred of England, arrived in the harbor of Honolulu, being in command of Her Britannic Majesty's ship-of-war Galatea. As soon as the king learned of the duke's presence he made special preparations for his reception; and for his better accommodation on shore he assigned for his use the residence of the late Kekuanaoa, who died in November of the preceding year."[209]

A more contemporaneous account is contained in the August 2, 1869, issue of *The Friend*: "The Duke landed twenty minutes after ten, accompanied by his suite, all wearing the plain dress of the navy, and were met by H.B.M. Commissioner and Governor Dominis, the Duke accompanying the Governor to the Royal carriage, which he entered together with Major Wodehouse and two members of his suite, and were driven to the residence of His late Highness M. Kekuanaoa, which had been fitted expressly for his occupancy."[210] Company B of the Hawaiian Cavalry escorted the Duke to ʻIolani Palace for a short visit with Kamehameha V.

During the visit Nicholas Chevalier painted a watercolor drawing titled, "View from the verandah of the residence prepared for and occupied by the Duke of Edinburgh while staying at Honolulu the 30th of July 1869."[211] Sadly, the watercolor was not one retained in the Royal Collection of the British monarchy.

The father of Olympic swimmer Duke Kahanamoku was the first to be named Duke, in honor of the Duke of Edinburgh. Albert Pierce Taylor called the visit one of the four most significant events in the history of Hawaiʻi.[212] Thus, Papakanene became known also as Edinburgh or Edinboro House and the grounds as Edinburgh premises.

The brief visit to Honolulu lasted just under two weeks, with the duke departing for Japan on Monday, August 2. Less than a year thereafter the property was sold at public auction, on July 3, 1870, to H.A. Widemann. The haste in which he bought the property had later repercussions. In letter to S.G. Wilder, the Minister of Interior, H.A. Widemann asked that consideration be given him for the removal of part of a building and a fence at the Papakanene premises, which he bought "for the sake of winding up and settling the liabilities" of the estates of Victoria K. Kamāmalu (died 1866) and Matiao Kekūanāoʻa.

Widemann explained: "The Edinboro House (Papakane) was one of the parcels of land then offered and sold and your memorialist became the purchaser thereof. About a year before this sale, in preparation for the arrival of the Duke of Edinburgh, said premises were put into repair for the reception of the Duke of Edinboro and the makai fence was then at that time new."[213]

Widemann was unaware of the encroachment of the building and fence and emphasized that the building and fence were in the exact place that they were when he bought the property: "The premises in question were sold on July 3, 1870 at public auction and your memorialist was put into possession and has remained in quiet possession ever since and has not made any alteration in the buildings or fences but has left them just as he found them or nearly so believing himself to be in the enjoyment of his own."[214] Nine years later Widemann discovered differently. He bought the land believing that the makai fence on the property marked the boundary, because the king and his ministers arranged for the construction of the fence. He found out later, however, "From surveys made lately it appears that this makai fence is beyond the metes and bounds given in the Land Commission Award and stands absolutely, as is alleged, on Government land as does also a large part of the building makai of the dwelling."[215]

Widemann continued: "Your memorialist now finds himself in this position that he is asked to remove his own building from land he bought—for which he certainly paid and paid a high price—and on which he had seen ministers of the sovereign then reigning and the sovereign himself making the arrangements for the buildings and fences."[216]

Even though Papakanene no longer remained in the possession of royalty, its associations with royalty were fondly remembered. In the case of Papakanene, the marriage of the daughter of the newest occupant to "a gentleman well known in Auckland," sent mention of the house to the farthest corner of Polynesia:

> Papakanene, the well-known mansion of the late Governor Kekuanaoa, now owned and occupied by Hon. H.A. Wideman, was on Saturday evening last the scene of the most brilliant and fashionable assemblage that Honolulu has witnessed for a long time. It was the occasion of the marriage of Mr. Widemann's eldest daughter Emma to Henry Macfarlane, Esq., Secretary to the Legislative Assembly. There were present, His Majesty the King, accompanied with his staff in uniform, H.R.H. Prince Leleiohoku, H.R.H. Luka Keehlkolani [sic], Governor and Mrs Dominis, Hon. A.S. Cleghorn and wife, their Excellencies the King's Ministers, and the American, British and French Ministers, the Consular Corps, with the officers of the U.S. ship Benicia.[217]

An account of the destruction of a building at the Papakanene premises reveals the original purpose for one of the structures when Kekūanāoʻa lived there: "An old coral building, corner of Queen and Kaumana streets, is being taken down. Many years ago it was used as a canoe house by Governor Kekūanāoʻa. It was purchased in 1869 by Hon. H.A. Widemann and has been used by him since as a warehouse."[218]

After the overthrow Widemann would serve as envoy from the deposed Queen Liliʻuokalani to England and Germany. Following Widemann's death, his estate leased the property to the Union Feed Company. On December 27, 1900, workers from the company demolished Papakanene.[219] The *Honolulu Republican* recognized both the historic nature of the property as well as the inevitability of its destruction: "In former days the old palace was the center of the aristocratic life of royalty. The demolition of this landmark emphasized the swift transition that is taking place on these islands. The steady advance of industry and the implacable sway of commerce have no regard for the reminiscent marks of the days of idleness." The article mistakenly attributed ownership to Kamehameha V rather than Kekūanāoʻa. The Associated Press, on the other hand, recognized the historic residence as that of Kekūanāoʻa. "A historic structure, the old home of Kekuanaoa. [...] has been torn down to make way for a more modern building."[220] Thus a feed store, albeit modern, supplanted the storied residence at the turn of the century.

Puuonioni, Honolulu (before 1852–), Kekūanāoʻa

Kekūanāoʻa owned a house called Puuonioni. Its name is known, but its location is not. When he leased the former house to W.C. Parke, Kekūanāoʻa recalled building his "wooden frame house called Puuonioni, on the North West of Halehuki situated in Honolulu."[221]

Residence of Kapiʻolani at Kaʻalaʻa, Pauoa, Honolulu (1855–)

The uncle of Queen Emma and first husband of King David Kalākaua's queen, Kapiʻolani, Bennet Namakeha, was awarded 17.28 acres at Kaʻalaʻa-luna as Royal Patent 4371, Land Court Award 7260, at the intersection of Booth and Pauoa roads. The site appears on an 1896 map titled *Part of Kaalaaluna, Nuuanu Valley, Kona, Oahu*.[222] Kapiʻolani, who was born in Hilo, on December 31, 1834, married Namakeha on March 7, 1852.[223] King Kamehameha IV and Queen Emma entrusted the raising of their child, Albert Edward Kauikeaouli Leiopapa A Kamehameha, to Namakeha and Kapiʻolani. Namakeha was the uncle of Queen Emma, brother of her father, George Naʻea.

Namakeha's will, dated September 7, 1858, reflects these relationships of husband and uncle: "I give to Kapiolani, my beloved wife […] my land at Kaalaluna […] to be divided between her and Emma, the wife of the King. The division is as follows: the inland side of that property (Number 4371), inland of the road to Pauoa, is for Emma and the two irrigated taro terraces, Nakamakaweuweu, lying on the seaward side of that road. The remainder of that property, the area 'Ulu,' the houses and all the goods are for Kapiolani, if she will quitclaim her lawful one-third dower interest."[224] He appointed G.P. Judd and J. Piʻikoi to administer and execute the will. On September 3, 1860, he amended his will to give to Kapiʻolani the two irrigated taro terraces, Nakamakaweuweu, and the area "Ulu." "And the remainder of that property, the houses and all goods there, this is my houselot, are for the Prince of Hawaii. The nature of this is as follows: During Kapiolani's lifetime she alone is to receive the revenues of that lot and upon Kapiolani's death it is to be inherited by the Prince of Hawaii."[225] Namakeha also appointed Levi Haʻalelea (who was the husband of Kekauōnohi) as replacement for J. Piʻikoi, who died April 26, 1859. Kamakee Piʻikoi is listed as the owner of an adjacent property. Namakeha died December 27, 1860. Among the receipts charged to the Estate of Namakeha was one for W.H. Cox for four dollars "For removing the body to Mrs. Rookes [*sic*] house." Sadly, the Prince of Hawaiʻi never inherited the property; he died on August 27, 1862. Kapiʻolani married Kalākaua on December 19, 1863.

Mary Kinoiki Kekaulike, youngest sister of Kapiʻolani, also lived at the Kaʻalaʻa residence. Kekaulike married High Chief David Kahalepoui Piʻikoi (listed in the marriage

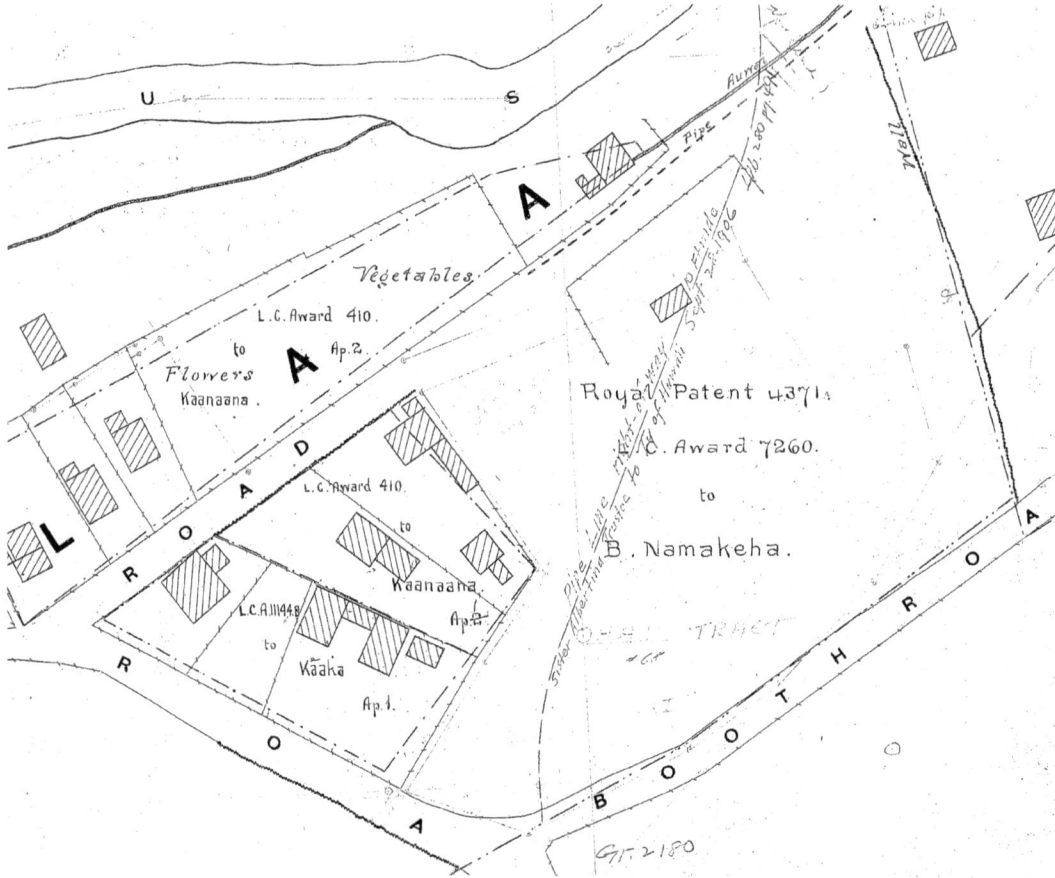

The will of Bennet Kamakeha gave his property at Kaʻalaʻa to his wife, Kapiʻolani, and Queen Emma's son, the Prince of Hawaiʻi. Detail of Registered Map 1791 (courtesy Land Survey Division, Department of Accounting and General Services, State of Hawaii).

record as Davida H. Piikoi) on February 25, 1861. The *Hawaiian Gazette* reported in his obituary that: "David Kawananakoa was born at Kaalaa, at the mouth of Pauoa Valley, Honolulu, on the old homestead of Kapiolani, queen-wife of King Kalakaua."[226] Maude Jones, librarian at the Hawaii State Archives (1931–1935 and 1937–1955), on the other hand, rejected Honolulu as the birthplace of Kawānanakoa and asserted that like his brothers he was born in Kōloa, Kauaʻi (Chapter 6).

Queen Emma bequeathed her portion of Kaʻalaʻa, a house lot, to her cousin, Stella Keomailani.

Residence of Iona Kapena, Peleula, Kaliu, Nuʻuanu, Honolulu

Another chief who had been elevated in rank along with Namakeha in 1845 was Iona [Jonah] Kapena, who maintained his residence just downstream from Kaʻalaʻa in Peleula, Kaliu, Nuʻuanu. According to the testimony of Kalehua, Kapena had lived in his residence, near a bend in Pauoa Stream, "at the time of Kamehameha I."[227] The testimony for Land Court Award 1090 revealed a dispute with his neighbor Mary Ann Aylett over the boundaries of the property. Another witness, Kahua, stated "I am capable of pointing out the boundaries in order to sever it (property)."²²⁸

Kapena, who had been appointed an assistant Supreme Court judge on May 10, 1842, was one of four witnesses on the deed of Kawaiahaʻo Church on July 21, 1842. The deed reflects the religious conversion of the *aliʻi*, especially the signatories, Kamehameha III and Kekāuluohi in Hawaii:

> In order to shew the nature of the doctrine believed by this church and in order that after generations may not mistake in this respect it is proper to commit to the custody of writing, in this instrument—the principal matter of belief of this Church, as follows—Will believe in Jehovah, that he is God, that He had no beginning, that He will have no end and that He will suffer no change, that He is not indeed visible to the bodily eye, but that He dwelleth everywhere that He Knoweth all things, that He is all powerful, all wise, and righteous altogether, that He possesses every glory and every good, that He created the earth and the heavens, and men and angels, both this world and the world to come and all things that are therein, that He continues and protects all things according to His own pleasure that he alone is God, and that all other things whatsoever which may be called god are vanity and the work of falsehood it absolveth sin and justifieth to Eternal life all the righteous who believe in Him—that there is no other name given under heaven among men whereby we may be Saved.—That He is the King of Zion, that His is all power in heaven and on earth, and that he will be the Judge of quick and dead.²²⁹

In 1845, Kapena was subject to what Hiram Bingham, pastor of Kawaiahaʻo Church, considered an extraordinary act: "About the same time, April 2, the people, in the exercise of the *right of suffrage* chose and sent to the legislature the following representatives, viz.: Iosua Kaeo, Iona Kapena, Paulo Kanoa, Namauu, Iona Piikoi, Beniti Namakeha, Kaisara Kapakea, and J.Y. Kanihoa [Kanehoa]."²³⁰ Actually, the named individuals were elected by nobles to the House of Nobles, a prerogative they continued to exercise until the Constitution of 1852, when the King named the members for life. The required notice of his election would not appear May 15, 1852. Kapena would later served as a Judge of the Supreme Court with Abner Paki, Iosua Kaʻeo, and Charles Kanaʻina.

He married Kahilipulu on September 2, 1846,²³¹ and later married Kalaikini on December 9, 1853. He died March 10, 1869, at Peleula.²³²

He adopted his nephew, John Makini Kapena,²³³ who served prominently during the reign of King David Kalākaua. It was John Makini Kapena who delivered the Hawaiian language address at the laying of the cornerstone for the current ʻIolani Palace (Chapter 3). Kapena married Emma, the daughter of Hawaiian historian David Malo.

Residence of Princess Ruth Keʻelikōlani, Emma Street, Kaakopua, Honolulu (c. 1860–October 15, 1873)

Princess Ruth Keʻelikōlani built a house on Emma Street, the thoroughfare named for the wife of her half-brother, Kamehameha IV. Although Kaakopua is better known as the site of the later Keōua Hale, an earlier house existed on the site that was destroyed by fire on the evening of October 15, 1873. Kaakopua appears on the list of lands given by the King to M. [Miriam] Kekauōnohi, governor of Kauaʻi and member of Privy Council. She was granddaughter of Kamehameha I. Prior to the introduction of Christianity, she was one of the wives of Kamehameha II. She was later the wife of A. Keliʻiahonui, son of Kaumuali'i, King of Kaua'i. After the death of Keli'iahonui, she married Levi Ha'alelea. She died in June 1851. The property eventually went to the husband of Princess Ruth, William Pitt Leleiohoku (March 31, 1821–October 21, 1848), and later to her. She in turn intended the property, indeed her entire estate, to go to her *hānai* son, William Pitt Leleiohoku Kalaho'olewa. Leleiohoku was brother of future monarchs David Kalākaua and Lili'uokalani. "Kaakopua Ili Aina Honolulu Oahu" is first on the list of properties deeded by Ke'elikōlani to William Pitt Leleiohoku Kalahoolewa on October 4, 1872.[234]

The house may have been built as early as 1860. Princess Ruth Ke'elikōlani wrote on September 3, 1860, from Hilo, a postscript to a letter in which she states: "My lot at Kaakopua must be fenced with a wooden one along the place that was measured. The caretaker of this lot, who is Kuhela k. is the bearer of this letter."[235] In a letter from Ruth to Lot, dated September 14, 1860, she asks him to "The lot at Kaakopua should be fenced with boards, and it is my desire that a large gate suitable for carriages to enter should be built at the front of the lot."

She also asks to him to furnish lumber for the residence: "You may buy some planed boards for me, and you can calculate the amount of the boards to build the house: Being as follows:

Length of the house,	26 feet;
Width of the house	16 feet
Height of the posts	12 feet
Width of the veranda	8 feet
Height of the veranda posts	7½ feet
8 windows	
4 doors	

It is my wish that you secure enough planed boards to cover the body of the house all around the posts, and the upper part of the house to be thatched Hawaiian Style. Also the planed boards to build two small rooms on the veranda, 12 feet long and 8 feet wide, the two being alike. I am forwarding a sketch of the house site so that you may know."[236] Unfortunately the sketch, like the house, no longer survives. The work at Kaakopua remained on her mind, even in a letter concerning the funeral expenses of her son, John William Pitt Kīna'u. She wrote on September 21, 1860: "You let me know the amount of money expended for the fence boards at Kaakopua, so that I may be able to know."[237]

If the Kaakopua house was built to specifications, it would have been a rare example of a hybrid wooden and thatched structure. Princess Keelikolani was known to prefer the *hale pili* over the western structures. Her death was in the *hale pili* on the grounds of Hulihe'e Palace rather than the nearby Western structure.

Later, on October 3, 1860, she writes that "she has been told the posts of her fence are small and wants him to put in large posts." She wrote to C.P. "Kale" Turner from Kailua, Kona, on July 15, 1861: "This is the first time I have written to you again. I let you know that what H. Kanuu told you in my name, you do a good job on my house which you spoke to me about in the way that you think to be proper. What you said about, what is still wanted for the house, I have informed L. Kamehameha, and you should wait, and [if] it does not arrive very soon, you write to Kamehameha in my name. If the brown cotton [*kūkaenalo*, unbleached muslin or beeswax] is all put on [the] inside, your [*sic*] let me know, the same also with everything else."[238]

The 1869 *Honolulu Directory* lists "Governess of Hawaii, residence 16 Emma street."[239]

The *Pacific Commercial Advertiser* reported that the destruction of the Emma Street house took place on the evening of Wednesday, October 15, 1873.

Queen Emma wrote about the fire in a letter to Peter Kaʻeo dated October 20, 1873: "The Governess Ruth's house was burnt to the ground last Wednesday night. Not a thing was saved from it. Next morning I went up and wilst [sic] viewing the ruins Ahala to get people to search amongst the ashes for trinkets. [We] found several rings [but] most of the natives stood by [and] never offered to help or quench the fire."[240]

How the fire started is unknown, but arson was suspected because "no kerosene lamp or lamp of any kind [was] lighted in the house that was burned. It is even asserted that there were no matches on the premises, the occupants for that reason going to a neighboring house to light their pipes a few minutes before the fire broke out."[241] The fire also resulted in the destruction of many valuables in the house. Strangely, the watch of William Pitt Leleiohoku found its way out of the burning building: "But by advertisement in another column it will be seen that someone actually 'saved' Mr. Leleiohoku's gold watch and chain."[242]

The inability of firefighters to locate the nearest fire hydrant also contributed to the total loss of the royal residence. The foremen of one of the companies looked in vain for the plug on the upper part of Emma Street. "Of course he did not find it," the newspaper wryly noted, "for as stated by us some time ago, there is but one hydrant in the whole length of Emma street, and that is below the square."[243] The fire and mix-up with the hydrant no doubt prompted a petition sent on August 13, 1874, regarding the water supply on Emma Street. The Minister of the Interior replied that a 4-inch pipe and hydrant were going to be installed.[244]

Residence of Archibald S. Cleghorn, Emma Street, Honolulu (c. 1869–1879)

On January 29, 1866, Archibald Scott Cleghorn bought five pieces of land from E.P. Kamaipeletani for $1,375.[245] The 1869 administrator's sale for the neighboring Kaikaika estate refers to "all that lot of land, on the eastern side of Emma Street, Honolulu, *makai* and adjoining the premises of A.S. Cleghorn."[246] The 1869 *Honolulu Directory* lists Cleghorn's residence as "35 Emma Street."[247] It was at his Emma street residence that Princess Kaʻiulani was born on October 16, 1875.

The proximity of his house to Emma Square and his demonstrated interest in horticulture most likely influenced the Minister of the Interior, W.L. Moehonua, to appoint Cleghorn "to take charge of 'Emma Square' now under the care of Jno. Montgomery Esqr."[248]

Cleghorn lived at the Emma Street until 1878, when he sold his residence for $14,000 to James Campbell. The next year Campbell married Abigail Kuaihelani Mapinepine Bright, and the house became a center of Hawaiian society. James Campbell, landowner, has his "p r" or "personal residence" recorded as "36 Emma street."[249] Four years later, James Campbell, now "capitalist and proprietor Kahuku Stock Ranch" is listed in the 1884 *McKenney's Hawaiian Directory* as living at "34 Emma."[250]

The first daughter of James and Abigail Campbell, Abbie Margaret Campbell, born September 26, 1880, died of convulsions on July 23, 1882, aged 21 months and 27 days.[251] Her funeral took place from the Emma Street residence. The couple's only son, James,

The former Cleghorn residence on Emma Street, where Princess Kaʻiulani was born, later served as the site of the Pacific Club (courtesy Hawaii State Archives, PPBAC-1-5-001).

who was born in Waikiki in 1886, died there on March 23, 1889, at age 3, and had his funeral at Kawaiahaʻo. Unlike her brother, the funeral for the two-year-old daughter of James and Abigail Campbell, Royalist Maddire Laakapu Campbell,[252] took place at the Emma Street residence on March 6, 1896.[253] She had died at Kapiolani Park. Four years later, her father, James Campbell, died at his Emma Street residence on April 21, 1900. The funeral took place at the same location two days later.[254]

Abigail Campbell married Col. Samuel Parker, owner of Parker Ranch on Hawaiʻi island, in at the Occidental Hotel in San Francisco on January 3, 1902.[255] Parker's first wife, Hattie, had died six months earlier. On January 6, 1902, Abigail Campbell Parker's daughter, Abigail Campbell, married Prince David Kawānanakoa at the same hotel where her mother's wedding took place.[256] The homecoming for the Parker and Campbell families was a greatly anticipated event. Abigail Campbell, now Mrs. Samuel Parker, shared what she planned upon her return to Hawaiʻi:

> I expect to be home at my Emma street house, which has been greatly improved and enlarged in the last few months. I have bought many statues and decorations in Europe, and have also ordered furniture from a house here. My daughter Alice will come of age on March 17, and I expect to give her a reception on that day. Besides I will give a reception to Prince David and his bride [her daughter Abigail Campbell], and will be at home to Mr. Parker's and my friends.[257]

In January 1902, Parker had been initially selected to replace Emma Street neighbor Sanford Ballard Dole as governor of Hawai'i, though George R. Carter eventually succeeded Dole in 1903.[258] A *Bulletin* reporter approached Samuel Parker in August 1902 at his Emma Street residence to ask him if he would be running for delegate. Parker told the reporter he would not run, but added: "I believe the Republican party can put up a man and win in this next campaign but I will not be that man."[259] The Republicans were indeed successful with their candidate for delegate in 1902, Prince Jonah Kūhiō Kalaniana'ole, the brother of Parker's son-in-law, Prince David Kawānanakoa. Although Parker himself would not run, his Emma Street house nevertheless was the location for political gatherings. In September 1902, his wife gave a poi lunch for the wives of members of the senatorial commission, and afterwards Samuel Parker returned with the members and "where they joined the jolly party."[260] Among the guests at the lunch were residents of other royal residences: Queen Lili'uokalani (Mu'olaulani), Mrs. Haalelea (Hōlani), and Mrs. Nāwahī (Mauna Kamala).

The residence was the site of a spectacular burglary the next year, when a blue diamond ring worth $4,500 and other jewels were taken from a jewel box kept at the Emma Street residence. The crime took place when Abigail Campbell was attending the dedication of the Alexander Young Hotel, which had been built over a portion of the childhood home of Lili'uokalani. Because several other jewels were left in the box, the police were "at a loss as to who [could] have perpetuated the crime."[261] The remaining jewels were worth $80,000.[262] In 2013 dollars the amount would be roughly $2.1 million.[263] The family's trusted coachman eventually confessed to the crime and most of the jewels were recovered.[264]

For several years Prince David Kawānanakoa and his wife, the Princess Abigail W. Kawānanakoa, lived in the Emma Street house before they moved to their Pensacola Street estate now occupied by Hawaiian Mission Academy.[265] The *Independent* announced in March 1902: "Prince and Princess Kawananakoa are now domiciled at the Campbell mansion on Emma street together with Col. And Mrs. Sam Parker."[266] On January 13, 1905, the *Hawaiian Star* announced: "Princess Kawananakoa will receive this afternoon from 3 to 5 o'clock at her Emma Street residence."[267] Princess Kawananakoa also entertained at her mother's home. The "Social Side of Life" column in the *Evening Bulletin* called a January 1905 gathering for Mrs. Edward Tenney: "One of the prettiest lunches of the season."[268] It noted that the decorations included an "historic centerpiece once owned by King Kalakaua."[269] A reception at the Emma Street residence for bride, Alice Kamokila Campbell, followed her wedding to Walter Macfarlane on June 21, 1905.[270] The *Hawaiian Gazette* gushed: "As one approached the Emma street residence of the Campbell-Parkers the display of electricity was such as to almost dazzle the guests, for the trees in the lawn were strung with electric lights and under the enormous tree in the center of the yard were globes of white light making a brilliancy which has never been rivaled in Honolulu."[271] Guests included Queen Liliuokalani, Archibald Cleghorn, the Prince and Princess Kawānanakoa and Prince and Princess Kalaniana'ole.

The probate of the estate of James Campbell was completed in 1905. The Emma street residence was valued at $20,000, and the furnishing valued at another $10,562.05, when the final accounts were approved in July 1905 by Judge Lindsay. The total estate, which included a mortgage to Queen Lili'uokalani for $35,000, totaled more than $1.9 million.[272] The $125,000 bond filed the trustee's attorneys, Robert W. Shingle and A. Lewis, Jr., was "said to be the largest on file in the local courts."[273]

On May 17, 1908, Abigail Campbell Parker gave a poi luncheon in honor of her husband's birthday.[274] Parker gave another luncheon on Friday, October 30, 1908, where she announced to friends that she was going in for an operation the next day.[275] Abigail Campbell Parker died October 31, 1908, from heart failure following a breast cancer operation.[276] Her body was moved from the hospital to her Emma Street residence.[277]

The funeral for Abigail K. Parker would take place in the "reception parlor" at the Emma Street residence on Wednesday, November 4, 1908.[278] The Hui Kaahumanu, of which Abigail Parker had been a member, kept vigil at the Emma Street house during the night before the services.[279] The service overflowed from the parlor: "In the makai drawing room were seated a number of prominent women, while in the rear lanai were seated the members of the Hui Kaahumanu and other Hawaiian Societies."[280] In Abigail Parker's will "the Emma Street house and lot," were left to Muriel Campbell, but the reference was not to the Emma Street residence that the Campbell-Parkers had lived in, but to a smaller residence makai of the property known as the Freeth cottage.[281] The will also split the income from her estate between her four daughters and her granddaughter, Princess Kapiʻolani, daughter of Prince David Kawānanakoa and Princess Abigail Kawānanakoa.[282]

Shingle would marry one of the Campbell daughters, Ethel Muriel Campbell, on February 18, 1909.[283] Shingle would also serve as the guardian of Mary Beatrice Campbell.[284] In 1911 the Emma Street residence was once again in the courts, this time concerning use and payment for repairs. The court decided that the $4,000 of repairs would be paid out of the "contingent interest of Mary Beatrice Campbell" and that she would receive the rental income. The case centered on the unmarried minor daughter because will directed that "each of the daughters should have use of the Emma Street residence for a home until married but not longer. Judge Robinson takes the view that it makes no difference whether the use is personal or by way of yielding a rental to the beneficiary."[285]

Like her sister Abigail and mother before her, the wedding of Mary Beatrice Campbell took place in San Francisco. She married George C. Beckley there on August 1, 1911.[286] Now that the last sister had married, no one was entitled to live at the Emma Street residence, so James Campbell's daughters (Abigail W. Kawānanakoa, Alice K. Macfarlane, Muriel C. Shingle and Mary Beatrice Beckley) in 1912 sold their interest in the Emma Street mansion to Robert Shingle, Muriel's husband, for $36,000.

Colonial Hotel

From 1912 The Colonial Hotel, managed by Mary Johnson, offered boarding at 1451–1451 Emma.[287] That year the hotel expanded the veranda and made repairs for a total of $475. It also built two cottages for $6,000.[288] In 1915 the Colonial was the site of a display of "unusual exhibit of Oriental embroidered art goods, lingerie and table linen."[289] The exhibit was shown by Mrs. L.W. Taylor, a guest at the hotel.

In 1924 the Shingles moved to Makiki [at 1927 Makiki Street] and sold the property for $100,000 to Lee Chong, C.S. Wing and Chong Kam. The Colonial Hotel, "A Select and Refined Private Hotel Within Easy Walking Distance of Business Section,"[290] continued to do business at 1451–1473 Emma.

Pacific Club

Two years later, on June 18, 1926, the Pacific Club paid $126,000 for the residence in which its former charter member and longtime president, Archibald Cleghorn, and his wife, Princess Likelike, had once lived. Before the sale to the Pacific Club, the mansion had been eyed by at least a couple of other parties. The University Club, which later merged with the Pacific Club, had been in negotiation in July 1909 to purchase the mansion.[291] On July 19, 1909, it was announced that "had very nearly completed negotiations."[292] The mansion was also proposed for the site of the U.S. Army headquarters.[293]

The Colonial Hotel moved to 1447 Pensacola Street;[294] the Pacific Club from Beretania and Alakea Streets to 1453 Emma Street.[295] In a foreclosure sale the Emma Street property was sold to Hugh Howell Jr. for $65,000. He in turn sold the property back to the Pacific Club on February 25, 1938, for $10. The club celebrated its 100th anniversary in the house in 1951.[296] A March 30, 1960, photo montage shows the destruction of the Emma Street house, with a photograph of its cupola at ground level.[297] The demise of the birthplace of Princess Kaʻiulani shared equal news value as the destruction of the popular eatery, the Kau Kau Korner, in an article titled "Landmarks Going Down." The current Pacific Club complex, designed by Vladimir Ossipoff, replaced the former Cleghorn house.

Honuakaha, Honolulu (c. 1860–1901), King Kalākaua and Queen Kapiʻolani

The residence of King Kalākaua, *makai* of Kawaiahaʻo Church, served as his residence before his election as king. During the smallpox epidemic in 1853 Honuakaha served as one of the hospitals where "persons in and about Honolulu who are desirous of receiving food, medicines and attendance at the expense of the Government"[298] came. The location was under the medical care of Dr. Edward Hoffman.[299] At that time Honuakaha was most likely still owned by Kinimaka, who had property on both sides of Punchbowl Street. Kinimaka received the property as Land Court Award 129. The early history of Honuakaha was remembered in 1901: "Away back in the 60's, when Kalakaua, then plain David Kalakaua, was the employee of the government, he had deeded to him these premises. They came to him through his kahua-Alii, Kinimaka, one of the chiefs who brought up David to manhood."[300] Chiefess L.H. Kaniu, the wife of Kinimaka, was the daughter of Kalailua, the sister of Aikanaka, the grandfather of Kalākaua. Registered map 861 shows a lot on the Diamond Head-makai corner of Punchbowl and Queen streets labeled "H.M. Kalakaua."

A story in the *Pacific Commercial Advertiser* in 1862 recounts a parade of the Prince of Hawaiʻi and the Honolulu fire department and the post-event gathering: "They then repaired to a luau prepared for them by the King near the dwelling of David Kalakaua, Esq, west of the stone church. The feast was spread under a large tent, erected for the occasion, and that it was fully appreciated by the guests, was amply attested."[301] The 1869 *Honolulu Directory, and Historical Sketch of the Hawaiian or Sandwich Islands* lists the address for the residence of "Kalakaua D., High Chief" as "9 Punchbowl."[302]

Besides the King and Queen retainers also took up residence at Honuakaha. The Hon. E.K. Lilikalani, "member Legislature and secretary to Her Majesty the Queen"

A depiction of the luau for the "Base-Ball Tourists" at Honuakaha. From *Athletic Sports in America, England and Australia* (1889).

has his residence listed in the 1884 *McKenney's Hawaiian Directory* as "Honnakaha [sic] Place."[303]

In 1888 Honuakaha provided the site for a feast for a group of "baseball tourists" that included Albert Goodwill Spalding, baseball manager and promoter of Abner Doubleday as the inventor of baseball. (Although he was still alive in 1892, no account lists the attendance of the true "Father of Baseball," Hawai'i resident Alexander Joy Cartwright.)

After being petitioned to play a game of baseball, and determining that playing on a Sunday violated Hawai'i law, the group went on a sightseeing tour of Honolulu. That evening:

> the party again rendezvoused at the Hawaiian Hotel, and from there went to Queen Kapiolani's private retreat, Honuakaha, at the corner of Queen and Punchbowl streets, to participate in a native feast provided by the King, Hons. S. Parker, J. A. Cummins, J. Ena, and Geo. C. Beckley.
>
> The grounds presented a charming appearance. Illuminations among the trees and shrubs were profuse and pretty.[304]

The event made such an impression on the attendees that a painting of the feast at Honuakaha was included in *Athletic Sports in America, England and Australia*.

When Robert Wilcox attempted to overturn the Bayonet Constitution, he did not find the king at 'Iolani Palace. King Kalākaua, "who was sleeping at Honuakaha, the Queen's private residence, Queen and Punchbowl streets, was apprised of the situation by telephone from one of the native women within the Palace. His Majesty immediately telephoned to Jas. W. Robertson, Vice Chamberlain, who repaired with all haste to the King, and they hurried off to the royal boathouse, where the King has remained ever since, the royal standard floating from the flagstaff."³⁰⁵ Testimony at the trial after the failed Wilcox revolution revealed that the leaders knew the king was at Honuakaha:

> The nature of the discussion was whether we should proceed to the palace Honuakaha. In reference to going to Honuakaha we heard the king was there and we wanted to take him to the palace for protection.
> We decided to go into the palace.³⁰⁶

In June 1891, Prince Jonah Kūhiō Kalaniana'ole started an organization that no doubt would have pleased his recently deceased uncle. Named for his cousin, Ka'iulani, the boat club met at the residence of his aunt, Kapi'olani, under the sponsorship of the prince.³⁰⁷

For Queen Kapi'olani's own charitable projects, her home on Punchbowl, which the newspaper inaccurately called Luakaha, provided an easily reached venue. A year after the death of her husband, King Kalākaua, during the reign of her sister-in-law, Lili'uokalani, an exercise in *noblesse oblige* took place for the maternity home that would later bear her name:

> H. M. Kapiolani, Queen Dowager, will give a grand luau on Friday next for the benefit of benevolent societies in general and the Maternity Home especially. It is intended the luau will be had at her Luakaha [sic] residence, Punchbowl street. A nominal sum will be charged. The lay out will be in the Hawaiian fashion. A large crowd ought to be present, to advance the feast's beneficent purposes. The Maternity Home, it has been found out, is deficient in certain things, and it is intended to enlarge the building and provide more convenient accommodations. The Queen Dowager was the prime mover in establishing the Home.³⁰⁸

Although no images of the interior of Honuakaha exist, a comprehensive list of its contents does. The inventory, by William Owen Smith, is undated, but probably dates to just after the overthrow, as does the inventory of Hale 'Ākala.³⁰⁹ The inventory of the Honuakaha included a multicultural mix of furnishings. Besides the Western furnishings like the oak sideboard and marble table, the residence also featured a Japanese screen and rolls of Japanese wallpaper.³¹⁰ Honuakaha was for a time the site of the Liloa Stone before its move to Pualeilani and then to the 'Iolani Place grounds in 1930.³¹¹

Less than two weeks after the Chinatown fire in 1900, Honuakaha was being offered by Lewers and Cooke for a shelter to house persons made homeless by the destruction of the "quarantine district." Albert V. Gear, secretary of the committee appointed by the executive "to devise ways and means for caring for persons after their release from quarantine" recommended to the cabinet several sites in Honolulu. Prominent on the list was "First, a portion of the land on Punchbowl street, known as 'Kapiolani premises.' This land was offered by Lewers and Cooke free of rent for one year, and the committee recommended it for immediate use. [...] It was decided to at once accept the Kapiolani premises and the same were taken in hand later in the afternoon."³¹²

Hundreds would soon thereafter fill the site. "Some 500 natives were taken to Honuakaha last night and this morning about half the number were removed to the Kakaako warehouse detention camp. [...] The natives remaining at Honuakaha are being taken care of today by the Hawaiian Relief Society and a number of others. There are about 60 natives in Prince Jonah Kalanianaole's place opposite Kawaiahao church on King street."³¹³

Not everyone favored the use of Honuakaha, not of respect for its historical significance, but because of the potential health threat posed by the overcrowded site. The *Independent* expressed: "Mr. C.M. [Charles Montague] Cooke is to be thanked for his generous offer in allowing the Board of Health to utilize his place but if some other site can be secured we think it would be good policy of the government to keep those who have lived in infected quarters as far away from the crowded center of town as possible."[314]

Within another year the physical structure on the property would be gone. Just eight years after the overthrow another lost palace would no longer serve as a site of remembrance of the monarchy:

> One by one the homes—once they were called palaces—of the former kings, queens, princesses and princes of Hawaii, are being disposed of under the auctioneer's hammer; in many cases to purchasers whom these royal owners would not have deigned to greet with even so much as a glance when they were clothed with the majesty of their royal prerogatives.
>
> Yesterday as the noon whistles were sounding a once royal residence was knocked down by Auctioneer Morgan to a Japanese to whom sentiment in matters pertaining to faded royalty, or relic-worshipping were foreign.
>
> To the buyer it was not sentiment, but dollars. One hundred and fifty dollars cash was paid for the house which was once the favorite recreation residence of the late King Kalakaua.
>
> Honouakaha [sic] is the name of the premises on Punchbowl street near Queen, where King Kalakaua and Queen Kapiolani were often wont to pass many days of quietude from the affairs of state, and where lately the two princes and heirs of Queen Kapiolani, David and Cupid, made their town home.
>
> Away back in the 60's, when Kalakaua, then plain David Kalakaua, was the employee of the government, he had deeded to him these premises.
>
> They came to him through his kahua-Alii, Kinimaka, one of the chiefs who brought up David to manhood. During the days before he was elected king, and when creditors pressed Kalakaua for money, Honouakaha [sic] was sold at public auction. It did not pass out of the hands of the family, for his wife, Kapiolani, bought the property back.
>
> During the palmy days of his reign as king the place was used as a resting place. It was near his boathouse, and at that time was somewhat secluded and apart from the busy portion of the town. In one part were houses for his many retainers, and many were the luaus and other entertainments given there. It was prettily hedged in with ti plants.
>
> Upon his death, Queen Kapiolani used the place for her town residence, and until ill health compelled her to keep to her Waikiki residence, where she died. Honouakaha [sic] was deeded to the two princes, and they resided there until their aunt's death, when they took up their residence at Waikiki.
>
> Since then the old house has gone into rapid decay.[315]

Healani Boat House, Honolulu (bef. 1883–after 1885), King Kalākaua

Besides his mainly residential buildings, King Kalākaua built a boathouse in Honolulu that he called Healani, or Heavenly Call. The boathouse combined several aspects

Opposite, top: Kalākaua stayed at Healani Boathouse during the 1889 Wilcox Revolution (courtesy Hawaii State Archives, PP-96-14-007). *Opposite, bottom:* King Kalākaua entertained Robert Louis Stevenson at the Healani Boathouse in 1889 (courtesy Hawaii State Archives, PP-96-14-001).

Chapter 5. Other Royal Residences of O'ahu   183

appreciated by the king: athleticism, pageantry, and entertainment. It was here that Kalākaua entertained Robert Louis Stevenson.

Kalākaua was at Healani when Robert Wilcox attempted to restore the rights of the monarch during the ill-fated Wilcox Rebellion of 1889.

Malamanui, Kalākaua's Hunting Lodge, Schofield Barracks, Wahiawā, Oʻahu

Besides the boathouse, Kalākaua maintained another specialty residence, this one devoted to the hunt. At Wahiawā, on the Leilehua plain of Oʻahu, the king built a hunting lodge he called Malamanui. Notes scribbled on the back of letterhead of Curtis P. Iaukea, Office of the Secretary of the Territory, record: "Alika Dowsett says that the Ranch Home now occupied by the Schofield Bk. Leilehua was built by King Kalakaua and C.H. Judd soon after they had bought out the Dowsett and Galbraith ranch interest in. The name 'Malamanui' was given to the House by the King. Kalakaua and Judd were partners. Name Leilehua was given the ranch after Judd and King bought."[316] The ranch was occupied by at least 1887. That year Kalākaua sent an agreement of sale for $3,000 to Alexander Joy Cartwright for "three hundred head of cattle now running at large on the land known as the Leilehua Ranch and especially running on the land of Waianae-uka and branded /drawing of brand/."

Trustees of His Majesty's Estate sold the 20,000 acres of Leilehua Ranch at auction on March 12, 1889.[317] On the Friday following the auction, March 19, 1889, Kalākaua's partner in the ranch, Col. C.H. Judd, relocated his family and his "movables" to Kualoa.[318]

Though primarily a cattle ranch, Leilehua Ranch continued its hunting legacy. In 1893, Henry Davis, E.I. Spaulding and S.G. Wilder held the private shooting rights to Leilehua Ranch. September marked the beginning of the hunting season for native ducks. The assessment of hunting at Leilehua Ranch concluded: "Good shooting for duck and pheasant are to be found thereon."[319]

Upon annexation of Hawaiʻi in 1898, the Leilehua Ranch lands were reserved for War Department use.[320]

The Army started an unnamed army post there in 1909. Rumors first suggested the post might be named for General Earl D. Thomas,[321] but the camp was eventually named for Major General J.M. Schofield, who had come to Hawaiʻi in 1872 to survey Pearl Harbor. The Leilehua Ranch House later became part of Schofield Barracks and the home of its commanding officer.

The large structure provided the venue for a double wedding in 1913: "Lieutenant Sheridan is at present at Fort Huachuca, where the Fifth Cavalry arrived last week and the time of his return to Honolulu is not yet known but it is likely that the young officer will return in a very short time and that the home of Colonel [George K.] McGunnegle, which was formerly King Kalakaua's hunting lodge will be the scene of a double military wedding in the very near future."[322]

As a young girl, Carita Rodby, lived at Schofield Barracks between 1911 and 1917. She recalled: "I know that where the golf course is now was King Kalakaua's hunting lodge."[323]

The use of the structure would shift from residential to recreational when the U.S.

Army started constructing housing at Schofield Barracks. The assessment of the structure by Major General William Giles Harding Carter, commanding officer of the U.S. Army Hawaiian Division from January 1914 to his retirement in November 1915, set into motion the transition of Kalākaua's hunting lodge to a military country club:

> Taking everything into consideration, I am of the opinion that the Leilehua Ranch House now occupied by the Commanding General, Schofield Barracks, should, when permanent quarters are completed for that officer, be set aside as a country club by officers of the garrison [...] The use of this house and grounds would admit of suitability for the entertainment of large parties of visitors. It was so used recently during the visit of the large congressional delegation here. It will be of great value if set aside for the use of the whole post, and this use will forestall any application by groups of bachelors to occupy this building when vacated. It is too good to be pulled down and if set aside for the officers an opportunity now exists for obtaining large quantities of suitable shrubs and trees from the agricultural station here, to increase its attractiveness. [...]
>
> The request was returned with the approval of the secretary of war and the following order has been issued: "Pursuant to authority of the secretary of war the building on the reservation at Schofield Barracks, known as the King's hunting lodge, is hereby set aside for use as a country club for the officers of the garrison and be dedicated to that use when quarters for the commanding general are completed."[324]

On Saturday, December 15, 1917, non-commissioned officers hosted a dance "in the officers' club at Schofield with the band in atteddance [sic]."[325] By 1928 the transition from royal retreat to military recreation center was fully realized, a was a shift from use by officers only to use also by enlisted men: "The new club house is located in a beautiful grove of Hawaiian trees, the former site of King Kalakaua's Hunting Lodge. In the old days of the Hawaiian royalty the king and his court would come here to the Uplands of Schofield for their summer sports and hunting. The old hunting lodge has been entirely remodeled and modernized in every respect for the golf club. Golf is a popular game the year around at Schofield Barracks, not only among the officers but among the enlisted men as well."[326]

Antoinette Withington wrote of the hunting lodge in 1937: "The site of Schofield Barracks was once a hunting-lodge of a king—a great plateau of open country lying between the Waianae Mountains and the Koolau range. King Kalakaua's hunting-lodge still remains on the reservation."[327]

Although less distant than Malamanui, Queen Emma often retreated to her remote residence at Puʻuloa, Oʻahu.

Residence of Queen Emma, Puʻuloa, ʻEwa, Oʻahu (before 1873–after 1883)

On land now occupied by Fort Kamehameha, on the Waikīkī side of the mouth of Pearl Harbor, Queen Emma maintained a residence at Puʻuloa. Indeed, the name of the installation originally honored her instead of the warrior king. Initially called the Reservation at Queen Emma Point, the land was purchased from the Queen Emma Estate in 1907 to site three and later four artillery batteries.

The remote location of her Puʻuloa house, eight miles by road back to Honolulu, made for a lengthy trip to her other residences at Rooke House, Hānaiakamalama and the Marine Residence at Waikīkī. Although Emma refers to the location of the residence as Puʻuloa, the former name of Pearl Harbor, her house on the Waikīkī side of the mouth of the anchorage was in the ahupuaʻa of Hālawa.

During her stay at Puʻuloa on March 13, 1883, Emma wrote to Flora Jones, who she called "Ihilani": "I have been so taken up with the carpenters have had very little time to scribble off my letter and the distance away from town is a nuisance." She closed her letter with her plans to return to Honolulu from Puʻuloa: "I shall go into town for Passion week and return directly after Easter Day."[328] Easter Sunday took place on March 25 that year. Emma stopped in Moanalua on her return trip to Puʻuloa. She told Jones in a letter from Moanalua, dated March 27: "On my way to Puuloa we have stopped here at the Governor's [John Dominis] cottage for a night to allow our boys time for cutting hay as feed for our animals down at the beach. I shall now remain at Puuloa till our house building is pau save only for riding up for the Sunday services."[329] Her letter to Jones on April 3, revealed the status of the building project:

> We are still here living like the Arabs in tents as the old house is being moved away to make place for the new cottage. You will never wish to come here twice if you only saw it once. It is precisely like the country between Capt. Makee's Landing [Makena, Maui] and Waikapu, open and barren but this has a greener appearance from being over grown with horrid Mimosa bushes. The houses are all on the coast with not a shade tree near them. The two and only trees throughout the place are in front and at rear of our house so that my expectant groves of cocoanuts Algerobas [Algarrobas], Monkey Pods, Ponciannas [Poincianas] etc etc. are yet in the shell as it were because they are only just above ground now. It is very hot during the summer out of the house but delightfully cool in the shade.
>
> I cannot give a good description of this marine residence or rather a flattering picture but I enjoy the freedom and quiet which reigns and I think like at least that, so whenever you are down again in Honolulu I will bring you here and then you can form your own conclusions of it.[330]

The "old house," labeled "Queen Emma," appears on an 1873 map titled *Pearl Lochs and Puuloa Entrance, Ewa, Oahu*, by C.J. Lyons.

Emma also asked Jones for a comparison of the weather: "I wonder if you are having fine weather again. It is broiling here."[331]

Emma records the construction of the new house at Puʻuloa "home" when next she wrote Flora Jones. In the intervening time, Princess Ruth Keʻelikōlani had died in her *hale pili* in Kailua, North Kona (Chapter 3). Emma wrote on Wednesday, July 10, 1883: "Your letter of last week is safely received, reading it in the carriage on my way home from Ruth's or Keelikolani's [Keōua Hale] where Mr. and Mrs. Bishop is for the present. I came direct here [Puʻuloa] from there [Rooke House] to oversee the carting of lumber from beach to this place, or rather to make arrangements for so doing. The girls come down tomorrow, then we all go up to town for spending Thursday, Friday and Saturday at Kahala with Mrs. Bishop at one of the late Governess' places on the other side of Telegraph station."

The activities kept Emma very busy after the death of Princess Ruth. Emma wrote: "then my school children [from St. Andrew's Priory] came out we have devoted our time to them besides moving about to my three houses of Nuuanu, Waikiki and here [Puʻuloa].[332]

Emma continued to spend time at each of her four houses. In a letter from Rooke House on August 7, 1883, she complained: "the place at Puuloa still goes on so slowly consequently taking me continually down there."³³³ The burden of managing four residences again came up in a letter to Flora Jones in October 9, 1883. In apologizing for missed chances to send letters to her friend, Emma noted: "but really we have been on the move so much between our various places of Waikiki, Puuloa and Nuuanu [Hānaiakamalama] that it takes time and people to manage it. I am now at Waikiki making a pond near the high road for my water lily but it has taken so much time and will keep us at it all this month. I think I will take a run to Puuloa in the mean time."³³⁴

The map titled *Mouth and Bar of Ewa or Pearl River, Island of Oahu, Hawaiian Group* also provides an element concerning the Puʻuloa residence unrecorded about most of the lost palaces—their color. The 1873 map labeled the residence: "House (yellow color)." Another 1873 map described the navigational aid as "Large square yellow house with two bushy trees in front."³³⁵ An 1885 navigation guide also noted the color: "near the entrance, on the eastern side, is a large yellow building, called Queen Emma's house."³³⁶ The new house retained the color of the old one.

Technology, too, has given a more precise indication of the location of the house. In 2005, Lawrence B. Conyers, of the department of anthropology at the University of Denver, and Samuel Connell, of the department of anthropology at Foothill College, identified the possible foundation of Queen Emma's residence using ground penetrating radar. They reported: "the square corner of what appears to be the foundation of Queen Emma's house became visible in the general area indicated by the historic maps."³³⁷

Princess Ruth Keʻelikōlani, the half-sister of Emma's husband, Kamehameha IV, chose a suburban residence much closer to town.

Residence at Mauna Kamala (1878, moved 1901, demolished after 1939), Princess Ruth Keʻelikōlani

During the fourth year of the reign of King Kalākaua, Princess Ruth Keʻelikōlani built her home in the suburb of Kapālama at Mauna Kamala. Her home at Kaakopua, an *ʻili* of Honolulu, on Emma Street (Chapter 5) had been destroyed by fire on October 15, 1873.

The first mention of residence appears in the *Pacific Commercial Advertiser* in a September 1878 account of a "house-warming on Saturday last [August 31], at her new residence on King street, beyond Liliha street, which was attended by a large number of personal friends and others, who thoroughly enjoyed themselves."³³⁸ Mauna Kamala was bounded by Asylum Road (now called Pālama Street) on the northwest, King Street to the southwest and what today is Pua Lane on the southeast. Kanoa Lane today bisects the Mauna Kamala site, though it did not extend to Pālama Street when Princess Ruth's house was located there. The earliest depiction, in an 1881 map titled *Main Part of Kona District Oahu* by R. Covington, shows the outline of a roughly square structure with a rectangular wing attached to the northern corner. It is labeled "R. Keelikolani's."³³⁹

The builder of the Kapālama house of Ruth Keʻelikōlani was S.D. Burrows, owner of Burrows' Planing Mill on Fort Street. His 1881 obituary notes: "Monuments of his skill exist in and around this city, specially in the suburban residences of Her Royal Highness Ruth Keelikolani and the Hon. Simon K. Kaai, on the Palama road [now King Street], and also in the mansion of her ladyship on Emma Street."³⁴⁰ The royal residence had its

Princess Ruth with *kahili* bearers Samuel Parker (left) and John A. Cummins. Parker would later marry Abigail Campbell and live in the Emma Street residence where Ruth's goddaughter, Princess Ka'iulani, was born in 1875, around the same year this photograph was taken (courtesy Hawaii State Archives, PP-97-18-015).

own water supply. On April 8, 1882: "The ortesian [sic] well of Princess Keelikolani, at Palama, struck flowing water at 10 o'clock on Saturday morning."[341]

Royal Deaths

Princess Ruth would live in her Kapālama home for just under five years. She died on Thursday, May 24, 1883. Her will gave most of her Kamehameha lands, including her Kapālama home, to Princess Bernice Pauahi Bishop. With the subsequent death of

Bishop on October 16, 1884, the former residence of Ruth Keʻelikōlani became part of the inventory of Bishop Estate properties leased to provide income for the Kamehameha Schools. Two January 1886 advertisements offered: "House to Let or Lease. At Palama opposite the Reformatory School, the house formerly occupied by Her Royal Highness the late Ruth Keelikolani."[342]

Nāwahī Place

When Joseph Kahoʻoluhi Nāwahī, Hawaiian legislator, started living at Mauna Kamala is not precisely known, though his main residence remained in Hilo, on the Big Island of Hawaiʻi. He served in the legislature from 1872 to 1892 representing that island in the House of Representatives. He was living in Kapālama at least by 1892. That year the city directory lists him as "Nawahi Joseph, atty at law, r King, Palama."[343] By 1893 Princess Ruth's former home was referred to in the *Daily Bulletin* as "the residence of J. Nawahi, opposite the Reformatory School."[344]

Following the overthrow of the Hawaiian monarchy in January 1893, Nāwahī sought to prevent the annexation of Hawaiʻi by the United States. As a key leader of the opposition, his Kapālama home was searched for weapons on the evening of Saturday, December 8, 1894. The *Daily Bulletin*, in an article titled "Treason and Conspiracy: The Government Does Not Wait for Overt Acts," described his arrest and the results of the search:

> When both [John E. Bush and E.C. Crick] had been locked up [for treason] Jos. Nawahi started for his home at Palama. On the way he was met by Lieutenant Holi, who with Captain Rosehill had been searching Nawahi's house for arms. The officers had a warrant for Nawahi's arrest on a charge of conspiracy. Nawahi was taken to the Station and locked up. No arms of any description were found, at his home.[345]

Despite the lack of evidence the Republic of Hawaiʻi imprisoned him for three months. Two years later, Nāwahī went to San Francisco to treat the tuberculosis he contracted during his imprisonment and died there on September 14, 1896. After the *Australia* brought Nāwahī home on Tuesday, September 29, 1896, and thousands of supporters showed their aloha for the Hawaiian patriot, the earthly remains of Joseph Nāwahī returned to his residence in Kapālama. The *Hawaiian Gazette* recorded the overwhelming response to the death of Nāwahī:

> During the afternoon hundreds of visitors called on the Mrs. Nawahi and said their respects, and at night the avenues leading to

When the Hawaiian patriot, Joseph Nāwāhī, lived at Mauna Kamala, it became known as "Nāwāhī Place." The drawing of Nāwāhī accompanied an article about his death in the *Hawaiian Gazette*, September 25, 1896.

the house were lighted with torches as a mark of respect to the deceased. The grounds were filled with people throughout the night.[346]

The memorial service for Nāwahī took place the following day, on Wednesday, September 30, 1896, at his home located at "ka pā o Mauna Kamala"[347] (the yard of Mauna Kamala): "The funeral services of the late Joseph Nawahi were held in the family homestead, Palama, shortly before 1 o'clock."[348] The march from his home included "two societies of women to the number of 500, and another, the Aloha Aina, of men. The hearse, drawn by sixty-four of the friends of the deceased, was next in order."[349] The mourners would not see his burial, for his final resting place would be in Hilo.

Emma Nāwahī would continue to coordinate anti-annexation efforts from her Kapālama home. In a letter from Kapālama dated January 28, 1897, to Lili'uokalani, who she addresses as "The dearly beloved Kamailealii," Nāwahī writes: "You shall be restored to the throne, that's the prayer the people always pray for night and day with tears."[350] A letter dated March 31, 1897, also details the efforts of Robert Wilcox to raise money by "expressing remembrance of Nawahi." She continued, "I ordered the young folks to put into opinion papers forbidding the people not to go there to register their names lest they be swindled. Perhaps this is why they are saying it's for a monument to Nawahi, but the intent is different."[351]

A letter dated July 21, 1897, refer to "Honolulu" rather than "Kapalama" as the location of the writer. Another one dated Nov. 19, 1897, again refers to Kapalama. Another dated January 12, 1898, again uses "Kapalama," though one dated January 6, 1898, uses "Honolulu." "Kapalama" appears in letters dated January 6, 1899, and February 4, 1899; February 9, 1899; Honolulu on February 21, 1899; Kapalama on February 28, 1899, Honolulu on May 16, 1899; Kapalama on August 18, 1899; Honolulu on August 2, 1899, and the rest of the year. "Kapalama" again appears on a letter dated February 20, 1900.[352] Emma Nāwahī may have moved to Waikīkī; she writes in an undated letter: "I tried to return to Waikiki and I was very fortunate. I'm quite strong these days. No more weakness."[353]

Pālama Chinese School

Following the death of Nāwahī, Seventh Day Adventist missionary H.H. Brand and his wife opened "in 1897, a boarding school known as the Palama Chinese School, which later became the Anglo-Chinese Academy."[354] Seventh-day Adventist elder Hideo Oshita wrote of the predecessor of Hawaiian Mission Academy: "In a mansion, called 'Nawahi Place,' which was formerly occupied by a Hawaiian princess, Mr. and Mrs. H. H. Brand started a boarding school, called Palama Chinese School, with fifteen Chinese boys."[355] Oshita also gave the street and landmark associated with the property: "This school was located at the end of Banyan Street in Palama. The old Banyan tree under which the students played still stands (in 1961 [and fifty-two years later in 2013]) in the center of Banyan Street."[356] The background of a photograph of the faculty and students shows a one-story building with a dual pitch, hipped roof, and a veranda or lānai on the front face and around the right corner. The building has a wing stretching to the left of the main structure that also features a lānai.

The school's principal, W.E. Howell, gives the most complete description of the royal residence in his account, "Among the Chinese in Honolulu," in the December 21, 1897, issue of *The Advent Review and Sabbath Herald*:

Accordingly, after careful searching, Brother Brand secured a place outside the business part of town, formerly the residence of a native chief named Nawahi (Nä-wä-heé), and now known as "Nawahi Place."[357]

Howell confirms the continued presence of the artesian well drilled in 1882: "In one corner of the grounds an artesian well furnishes an abundant supply of the best water obtainable in Honolulu."[358]

Howell also noted the use of neighboring properties: "Adjoining our lot is the residence of the British consul [Muʻolaulani, the palace of Liliʻuokalani]; on the opposite side of the street is the government reform school; a little beyond is the Chinese hospital recently erected."[359]

He also gives the only description of the extensive plantings at Mauna Kamala:

> The driveway is lined on both sides by eighteen stately royal palms and thirteen smaller ones. Alternating with these are oleander bushes from ten to fifteen feet high, some bearing red and some white blossoms. Near the main building, on each side of the entrance, is a banian-tree, whose branches measure about eighty-five feet from tip to tip, affording abundant shade for our boys to enjoy the open air. Still nearer the building are two Norfolk pines, imported from the Norfolk Islands, straight and slender, reaching thirty or forty feet skyward. In other parts of the grounds are six ponciana [Poinciana] regias, two small magnolias, and one native plum-tree. Directly in front of the entrance is a small fish-pool encircled with foliage plants and ferns.[360]

Constructed less than two decades earlier, the royal residence was already in poor condition in 1897. Howell gave the following assessment: "The buildings are very old and badly run down, though once, doubtless, the main one was a mansion."[361]

Howell also provides the dimensions of the house, the "main part thirty by forty feet in size," with a wing "thirty-seven by fifteen feet." He also notes that: "Three sides of the main part and one side of the [wing] contain a veranda seven feet wide."[362]

By the 1900–1901 school year the Palama Chinese School had relocated, necessitating a name change to the Anglo-Chinese Academy.[363]

Subdividing Mauna Kamala

From October 1900 to August 1901 Bishop Estate undertook a project to fill the portions of Mauna Kamala that were used for growing rice and sweet potato. The principal of the Palama Chinese School provided a description of the extent of the wetlands at Mauna Kamala:

> About the most unfavorable feature of our situation is that we are surrounded on four sides by rice-lots and sweet-potato patches, the only outlet being a driveway about three hundred feet long by thirty-six feet wide, leading to the street in front. Rice-lots have standing water in them constantly, except a short time before the grain ripens and during harvest.[364]

The estate paid Hawaiian Ballasting Co., H.R. Hitchcock and R.M. Duncan for more than 24,000 wheelbarrow loads of fill for Mauna Kamala.

A 1900 Bishop Estate map of Mauna Kamala shows the former residence of Princess Ruth Keʻelikōlani with two stairs on the southwest side, one stair to the southeast, and two curved bays and stairs on the northeast exposure, the most detailed drawing of house.[365]

By 1901 Ruth Keʻelikōlani's house had changed hands, going to a local real estate agent: "Mr. [Paul E.R.] Strauch bought from the Bishop Estate the home immediately behind the banyan tree in 1901...."[366] The Bishop Estate receipts for September 1901, under the category "Sale of Improvements" include one for $100 to "Mrs. F. [Fanny] Strauch, old buildings at 'Mauna Kamala,' Hon."[367] A structure, labeled as "Old House" in a 1901 map titled *Mauna Kamala Premises* by J.A. McCandless, sits in the middle of a planned extension of Kanoa Street.

The Trustees of the Bishop Estate were pleased to report in 1902 that "the laying out and fencing of the property at King Street and Asylum Road known as 'Mauna Kamala', begun last year has been fully completed this year; and this section is now ready for occupancy."[368] The property was divided into quadrants: Block A to the southwest, B to the southeast, C to the northwest and D to the northeast. The 1902 report of the Bishop Estate's activities noted: "The Trustees have agreed to accept from the American Board of Commissioners for Foreign Missions the old Kaumakapili Church site in the District of Kamanuwai" in exchange for Mauna Kamala lands.[369] The original plans of the trustees to lease the subdivided lot at Mauna Kamala in Kapālama did not experience any demand, so they decided in 1903 to "offer the lots for sale, in fee, at schedule prices."[370]

Political Rally Site

The location of the former royal residence, a large open space, served as a venue for several political rallies in 1904: "Under the branches of a large banyan tree on the old Ruth Keelikolani premises out Kapalama way and almost directly opposite the Kaiulani school, the Republicans held forth to quite a goodly crowd of spectators."[371] A month later they met again: "Republicans ... Fifth District, 'under the banyan tree' across the way from the Kaiulani school, King Street, at the former residence of Princess Ruth Keelikolani."[372]

More Sales

The sale of the lands surrounding the former site of the Kapālama residence of Princess Ruth Keʻelikōlani began in earnest in 1904. The largest purchases were by the trustees of Kaumakapili Church[373] and the Protestant Episcopal Church in the Hawaiian Islands.[374,375,376] In 1906, the swap of former site of Kaumakapili Church at the mauka end of Smith Street for 72,251 square feet of Mauna Kamala property was finally completed.[377] On May 7, 1910, Kaumakapili Church broke ground at its new site in Block A of Mauna Kamala.[378] The Protestant Episcopal Church in the Hawaiian Islands also continued to increase its presence in the area by another 33,000 square foot portion in 1911[379] and 23,000 square foot parcel in 1912.[380] Daizo Sumida and E.L. Schwarzberg also bought 11,500 and 33,532 square feet of Mauna Kamala respectively in 1912.[381] By July 29, 1912, Ching Chow and Lum See had bought the property from Schwarzberg and subdivided it into sixteen lots ranging in size from 1,850 square foot to 2,264 square feet. They called the subdivision Banyan Tract after the banyan tree anchoring the southwest end of the street named for the same tree. Chinese revolutionary Sun Yat-sen stayed in Ching Chow's home there at 1127-C Banyan street.[382]

Relocated House

A description of the original location of Princess Ruth Keʻelikōlani's house at Mauna Kamala and the site of the relocated royal residence comes in a 1934 interview by Gwenfread Allen of real estate agent Paul E.R. Strauch. Strauch said that he: "moved it from its location near what would now be the corner of Kanoa lane and Banyan Rd. to the end of Banyan St. near N. Kukui St. Here cut into two buildings and remodeled it still stands and is used by the American-Hawaiian Soy Co."[383]

In the September 23, 1905, edition of the *Evening Bulletin*, a "For Sale" advertisement appeared: "Two houses and lot, 100 × 130, at Kapalama, near Kaiulani School, formerly residence of H.R.H. Ruth Keelikolani. Two lots, 50 × 130, adjoining same. At a Bargain. P.E.R. Strauch, Walty Bldg. No. 74 King St."[384] Contemporaneous maps agree with the real estate agent's account of the relocated residence. The house at the end of Banyan Street at N. Kukui Street in the 1906 Dakin Fire Insurance maps, numbered 461, and the dwelling behind it labeled 462, fit the description of the relocated house referred to by Strauch. The larger building includes verandas on three sides of the house's main room. The long rectangular wing separated from the house also has a lānai.

The 1914 Sanborn Fire Map further confirms Strauch's 1934 account of Ruth Keʻelikōlani's relocated home. At the end of Banyan Street on the map is the American Soy Brewing Company Ltd. The site referred to as the "American-Hawaiian Soy Company" in a 1934 interview of Strauch includes a building labeled Office and Dwelling (758 N. Kukui) and a building labeled Storage (758B N. Kukui) which fits his description of the two parts of the house relocated from the site at Kanoa and Banyan streets. The larger structure in 1914 has part of the open lānai shown in the 1906 Dakin Fire Insurance map enclosed, which agrees with Strauch's use of the term "remodeled." Kanekichi Iida was president and manager of American Hawaiian Soy.[385] The 1927 Sanborn Fire map shows the two structures still standing. The two buildings are gone in the 1950 Sanborn Fire Map, the American Soy Brewing Company replaced by the Hayashi Hongwanji Mission of Hawaii.

Keōua Hale (1882, Demolished 1925), Princess Ruth Keʻelikōlani and Princess Bernice Pauahi Bishop

Built by Princess Ruth Keʻelikōlani to rival nearby ʻIolani Palace, Keōua Hale dominated Emma Street with its imposing Second Empire architecture. Taller than ʻIolani Palace, the residence of one of the last members of royalty from the Kamehameha dynasty would have been clearly visible from the residence of the new dynasty of King Kalākaua. Henry Whalley Nicholson made the comparison while ʻIolani Palace was still being built: "Her new palace on Emma Street rivals, if it does not surpass, that under construction for the King."[386]

The announcement of the new residence appeared in the *Daily Bulletin*: "Her Highness the Princess Ruth Keelikolani will open her new mansion on Thursday [February 9, 1882] next. A luau and a ball will be given on the occasion."[387] The opening took place a year before Kalākaua's coronation (in the ninth year of his reign) on February 12, 1883, an event that Princess Ruth, Queen Emma and Princess Bernice Pauahi Bishop refused to attend. King Kalākaua, nevertheless, did attend the formal opening of Keōua Hale, dancing with Ruth Keʻelikōlani. A narrative in the *Memoirs of Bernice Pauahi Bishop* recounts the ball: "In the Quadrille of Honor at the ball the Princess Ruth danced with the King, wearing a dress of rich yellow brocade with a train the prescribed three yards and a half in length. Mrs. Bishop also took part in the quadrille, enjoying it thoroughly,

Keōua Hale in 1883 (courtesy Hawaii State Archives, PP-92-10-004).

laughing heartily as her cousin and the King went through the intricate figures, the Princess being a woman of great size and weight."[388]

The day following a dinner at the Hawaiian Hotel given by King Kalākaua, on March 29, the Japanese Envoy "made a call by appointment on Her Highness Keelikolani at her mansion on Emma street."[389] On March 30, 1882, "H.H. Keelikolani, accompanied by the Hon. Mrs. Pauahi Bishop, held a levee [levée, a court reception] at her town mansion, at which were present H.R.H. Liliuokalani, the Cabinet Ministers and their ladies and other Government notables."[390]

Ke'elikōlani would die soon after at the *hale pili* on the grounds of Hulihe'e Palace in Kailua, Kona on Hawai'i island (Chapter 1).

The *Daily Bulletin* in her obituary announced: "The coffin will be laid in state at the house, on Emma street. The funeral will take place on June 15."[391] The funeral actually took place on June 17, 1883. Her funeral postponed the celebration of Kamehameha Day that year.[392] The court went into full mourning from May 31, 1883, to the day after the funeral and half mourning for another two weeks after that.[393] The Emma street residence provided the focal point for the funeral: "The closing ceremonies connected with the funeral of the late Princess Ruth were performed in her late residence on Emma street on the afternoon of the 17 inst., Rev. H.H. Parker officiating, and they were most impressive [...] A large attendance, was present in the rear parlor in which the body lay in state [...] The room in which the body lay displayed very few outurned [*sic*] tokens of mourning the walls being decorated with clusters of flowers here and there and large bunches of flowers being noticeable in the windows."[394] Unlike the funerals of other royalty that went from their home to Kawaiaha'o and then to the Royal Mausoleum, Princess Ruth's last rites took place at her Emma Street residence and then the procession went up Nu'uanu avenue to the royal burial grounds.

The question regarding ownership of Keōua Hale continued long after the death of

Princess Ruth. In October 1883 the *Daily Bulletin* announced: "The case of His Majesty v Mr. Samuel Parker, concerning the rights of ownership to certain lands, has been settled out of court. Hon. C.R. Bishop pays His Majesty and sisters the sum of $30,000. In return His Majesty gives up all claims to certain lands in Kau and to the Emma Street property of Her late Royal Highness, Princess Ruth."[395] The death of Ruth also meant a sale of the items stored at the Emma Street residence. An auction by E.P. Adams took place on Wednesday, March 12, 1884. Many of the items, "valuable gourds, calabashes, kappa cloths and other specimens of ethnographic interest," were bought "at the sale at the residence of her late residence of H.R.H Princess Ruth"[396] by Mrs. [Emma Kaili Metcalf] Beckley [Nakuina] for the Hawaiian Government Museum.

Bishop Residence

Princess Ruth gave her Emma Street house to Bernice Pauahi Bishop. Bishop had iron gates with the prominent initial "B" manufactured for the residence, but she would never see them. She would die on October 14, 1884. Bishop lay in state at her Emma Street residence. The arrangement reflected her chiefly rank:

> In the centre of the drawing room stood a bier covered with white silk, upon this was laid the body draped in snowy satin, the arms crossed on the breast. The clear cut features, and hair just tinged with gray, of her who had been once so full of life, alone were visible, she might have just sank to rest: she *had* sunk to rest, the long, deep sleep of death. On each side of the bier stood two female attendants. Four kahili bearers on either side, waved monotonously their mournful plumes, while four officers of the king's staff stood on guard. At the head and feet were placed large kahilis, emblems of the rank of the deceased. Between the kahilis were arranged massive silver candelabra, with lighted candles, and a mass of pure white blossoms, woven into crosses and wreaths by many mourning friends.[397]

Charles Reed Bishop continued to live in the house following the death of his wife and to make improvements to the property. In April 1886 Bishop sought his own water supply when he contracted with McCandless Brothers to drill an artesian well at the Emma Street location.[398] He moved to California in 1894. In March 1895, the public gained entry to the Bishop mansion in preparation for an auction of the furnishings. Among the items were the "state bedstead, mirrors, rich upholstered and finely polished wood pieces."[399]

Public School

The empty mansion of Princess Ruth Ke'elikōlani became the site a public school after the passage of Act 22 of the Republic of Hawaii in 1895, titled "An Act Making Special Appropriations for the Use of the Board of Education for the Purchase of Real Estate and Repairs on Buildings on Emma Street known as 'Keoua Hale.'"[400] The $17,000 appropriation provided $15,000 for the purchase and $2,000 for repairs derived from government bonds with a 12 percent interest rate. Another $15,000 was appropriated to "purchase the building known as 'Keoua Hale' on Emma Street."[401] The building and land were purchased for $30,000 but listed as an asset worth $100,000 on the books of the Republic of Hawaii.[402] The writer questioned whether the property could be sold for the amount of the appraisal. Like many other Second Empire residences, the house was too large to be rented. The rationale behind the Board of Education buying the property

Keōua Hale still stands with a two-story concrete building on the grounds to its left, the first of three buildings that would eventually replace the wooden palace of Ruth Keʻelik?lani (courtesy Hawaii State Archives, PP-92-10-009).

for roughly a third of its value was that it was "impossible to obtain a tenant willing to pay $1800 a year rent."[403] Interestingly, Liliʻuokalani was able to rent Muʻolaulani Palace in nearby Kapālama for six times that amount a year.

The dedication of the school took place on Friday, November 1, 1895, with addresses by the president of the Republic of Hawaii, Sanford Ballard Dole, and historian W.D. Alexander.[404] The "former Princess Ruth premises" would remain a school, first Honolulu High School and later Central Grammar School, for three decades. The remaining examples of select schools were: "Honolulu High School; [and] the Kaakopua school under Miss Coursen which is preparatory thereto."[405] By 1897 the teachers had discovered the shortcomings of teaching in a former mansion. The board of education granted their petition for "inside blinds for Kaakopua school."[406] The next month the board worked to "correct the very bad lighting."[407]

One of the buildings comprising the Central Middle School today still bears the name of the original owner of Keōua Hale, Princess Ruth Keʻelikōlani. On the *makai* wall of the building bordering Kukui street, in raised letters, is the name "Keelikolani School." The twelve-classroom building, dedicated in 1916, was built while the mansion still stood on the grounds. Sealed tenders had gone out May 2, 1916, for construction of the "2-story Concrete and Frame School Building, in Central Grammar School Grounds, Emma Street."[408] Superintendent Henry W. Kinney in accepting the new

Chapter 5. Other Royal Residences of O'ahu   197

The raised words "Keelikolani School" on the wall of the *makai* building of Central Middle School once provided the only clue to the connection between the property and Princess Ruth Keʻelikōlani (photograph by the author).

structure, on the *makai* side of Keōua Hale, said: "The new building certainly is a fine one, and is a credit to the architect and to the building inspector's office."[409] Although in reports the school was called Central Grammar School. An appointment in 1917 referred to "Keelikolani School."[410] The 1919 report of the superintendent of public instruction to the governor recommended the purchase of the "so-called King property on Vineyard Street, adjoining the Kaakopua School premises. As the Kaakopua School lot is too narrow to admit any further construction, and as this addition would allow such, it seems as if it will be a very good plan to secure it, in order that some day one of the standard twelve-room concrete buildings may be placed thereon to take care of the great demand which is being made upon the primary departments in the centre of the city."[411] The enrollment at Central Grammar School that year totaled 1,337.

Unlike its brick and concrete rival, 'Iolani Palace (1882), and its concrete neighbor across Queen Emma Street, St. Peter's Episcopal Church (1914), the wooden structure, Keōua Hale, suffered from the decay caused by termites and in November 1925 was "torn down to make way for the second unit of the handsome new Central Grammar school."

Soon after the destruction of Keoua Hale efforts took place to remember the residence and its resident. To maintain a remembrance of Princess Ruth and her connection with the Kaakopua site, the Kaahumanu Society, in a letter dated April 13, 1927, "requested that the name of Central Grammar School be changed to 'Keelikolani School.'"

The response clearly opposed the request: "It was moved by Mr. [John K.] Clarke, seconded by Mrs. [Mary Louise] Rothwell, that no action be taken, but that a suitable reply be made to the request. Carried unanimously."⁴¹²

On September 16, 2021, the State of Hawaii Board of Education voted to change the name of Central Middle School to Princess Ruth Keʻelikolani Middle School.

ʻUlulani, Kulaokahuʻa, Honolulu (–1884), Princess Kekaulike

Less than a year after the death of Ruth Keʻelikōlani, one of the last royal members of the Kamehameha dynasty, the Kalākaua dynasty suffered it own loss with the death of the sister of Queen Kapiʻolani. She was the mother of the last princes of the Kingdom of Hawaiʻi: David Kawānanakoa, Edward Abnel Keliʻiahonui, and Jonah Kūhiō Kalanianaʻole. Princess Mary Kinoiki Kekaulike died at her house, called ʻUlulani, on the morning of January 8, 1884.⁴¹³ Kekaulike was born May 12, 1843. She also lived at Kaʻalaʻa, Pauoa, Honolulu, and Kōloa, Kauaʻi (Chapter 6). She accepted the position of Governess of Hawaiʻi island in September 1880, succeeding her sister, Princess Likelike.⁴¹⁴ As with many of the appointed governors of the neighbor islands, Kekaulike maintained residences there. In 1882, she received permission "to construct a Boat-House upon the land of the Government at Piihonua, Hilo, Hawaii."⁴¹⁵

The house at Kulaokahuʻa had not been hers for very long. An advertisement announced the May 27, 1882, sale of the "House Lot and premises known as ʻUlulani,' the late homestead of James S. Lemon. Grant No. 500."⁴¹⁶ Lemon also named his son "Ululani." Lemon had bought the property from Eliza Macfarlane on February 22, 1870.⁴¹⁷ According to the Bureau of Conveyances, H.R.H Kaulike [sic] bought the property for $4,900 from the estate of J. [James] S. [Silas] Lemon [R.P. 3336 and a portion of R.P. 500].⁴¹⁸ The property lines ran 324.6 feet along Makiki Street, 383 along Beretania Street, 300 along R.P. 500, and 260 along Kinau Street.⁴¹⁹ The deed was recorded January 15, 1883.

Princess Kekaulike was sister of Queen Kapiʻolani (courtesy Hawaii State Archives, PP-97-19-001).

Shortly thereafter,

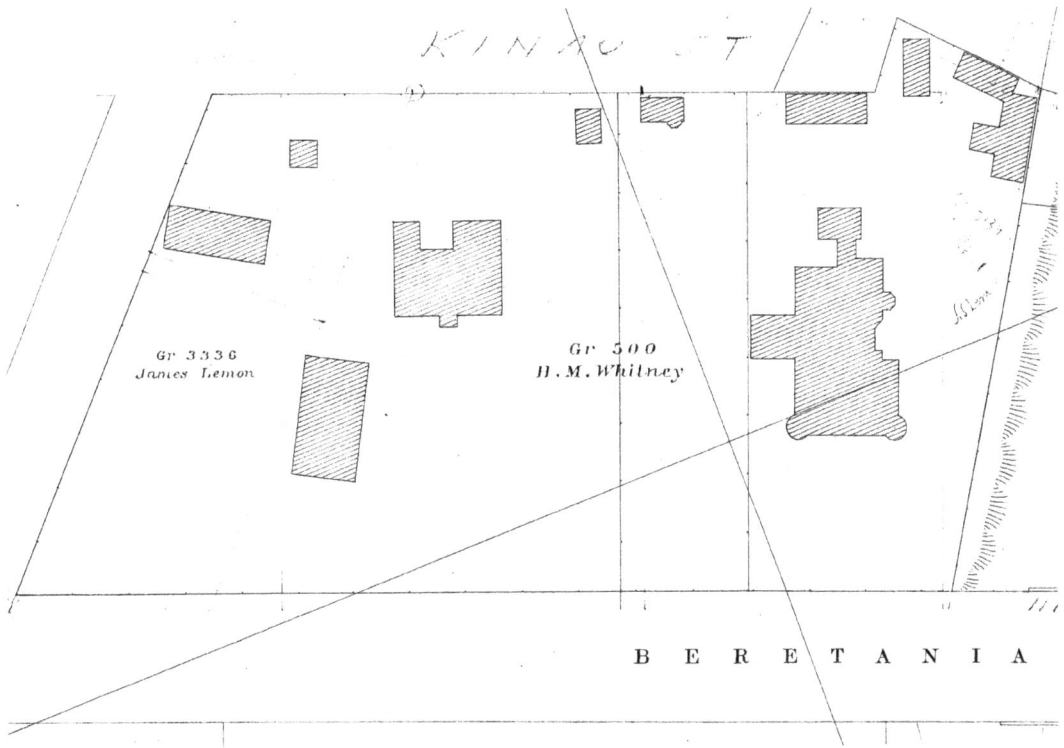

Princess Kekaulike purchased the ʻEwa half of the property of James S. Lemon, called ʻUlulani, in 1883. In 1917 the Kapiolani Maternity Home bought the Diamond Head portion of ʻUlulani with the old Lemon residence from August Dreier. Detail of Registered Map 2285, "Beretania Avenue and Makiki Street East," 1903 (courtesy Land Survey Division, Department of Accounting and General Services, State of Hawaii).

following the dedication of the statue of Kamehameha I in Kohala, on Hawaiʻi island, in April 1883, she took ill and her physicians diagnosed her with heart disease.[420] She retired to ʻUlulani where she died January 8, 1884.

The "Order of Procession" for the funeral of Princess Kekaulike gave the following instructions: "Those who are to precede the catafalque will form on the west side of the entrance to the residence of Her late Royal Highness."[421] The report of her funeral also places her house "at Ululani on Beretania street."[422] The January 12, 1884, issue of *Ka Nupepa Kuokoa* announced: "Ma ka Poalua nei ma Ululani, Kulaokahua, ke ʻlii Kiaaina Kekaulike o Hawaii."[423]

Kēhaulani

The house may also have been known as Kēhaulani. Mrs. Jennie K. Wilson, in her notes on the Music Collection of Queen Liliʻuokalani, wrote regarding the composition titled Kēhaulani: "Kēhaulani, the home of Kino-iki, Queen Ka-piʻo-lani's sister. I think at the corner of Young and Makiki Street. A first playground for children and field for sports was opened there."[424]

Kapiolani Maternity Home

Princess Kekaulike bequeathed the property to her sister, Queen Kapiʻolani, who used the residence of Princess Kekaulike for one of her projects, a maternity home for Hawaiian women.

The *Daily Bulletin* announced the completion of the facility: "A lying-in hospital for Hawaiian women, long projected, is now an institution of the land. It is located at the corner of Beretania and Makiki streets and is now known as the Kapiolani Maternity Home. The premises are the property of Queen Kapiolani [....] Her Majesty gives the premises for one year free of rent."[425] The *Hawaiian Gazette* also related the connection with Kekaulike: "The Kapiolani Maternity Home was started by the Hooulu Lahui Society. It is situated at the corner of Beretania and Makiki streets being the residence at one time occupied by Princess Kekaulike."[426]

In November 1890, a former owner of the property, Mary Ann Lemon, widow of James S. Lemon, was "asked to take the position of Matron of the Home, giving her the privilege of having the children [son, Ululani, and daughter] with her."[427]

Even after her husband's death, Kapiʻolani, now Queen Dowager, continued her support for the institution. She gave a benefit luau to support the Kapiolani Maternity Home at the Armory on Beretania Street.[428] A month earlier she held another luau at her residence at Honuakaha.

In August 1897 Mary Ann Lemon resigned her position as matron,[429] prompting an inquiry by the home's namesake. On September 8, 1897, Kapiʻolani, president of the Kapiolani Maternity Home, sent a letter to J.A. King, minister of the interior, asking him: "Did you make known to a member or members of the Board of Directors of the Kapiolani Maternity Home, that the Government is thinking of withholding and keeping the appropriation which was given for said Home by the Legislature, if Mrs. Meleana Lemon is continued to manage said Home? And whether it is true?"[430] The minister replied the same day that he "has not met any members of the Board of Directors of the Kapiolani Maternity Home, nor has he expressed any opinion pertaining to the Home, the appropriation for the Home, or matters pertaining to Mary Ann Lemon— the opinion of the Minister pertaining to this lady are of the best."[431]

On March 19, 1918, the two heirs of the Kapiʻolani estate, Jonah Kūhiō Kalanianaʻole and the estate of David Kawānanakoa, signed over their interest in the property that Kekaulike had purchased thirty-five years earlier, comprising the ʻEwa portion of the Lemon estate. A little over a year later, on June 17, 1919, Kapiolani Maternity Home, represented by its president, Jonah Kūhiō Kalanianaʻole (Kapiʻolani's nephew), and treasurer, Muriel Shingle (sister-in-law of Kapiʻolani's other nephew, David Kawānanakoa), purchased the Diamond Head portion of the Lemon property from the estate of August Dreier.[432] The Kapiolani Maternity Home would remain at Kulaokahuʻa until their move in the 1940s to their current Bingham Street location. Today, an empty paved lot is all that remains of ʻUlulani, the lost palace of Kekaulike.

Residence of Peter Young Kaʻeo on Emma Street, Kahehuna, Honolulu (–1880)

After his return from Kalawao, Molokaʻi, Peter Young Kaʻeo again took up residence at his house on the street named for his cousin, Queen Emma. Free of the disease that had sent him to Molokaʻi, Kaʻeo also resumed duties as a member of the House of Nobles for the session of 1878, from April 30 to August 6,[433] and the session of 1880, from April 30 to August 13.[434] During the latter session, the Kapālama neighbor of Princess Ruth Keʻelikōlani, Samuel Kaloa Kaʻai, died and left a vacancy in the House of Nobles. A little more than three months after the end of the session, on November 26, 1880, Kaʻeo himself would die at his Emma Street residence. He was interred in the Royal Mausoleum on Sunday, November 28, 1880. "The hearse was surrounded by Kahili bearers as becomes the dignity of a chief."[435]

As with many of the lost palaces, the precise address where Kaʻeo lived on Emma Street is unknown. John Tayman, however, in *The Colony: The Harrowing True Story of the Exiles of Molokai*, places the residence close to the house of Sanford Ballard Dole, on the *mauka* and ʻEwa portion of the street: "Dole's lushly gardened residence in Honolulu was on Emma Street, near the home where Peter Kaʻeo had died. Dole's wife believed leprosy hung over their residence like a thunderhead. Anna Dole wore her gloves indoors, and used her dress hem to turn doorknobs."[436] Dole had bought the property [R.P. 3126] from Afong and wife on December 8, 1875. The Royal Patent Grant had been issued to Afong in 1874. He had married Anna P. Cate that year in Castine, Maine. The couple moved in on April 29, 1876. Their *makai* neighbor, Mrs. Thomas Lack, lived on land originally granted to Kaniho [NT 482v3, FT 158v3]. The *mauka* neighbor, Hugh McDonna had purchased the land in 1875.

Residence of Prince Albert Kukailimoku Kūnuiākea, Kapālama

Peter Young Kaʻeo's half-brother, Prince Albert Kukailimoku Kūnuiākea (whose name also often appears as Kuniakea), was son of Kamehameha III and Jane Lahilahi Young Kaʻeo, daughter of John Young. He was born at Kuaihelani (Chapter 4) and reared by Queen Kalama at Kīnaʻu Hale (Chapter 4) and Pihanakalani at Haʻimoeipo (Chapter 4). The 1884–1884 *McKenney's Hawaiian Directory* lists his residence as "46 Richard."[437]

Kūnuiākea was living in his Kapālama house by at least 1886 when a news account places a death at his residence. The 1890 city directory lists his residence as "Kapalama uka near King." He bought his Kapālama residence for $1,700 from William C. Achi and his wife, Isabella A. Achi. The deed for the 21,120-

Prince Albert Kūnuiākea (courtesy Hawaii State Archives, PP-98-6-006).

square-foot property was recorded on April 28, 1891.[438] His address in the 1900 U.S. Census is listed as "Achi & Maile Roads."[439]

The residence of Prince Albert Kūnuiākea in Kapālama exemplifies Ralph S. Kuykendall's observation that: "with the lapse of time and the progress of improvement and development, the exact location of historically important spots frequently becomes a matter of uncertainty."[440] When Paul E.R. Strauch bought Princess Ruth Keʻelikōlani's house at Mauna Kamala in Kapālama, some thought the home belonged to Queen Emma's cousin Prince Albert Kūnuiākea. Strauch rejected the notion, noting that "at the time he bought the property Prince Kuniakea was occupying a house up the present Kanoa lane, towards Austin lane."[441] The 1907 File Plan for Peterson Tract confirms Strauch's description of the location of Albert Kūnuiākea's home. The lot is labeled on the map as "Est[ate]. A. Kuniakea" (Kunuiakea died in 1903), which locates the home in the exact spot Strauch described.

Unlike the residences of other royalty in Kapālama, few politically significant events happened in Prince Albert's house. Instead the newsworthy events usually reflected odd news. For instance, on April 18, 1886, a visitor to the residence of Prince Kūnuiākea in Kapālama suddenly died. Mrs. Kapena "had been troubled for sometime with heart disease, but yesterday she was feeling well and in good spirits. At half-past four o'clock in the afternoon while visiting at the residence of Prince Kunuiakea, at Palama, she dropped dead without speaking a word."[442]

Prince Kūnuiākea's Kapālama residence is also mentioned in another odd account in the *Hawaiian Gazette*:

The other day Prince Albert Kuniakea sat on the veranda of his royal residence at Palama. Apparently with that tired feeling on him he commenced to think with sadness and regret of the kingly throne that is fading day by day away from him. He had a revolver in his hand while in this deep study and no doubt remembering that old saying about man's inhumanity to man etc commenced firing the revolver. It happens that Dr. Hammond the eminent letter writer for the outside pages of the daily papers lives next to the prince The doctor was in his garden watering some favorite plants that are expected to grow twenty dollar bills in the shape of bananas perhaps ever and anon devoting a thought to a hoped for rise in real estate values. At first the doctor was a little annoyed at the shots whistling in close proximity to his clerical garb but when the firing continued for some time he decided to do more ducking than he ever did at Waikiki. When he looked around and saw the prince with a revolver the doctor's long hair commenced to stand until it stood up straight. He lost no time getting into the city driving rapidly to the Police Station and asking for a warrant to arrest his blood thirsty neighbor. The police were happy to oblige the doctor and when the usual formalities were through they wished him to take the prescribed oath. He true to his reputation objected and would not swear but merely affirm. It is not known how he fixed it but he received the warrant that caused the arrest of the prince on a charge of nuisance.

The trial will take place Tuesday and Deputy Marshal Mehrtens is seriously thinking of hiring the Armory to accommodate the large crowd expected to witness this very important case.[443]

Another complaint again caused the arrest of Kūnuiākea four months later in March 1892:

Prince Albert K. Kunuiakea was arrested on Sunday morning on the complaint of residents of Palama, where he lives, that the Prince had been recklessly firing pistol shots, he was arraigned in the Police Court this morning, when he pleaded not guilty. The evidence of W. C. Achi, M. R. Colburn and others went to show that, about 3 or 4 o'clock Sunday morning,

Detail of Peterson Tract File Plan 12 shows "Est. A. Kuniakea" in the upper right-hand corner (courtesy Land Survey Division, Department of Accounting and General Services, State of Hawaii).

pistol shots numbering nearly ten were fired from the vicinity of the Prince's house, but who was doing the firing the witnesses could not testify. They, however, had all been frightened out of their houses. Suspecting it was the Prince again at his tricks, he having been tried before on a similar charge, he was arrested and brought to the Police Station. C. W. Ashford, who appeared for the Prince, moved for a dismissal on the ground that it had not been proved that the shooting was done by the defendant. His Honor granted the motion, but took occasion to caution the defendant as in the former instance.[444]

The Kūnuiākea residence was the site of a crime against them in 1896: "A robbery was committed a day or two ago at the house of Prince Albert Kunuiakea. A secretary desk was broken open and $250, the pin money of Mrs. Kunuiakea abstracted. Detective Kaapa is on the trail and thinks he has a solid clue."[445] To put the robbery in perspective, $250 would be the equivalent of nearly $7,000 today.[446]

The location of the residence of Prince Albert Kūnuiākea may be seen on maps of the area for more than four decades, appearing on the 1906 Dakin Fire Insurance Map,

1914 Sanborn Fire Insurance Map, and 1927 Sanborn Fire Insurance Map, and 1950 Fire Insurance Map. Today, the dwelling of the last of the Kamehamehas no longer stands.

Muʻolaulani (1885–c. 1940), Queen Liliʻuokalani

Although Queen Liliʻuokalani is most often associated with ʻIolani Palace, the site of her reign and later imprisonment, and Washington Place, the location of her residence following her release and the place of her death, her Kapālama residence, Muʻolaulani Palace, held a special place in her heart, because it was hers alone; ʻIolani Palace was the royal residence envisioned and built by her brother and Washington Place the house of her mother-in-law. Liliʻuokalani chose Muʻolaulani and paid for it herself. It had no family associations.

The house was sold by Becky K. Kaʻai, the widow of Simon Kaloa Kaʻai, on December 1, 1884, to Albert G. Ellis for $7,000 and then sold by Albert G. and Delia Roberts Ellis, on December 3, 1884, to Lydia L.K. Dominis for $8,000.

The house may have been one built by S.D. Burrows for Kaʻai. An obituary for Burrows had made reference to residence of "the Hon. Simon K. Kaai, on the Palama road" as one of the "[m]onuments to his skill."[447] The advertisement for the sale mentions "Residence of the late Simon K. Kaai at Palama Honolulu, [...] with dwelling house and commodious out-houses situate thereon. The buildings are capacious and nearly new and in good repair, the main house containing eight large rooms. The grounds are planted with flowering plants and shrubs. This is a most desirable property for any one wishing a residence just out of town."[448] The curved stairways are certainly reminiscent of one at Keōua Hale, another house design attributed to Burrows.

Princess Liliʻuokalani first mentions her Kapālama residence in a diary entry on Friday, February 6, 1885: "Took a drive with Mrs U & Mrs Wilson to my new house."[449] Whether Liliʻuokalani was referring to a newly constructed house or one that was simply newly acquired is not certain, but in either case Liliʻuokalani had carpenters on site. The advertisement called the existing Kaʻai residence "nearly new and in good repair," so Liliʻuokalani may have been making modifications to the existing structure and putting on a fresh coat of paint. On Friday, February 13, 1885, she commented on the progress of the construction: "4 p.m. went to Kapalama—found carpenter and painters work almost complete."[450] The subsequent diary entry, however, recorded a delay: "Came out here was disappointed the carpenters did not come out—planted trees before going home."[451] On Tuesday, February 24, 1885, she commented on the start of part of her gardens: "Went to Kapalama to plant roses."[452] On Sunday, March 8, 1885, she again noted progress on her residence: "Mr Wilson says they will be through painting my house at Kapalama—welcome news."[453] His report was accurate, for on March 12, 1885, Liliʻuokalani recorded: "was pleased to find painters had got through with large house—Mr Wilson says I must not move in till next week—How slowly everything seems to progress."[454] On Sunday, March 15, 1885, she wrote about her preparations for moving in: "King called & warned me about new house.... Mary Ailau Kaae Kaipo went with me to Kapalama—Matting al [sic] ready—Must move in Wednesday [March 18]—Two fish to get Manewanewa for gate Mananalo for piko hale. M. dine—Must drive in side gate. *Komo mai maka welau hopa* [sic] *oka hale a hiki ika humu oka hale—Mai poina.*"[455] A note to the transcription of the diary translates the Hawaiian as: "Enter at back of the house up to the tabu enclosure of the house—Don't forget." The appointed day for her to occupy the house came and went, and on Saturday, March 21, 1885, Lili'uokalani wrote in her diary: "I am getting despondent—for one reason or another I cannot move into my house."[456] Finally, on Sunday, March 29, 1885, Lili'uokalani moved into her Kapālama home. She recorded in her diary that day: "This is the day that I am supposed to take possession of this house—I think that I shall call it Muolaulani."[457] Mu'olaulani may have been named in honor of Princess Ruth Ke'elikōlani. Mu'olaulani is the name used for her in an 1861 set of songs titled "He Inoa Ka Haku o Hawaii," listed with her half-brothers Kapuāiwa [Kamehameha V] and 'Iolani [Kamehameha IV] and half-sister Kalohelani [Kamamalu].[458] The residence consisted of two single-story wings forming an L-shaped footprint. The wing facing King Street featured a ten-foot-deep veranda that stretched across the 100-foot-wide front face of the building (the same width as 'Iolani Palace) and a similar one on the back face. The other wing, set at a right angle to the main wing, ran perpendicular to King Street. It, too, was 100 feet in length, with a veranda facing southeast toward Diamond Head.

Confusing References

Despite detailed diary entries about the timing of the completion of the residence and plantings, the location of Mu'olaulani is plagued with confusing references. The earliest depiction of the L-shaped outline of Lili'uokalani's residence appears on an 1887 map titled *Honolulu and Vicinity* by W.A. Wall. That map inaccurately labeled the site: "R Keliikolani," a misspelling of "R Keelikolani," who had died four years before the creation of the map. The location of Mu'olaulani is also obscured by modern written references to it. *Place Names of Hawaii* indicates: "[Robello] lane was the site of Queen Lili'uokalani's Pālama home."[459] Further adding to the confusion is another reference in *Place Names of Hawaii* to Mu'olaulani: "Site of the Queen Lili'uokalani Children's Center, Kapālama section. Honolulu. Lili'uokalani had a home here. *Lit.*, innumerable royal buds."[460] Although sharing the name of the original King Street site, the Hālona Street location of the children's center, eight-tenths of a mile to the north, was not the site of Queen Lili'uokalani's Kapālama home. Even the *Queen's Songbook*, sponsored by the Queen Lili'uokalani Trust, is vague regarding the actual site of Mu'olaulani, locating it "somewhere in the vicinity of King Street, Auld Lane and Robello Lane."[461] The more recent mele, Pu'uhonua Nani, by Val Kepilino and Malia Craver, which praises the Queen Lili'uokalani Children's Center, also conflates the two different locations: "Famed indeed, is Mu'olaulani/A preserver of life for youth."[462] The first line refers to Lili'uokalani's home; the second refers to the Lili'uokalani Children's Center.

The earliest printed reference to the property, in the May 11, 1885, issue of the *Daily Bulletin*, did not even mention the house, instead noting that "Out along the Palama Road the country looks like Dutchland with the dykes bursted. Princess Liliuokalani's garden was like a miniature archipelago, the water flowing deep on all the paths."[463] Missionary Charles Stewart had described the area in 1824: "On leaving this stream [Nu'uanu], our path led to the west; and for the first mile lay through an uninterrupted succession of taro plantations."[464]

Soon after its opening, Lili'uokalani composed a song in May 1885, simply titled "Nohea I Mu'olaulani," to praise her new suburban home:

He mea nui ke aloha	This great love of yours
Ke hiki mai i oʻu nei	Has come here to me
Meheʻo kuʻu lei kaimana ala	It is like my diamond necklace
Kāhiko o kuʻu kino	To adorn my person
Kuʻu lei popohe i ka laʻi	My lei so shapely in the calm
Nohea i Muʻolaulani	Handsome at Muʻolaulani
Ka beauty lā he mau ia	It is a beauty, always a thing forever
No nā kau ā kau[465]	For all seasons

Shifting Locus

By May 21, 1885, Liliʻuokalani had already started relocating the site of her royal duties to her Kapālama home. The *Hawaiian Gazette* noted the inaugural event: "H.R.H. Princess Liliuokalani held the first reception at Palama on the afternoon of the 21st inst. The Band was stationed on the grounds and played a number of choices selections during the reception hours."[466] The site also provided a venue for meetings of the Liliuokalani Educational Society, whose aim was the "care and education of needy orphan children."[467] The hospitable Kapālama home and gardens also provided an ideal social gathering spot to support Liliʻuokalani's newly formed charitable venture.

The *Daily Bulletin* described the "ice cream sociable" that the society held on Tuesday evening, August 3, 1886:

> The cool atmosphere of the evening, the refreshing greenery surrounding the premises, the subdued light reflected from the Japanese lanterns disposed around the verandahs and garden, the informality of the gathering, and the genial affability of the royal lady who presided, all combined to make the occasion extremely pleasant and delightful, the memory of which will mark a sunny spot in the past of every participant.[468]

In contrast to the "informality" of the August gathering, the home also served as a site of more formal visits a month later. She made a special invitation at to the "first and second divisions of Liliuokalani Educational Society, Hookuonoono Society and Nihoa Society"[469] to visit her "at home" at Muʻolaulani at 2 p.m., September 2, 1886. Then, that evening, Liliʻuokalani hosted nobles and representatives at a luau at Muʻolaulani. The *Pacific Commercial Advertiser* reported: "The Palama residence of the royal lady was beautifully decorated with maile and fern wreaths, and bouquets of flowers, and during the early part of the day was thronged with visitors, who called to congratulate the Princess and pay their respects."[470] King Kalākaua made a special presentation there in honor of his sister's forty-eighth birthday:

> Princess Liliuokalani, by request of His Majesty, presented herself before him, and thereupon, after a short introductory address by His Majesty, whilst kneeling, was invested with cordon and decoration of the Royal Order of Kapiolani, the insignia of which Order was also displayed by His Majesty.[471]

Besides the ordinary, regularly scheduled occasions, the home would also serve as the site of a number of major events in Liliʻuokalani's life. It was there that Liliʻuokalani was asked if she would replace Kalākaua as sovereign if he was dethroned.[472] Liliʻuokalani also received, in 1887, while at Muʻolaulani her invitation to accompany Queen Kapiʻolani to Queen Victoria's Golden Jubilee, celebrating the fiftieth year of the British monarch's reign.[473]

The large house also allowed Liliʻuokalani the opportunity to show hospitality to one of her supporters, Robert Wilcox, and his new bride upon their return to Hawai'i in October 1887: "I gave them comfortable rooms in the long building attached to the main house at my Palama residence."[474] Gina Wilcox would later name her daughter Mu'olaulani as a favor to Lili'uokalani.[475]

The last major receptions given by Lili'uokalani at Mu'olaulani marked her birthday and that of her brother, the king. The fiftieth anniversary of Lili'uokalani's birth, held September 2, 1888, was attended by more than 200 well-wishers. The *Hawaiian Gazette* reported: "Princess Liliuokalani was dressed in cream colored satin with silk trimmings and was generally congratulated upon her hale and hearty appearance in turning the half century of life."[476] Two months later, in November

Lili'uokalani in 1887, the year she was asked to attend Queen Victoria's Golden Jubilee with Queen Kap'iolani. She received the invitation while living at Mu'olaulani. Photograph by Walery, London, England (courtesy Hawaii State Archives, PPWD-16-4-014).

1888, Lili'uokalani feted her brother: "The King's Birthday was ushered in by native serenaders in different quarters. There was a fine concert in the wee sma' hours on the veranda of Princess Liliuokalani's residence at Palama."[477] By 1888, Lili'uokalani's place of residence was firmly established in Kapālama. The 1888 *Hawaiian Directory and Hand Book of the Kingdom of Hawaii* lists: "Lileuokalani [sic] HRH, the Princess Regent, res Muolaulani, King."[478] All that would change the following year.

Upon the death of her mother-in-law, Mary Dominis, on April 25, 1889, Lili'uokalani returned to live with her husband, John Owen Dominis, at Washington Place. Despite her move from Mu'olaulani, her Kapālama home continued to play a historically significant role.

Mu'olaulani and the Rebellion of 1889

In the spring of 1889 Robert Wilcox returned to Hawai'i from San Francisco and once again resided at Mu'olaulani. Lili'uokalani relates in her biography, *Hawaii's Story by Hawaii's Queen*:

Robert Wilcox and his wife, Gina Sobrero, lived as guests of Liliʻuokalani at Muʻolaulani (from "Romantic Career of Robert W. Wilcox, Hawaii's Representative in Congress," *St. Louis Republic*, December 16, 1900).

> As the rooms formerly occupied by him and Mrs. Wilcox were not at that time used, and I was then living in Washington Place, I told him that he was welcome to go to Palama, and remain there until such time as he should be able to provide for himself elsewhere. I could not foresee that my kindness and hospitality to these persons in need would be used by suspicious parties to connect my name with a foolish and ill-organized attempt subsequently made by Mr. Wilcox to restore some part of the authority of which the missionary party had deprived the king."[479]

Upon her return from a trip to Kauaʻi in July 1889, Liliʻuokalani visited Muʻolaulani to inspect the house and grounds.[480] She provides an account of her encounter with Wilcox at Muʻolaulani:

I had finished my examinations, and was just on the point of leaving, when I heard steps on the front staircase; and knowing that some person was without, I advanced to the door, which I did not open, but drew down the grating, and met the gaze of a young man with haggard, anxious countenance. It was Mr. Robert W. Wilcox who was standing before me, trying with all his self-control to appear calm, but evidently much excited. He told me in a few words that he was ready to release the king from that hated thraldom under which he had been oppressed, and that measures had already been taken.[481]

In an interview just after the revolution, Liliʻuokalani indicated that "she ordered [Wilcox] away from the house and he took up his quarters in the servants' cottages in rear."[482] Nevertheless, the presence of Wilcox at Muʻolaulani implicated Liliʻuokalani by association. One of the headlines for the *Daily Bulletin* story following the revolution was clearly designed to imply the connection: "Residence of the Heir Apparent the Starting Point of the Rebel March." The ties continued in the article: "The rebels met at Princess Liliuokalani's Palama residence Monday evening, and in the early morn of Tuesday marched from there, 180 strong, right along King Street to Richards Street, from there along Palace Walk to the rear gate of the Palace yard."[483] Chief Justice of the Hawaiʻi Supreme Court, Albert Francis Judd, also made the connection: "Liliuokalani disavowed to me her knowledge or connivance with Wilcox's plans, but the fact that the armed party under Wilcox assembled at her own house in the suburbs and started from there to the Palace, gives credence to the belief that she knew of it."[484]

Such a belief was the basis of a question posed by a *Daily Bulletin* reporter to Liliʻuokalani during an interview at Washington Place: "Reports being around that you were implicated with Wilcox in his designs, and that he held secret meetings at your Palama residence which you attended, will you say whether or not such is the case?"[485] Liliʻuokalani denied involvement in the plot:

> The Princess replied that she knew nothing whatever of Wilcox's intentions until the Ministers informed her after her return from Hilo in June; that after being so informed she at once told Wilcox she did not approve of his designs if such was his intention, and told him he should desist without further delay; that she had never been present at any of his meetings.[486]

Nevertheless, a song written in praise of the Robert W. Wilcox makes prominent mention of Liliʻuokalani and Muʻolaulani, associating both with the rebellion. Composed by Mrs. Kauakipuupuu, the *mele* "Aia E Ka Nani I Muolaulani," or "He Mele no Wilikoki," first appeared a month and a half after the rebellion in the newspaper, *Ka Leo o ka Lahui*,[487] and was later reprinted in 1890 biography of Robert W. Wilcox, *Ka Buke Moolelo O Hon. Robert William Wilikoki*.[488]

The Lease of Muʻolaulani

Linked in newspaper accounts and song with the failed rebellion, Liliʻuokalani further distanced herself from Muʻolaulani with a six-month lease of the property starting October 10, 1890, to Ernest Hutchinson.[489] By 1892 Hutchinson is listed as living in Makiki.[490]

Even with her move to ʻIolani Palace as Queen following her brother's death in 1891, Liliʻuokalani continued to use Muʻolaulani for meetings. An empty Muʻolaulani provided now Queen Liliʻuokalani with a venue for an 1892 gathering that brought together various proponents for a new constitution. Liliʻuokalani recounts: "Accordingly a meeting was called to be held at Muolaulani Palace, at which there was to be an opportunity for them to compare their opinions and discuss them in my presence."⁴⁹¹ The meeting helped produce the "Draft of Constitution of January 14, 1893," which sought to "annul and abrogate the constitution promulgated by Kalakaua on the 7th day of July, A.D. 1887."⁴⁹² The proposed constitution never went into force as the Committee of Safety took control of the government on January 17, 1893. Mention of Muʻolaulani temporarily ceases following Liliʻuokalani's overthrow, her imprisonment at ʻIolani Palace on January 16, 1895, and her subsequent house arrest at Washington Place. The "land known as Muolaulani, situated in Kapalama" is part of a list of properties mortgaged to supporter H.A. Widemann for $32,000 in November 1893.⁴⁹³

Muʻolaulani would once again come into the society spotlight when Liliʻuokalani leased her Kapālama residence to British Commissioner and Consul-General Albert George Sidney Hawes. An announcement appeared in the July 13, 1895, issue of the *Hawaiian Star*: "Maj. A.G.S. Hawes, the British Commissioner, has taken Liliuokalani's Palama residence for five years."⁴⁹⁴ With a diplomatic representative in residence, the halls of Muʻolaulani once again provided a venue for social gatherings. On Tuesday, December 23, 1895, Hawes "gave a delightful musicale and dance at the Legation, Palama."⁴⁹⁵ The formal lease was signed in May 1896 for $65 a month.⁴⁹⁶ The house also featured more intimate gatherings as reported in the "The Week in Society" column of the *Hawaiian Gazette*: "British Commissioner A. G. S. Hawes gave a luncheon to Miss Gay of Hawaii at his home in Kapalama yesterday [November 23, 1896]. There were present Mr. and Mrs. Cropp, Miss Kate McGrew, Miss Marie Von Holt, Mr. Aubrey Robinson, Mr. Sinclair and Dr. Cooper."⁴⁹⁷ The Sinclair and Robinson families owned the island of Niʻihau. Six months later, in May 1897, Hawes would announce a major social event: "The Britannic Majesty's Commissioner and Consul-General extends a general invitation to the celebration of Queen Victoria's birthday on May 24th from 3:30 to 6:30 p.m. at his Palama residence."⁴⁹⁸ The events in Hawaiʻi celebrating Queen Victoria's Diamond Jubilee, recognizing

Albert George Sidney Hawes, British Commissioner and Consul, returned Muʻolaulani to prominence as a venue for major social events (courtesy Hawaii State Archives, Glass Neg. 9668).

the sixtieth year of her reign, rose to a crescendo on Friday evening, June 25, 1897, when music and merry-making once again graced the rooms of Muʻolaulani:

> The reception and ball given by the Commissioner were a proper end of the Jubilee festivities....
> The Commissioner occupies the Palama residence of Queen Liliuokalani and the handsome rooms of that dwelling were decorated in a very artistic manner by lady friends of the genial host.
> A magnificent floral structure, representing the crown of Hawaii in emblematic colors had been sent to the Commissioner by the retainers of Queen Liliuokalani, at her special request, and had a prominent place in the library....
> Exquisite refreshments were served during the evening and when the doors of Mr. Hawes residence closed he was again voted by all his guests the host *par excellence* of Hawaii-nei.[499]

His role as host would be tragically cut short when Hawes died little over a month later on August 6, 1897,[500] from an infected abscess related to a shipboard fall. The genial host, who had opened his leased home for diplomatic functions, was fondly remembered for his social gatherings: "At his establishment at Palama he entertained royally, and his door was always open to the cultured people of the Islands."[501] He had two months earlier proposed to Miss Eliza Gay, granddaughter of the owner of Niʻihau, and planned to continue to reside at Muʻolaulani after his wedding.[502] Instead the residence was the site from which his body was borne to his funeral at St. Andrew's Cathedral. The *Friend* noted the sadly ironic timing: "Only a few days after the date of his death was the time appointed for the wedding of Captain Hawes with Elise Gay of Kauai. He was thus without one tenderly to mourn his passing." The juxtaposition, too, with the social events at Muʻolaulani prompted community members to reflect: "Death so untimely," wrote *Paradise of the Pacific*, "coming in the wake of the Jubilee festivities impressed one sadly that in the midst of life we are in death."[503]

The popular Hawes was replaced by W. J. Kenny, Esq. who served as acting British Commissioner and Consul-General.[504] Kenny had previously held the position of "British Consul at Tainan, Formosa."[505] The passing of Hawes also resulted in a renegotiation of the lease of Muʻolaulani. The *Evening Bulletin* reported on Friday, November 12, 1897, that Kenny would "likely occupy the premises of the late Commissioner Hawes at Palama. Negotiations to that end were practically concluded today. Mr. Hawes' lease of the place will run nearly four years longer, it having been originally made out for five years."[506] The 1898 *Husted's Directory and Hand-Book of Honolulu* listed Kenny's address as "King opp Dowsett lane [today called Akepo Lane]."[507] This address agrees with contemporaneous maps of the area. An 1897 Monsarrat map has Liliʻuokalani's name attached to the residence as well as the outline of the house of Princess Ruth Keʻelikōlani.

The extensive grounds of Muʻolaulani provided Kenny with a resource to support the British national sport in Hawaiʻi. In January 1898 the "Local and General News" column of the *Independent* reported, "Cricket to-morrow afternoon," and that "British Commissioner Kenney is having a cricket practice ground arranged at his Palama residence."[508] The Honolulu Cricket Club thanked its patron at a meeting in February 1898 "for his hospitality in preparing and placing at the use of the Club a practice ground at Palama...."[509] A reception on May 24, 1898, celebrated Queen Victoria's 78th birthday. "The home in Palama was beautifully decorated, the flowers sent in by kind lay friends playing a most important part. A picture of Queen Victoria held a place of honor in the library of the Commissioner."[510] Among the attendees were A.S. Cleghorn, vice chairman of the event, and his daughter, Princess Kaʻiulani.[511]

That year Hawaiʻi was annexed to the United States on August 12, 1898. The annexation resolution specified that the "existing treaties of the Hawaiian Islands with foreign nations shall forthwith cease and determine, being replaced by such treaties as may exist, or may hereafter be concluded between the United States and such foreign nations."[512] In January 1899, President William McKinley "granted the first exequaturs to foreign Consuls to discharge their functions in the Hawaiian Islands. In the list of Consular officers recognized for such purposes appeared to-day the [name] of William Robert Hoare to be British Consul at Honolulu."[513] Although named, Hoare was not physically present in Hawaiʻi, and so duties were not yet transferred from Kenny. On February 3, 1899, the visit of Lord Charles Beresford occasioned another round of social events at Muʻolaulani. After the speech by Dr. Robert McKibbin that spoke of the mutual interests of the Americans and British, Lord Charles responded, making comment on the recent annexation:

> With regard to the native Hawaiians I cannot say that I know very much about their position. It may be presumed, however, that they feel a degree of soreness over the change in the political conditions of their country. Nevertheless looking back to my own country not so very long ago there was considerable soreness in Ireland over its union with Great Britain.[514]

Hoare would not arrive in Honolulu until February 16, 1899. The journey of several thousand miles from London took its toll on Hoare, who, the *Hawaiian Gazette* reported: "did not yesterday consult with Commissioner Kenny regarding the time for the transfer of the Consulate, but Mr. Hoare states that the transfer will be made within a few days."[515] The Honolulu Cricket Club visited Muʻolaulani in late February 1899 after the transition to bid a fond farewell to Kenny. His friends expressed their appreciation for the "tactful discretion displayed by you during a most delicate and most important era of political change in which indiscretions would have been follies worse than crimes."[516]

With the passage of the Organic Act, Hoare became H.M. Consul for the Territory of Hawaiʻi in 1900. The 1900–1901 Honolulu city directory lists "Hoar [sic] W R, Consul Great Britain, Office King opp Dowsett's lane [now named Akepo Lane]."[517] Hoare brought with him a strong understanding of the United States. In the 1882 he had been named as 2nd Vice Consul to the United States for New York, Delaware, New Jersey, Rhode Island and Connecticut.[518] With the new consul in residence the entertaining of guests once again resumed. Queen Victoria's birthday celebration in May 1900 provided Hoare an opportunity to draw Honolulu's elite to Muʻolaulani:

> The reception at the British Consulate, Palama, in honor of Queen Victoria's birthday was largely attended. Many ladies were among the callers. Consul Hoare and Miss Hoare received the guests in the parlor.... The government band played on the grounds during the reception. "God Save the Queen" was timed for high noon, when the Queen's health was drunk on Judge Stanley's proposal. A fine collation was spread in the lanai.[519]

In August 1900 Hoare convened a British Naval Court, "at his residence adjoining the British Consulate, King Street,"[520] to make a determination regarding the grounding of the British barque *Dunreggan* on the reef off of Diamond Head. The court ultimately decided an uncharted strong current off Diamond Head caused the stranding of the vessel.

The turn of the century would soon mark the end of the Victoria's long reign. Hoare made special arrangements at Muʻolaulani to commemorate the death of Queen Victoria in 1901, inviting British residents "to attend a meeting to be held at the British Consulate 651 King Street Honolulu on Saturday next the 2nd February at 2:30 p.m."[521]

Japanese Hotel

A July 8, 1901, inventory of the Kapālama property helps identify the various rooms and parts of the residence that included a veranda, three parlors, a music room, dining room, kitchen, three bedrooms and three closets.[522] The inventory marked the end of the lease to the British Consulate, for on July 8, 1901, Liliʻuokalani leased to Nakata (中田) "that lot of land on King street at Kapalama known as Muolaulani lately occupied by W. Robert Hoare" for five years at $780 per annum. Nakata, in turn, subleased Muʻolaulani to K. Koyasu on July 30, 1901.[523] In August 1901, *The Honolulu Republican* announced the new use for the property: "The old British Consulate, opposite the Dowsett homestead on, the Palama road, is now being used as a Japanese hotel."[524]

That same year, Prince David Kawānanakoa would name one of his canoes "Muʻolaulani."[525] The six-paddle canoe would compete in the Regatta Day Races for a $20 prize.

Territorial Political Activity

Muʻolaulani, a site for revolution a decade earlier, became a center for political activity during the early years of the Territory of Hawaiʻi. The large residences of Kapalama provided meeting sites for political parties. "A Republican meeting will occur at the Achi residence in Kapalama and a Home Rule one also at a near-by place at Muʻolaulani, at the servants' quarters of the Queen."[526] Another 1902 political rally of Home Rulers at Muʻolaulani drew 300 to 500 persons and Speakers, including Delegate Robert Wilcox "held their attention to a late hour bordering on to midnight."[527] Another large gathering of the Home Rule party took place at Muʻolaulani the next year. The site of the planning of the Wilcox Rebellion of 1889 had become the rally place for Wilcox's party in 1903.[528] In early 1904, Muʻolaulani, a gathering place for the Home Rule party, saw the formation of a new precinct club of the rival Democratic party "at the present abode of F. J. Testa at Muolaulani."[529] An October 12, 1904, list of political meetings included the Home Rulers in the Fifth District "at Muolaulani, Queen Liliuokalani's premises."[530] Three days later, on October 15, 1904, the Democrats once again held their meeting at Muʻolaulani.[531] References to events at Muʻolaulani cease in 1904.

Tenements

By 1906 Muʻolaulani is divided into fourteen separate residences and labeled as a tenement. Although used in the pejorative today, the term "tenement" was used to refer to any property rented to multiple families. The 1906 Dakin Fire Insurance Map gives the most detailed drawing of the residence, which featured a pair of curved staircases on the King Street face of the building. A veranda ran along the entire King Street side of the house. Another curved staircase connected to the veranda from the southeast side. The northeast side of the building also featured wide verandas and two rooms with curved bays. From the north corner a long narrow wing stretched northeast. A veranda

Detail of an 1897 map by M.D. Monsarrat shows the location of Muʻolaulani, marked as "Liliuoklani" [sic]. The rectangular building across King Street from the Reform School indicates the unlabeled location of the house of Ruth Keʻelikōlani. The small circle indicates the location of the artesian well. Registered Map 1910 (courtesy Land Survey Division, Department of Accounting and General Services, State of Hawaii).

ran along the entire southeast face of the wing. On the 1906 map the residence is given two addresses. The five-room wing that parallels King Street is numbered 430 King Street; the nine-room wing parallel to Pua Lane is 438 King Street.

In 1908, Liliʻuokalani mortgaged her land holdings. A $70,000 mortgage taken by Liliʻuokalani in 1908 from Claus Spreckels included "the land at Kapalama known as Muolaulani."[532] The mortgage, at a six percent rate, paid off the 1901 mortgage to H.A. Widemann.[533] On June 13, 1909, Liliʻuokalani wrote a codicil to her will regarding Kealohilani and Muʻolaulani: "It is my will that Joseph Kaiponohea Aea shall at my demise, inherit my house and lot at Kapalama, known as 'Muolaulani.'"[534] Aea never received the property. Six months later, in December 1909, Liliʻuokalani created a deed of trust that gave in part: "Loe, of Honolulu, the house and premises, now occupied by her at Muolaulani, Kapalama, Honolulu, and $180 a year [Loʻe was the maternal grandmother of Liliʻuokalani's hānai daughter Lydia Kaonohiponiponiokalani Aholo]; Hakaui and his wife Kainalu, of Honolulu, the lot of land enclosed and occupied by them at Muolaulani, and $150 a year."[535]

In 1911 the Hawaii Territorial Senate received a resolution from the Board of Supervisors of the City and County of Honolulu proposing: "that those premises situate at Kapalama, lying on the Waikiki side of Pua Lane, and known as 'Liliuokalani Premises', should be made a park for the use of people living in that locality."[536] The request was ultimately tabled by House of Representatives, ending any further consideration.[537] That same year Liliʻuokalani asked that some of the property of her trust be gifted to the city. That land at Waikahalulu still bears her name as Liliʻuokalani Gardens.

The residence appears in the 1914 Sanborn Fire maps labeled as "Tenements." The addresses are changed to 642A and 642C. A kitchen building *mauka* of the King Street wing is labeled 642B.

Liliʻuokalani died on November 11, 1917, and Muʻolaulani passed to her trust.

Sometime before 1922, the main house was demolished. A map of Kapālama that year shows an empty lot where the main house once stood.[538] Only the wing parallel to Pua Lane remains in the 1927 and 1950 Sanborn Fire maps. The King Street wing was replaced by six buildings labeled 642A, 642B, 648A, 648B, 642F, 642G. The only picture of Muʻolaulani (just the remnant wing) is part of a 1939 aerial photograph of the Hawaiian Housing Commission Tract. The wing disappears entirely in the 1956 Sanborn Fire Map, supplanted by a public housing development that replaced many of the tenements *mauka* of King Street between Pua Lane and Liliha Street.

Residences of Liliʻuokalani, Mānoa, Oʻahu

Although not on the scale of Muʻolaulani, Liliʻuokalani maintained residences in other suburbs of Honolulu. Thomas G. Thrum, in his discussion of the royal residents of Mānoa in the *Hawaiian Almanac and Annual for 1892*, mentions that Boki and Haʻalilio "were high chiefs who held Manoa in high favor," lists "Princess Victoria, Kanaina, Lunalilo and Keelikolani of more recent times" and concludes the roster of residents with "the present queen Liliuokalani." Liliʻuokalani bought her properties in Mānoa in 1881 and 1889–1890.

East Manoa Road property

On March 26, 1881, Liliʻuokalani bought land on both sides of East Manoa Road in Kolowalu. ["J.L. Aholo and wife, of Honolulu, to J. Ewaloa et al., of the same place. Articles of Adoption, dated May 24, 1899; Liber 198, folio 151. Adopts D.K.M. Malo, a male child."] The property, originally Land Court Award 1926, Apana 1 and 2, to Nanauki, consisted of two pieces of land. His neighbor, Halawa, testified: "The house lot is enclosed with a stone wall. The kula land is not cultivated. He got the kalo patches from me [Halawa] in the life time of Kinau."[539] A survey of L.C.A. 1926 identified Apana 2 as "A House Lot."[540]

On July 20, 1900, Liliʻuokalani wrote a letter from Kealohilani to J.O. Carter asking him to communicate with a tenant of the East Manoa Road property: "Will you kindly write to Mrs. Hilo Ewaloa [The Ewaloa family had been granted LCA 1828 at the mouth of Manoa Valley] that as she has not paid rent for the Kuleana of Nanauki for the past two years—neither for the loi's or for the house lot—that she is in default of payment; is notified that at the end of ten days from the day of notification—she is to move away from the house and deliver up the keys to Akana—and that she has no more kuleana to house lot and loi's."[541]

On December 13, 1928, "K. Okimura, M. Masunaga, I. Okamura, R. Okinaga, U. Suehiro, S. Kamemoto, as Trustees for and on behalf of the Manoa Japanese Language (a voluntary unincorporated association)"[542] bought the portion of the property on the northwest side of East Manoa Road (LCA 1926, Apana 2) for $15,924.15. Fred Kinzaburo Makino headed the school's education committee.

The language school, which celebrated its centennial in 2010, still occupies the house lot of Lili'uokalani on East Manoa Road. The Manoa Church Lot diagonally across the street is now Manoa Valley Theatre. The Manoa Valley Shopping Center sits on the former agricultural portion of the Lili'uokalani purchase.

Manoa Road Property

Across the valley Lili'uokalani bought adjacent pieces of property at foreclosure auctions in 1889 and 1890. Lili'uokalani and the property there is mentioned in relation to other prominent landholders in Mānoa. An article in *The Hawaiian Almanac and Annual for 1892* reported: "Another name identified with Manoa early days is that of John Stevenson, known also as 'Col. Stevens.' Among his properties in the valley was the tract lying between the old Brenig premises (the latter now a portion of Her Majesty Lili-iuokalani's estate), and the Ehu homestead at Kaipu [Ka'aipū]."[543] The Brenig property, named for Karl Brenig, comprised a 1.5 acre portion of a 15.5 acre Royal Patent Grant 136 to Komaia. Komaia died of smallpox on August 7, 1853, survived by a wife and older brother. Brenig bought the property in 1855 and sold it in 1867.

On December 23, 1889, Lili'uokalani acquired 1.5 acres at a foreclosure auction for $380. She bought another 2.14 acres for $650 at another auction on June 16, 1890.

Lili'uokalani wrote from Washington Place to J.O. Carter on September 19, 1904, regarding the lease of the Manoa Road property: "The bearer of this [letter] Mr. Makino would like to lease the Manoa lot for Fifteen years at Fifteen dollars a month. I think this is a fair offer and you can of course make out the papers according to the usual stipulations made in all leases and papers of agreement."[544] She wrote again to Carter the following month: "Mr. Makino is applying for my land in Manoa. I mean the makai lot that you leased to Mrs. Joseph Emmerson at $10.00 a month. He—Mr. Makino is willing to give $15.00 a month and I have agreed to let him have it for fifteen years. There is five acres in this lot more or less and he is anxious to improve on it."[545] On November 4, 1904, Lili'iokalani leased her Manoa Road property to F. K. Makino for 15 years at $180 a year.[546] In 1909 Makino would lead the Japanese Strike against the sugar planters. Called a "labor agitator," Makino was jailed in 1910. In 1912 he started the Japanese language newspaper, *Hawaii Hochi*.

Just before the Makino lease expired, in a letter dated August 27, 1919, Carrie A. Sabine, superintendent of the Salvation Army Home Girls' Department, asked the trustees of the Lili'uokalani Trust to sell to them the property "now occupied by Mr. Makino" for a "Home of Refuge."[547] The superintendent appealed to the memory of the Queen: "We are positive that Hawaii's gracious Queen who did so much to uplift the weak and helpless, would if she were here, voice her feelings of approval in the matter, and the property could not be put to a better use other than a home of refuge for our wayward women."[548] Ultimately the trustees declined the request. They noted that the "alienation of any portion of the real estate at this time whilst litigation against the Estate is pending will only tend to further complicate matters."⁵⁴⁹ On May 31, 1927, the trustees for the Liliuokalani Trust sold 5.201 acres to Hawaiian Trust Company for $30,000, reserving a .462 acre portion for a Salvation Army lease.

Residence of Liliʻuokalani at Kahala, Oʻahu

The residences of royalty would often serve as a magnet for other residences. William Auld, the head of the Insane Asylum, a "personal and intimate friend of Liliʻuokalani by whom he was held in high esteem" and "fast adherent to the royalist cause,"⁵⁵⁰ built a house near hers. His obituary noted that he had "just completed a new beach residence adjoining that of Queen Liliʻuokalani, at Kahala, beyond Diamond Head."⁵⁵¹

The Kahala land, called the "Queen's Place" at Kahala, was part of a "life estate under the Will of Bernice P. Bishop."⁵⁵² According to the will, Liliʻuokalani could lease the property, but not for periods beyond ten years. At least one lessee was willing to pay for the months before the date he wanted because he recognized that if she died before the lease went into effect it might not be valid.⁵⁵³

Many other supporters would host royalty at their residences. Although *Lost Palaces of Hawaiʻi* looks primarily at the residences owned by royalty and high chiefs, one frequently visited house deserves mention.

Residence of John Dominis, Waialua, Oʻahu

Although most often remembered as Prince Consort of Queen Liliʻuokalani, John Owen Dominis served on the Privy Council of Kamehameha V, Lunalilo, and Kalākaua; as a member of the House of Nobles from 1864 to 1886, Governor of Maui from 1878 to 1886, and as Governor of Oʻahu under Kamehameha V, Lunalilo, Kalākaua and Liliʻuokalani. Like many other members of royalty Dominis also maintained a distant retreat, his near the mouth of the Anahulu River in Kawailoa, Waialua, on the north shore of Oʻahu. On June 12, 1867, Dominis bought land bordering the Loko Ea fish pond from J.W. Keawehunahala.⁵⁵⁴ The following year, on October 7, 1868, he purchased an adjacent piece of property, also bordering the fish pond, from Ki and James Robinson.⁵⁵⁵ He later secured from Princess Ruth Keʻelikōlani, on August 27, 1874, the land that stretched to the Anahulu River from his two earlier purchases.⁵⁵⁶ Labeled the "Gov. Dominis House" on the October 1884 map of Waialua Bay, the residence sat across the Anahulu River from the [William A. ?] Dickson and J.S. Emerson houses and the Protestant Church, linked by a footbridge.

Liliʻuokalani mentions the residence in *Hawaii's Story by Hawaii's Queen* in reference to her tour of the islands at the start of her reign. Dominis had built an addition to the Waialua house that Liliʻuokalani called a "great surprise." The gift presented for his wife consisted of an addition to the riverside house: "A large wooden lanai, or outer room, had been built, capacious enough to accommodate some one hundred and fifty or more persons. He had thought what a pleasure it would be to have this cool and pleasant resort, where, after the heat of the day or a row up the stream of Anahulu, I might take my comfort in sitting under the grateful shade, with all the friends I might select and invite to meet and rest with me there. It proved to be all that his kindness foresaw and desired, and also served as a reception-room for pleasant dances and other festivities."557

Following the death of John Owen Dominis on August 27, 1891, and the probate of his will, the property passed to his wife, Lili'uokalani. On April 4, 1892, Lili'uokalani received "Deed Keelikolani to J.O. Dominis Lot in Kawailoa, Waialua, O'ahu."558 After the overthrow of the monarchy the Waialua residence continued to serve as a venue for social gatherings. The Society page of the *Pacific Commercial Advertiser*, in reporting in 1904 about the visit of Prince and Princess Kawananakoa, referred to the location as "Queen Lili'uokalani's old cottage at Waialua."559

In 1909 Lili'uokalani made provisions in her Deed of Trust regarding her Waialua property: "For S. K. Mahoe, and Emalia his wife, of Waialua, Oahu, the premises known as 'Punamoenui' and 'Punamoeiki,' at said Waialua; reversion to the Trustees."560 Lot Kamehameha, then Prince, made an agreement with W.C. Lane for the "Kalo lands of Kealia and Punamoi of about four acres."561 Whether "Punamoe" and "Punamoi" refer to the same location is uncertain, but both were situated in Kawailoa, Waialua, Oahu. The agreement also makes reference to Lauhulu. One of the properties just *mauka* of the John Dominis residence is listed as being in the *'ili* of Lauhulu.

Residence of Gideon La'anui at Waialua, O'ahu

One of the other venues for social gatherings at Waialua stood across the Anahulu Stream from the residence of John Dominis and Lili'uokalani—the Haleiwa Hotel. Before the hotel was built the site had been the residence of high chief Gideon Pele'ioholani La'anui, overseer of Waialua. Indeed, the claim by La'anui included all of Kawailoa, "from the uplands to the sea, from that side to this side."562 His claim to the land came through his marriage to Lydia Nāmāhana, also known as Pi'ia: "The origin of my right to the land in Waialua is from my *wahine*, Kuaipiia, and I have become

Piia, referred to as "Nomahanna, Queen of the Sandwich Islands." Frontispiece of *A New Voyage Round the World, 1823–1826*, by Otto Von Kotzebue (courtesy Hawaii State Archives, Paul Markham Kahn Collection, 03/191).

A descendant of High Chief Gideon Pele'ioholani La'anui, Elizabeth Kahanu Kalaniana'ole, wife of Prince Jonah Kuhio Kalaniana'ole (left), appears with her mother Muolo La'anui (right). Marie Nalanielua Jones stands between them (courtesy Hawaii State Archives, PP-97-1-054).

a genuine *kama'aina* of this place, as though native-born of several generations of ancestors."[563] Pi'ia was sister of Ka'ahumanu and Kaheiheimālie. All were daughters of Keeaumoku and wives of Kamehameha I. La'anui was given just five acres in Waialua as LCA 9951.

After the death of Pi'ia in 1829, La'anui married Owana Rives, daughter of Jean

The residence of Gideon Pele'ioholani La'anui stood *mauka* of the Haleiwa Hotel, near the grove of trees on the left side of the photograph (courtesy Hawaii State Archives, PPWD-10-2-007).

Baptiste Rives, who as a translator had accompanied Kamehameha II to England. Their daughter, Elizabeth Keka'aniau La'anui, was born September 12, 1834, at the Waialua residence, and later attended the Chiefs' Children's School. Gideon Kailipalaki La'anui was born at the residence in April 1840. His mother died two months later, on June 20, 1840. A third marriage with Amelia Puoho gave him a daughter, Muolo Keawe-heulu La'anui, mother of Elizabeth Kahanu, who married Prince Jonah Kūhiō Kalaniana'ole. Gideon Pele'ioholani La'anui, died on September 11, 1849, and was buried at Lili'uokalani Church.

The properties eventually became part of the Bernice Pauahi Bishop Estate that leased the La'anui homestead to B.F. Dillingham's Oahu Railway and Land Company.

In October 1898 the *Pacific Commercial Advertiser* announced that plans for a new hotel at Waialua, designed by O.G. Traphagen for Oahu Railway and Land Company, had been completed.[564] (Traphagen would also design the Moana Hotel in Waikīkī in 1901.) The Waialua hotel opened on August 5, 1899, with Curtis Iaukea, a former member of Queen Lili'uokalani's personal staff, as its manager.[565] In 1914 Justin Emerson delivered an address at a reception held to honor the three Emerson children. Reprinted in *The Friend*, the speech titled "Emersosoniana," located the first church and the residence of La'anui: "The first 'Hale pule,'—a large thatched building which would seat 1000 persons on the floor of mats or rushes, was located near where the Haleiwa Hotel now stands, a few rods from Laanui's residence."[566] In a 1925 account J.S. Emerson reminisced in *The Friend* about the first church at Waialua and Laʻanui, who had helped build it.[567] Albert P. Taylor added to an entry about the story in the subject catalog at the Hawaii State Archives: "Across the way, mauka, in a grove where autos park was the site of Laanui's house." By January 1943 the hotel had become a club for Army officers.

Chapter 6

Royal Residences of Kaua'i

O Kaua'i Nui moku lehua, 'āina nui makekau
Great Kaua'i, isle of warriors and land of men ever on the defense.[1]
—Hawaiian proverb

The island of Kaua'i, the last portion of the archipelago incorporated into the Kingdom of Hawai'i, maintained its independence under King Kaumuali'i [Ka-umu-ali'i] until 1810, when he became a vassal of Kamehameha. This history had a profound impact on the number of palaces on the island as well as the adoption of Western building practices and styles.

Residence of Kaumuali'i, Waimea, Kaua'i

The earliest description of King Kaumuali'i comes before the voluntary cession of Kaua'i in the account by John Turnbull, who arrived at the island on December 26, 1802, aboard the *Margaret*. Unfortunately, Turnbull does not describe the residence of Kaumuali'I, since his encounter with the island ruler took place only on deck of his ship. Turnbull did, nevertheless, record the presence of Western carpenters and blacksmiths supporting the Kaua'i ruler.[2] The efforts of those Westerners, however, seem to be devoted solely to the construction of a Western style "vessel suited to an attempt of a long voyage, and in the event of the expected invasion, they proposed to escape from the island."[3]

A description of the king's residence does appear in an 1868 narrative by the Hawaiian Club of Boston. The reference in the account to Kamehameha threatening to invade the island places the time of the encounter to prior to 1810. Although the expatriate organization published the account more than half century after the actual meeting of King Kaumuali'i at his residence, the description includes rich detail:

> On one occasion, during the reign of Kaumualii, King of Kauai, Captain Wiles who was about to sail for the States, called on him at his royal residence at Waimea, to receive his orders. The captain and his supercargo were ushered into one of the apartments of the grass palace, and after respectfully saluting the king who reclined *en dishabille* on his *hikie* seated themselves at a small table, which stood against the side of the room, and prepared to take down the items on paper. Kaumualii, who had been taking his afternoon nap, and was attended only by his *Iwikuamoo*, immediately arose, and wrapping a light *kapa* around his form, seated himself on a brilliant Niihau mat in the coolest part of the room, and after sending out his attendant to order a repast of fish and fowl, for his guests proceeded to business. As he had doubtless already made up his mind as to the articles he wished to order, the list was quickly told off and

written down, showing by its contents the character of the man and the circumstances of his little kingdom, as well perhaps as the message of a president or the speech of a premier usually exhibits the condition of a nation. Besides a large assortment of dry goods and hardware, articles of adornment and implements of peace, there was a large order for powder and muskets, and a battery of field-pieces for the benefit of that insolent Kamehameha, who was even then threatening to invade his dominions.[4]

The author refers to the structure as a "palace," albeit modified by "grass." The division of the interior into apartments reflects the adoption of the Western practice of rooms. Ultimately, though, the account ridicules Kaumuali'i, whose unfamiliarity with the characteristics of gems resulted in his request for a coconut-sized diamond. The description of the residence also reveals once more an aspect of an early transitional phase of royal houses—the use of Western furnishings in the traditional Hawaiian house.

Although Kamehameha I allowed the continued rule of Kaumuali'i after 1810, his heir, Kamehameha II, kidnapped the Kaua'i ruler soon after his father's death in 1819, having a profound impact on the royal residences of that island. Fornander notes in his history of Kaua'i that, "after the death of *Kamehameha, Kaumualii* the last independent king of Kauai removed to Honolulu and became the spouse of *Kaahumanu*, most of his nobles followed him thither."[5] The migration of the king and his court to O'ahu explains the dearth of royal residences on Kaua'i. The relocation of Kaumuali'i to O'ahu also necessitated the appointment of a series of island governors. Ke'eaumoku, also known as Governor Cox, was appointed as the first governor of Kaua'i. He was the brother of powerful Kuhina Nui, Ka'ahumanu; governor of Hawaii island, Kuakini; and future Kuhina Nui, Kekāuluohi. Ke'eaumoku died on March 23, 1824.[6] His successor was Kahalai'a, son of the brother of Kamehameha I and Wahinepio (Stewart gives parentage). The governor was married to Kīna'u, who was given to him by Kamehameha II when the king departed on his ill-fated journey to London. Thus, what amounts to royalty on Kaua'i primarily comprises the island governors appointed during the Kamehameha and Kalākaua dynasties. On August 8, 1824, the son of Kaumuali'i, called Humehume, attempted to capture the Russian-built Fort Elizabeth. Following the suppression of the revolt, Kahalai'a was replaced by Kaikio'ewa as the island's third governor.

Humehume, also known as George Tamoree, was the son of King Kamuali'i, the last ruler of Kaua'i. Detail from the painting *Four Owyhean Youths* (1822) by Samuel Finley Breese Morse.

Residence of Humehume and Peke, Wahiawa, Kaua'i

The instigator of the rebellion, Humehume, was married to Peke, Elizabeth "Betty" Davis, daughter of Isaac Davis, who had helped Kamehameha I conquer the island chain. Hiram Bingham wrote of the couple: "At the foot of this valley [Wahiawa, Kaua'i], I found George living much in the original native style in a dingy, dirty, thatched house at the sea-side, just where the surf washes a small beach between two rocky cliffs. His wife, Betty, was a daughter of a Hawaiian mother [Kaiona] and Isaac Davis [...] who afterwards assisted Kamehameha in his wars."[7]

The residence of Humehume stands in stark contrast with the *hale pili* of Kaikio'ewa, the man who defeated the Kaua'i rebel.

Residence of Kaikio'ewa and Keaweamahi, Waimea, Kaua'i

The earliest account of the residence of Kaikio'ewa, and his wife, Keaweamahi, comes from Jacobus Beolens, Dutch captain of the *Wilhemina & Maria*, who visited Kaua'i from March 8 to March 10, 1828. His log described the location of the residence of the island governor: "The guide first conducted us to the east side of the village, to the bank of the lake. On our left hand we had among other Indian dwellings that of the chief of this island, whose name was Quequaheva [Kaikio'ewa]."[8]

Captain Beolens also described a meeting that took place in the residence of Kaikio'ewa:

> We then paid a visit to the chief Quequaheva, who we met sitting at the entrance of his home, surrounded by many men of his retinue. They sat in two rows, to the left and right of their chief, and helped their lord kill time by telling stories and fantasies. We approached Quequaheva with "*Aroga*, Governor," to which he replied in his usual way. We then sat down on a bed

Village of Waimea, Kauai, from Hiram Bingham's *A Residence of Twenty-one Years in the Sandwich Islands*. The residence of Kaumuali'i would have been next to Fort Elisabeth on the left side of the sketch. The house of Kaikio'ewa, the governor of Kaua'i, was located across the river.

consisting of a pile of mats. In the shadows or in the background of the building I perceived Mrs. Quequaheva [Keawemahi], lying on a matress of mats with her head protruding from under a cover. Although this lady appeared more talkative and because of her fewer years more mobile than the old Queen Kaahumana [Kaʻahumanu], she was no less large and fat, like the best of her *erie* [aliʻi] dynasty.[9]

The missionaries gave high praise for the efforts of Kaikioʻewa and Keaweamahi:

The change of Kauai administration through the removal of its king, led to the appointment of Kahalaia, of Maui, as governor, a nephew of Kalanimoku, a man of excellent qualities, who, outwardly at least, made a show of favoring religion and built a church at Waimea. Consequent upon the rebellion of George Kaumualii, in which Kahalaia was killed [Kahalaia actually died of whooping cough[10] in 1826, two years after the 1824 rebellion], Kaikioewa, an aged chief of high rank, a warrior with Kalanimoku under Kamehameha, headed a body of men from Maui, and with Hoapili and Kahekili, hastened to the scene of conflict. At the close of the war Kaikioewa was made governor of Kauai, who with his wife, Keaweamahi, restored order rendered important service to the cause of instruction and religion, and took pleasure in erecting as he said, "the best built chapel in the islands," a building ninety by thirty feet. With his wife he made tours from time to time to instruct and encourage the people. Their support of schools and teachers was commendable. Keaweamahi herself conducting a school of forty children.[11]

John Kirk Townsend, who visited Kauaʻi on February 10, 1835, gave an account of the relocation of the house of King Kamehameha III on Kauaʻi. The king and his former guardian, Kaikioʻewa, had earlier sailed to Kauaʻi on the *Avon* on January 21, 1835. Levi Chamberlain recorded the purpose of the king's visit in his journal: "The King & Kaikioewa sailed for Kauai in the Brig. Avon. Kaikioewa is considered to be deranged and it is said one object of the King in going to Kauai at the present time was to get the old chief home to his own island."[12] The king, eager to return to Oʻahu, had his house moved so he could view the ship's arrival. He had earlier allowed Townsend to stay in his house but later decided to use the residence. Townsend recorded: "The principal object of the king in calling upon us was to request, which he did with great apparent diffidence, the *loan* of his house for a few days, as he wished to move his residence to a point nearer the sea, in order to catch the first glimpse of the white sails of the Avon, the arrival of which he is expecting with great anxiety."[13] The subjects of the king turned out in large number and moved the king's house and other *hale pili* for his servants: "Little houses were put up all around the vicinity, and thatched in an incredibly short space of time, and when Mr. N. and myself visited the royal mansion after nightfall we found the whole neighbourhood metamorphosed; a beautiful little village had sprung up as by magic, and the retired studio of the naturalists had been transformed into a royal banquet hall."[14] The account demonstrates the highly transportable nature of the *hale pili*.

On December 24, 1846, Keaweamahi made her claim for a house lot in Waimea, giving the history of the property: "From the time of my *kane alii*, Kaikioewa, I had all these things which I have now and on his death I continued his rulership, which was given to me. *A nana aku no au iaia mawaho o kona moe ana*. ... For your information, O Land Commissioners, that is my claim for my place which I occupy. We held it from the time of the fighting [1824] and in the year 1837 Kailinaoa and from thence until this time."[15] The land described by Keaweamahi was surrounded by two ponds on the west, two on the north and one on the east. Land enclosed for pigs formed the southern boundary. "This was the nature of the house lot, which was from Kaikioʻewa. When he died, Kekuanaoa was the one from whom I held it. Therefore there are three with the right to the place—mine is from the year 1831 to 1847, this being the place to which the right was conveyed in the previous letter."[16] Keaweamahi followed the claim with further testimony on January 10, 1848: "The first of the diagrams of the places I occupy is a little suitable, but best of all is the place I now occupy with all our retainers living in one house lot. This land claim was acquired in January 1824."[17]

Residence of Kaikioʻewa, Kōloa, Kauaʻi

Kaikioʻewa also erected a residence at Kōloa. The Rev. Reuben Tinker, who had arrived with the fourth company of missionaries on June 1831, reported in September 1836: "At this place of the stream [Kōloa] the governor of Kauai has built a hay house where he spends a part of his time though his home is commonly at Waimea."[18] The chief's residence remained on Kauaʻi for the rest of his life: "He died at Kōloa in April 1839."[19] Kaikioʻewa was the hānai father of Moses Kekuaiwa, brother of Kamehameha IV and Kamehameha V. The young Moses suffered a double loss. His mother, Kīnaʻu, had died a week before his hānai father. Both had died of mumps brought to the kingdom on board the *Quixote*.[20]

After the death of Kaikioʻewa, his widow, Emelia or Emili Keaweamahi, served as governor from 1839 to 1842. The missionaries reported: "That island is now left without any suitable person to act as governor. It is probable that the oldest son of Kinau [Moses Kekuaiwa, born July 20, 1829] will be appointed governor, with the widow of Kaikioewa to act as his guardian and agent."[21] Like her late husband, Keaweamahi exhibited a domineering style in conducting duties as *konohiki* and her role as overseer of the island. On August 5, 1839, she received instructions from the King, Kamehameha III, and the *Kuhina Nui*, Kekāuluohi, regarding the workers in her charge. Their complaints to her include her making the weak and blind work on *koele* days and hassling persons cultivating new lands. In a letter signed by the King and Kuhina Nui, the two wrote: "This trouble that I and the King have heard about you, you stop it right away, and you carefully study the law pertaining to the taxes of the Kingdom.

You or your son will not be able to get away from me, if you accept the doings of those under you, your being deprived of high office will be the consequence, and the continuing to be a lord in these islands."[22] Keaweamahi must have reformed, for she continued in office for another three years, until 1842.

The journal of "Peter Goabout to his cousin Job Stayathome," published in the *Polynesian* in August 1841, described the residence of Kauai's third governor, Keaweamahi, as "a very good wooden dwelling house, prettily situated upon a hill, which was built by her late husband by foreign mechanics; but it is kept in very poor repair, and is seldom occupied."[23] The same article observed the practice of using the Western houses for ceremonial purposes and traditional houses for daily living: "However good houses the chiefs may have, they prefer to sleep in thatched huts, after the good old custom of their ancestors, while their finer dwellings are kept only as matters of state, and to gratify their pride in the eyes of foreigners."[24] The account also gives a detailed description of the *hale pili*. "Amelia [sic], however prides herself upon possessing the finest thatched house after the Hawaiian style, upon the islands. It was a work of gallantry on the part of her late lord, and one of his last works of any nature. Not long before he died, which was in 1839 [April 10, *Sandwich Island Gazette*, May 4, 1839; Hawaiian Spectator, p 494, v.2], she expressed a wish to have such a building."²⁵

Like Mokuʻula on Maui (Chapter 2) and the residence of Ruth Keʻelikōlani at Mauna Kamala in Kapālama on Oʻahu (Chapter 3), Keaweamahi chose to locate the site of her house in the midst of land cultivated with taro:

> Gov. Keikioewa, who by the way was a bit of taskmaster, and Napoleaon-like had a most aristocratic, or rather despotic contempt for the word impossible, issued his orders, and the work was commenced.—Amelia with an equal disregard to any obstacles which nature might present, or moved by that spirit which enhances the value of an object by the effort to obtain it, selected not just the site which was most eligible, and of which there was an abundance, to wit, dry ground, but the miry beds of some fish ponds and kalo patches.²⁶

After several month of filling the wetlands site, the foundation for the residence reached completion. The dimensions and aspects of the *hale pili* are also described. Interestingly, the residence was 20 feet longer and 4 feet wider than the house of God they had built for the missionaries across the river:

> The building erected was 110 feet in length, 34 in breadth, and 30 to the ridgepole. It is a neat and pretty house, with an air of savage grandeur about it which is pleasing.—The interior was one fine hall, but has since been divided into two rooms, and from the fineness of the cinet [sennit], and the neatness with which it was laid on, the whiteness of the rafters, even size of the great posts, smoothness of the thatch, and good proportions of the whole, presents quite a regal appearance, and is well worth the attention of the traveller, particularly as such governors as Kaikioewa are getting scarce and the chance of there being more such buildings erected, somewhat small.²⁷

Thus the author identifies the primary reason why the great *hale pili* ceased to be constructed—lack of leaders to mobilize the many hands necessary for such projects. The account also identifies at least major one item placed in the residence—"a canoe belonging to Moses the governor apparent, of most beautiful workmanship. It is made of one koa log, and is 44½ feet long, three feet deep, and 21 inches wide, with high prow and stern neatly attached to the main body by fine cord. The whole is finely polished, and from the care with which it is preserved, can be but seldom used."²⁸

The storing of the canoe there shows the role of Keaweamahi as a governor in place of the twelve-year-old Moses Kekuaiwa.

She was followed as governor by Miriam Kekauōnohi from 1842 to 1844. Kekauōnohi, a widow of Kamehameha II, was married to Aarona Keliʻiahonui, son of the former king of Kauaʻi, Kaumualiʻi. In the Great Mahele Keliʻiahonui received Kalihikai, an ahupuaʻa in Halelea, Kauaʻi. By 1845 they were living at Hōlani House in Honolulu (Chapter 4).

Paulo Kanoa, a cousin of Moses and Kekūanāoʻa, started as governor of Kauaʻi on October 21, 1846. Kanoa was one of the eight who had been "advanced a degree higher in the rank of chiefs" during the Legislative Session of 1845 (April 2 and April 23). The others were J. Kaʻeo, J. Piʻikoi, J. Kapena, Kaisara Kapaʻakea, B. Namakeha, Nueku Namauu (cousin of M. Kekūanāoʻa) and J.Y. Kanehoa.

Moses Kekuaiwa and his *hānai* mother, Emilia Keaweamahi, the presumptive governor and past governor of Kauaʻi respectively, both died on November 24, 1848. With the death of Moses, called Moses Kaikioʻewa in his death notice, Kanoa continued in the position.

In 1850 the Privy Council approved that the building of a "two small cottages" at Huleiʻa, today called Hulāiʻa, Nawiliwili, in the Līhuʻe district, for a courthouse and a residence for the island governor. The cost was "not to exceed three thousand dollars."[29] "The council also approved the purchase of the property and that "until this is secured no building be purchased."[30] In August 1851 Edward P. Bond reported on expenses for building of the residence and courthouse amounted to $856.67.[31] A list of the island governors in 1860 reported that Paul Kanoa still maintained his residence in Nawiliwili, Kauaʻi.[32] Chief Kanehoa of Keauhou, Kona, died while visiting Kanoa on February 22, 1860.[33] Another dozen years later, in April 1872, the *Pacific Commercial Advertiser* reported that "Rumor has it that the venerable Paul Kanoa, who has for so many years held the office of Governor of the Island of Kauaʻi, is to resign."[34] The rumors proved false, and Kanoa served until January 4, 1877, having held the office under five kings, from Kamehameha III through Kalākaua.

Of the remaining Kauaʻi governors, only two were chiefs: John E. [Edward] Bush (January 4, 1877–1880) and Paul P. Kanoa (January 12, 1881–1886). The younger Kanoa was the last chief to serve as Governor of Kauaʻi. Anna Lanihau, keeper of the Royal Mausoleum from March 6, 1885, took on the role of governor from July 31, 1886, to 1888. William Hyde Rice, who had been one of thirteen committeemen who waited for Kalākaua to sign the Bayonet Constitution, was governor of Kauaʻi from February 8, 1892, until February 28, 1893, more than a month after the overthrow.

Residence of Debora Kapule, Pohoula, Wailua, Puna, Kauaʻi (1829–after 1848)

Debora Kapule, the favorite wife of the last king of Kauaʻi, Kaumualiʻi, continued to live on the island where she had once reigned as queen. When Kaʻahumanu spirited away her husband and son to Oʻahu, at one point marrying both, she suffered a double loss. But despite her plight she was one of the defenders against the revolt of Humehume.

Kapule makes no mention of her royal past in her land claim, calling herself in the native testimony: "Debora Haakulou Kapule, a woman of the Hawaiian Islands living at Wailua on the Island of Kauai."[35] She told the Commissioners to Quiet Land Titles on January 6, 1848: "I have occupied this parcel of *kula* land from the year 1829 until the present."[36] On January 11, 1848, Kapule continued her testimony, giving an account of the changing status of her property: "After the war, the land was given to the chiefs, and Kaahumanu I gave me this land of Wailua, saying to me that I was to be the *HakuʻAina* [landlord] and that the revenue from it was mine. When Kaahumanu I died and the land passed to Kaahumanu II [Kīnaʻu] and I continued in occupancy. When Kaahumanu II died and the land passed to Kaahumanu III [Kekāuluohi]—then my occupancy changed. I did not receive certain revenues of the land and what I did receive, from my animals on the land was paid for by the head in Government, and I had to cultivate with my own woman's hands for my sustenance and not by means of the *poʻalima*."[37] Her Wailua house most likely was a *hale pili*. George Washington Bates in his *Sandwich Island Notes* described his visit to Wailua in 1852, and the decaying structures he found: The only interest it (the village of Wailu) now retains is its having once been the abode of royalty. Everything was going rapidly to decay. The canoes that were once occupied by her majesty and her friends I found rotting in a shed that stood near the banks of the stream."[38] Though no explicit depiction of the Wailua house exists, a description of her house at Waimea is found in *Sandwich Island Notes*.

Residence of Debora Kapule, Waimea, Kaua'i (–1853)

The house of Debora Kapule in Waimea, Kaua'i, described by Bates in his 1854 book, reflects both Western and traditional elements: "She had removed her residence from Wailua and taken up her permanent abode at this village, once the seat of her ancestors. I found her occupying a neat stone house, handsomely matted on the floor of the apartment; for there was only one, and that served for every purpose."[39] Like the *hale pili* the residence consisted of an undivided room. It was, however, constructed of stone in the Western fashion of building. The matting in the house, too, reflects the traditional floor covering for a *hale pili*. Kapule died in Waimea on August 26, 1853.

Residence of James Young Kanehoa at Kōloa, Kaua'i (After 1839)

James Young Kanehoa, son of John Young (Olohana) and Namakaelua, who like Paulo Kanoa had been "advanced a degree higher in the rank of chiefs" by the Privy Council in April 1845. He married Kale [Sarah Davis], daughter of Isaac Davis, another of the Western advisors of Kamehameha I. The couple were the *hānai* parents of Keli'imaika'i Ka'eo (also called Alebada), the son of Joshua Ka'eo and Gini Lahilahi Young, sister of James Young Kanehoa. In 1847 he asked for the award of a house lot in Kōloa, Kaua'i, near the jail: "The reason that I acquired this place was that when Ladd *ma* began to plant sugar cane at Koloa, the Ali'i was also a planter of cane. The Ali'i [Kamehameha III] appointed me as Luna over the planting of the cane. Because I had no residence I asked Keawemahi [Keaweamahi] who succeeded Kaikoewa [Kaikio'ewa] as governor, for a place. I have had this place until the present time and do not know of any objections. I myself made the fence and the houses and everything in that lot which had been formerly unused land. John Ii knows of my living there, in his sailings to Kauai."[40] Kanehoa died October 1, 1851, and his claim was not awarded. He did receive, however, the ahupua'a of Lāwa'i, which he inherited from his father [Mahele Award 43, Royal Patent 4512]. In a will dated September 21, 1851, Kanehoa gave one-third of Lāwa'i to his niece, Emma, daughter of his half-sister, Fanny. The probate court ultimately refused to recognize the will because it had no witnesses. Lāwa'i instead went to his wife, Hikoni, who eventually deeded the land to Emma.

Residence of Princess Kekaulike at Ho'ai, Kōloa, Kaua'i

The dynasty that succeeded the Kamehameha rulers traced its genealogical roots to Kaua'i. The youngest granddaughter of King Kaumuali'i of Kaua'i, Princess Kekaulike, lived in Kōloa, Kaua'i, where she gave birth to her sons, Edward Keli'iahonui on May 13, 1869, and Jonah Kūhiō Kalaniana'ole on March 26, 1871.

Their brother, David La'amea Kawānanakoa Kahalepouli Pi'ikoi, had been born

Left: Young Prince Jonah Kūhiō Kalaniana'ole, the other prince born on Kaua'i (courtesy Hawaii State Archives, PPWD-15-8-005). *Right:* Charcoal drawing of Edward Keli'ihonui, one of two princes born on Kaua'i. Prince Edward Street in Waikīkī is named for him (courtesy Hawaii State Archives, PP-98-3-001).

earlier at a residence at Ka'ala'a, Honolulu (Chapter 5), on February 19, 1868. After the death in 1922 of Prince Jonah Kūhiō Kalaniana'ole, the second delegate to the U.S. Congress from Hawai'i, the Order of Kamehameha honored him by marking his birthplace with a monument.[41] They had announced the project in 1924[42] and completed it in 1928. Prince David Kawānanakoa draped lei on the monument at the dedication ceremony.

Royal Residences of Ni'ihau

The nearby island of Ni'ihau formed a portion of the kingdom of Kaumuali'i later absorbed by the Kingdom of Hawai'i but had no royal residence. A lament regarding the absence of a suitable residence there for ali'i formed part of a missive sent to the kingdom's Kuhina Nui. Kauukualii wrote a letter to Keoni Ana asking about a rumor he had heard concerning the sale of the island. He observed: "I feel sorry should the Chiefs come here, and there is no house, we, the people are satisfied with a small house, but we pity the masters."[43] True to the rumor, the island was sold, albeit a dozen years later, to the Elizabeth Sinclair in 1864.

Chapter 7

Preservation of Lost Palaces

E uhi ana ka wā i hala mea i hala.
Passing time obscures the past.[1]
—Hawaiian proverb

On all of the islands the residences of royalty suffered from natural decay and man-made destruction. The deaths of the chiefs, along with their debts, resulted in the sale and often dismantling of the structures. For other lost palaces, businesses often supplanted the houses built in prime commercial locations. The disappearance of the palaces in turn resulted in the loss of the memory of the individuals and events associated with the palaces.

Historic Preservation in Hawai'i

Sadly, the destruction of the vast majority of the lost palaces took place despite an interest in historic preservation in Hawai'i. Indeed, interest in historic preservation existed from the very beginning of the government that succeeded the Kingdom of Hawai'i. The ability for the government to preserve places of historic interest dates back to the Laws of the Republic of Hawaii of 1898. Act 43 authorized the minister of the interior to "acquire and preserve for and in behalf of the Hawaiian Government ancient Heiaus and Puuhonuas or the sites or remains thereof throughout this Republic...." The act also authorized the government to condemn sites and to "promulgate all necessary or proper rules for the preservation and management of the property...."[2] The act, signed by Sanford B. Dole, president of the Republic of Hawaii, took effect on June 15, 1898. Private organizations, too, made efforts to preserve historical sites, the most notable being the Hawaiian Historical Society. Historian Ralph S. Kuykendall dated such efforts of that organization to January 12, 1903. He recorded from 10th Report of the organization: "Mr. Wm. A. Bryan moved that a committee of five be appointed to bring before other organizations and the legislature the matter of marking the sites of important historical events. This was seconded and carried. The president stated that he would name the committee later."[3] The 12th Report of the society recorded the names of the Committee on Landmarks: Mr. [William Alanson] Bryan [Jr.] [...] Dr. N.B. [Nathaniel Bright] Emerson, Prof. W.D. [William De Witt] Alexander, Prof. W.T. [William Tufts] Brigham and Mr. L.A. [Lorrin Andrew] Thurston" and that "more than one hundred spots of interest had been indicated." Emerson, Alexander and Thurston all descended from missionaries; Emerson was the son of John Smith Emerson and Ursula Sophia

Newell Emerson, missionaries in the fifth company (1832); Alexander (1833–1833) was son of missionaries William Patterson Alexander and Mary Ann McKinney who arrived aboard the whaling ship *Averick* in 1832. Lorrin Andrew Thurston's name preserves his missionary forebears, Lorrin Andrew and Asa of the first missionary company (1820). A friend of Charles Reed Bishop, William Tufts Brigham took up his post as first director of Bernice Pauahi Bishop Museum in 1891, though he had cataloged botanical specimens in Hawai'i and taught at Oahu College a quarter century earlier during the reign of Kamehameha V. In his *Additional Notes on Hawaiian Featherwork* Brigham referred to the "kindness of Her Majesty" (16) regarding permission to photograph a feather cloak belonging to Queen Lili'uokalani. William Alanson Bryan, Jr., chairman of the committee, arrived in the territory of Hawai'i in 1900 to work at Bishop Museum. Such was the composition of the earliest group tasked with the preservation of historic sites. The 13th Report in 1905 noted further progress and widespread support. "It is believed that the general interest, which is everywhere manifest in this matter, will crystallize in such a way that the next legislature will see fit to provide funds to carry on the work, which has been so well begun, and cause suitable marks to be established at such places as the committee may be marked."[4] The next legislature did indeed see fit, providing Act 128 for a "Memorial to Commemorate Signing of the First Constitution by Kamehameha III."[5] The 1907 legislation provided an appropriation of $500 to erect the Lahaina monument. A year earlier, the Papers #13 of the Hawaiian "Historical Society record, "The Committee on Ancient Land Marks was instructed to take necessary steps for marking the place where the first constitution was proclaimed at Lahaina."[6] The name of the committee now included "Ancient" and its focus would tend in that direction, though the proclamation of the constitution was clearly not ancient.

So it fell upon private organizations rather than government to take the lead in attempts to preserve the homes of royalty. The Daughters of Hawai'i in 1915 renovated Queen Emma's Hānaiakamalama, the first of its preservation efforts.

Government did protect one of the surviving royal residences. At the urging of Prince Jonah Kūhiō Kalaniana'ole, the territory purchased Washington Place in 1921. The circuit court granted, on May 11, 1921, the territory's petition to condemn Washington Place through eminent domain "in fee simple absolute for public use and purpose of an executive mansion."[7] Absent his influence Washington Place might also have passed into memory or worse.

Historical Commission

The same year that the Territory of Hawaii purchased the home of the late Queen Lili'uokalani for the governor's mansion, Governor Charles James McCarthy signed Act 120 into law, on April 18, 1921, creating a Historical Commission. Part of the function of the commission was placed prominently in its title: "to Secure Information in Regard to Historical Places."[8] S.L. Desha, Sr., the senator representing Hilo on the Big Island of Hawai'i, introduced Senate Bill 7 for "An Act creating a Commission to Compile and Publish a revised history of the Hawaiian people, authorizing the Commissioners to compile same and making an appropriation therefor." The importance of the bill is reflected in its number, SB 7, and its referral to the Committee on Ways and Means on the third day of the session.[9] The aspect of historical places was added to the title in an amendment on second reading of the bill. The Ways and Means Committee amended Section 2 of the bill to include additional duties: "Said commission shall investigate and compile information upon places, structures, monuments and things in the Territory of Hawaii of historical importance and interest, and report back to the next legislature the advisability of preservation and restoration of such historic places, together with the cost of doing so."[10] The bill also included a $15,000 appropriation. The bill passed third reading with all senators voting in the affirmative. The senate bill passed third reading in the house on April 12, 1921, with minor amendments. The senate concurred with the amendments and the bill passed final reading on April 16, 1921.[11] The bill was signed into law as Act 120.[12]

Although the Senate bill amended by its ways and means committee called for a commission consisting entirely of "members of the faculty of the University of Hawaii,"[13] the final act specified: "One member of said commission shall be appointed from the faculty of the University of Hawaii."[14] The governor, in accordance with the act, appointed Prince Jonah Kūhiō Kalaniana'ole, former governor George Robert Carter and Dr. Karl Clayton "K.C." Leebrick to the commission. Prince Kalaniana'ole, cousin of King Kalākaua, was Hawai'i's second delegate to Congress. Carter was son of Henry A.P. Carter, Hawaiian minister to Washington, D.C., and Sybil Augusta (Judd) Carter; He was also a member of the Hawaiian Mission Children's Society and Hawaiian Historical Society.[15] Leebrick filled the faculty member position on the commission. At the initial meeting of the commission Prince Kalaniana'ole was elected president. The death of Prince Kalaniana'ole shortly thereafter resulted in the appointment Emma Ahuena Davison Taylor, a member of the Hawaiian Folklore Commission, to fill the vacancy. George R. Carter was chosen as president. The volunteer commission voted to "secure the appointment of some trained historian to direct the work of the Commission, since it was clearly not the duty nor within the temporal ability of the members to personally carry on this work."[16] To that end the position was offered to Ralph S. Kuykendall in June 1922.[17]

Kuykendall would have six months with the commission before the first report to the legislature became due. He wrote in the first report of the commission:

> History becomes more real when we can stand upon some spot of ground and in imagination picture the great events that happened there. Such places should be identified and marked, so that memory of these great events may forever adhere to them. It is a well known fact that with the lapse of time and the progress of improvement and development, the exact location of historically important spots frequently becomes a matter of uncertainty.[18]

Governor W.R. Farrington reported to the following legislature: "The Commission has undertaken an investigation and marking of places of historical interest."[19]

Representative and vice speaker Emil M. Muller of District 2 on the Island of Hawai'i introduced HB 393, titled "An Act to amend Sections 1, 2 and 3 of Act 120 of the Session laws of 1921, relating to the historical commission." The legislation resulted in Act 139, signed May 2, 1923, that further authorized the commission "to advise and cooperate with local organizations in work of preserving, marking and restoring such places and objects, to take independent action where local organizations do not exist, and to make recommendations to the governor and to the legislature in reference to such matters."[20] Though titled "Landmarks and History," Governor Farrington made no mention of progress regarding landmarks in his message to the legislature on

February 18, 1925.[21] Nevertheless, Act 49 of 1925 did make a $2,500 appropriation for "Marking and Preserving Historic Places in the Territory of Hawaii" though none of the lost palaces were included on the list. The historic places comprised the Poliahu and Malae heiau and Menehune Ditch on Kauaʻi, the battle site in Iao Valley, the birthplace of Kaʻahumanu in Hana, the Puʻukoholā and Mailekini heiau in Kawaihae on the Big Island, and the Upo (or Ulupo) heiau in Kailua on Oʻahu.[22] The act did allow that any fund not spent could be used "in preserving and marking other historic spots in the Territory."[23] The 1927 message makes no mention of landmarks at all in the section titled "Historical, Folklore and Other Commissions."[24] That year the Daughters of Hawaiʻi renovated Huliheʻe Palace.

The commemoration of one hundred and fiftieth anniversary of the "discovery" of Hawaiʻi by Captain Cook occasioned increased interest in Hawaiian history. Albert Pierce Taylor, librarian with the Hawaii State Archives and member of the commission charged with planning the commemorative events, noted: "There has also been aroused a sense of the importance of marking historic places."[25] That interest came in part from the discovery of the post and copper plate that Lord Byron placed in 1825 to mark the spot where the flesh of Captain Cook was separated from his bones, according to Hawaiian practice.[26]

The governor's 1929 message, too, makes no mention of landmarks in the section titled "The Historical Commission," only referring to commission's other mandate—history publications. Curiously, the message does make a plea for the preservation of

Stonehouse, the former residence of Richard Armstrong, housed the Punahou Preparatory School (courtesy Hawaii State Archives, PP-89-5-013).

a home, albeit not a royal one, in a section titled "An Armstrong Memorial," immediately preceding the historical commission section. Farrington calls for preservation of Stone House, the home of the Rev. Richard Armstrong and General S.C. Armstrong. "This Armstrong home should be preserved as a museum of Hawaii's educational progress. The land may be purchased and will properly become a part of the Governor's official residence."[27]

The preservation of a residence such as Stone House would have been outside the scope of what the Hawaiian Historical Society recorded as its efforts in "Preserving Old Hawaii." The 1930 report of the society noted that members were "endeavoring to preserve from loss of the rare things of *ancient* [italics mine] Hawaii."[28]

The 1931 message to the legislature by the new governor and missionary scion, Lawrence M. Judd, included no reference at all to the historical commission and recommended a reduction in the number of boards and commissions.[29] Despite the absence of mention to the commission, Act 35, passed by the 1931 legislature, did authorize the governor to "declare by public proclamation, historic land marks, structures and other objects of historic, scientific, scenic and botanic interest ... to be territorial monuments or preserves."[30] The designation was only for territorial lands and private lands with the "consent of the owner." A list, dated December 15, 1932, specified "Objects to be Considered for Designation as Territorial Monuments by the Governor of Hawaii under Act 56, S.L. 1931." The seventy-six objects of prehistoric, historic, botanic and scenic interest included just one royal site. The twelfth item on the list was "Pukaomaomao, Kaahumanu's summer home, Honolulu" (Chapter 5).[31]

The Historical Commission lasted a little more than a decade. Act 9 of the Second Special Session Laws of 1932 abolished the Historical Commission effective July 1, 1932, transferring "all functions and powers of the historical commission" to the regents of the University of Hawai'i. The transfer of responsibility would not result in any action by the university for another decade, when "At the request of President [Gregg M.] Sinclair, Professor Henry P. Judd and Associate Professor Ralph S. Kuykendall met with him to devise some means of assisting the Regents of the University in carrying out the duties imposed upon them by Sec. 835 of the Revised Laws of Hawaii 1935 [Revised Laws 1945, Sec. 1963], in regard to places of historical interest in the Territory."[32]

An August 1942 report by Henry P. Judd, professor at the University of Hawai'i, listed 33 "places for designation because of their prehistoric interest, or their historic interest, scenic interest or otherwise."[33] The report again mentioned Puka'ōma'oma'o, this time as the fourth item in the list.

By 1945 the miscellaneous duties of the department of public works, under section 4905, expanded beyond ancient sites, allowing for the acquisition and preservation of "other places of historic interest, or the sites or remains thereof throughout the territory."[34] The following chapter empowered the superintendent of public works to "promulgate all necessary or proper rules for the preservation and management of the property ... when acquired, and to regulate the admission and control of all persons visiting or entering the same."[35]

Conservation Council for Hawaii

In 1950 attempts to protect historical structures would mesh public and private efforts. That year, the private Conservation Council for Hawaii was established on

August 9. Its stated objectives were "furthering conservation in its various aspects in the Hawaiian Islands to the end of betterment of human welfare therein."[36]

The sites committee was just one of the council's divisions; the others were land, water, flora and fauna. Alice Spalding Bowen was installed as chairman of the sites committee, a position she would hold for three years. The private organization recognized that much of the effort occurred outside of government. "To date, efforts have been largely by groups of a private nature—Daughters of Hawaii (Hulihee Palace, Queen Emma Home), Bishop Museum (noting archeological sites and repository for items of historical interest); preservation of Iolani Palace as a government building with retention of many features of historic importance."[37]

Commission on Historical Sites

Historic preservation would take a more prominent role when the Commission on Historical Sites was established by Act 36 on May 4, 1951. The commission consisted of five members, one each from the four counties and the city and county of Honolulu. The executive secretary of the Hawaii Visitors' Bureau served as the secretary of the commission. The act charged the commission "to locate, identify, and preserve in suitable records information regarding heiaus [sic], ancient burial places, and sites of historical interest." The act also established five three-person county advisory committees chaired by the county representative on the commission. The commission also needed to concur with any construction affected any heiau, ancient burial place or other place of historic interest.[38]

From the start, the Territory of Hawaii Commission on Historical Sites and the Sites Committee of the Conservation Council for Hawaii shared goals and membership. The 1952 annual meeting minutes of the council note:

> With the exception of our Kauai representation the Governor appointed as members of the Commission the same individuals who serve your committee. For Oahu, Miss Maude Jones and Mrs. Alice Spalding Bowen; for Maui, Mrs. Inez Ashdown; for Hawaii, Mr. Homer Hays; and for Kauai, Miss Elsie Wilcox and the Executive Secretary of the Hawaii Visitors' Bureau to serve as Commission Secretary.
>
> It was the unanimous opinion of members of the Sites Committee in its May meeting that our work need not conflict and that we continue to render all possible assistance to the official commission.[39]

One of the early acts of the commission was to ascertain the extent of its powers. William Cogswell, executive secretary of the commission sent a letter dated December 11, 1951, to the attorney general, particularly focused on what the commission could do if a heiau or historical site was threatened by public construction.[40] The answer from John R. Canright, deputy attorney general, identified the duties of the commission as two-fold: "1. Locate, identify and preserve records relating to heiaus, ancient burial places, and other historical sites. 2. To pass upon applications for construction of public improvements in the areas of such sites and, where appropriate, make objections to such construction."[41] Alice Spalding Bowen, chairman of the commission, in a letter dated August 2, 1954, requested an opinion of the whether the territory of Hawaii could condemn "a privately owned heiau or other historical site of importance." The opinion of Norito Kawakami, deputy attorney general, was that "such heiau or other historical site may be condemned."[42]

With Bowen heading the commission, the Conservation Council chose Bryant Cooper to head its sites committee.[43] Bowen expressed her high regard for the sites committee and its "very earnest and energetic chairman, Mr. Bryant Cooper"[44] in a February 5, 1955, letter to R. L. Cushing, president of the Conservation Council for Hawaii. She wrote of the symbiotic relationship between the two groups: "Because of the nature of our affiliated groups, projects started by the Council's Sites Committee can often be carried on and brought to completion by the Commission."[45] Bowen cited as examples of cooperation the Nuuanu Petroglyph Park and the study of the Summer Palace of Kamehameha III (Chapter 5).

On May 6, 1955, three new sections of chapter 316A of the Revised Laws of Hawaii 1945 took effect, whereby the governor could "declare by public proclamation historic landmarks, historic and prehistoric structures, and other objects of historic or scientific interest that are situated upon the lands owned or controlled by the Territory of Hawaii to be territorial monuments."[46] The act also established penalties for the destruction of "any historic or prehistoric ruin or monument."[47]

In 1955 Bowen accepted an appointment to the governor's advisory committee for the proposed capitol building. In her acceptance, she gave the opinion of the sites commission "regarding the proper location of that building and the protection which we consider so necessary for Iolani Palace and its grounds." She continued:

> It is considered by the Commission on Historical Sites as the foremost historical site in the Territory. This is not a biased opinion of site-minded people for I quote that of the group of associated architects for the Territorial Department of Public Works, which studies plans for the new capitol buildings in 1933: "Every effort will be made to enhance the setting of Iolani Palace and to preserve to perpetuity what is in all probability Hawaii's most historically significant building."[48]

The letter also opposed the building of the new Archives building on the 'Iolani Palace grounds.

On April 17, 1956, Bowen and Osborne had a discussion with Wadsworth Y.H. Yee of the attorney general's office regarding the best way to exercise the condemnation process. Yee responded in a letter to Bowen: "Since the Territory or public lands office does not have the funds for acquisition of this type of property, it is suggested that you contact Mrs. Osborne [of the Conservation Council for Hawaii] to raise enough money to purchase said site for the Territory of Hawaii."[49] The letter points to the necessity of public-private partnerships to the protection of historical sites. The relationship between historic preservation and the territory's growing industry of tourism was outlined in testimony by Bowen to the pre-session hearing of house committee on tourist development. The committee vice chair was future member of the U.S. House of Representatives and later U.S. Senate, Spark Masayuki Matsunaga, and committee member and future Hawaii state governor, George Ariyoshi. An "imaginary" tour in the testimony took the committee members to one of the lost palaces of Hawaii, Kaniakapupu (Chapter 5), the summer palace of Kamehameha III and Queen Kalama.[50] Bowen established the need for monies to carry out the work of the commission: "Heiaus, petroglyphs, historic buildings, both on public and private lands, have been destroyed in the past and unless they are given complete protection now, the remaining ones will deteriorate or be destroyed by construction work and by vandals. Every delay in making the funds to protect these sites available means the loss of more of them."[51]

A 1957 report of the sites committee of the Conservation Council for Hawaii justified its presence within a conservation organization by linking its efforts to economic issues: "The Sites Committee, while not directly concerned with natural resources, is an integral part of the Conservation Council. The preservation of historic sites in the Territory is important, not only for their historical value, but also because of their added attraction to tourists."[52] The report also outlined the committee's partnership with the territorial sites commission, noting the forces in play that resulted in the destruction of historic sites: "The Sites Committee supports and assists the Territorial Sites Commission in its work (without funds) of preserving historic and legendary sites from destruction is [sic] the face of public apathy and hunger for land to exploit for modernization"[53]

Clarice B. Taylor, secretary of the Historic Sites Committee, Conservation Council of Hawaii, sent on November 5, 1958, a letter to Mrs. Lloyd B. Osborne, the committee chairman, that included "listings and pertinent information on the most important Historic Sites of the Islands of Oahu, Molokai, Maui, Kauai and Hawaii." The sites reflected the work of the select committee of the historic sites committee comprised of Dr. Kenneth P. Emory, Walter Horschler of the Territorial Planning Office, Mrs. Lloyd Osborne and Clarice B. Taylor. Taylor ended the letter: "There is sufficient information on each site to assist Mr. Horschler in making a report for the Governor" [William Francis Quinn].[54]

An undated List of Territorial Historic Sites developed by the Committee on Historic Site Conservation divided sites into three classes: Class I, "Those sites which should be cleared, maintained, made accessible and preserved"; Class II, "Those sites which are now in no danger of destruction but rank in importance with sites classified as #1" and Class III, "Those sites of lesser importance which should be zoned as historical sites for future preservation." The list included under Kona, Hawaiʻi, sites: "Kamakahonu and Ahuena Heiau" in Class I and Huliheʻe Palace in Class III, ʻIolani Palace and "Hanaiakamalama (Queen Emma's Home)" in Class II, on Molokaʻi "Malama (house site of Kamehameha V)" in Class III.

Agnes C. Conrad, chair of the commission on historical sites, specifically addressed Hānaiakamalama in a memorandum to Gov. William F. Quinn on December 12, 1958. The memorandum is especially insightful regarding the focus of historic preservation in Hawaii:

> There has been a great deal said about saving the historic sites in the Territory, with the stress usually placed upon archeological sites. Equally important are those sites from the nineteenth century which so well represent the amazing transition made by the Hawaiian people in a comparatively short time from an isolated to a highly civilized culture. Hanaiakamalama, country estate of King Kamehameha IV and Queen Emma, is one of the outstanding reminders of this transition. The land in the park is the same as that which constituted the original estate. It has remained as a unit since Queen Emma inherited it from her uncle in 1857. To the Hawaiian people, it is particularly important as a site connected with the Kamehameha dynasty, just as Iolani Palace is closely connected with the Kalakaua. Left intact, it will continue to serve not only as a park, but as one of the most important historic areas in Honolulu.[55]

Hānaiakamalama, though, was not included in the 1960 resolution that made recommendations for a proclamation of the governor. The resolution, passed at the August 27, 1957, meeting of the commission, combined two motions. Member Colin Lennox made the first motion requesting the governor to declare ʻIolani Palace a state historical monument. The motion passed unanimously. A subsequent motion by Beatrice Savage of Maui to also make the same recommendation for ʻIolani Barracks, Washington Place and Aliʻiolani Hale also passed, by a vote of three to one, with Lennox voting against the additional sites.[56] Lennox explained his vote in a minority report that reasoned questioned whether the restoration of the three structures was possible. He also reasoned: "The designation of these structures as State Monuments also encumbers the ground on which they stand," and would "seriously curtail the efficient use of the whole area."[57] Conrad, in a January 26, 1960, letter to Gov. Quinn, recommended the "proclamation by the Governor of Iolani Palace and grounds, Iolani Barracks, Washington Place and Aliʻiolani Hale as state historical monuments."[58] Although recommended as state historical monuments, only ʻIolani Palace appears in a "list of the most important historical buildings and sites that have been preserved"[59] that Conrad sent in answer to a request by the National Geographic Society. Both Queen Emma's Home and Huliheʻe Palace appear on the list.

With the transition from territory to state, the commission was disbanded by Act 1, 2nd Special Session, State Laws of Hawaii 1959.[60] The duties were taken over by the state department of land and natural resources in May 1960.

Historic Marker Program

It was another state entity, the department of economic development, however, that initiated another effort to mark historical sites. George Mason wrote a 1962 letter to Gov. William F. Quinn concerning a recommendation from the state department of economic development that supported a statewide system of marking Hawaii's historical sites. The letter noted:

> The objectives of the historical marker program are to give recognition of permanent nature to a historical site and center attention on its significant role in shaping Hawaii's history; to give the visitor essential facts about a site because these sites are not entirely self-explanatory; for example, a heiau looks like just another pile of stones until its impact on Hawaii's culture is explained; and to cultivate a continuing interest and appreciation of the history of Hawaii which can best be done at the site itself.[61]

The priority list of marking sites in the department's report, titled "Marking Hawaii's Historical Sites: A Recommended Six-Year Program," reflects the prehistoric and missionary bias of historical preservation efforts. The first ten on the list include just two sites related to the monarchy—ʻIolani Palace and the Royal Mausoleum. In contrast the same list features two fishponds (Menehune and Ualapue), three missionary sites (Lahainaluna School, Waioli Mission, and Wainee (Waiola) Church and Cemetery) and three ancient sites (Mookini heiau, Palawai petroglyphs and Kaimu-Makena ancient burial grounds. The royal residences were ranked 2 (ʻIolani Palace), 20 (Huliheʻe Palace), 50 (Washington Place) and 56 (Queen Emma's home). In contrast, the Gulick-Rowell Home (26) in Waimea, Kauaʻi, residence of the first Kauaʻi missionaries, ranked higher than Washington Place and Hānaiakamalama. Other royalty related sites include Kalaupapa Lookout (13) [the establishment of Kalaupapa was credited to Kamehameha V]; Lunalilo's tomb (22), Kapuaiwa Grove [planted in honor of Kamehameha V] (23), Royal Slide (43), and Kamehameha water tunnel (52). The royal sites, residences and otherwise, were vastly outnumbered and outranked by missionary sites, ranked 4,

6, 8, 15, 17, 19, 24, 26, 28, 31, and 60 and heiau (5, 14, 18, 21, 25, 27, 30, 32, 33, 35, 37, 40, 42, 45, 46, 48, 54, and 55). If you add fishponds (1, 3, 41), petroglyphs (8, 39, 51,) and other ancient sites (10, 29, 49, 57, 58), to the ancient temple locations, prehistoric sites account for just under half of the historical sites identified for marking.

Although the governor recommended appointing an advisory committee for the marking project, another body was still looking at historical sites. Even after the demise of the Historical Sites Commission, the Sites Committee of the Conservation Council for Hawaii continued its historic preservation efforts. Starting in November 1964 the council's sites committee, through the efforts of Alice Brown, produced a series of radio programs aired on KAIM titled "Stones and Stories." The Sunday evening program covered several lost palaces of Hawaii including by title: "Kamakahonu," "The Three Palaces of Kamehameha III (in three parts)," and "Ainahau and Princess Kaiulani."[62] These efforts would at times put them at odds with other preservation efforts, such as the Lahaina Restoration Project, which had an impact on the sites of three lost palaces: Lahaina Palace or Brick Palace or Kamehameha House; Moku'ula, Lahaina; and Hale Piula (Chapter 2). The council in 1966 pressed the state to establish a position of park historian. In a letter to the state senate ways and means committee Doak C. Cox, president of the council, noted: "An extensive study on marking sites was prepared by the Department of Economic Development in 1962 and sixty sites were identified as important enough to mark; since that time only two plaques have been installed. Nineteen of these sites have been given national recognition by being designated as Registered National Historic Landmarks; only three now have markers explaining their national significance. Funds to buy markers are not sufficient; there must be personnel to research and compile the text. The lack of a Park Historian to do the necessary research and write the text has been one of the primary causes of the delay."[63]

The Sites Committee was pleased to announce at the March 9, 1966, meeting that "The Park Historian position is on a contract basis for the first year and as a regular position next year. This Park Historian is included in the operating budget of the house and is to go next to the Senate."[64]

Agnes C. Conrad, in a 1966 letter endorsing a proposed Honolulu Historical Center, highlighted the preservation role of the Conservation Council for Hawaii: "The Conservation Council for Hawaii and its Historic Sites Committee has long been interested in preserving Honolulu's historic buildings."[65] The Hawaiian Mission Children's Society, preparing for the Mission Sesquicentennial in 1970, had asked Charles E. Peterson, FAIA, to create a master plan for the Mission Houses Museum. The request resulted in a proposed Honolulu Historical Center Plan.

The council approved in January 1967 a letter to Governor John A. Burns "urging that the Historic Preservation plan of the federal government be implemented in Hawaii by the Parks Division of the State."[66]

Even the Conservation Council recognized the limitations of a committee looking primarily at ancient sites. Richard H. Cox in a letter to Dorothy Lindley, chairman of the Preservation Committee of the Model Cities Advisory board, concluded: "The only organized group with a dedication to preservation of *buildings* [italics mine] is the Mayor's Historic Building Task Force. This group spearheaded by Miss [Nancy] Bannick continues to survey buildings throughout Honolulu."[67]

Historic Buildings Task Force

Started in 1965 as an advisory body to Mayor Neil S. Blaisdell's Action for Beautification Executive Committee, the Historic Buildings Task Force identified more than 400 historic sites, including one the lost palaces, Kaniakapupu, [M_488-4-36] and two surviving royal residences: Hānaiakamalama and Keawemalie, cottage of Kamehameha V at Moanalua, O'ahu. Task force chairman Nancy Bannick noted: "But Oahu still has many buildings which if attended to now can be preserved and need not become mere historic sites."[68] Unfortunately for the lost palaces, Bannick's voice was not available a half-century earlier.

Even with laws in place to protect them, the remaining palaces, nevertheless, have been threatened by destruction. A baseball diamond was once proposed for the site of Hānaiakamalama. The Inter-Island Steam Navigation Company wanted the Hulihe'e location for a waterfront hotel. Even 'Iolani Palace faced the threat of demolition for a parking lot for the nearby State Capitol building. Kamehameha V Cottage at Keawemalie, Moanalua, O'ahu has been moved twice.

'Iolani Palace was named a National Historic Landmark on December 29, 1962, and placed on the National Register of Historic Places October 15, 1966. The Friends of 'Iolani Palace started in 1966 to protect that royal site. Queen Emma's Summer Home was placed on the register on August 7, 1972; Hulihe'e Palace on May 25, 1973; and Washington Place, June 18, 1973. In addition to the extant royal residences, a handful of sites of the lost palaces have found their way on to the National Register of Historic Places.

By the time Act 216, titled "Relating to the Preservation and Protection of Prehistoric and Historic Sites and Archeological Remains" took effect, on July 14, 1969,[69] all of the lost palaces were no longer standing.

Lost Palaces on the National Register of Historic Places

Four of the lost palaces of Hawai'i have been placed on the National Register of Historic Places, one every decade since the establishment of the register: The earliest Kamakahonu, residence of King Kamehameha I (Chapter 1), was placed on the register on October 15, 1966, the same day as 'Iolani Palace; Kamehameha III's Birthplace (Chapter 1) on July 24, 1978; Kaniakapupu, the summer palace of Kamehameha III (Chapter 5), on October 15, 1986; and Kamehameha III's Royal Residential Complex (Chapter 2) on May 9, 1997.

That most of the lost palaces remain unmarked is not surprising. In his *Narrative of a Voyage Round the World*, Jacques Arago lamented in 1819 during a visit to Hawaii:

> His [Captain James Cook's] mutilated corpse was committed to the ocean he had conquered, and no lasting monument points out to the navigator the exact spot where he perished. The narrative of his brave successor has consecrated the point between Kayakakooa and Karakakooa; but the eye looks in vain for the cenotaph which should immortalize the memory of this deplorable event.[70]

That oversight was rectified ninety-five years after Cook's final encounter with Hawai'i when Princess Miriam Likelike gave, in 1874, the site of his death to the British government. A stone monument and obelisk still mark the spot.

It is entirely fitting, therefore, that the site of the lost palace of Princess Likelike on Emma Street (Chapter 5), the birthplace of Princess Ka'iulani, was one of the earliest to have a marker. The plaque marking the location was, most appropriately, installed at the Pacific Club, the successor of the British Club, where her father was a member.

The medallion includes an inscription around the bas relief visage: "The island flower, the island rose." Robert Louis Stevenson called Princess Victoria Ka'iulani "the island rose" in his poem "Kaiulani." The small plaque next to the larger disc explains, "This medallion marks the birthplace of Princess Kaiulani, 1875–1899, Daughters of Hawaii" (photograph by the author).

Conclusion

> Ke kau mai nei ka haili aloha
> The loving memory returns.[1]
> —Samuel H. Elbert. *Selections from Fornander's Hawaiian Antiquities and Folk-lore*

Hundreds of visitors and Hawaii residents don booties that cover their shoes each day to protect the floors of ʻIolani Palace, allowing them to walk the same halls that King Kalākaua once trod and visit the room where Queen Liliʻuokalani endured imprisonment. The docents share the history of the overthrow of the monarchy in that dimly lit room.

At the same time, others drive down Kanoa Lane in Kapālama with no notion that their vehicles are passing over the place where Hawaiian patriot Joseph Nāwahī lived and fought against annexation. Down the road children play around building 2 in Mayor Wright Homes without the knowledge of Queen Liliʻuokalani's attempts to revise the constitution of Hawaiʻi there before her overthrow. As Ralph S. Kuykendall presciently noted in 1923, when both royal residences were still standing: "It is a well known fact that with the lapse of time and the progress of improvement and development, the exact location of historically important spots frequently becomes a matter of uncertainty."[2]

The causes for loss of the royal residences in Hawaiʻi vary across the board. Though a number fell following the overthrow of the monarchy, many of the lost palaces disappeared during the monarchy. The materials of the *hale pili* were not used with permanence in mind; indeed, a house that could be moved in a day so the king could see the arrival of a ship shows the all too transitory nature of the *hale pili*. Even the grand *hale pili* of the 1820s like Haleuluhe and Halekauwila disappeared long before the end of the monarchy.

ʻIolani Palace with its brick core survived while its wooden rival, Keōua Hale, fell to the effects of termites. With care and repair, even wooden palaces like Hānaiakamalama and Washington Place and the cottage of Kamehameha V have survived. The lost palaces that remain possessed intentional advocates for their continuing existence. Nor can blame for their disappearance be placed solely upon the individuals who overthrew the monarchy. Even monarchs displayed indifference to the palaces of their youth; Kamehameha V sold the coral blocks that comprised Haliʻimaile, the house of his father, brother and sister. Several residences in the palace yard, too, were eliminated when Kalākaua built his palace in 1879 on the site of the 1845 structure.

The death of many chiefs in a relatively short period established a pattern of auction and destruction. As the *Hawaiian Gazette* writer noted at the sale of Honuakaha (Chapter 5): "One by one the homes—once they were called palaces—of the former kings, queens, princesses and princes of Hawaii, are being disposed of under the auctioneer's hammer." The residence of Kekāuluohi was sold in two parts, land and structure, at an auction following the death of its owner. Honuakaha fell after the death of Kapiʻolani; Haleakalā saw destruction several years after the death of Princess Bernice Pauahi Bishop, but within the lifetime of its one-time resident, Queen Liliʻuokalani.

As clearly demonstrated by the transition of Haleakalā to Hamilton House to the Arlington Hotel, houses designed as royal residences did not adapt well to other purposes, whether commercial or public. Two houses of Princess Ruth Keʻelikōlani served as schools; her Kapālama home hosted the predecessor of Hawaiian Mission Academy and Keōua Hale provided classroom space for Honolulu High School.

The charitable trusts established by royalty fulfilled their fiduciary responsibility by either subdividing the land or building multiple units to replace the single, large mansions. The trustees of the Liliʻuokalani Trust replaced the main section of Muʻolaulani with six identical two-story apartment buildings. The Manoa Uplands subdivision obliterated any remains of the residence of Kaʻahumanu at Pukaʻōmaʻomaʻo. The road that opened the Mauna Kamala property for development forced the removal of the Kapālama palace of Princess Ruth Keʻelikōlani.

Lessons Learned

The lost palaces of Hawaiʻi present valuable lessons about the importance of historic preservation. Fortunately, leaders in Hawaiʻi early on placed an emphasis on the need to preserve historic sites. The national historical park Puʻuhonua O Hōnaunau and the Mission Houses Historic Site and Archives are appreciated legacies of the early preservation efforts. While structures like Hānaiakamalama and Huliheʻe Palace met the fifty year criteria necessary for inclusion on the National Register of Historic Places when the Daughters of Hawaiʻi started their drive for its preservation, other lost palaces suffered destruction long before the half-century mark, including the supplanting of Hale Aliʻi by ʻIolani Palace.

Despite the loss of roughly ninety percent of the identifiable royal residences of Hawaiʻi, remembering the lost palaces, their locations and history still provide valuable links to the past. As Kuykendall noted: "History becomes more real when we can stand upon some spot of ground and in imagination picture the great events that happened there. Such places should be identified and marked, so that memory of these great events may forever adhere to them."[3]

Marking Sites

Although *Lost Palaces of Hawaiʻi* preserves the memory of the former residences of royalty in Hawaiʻi, a much more accessible marking of the locations is necessary, a project that would identify the lost palace at the site itself. Like the plaques that highlight significant buildings in Chinatown, the project would provide a short history and significance of the location. With the advent of QR codes, inclusion of a barcode could provide easy access of individuals with smart phones and tablets to expanded information regarding the sites. GPS coordinates, too, could provide Internet-capable devices with easy access to directions to the lost palaces sites. As the signs marking the boundaries of ahupuaʻa on Oʻahu have brought increased awareness to place names and ancient boundaries, the marking of the sites of the lost palaces could help restore a Hawaiian sense of place to communities.

Clearly having an historic structure engenders a more powerful response than an historical marker, and the preservation of buildings should always take first priority. Nevertheless, the Franklin Court "Ghost Structures," steel outlines of the buildings that comprised the now razed Benjamin Franklin compound, provide a creative model for lost buildings. Imagine standing at the foundation of Pukaʻōmaʻomaʻo, the Mānoa residence of Kaʻahumanu, as nearly sixty members of the Daughters of Hawaiʻi did in 1932. Though not as powerful, a plaque explaining the significance of Halelani Drive would at least honor the now lost palace site. An outline on the roadway where the residence of Princess Ruth Keʻelikōlani once stood would give a visitor an idea of the dimensions of her Kapālama house, as well as honor the last place that the Hawaiian patriot, Joseph Nāwahī, called home. A sculpture of the set of curved stairways that led into Muʻolaulani Palace would allow the viewer to locate Liliʻuokalani's house, where Robert Wilcox planned his ill-fated rebellion.

Not surprisingly, the greatest concentration of marked lost palaces occurs in Waikīkī, where markers exist for Paoakalani (#3 Ala Wai/Liliʻuokalani Site), Uluniu (#7 King's Alley Entrance), ʻĀinahau (#8 ʻĀina Hau Park/Triangle) and Marine Residence (#9 International Marketplace), Helumoa (#12 Back Lawn Royal Hawaiian Hotel). Hawaiian historian George Kanahele wrote the descriptions on the markers.

Private-Public Partnership

Private organizations like the Daughters of Hawaiʻi, Friends of ʻIolani Palace, Friends of Washington Place and Moanalua Gardens Foundation have played an invaluable role in preserving the royal palaces that remain. The preservation of historic buildings continues to be the focus of organizations like the Historic Hawaiʻi Foundation and its listing of most threatened buildings, but that does not negate the power of marking sites of buildings that no longer remain.

Certainly the Korean community in Hawaiʻi has been successful in marking sites of importance to the history of Koreans. Bilingual signs mark the locations of the Korean Boarding School for Boys and Korean Methodist Church Site (1906–1906) and Korean National Association Headquarters Site (1914–1914), now on the grounds of the Kalanimoku building on Punchbowl Street and adjacent to the Diamond Head side of Washington Place respectively. The Hawaii State House of Representatives passed House Concurrent Resolution 51 calling for the State Historic Preservation Division to "provide comment on signage, such as the plaque, affecting historic property" and that the Department of Accounting and General Services "be responsible for installation of any plaque."[4]

Marking the sites of the lost palaces, too, despite the lack of physical remains, serves a purpose so that, as Ralph S. Kuykendall observed, "memory of these great events may forever adhere to them."

With the rise of the Hawaiian sovereignty movement following the Constitution Convention of 1978 and the commemoration in 1993 of the centennial of the overthrow, the marking of sites of resistance like Muʻolaulani, where Robert Wilcox planned the 1889 attempt to counter the Constitution of 1887, and Mauna Kamala, where Joseph Nāwahī worked to prevent annexation, become even more important in providing another perspective of history here. Picture the centennial observances of the overthrow if ʻIolani Palace had been razed. Recognizing the sites of the lost palaces of Hawaiʻi links history and place, even in the absence of physical remains. Following the centennial remembrance of the overthrow of Queen Liliʻuokalani, Hawaiʻi saw the creation of other symbols of resistance, permanent and temporary.

A plaque, in English and Korean, marks the site of the Korean National Association Headquarters. Like the lost palaces, the building no longer stands, replaced by the residence of the governor of the State of Hawaiʻi (photograph by the author).

One such symbol, the statue of Robert Wilcox in his Garibaldi jacket on King Street, unveiled by the City and County of Honolulu in September 1993, provides a needed focal point to discuss his role in history. It fittingly looks out over the route he marched on to his ill-fated armed stand at ʻIolani Palace, but the key place for planning the rebellion, Muʻolaulani, still sits unmarked in Kapālama. The banyan tree in the center of Banyan Court Mall is gone, felled by disease. Now no tree or marker recognize the site as the gathering place for the hundred-strong group of men who marched with Wilcox in an attempt to restore the powers of the monarchy.

The more than seven dozen lost royal residences provide examples throughout the state of Hawaiʻi of the response of the Hawaiian people to rapid change. Recognizing the lost palaces fills the gap in the historic record—a record of a people who responded to rapid change with vigor and achievement, who adopted the best of the world's advances to establish its place in world. As Hawaiʻi responds once again to rapid change, the lost palaces provide this generation an opportunity to ponder not only the buildings but their builders.

Chapter Notes

Introduction

1. Pukui, *Hawaiian Dictionary*, s.v. "loaʻa."
2. "The New Palace," 2.
3. "New Palace," 3.
4. *Webster's*, s.v. "palace.
5. Campbell, *Voyage Round the World*, 88.
6. Eveleth, *History*, 111.
7. Interior Department Index to Commissions, May 28, 1873, Series 415, Foreign and Executive, Hawaii State Archives, 70.
8. Hopkins, *Hawaii*, 55.
9. Turnbull, *Voyages*, 203.
10. Turnbull, *Voyages*, 206.
11. Silliman, "Hawaii," *American Journal of Science*, 247.
12. Stewart, *Visit to the South Seas*, 124.
13. Ellis, *Polynesian Researches*, 21.
14. *Missionary Album*, 17.
15. Barrot, *Unless Haste Is Made*, 51.

Chapter 1

1. Pukui, *Ōlelo Noʻeau*, 203.
2. George Mortimer," *Observations and Remarks*, 52.
3. Lisiansky, *A Voyage Round the World*, 105.
4. Committee on Historic Sites, Sites—All Islands, List, n.d., 1958–1960, Hawaii State Archives, 201-1-16 [page 1 of list by Violet Hanson of "Historical Sites on Hawaii Which Should Be Preserved," Feb. 1960.]
5. National Register of Historic Places Inventory—Nomination Form, http://pdfhost.focus.nps.gov/docs/NRHP/Text/78001018.pdf
6. National Register of Historic Places Inventory—Nomination Form, http://pdfhost.focus.nps.gov/docs/NRHP/Text/78001018.pdf
7. National Register of Historic Places Inventory—Nomination Form, http://pdfhost.focus.nps.gov/docs/NRHP/Text/78001018.pdf
8. Ii, *Fragments*, 59.
9. Turnbull, *Voyages*, 223.
10. James Jackson Jarves, *History*, 214–215.
11. Arago, *Narrative*, 65.
12. Dibble, *History*, 81.
13. Eveleth, *History*, 111.
14. Ii, *Fragments*, 147.
15. Jarves, *Scenes and Scenery*, 214–215.
16. *Kailua Bay, Hawaii*.
17. Taylor, "Historical Notes," 15.
18. Alice Bowen to President and Directors, American Factors, Limited, Feb. 7, 1955. Blue Binder, Conservation Council for Hawaii, U-9, Archive of Hawaii.
19. Report of the Committee on Site Conservation, Conservation Council for Hawaii, Sixth Annual Meeting, February 24, 1955. U-9 Minutes-Exec. Bd. Conservation Council-1950–1956, 10.
20. Committee on Historic Sites, Sites—All Islands, List, n.d., 1958–1960, Hawaii State Archives, 201-1-16 [page 1 of enclosure to letter from Clarice B. Taylor to Mrs. Lloyd B. Osborne, Nov. 5, 1958].
21. Committee on Historic Sites, Sites—All Islands, List, n.d., 1958–1960, Hawaii State Archives, 201-1-16 [page 1 of enclosure to letter from Clarice B. Taylor to Mrs. Lloyd B. Osborne, Nov. 5, 1958].
22. Committee on Historic Sites, Sites—All Islands, List, n.d., 1958–1960, Hawaii State Archives, 201-1-16.
23. Committee on Historic Sites, Sites—Kamakahonu (site), Kailua-Kona; Corres., Memo, Map—n.d., 1959, Hawaii State Archives, 201-1-16 [letter from Richard H. Howland to C. Hutton Smith, May 7, 1959].
24. Committee on Historic Sites, Sites—Kamakahonu (site), Kailua-Kona; Corres, Memo, Map—n.d., 1959, Hawaii State Archives, 201-1-16 [letter from Walter F. Dillingham to Commission on Historic Sites, May 22, 1959].
25. Kekahuna, "Ka-Maka-Honu," 1.
26. Kekahuna, "Ka-Maka-Honu," 1.
27. Kekahuna, "Ka-Maka-Honu," 1.
28. "History of the Courtyard."
29. "Courtyard King Kamehameha's Kona Beach Hotel," https://www.marriott.com/hotels/travel/koacy-courtyard-king-kamehamehas-kona-beach-hotel. Accessed June 30, 2021.
30. Black, *Round the World*, 28.
31. "Chamisso's Account," 5.
32. Registered Map 1323, Land Survey Division, Department of Accounting and General Services.
33. Jacques Arago, *Narrative*, 100–101.
34. Arago, *Narrative*, 101.

35. Foreign Office & Executive, Chronological File, 1790–1849, 1801, Series 402-2-2 J17a, Hawaii State Archives.
36. Judd, *Honolulu, Sketches of Life*, 44–45.
37. Judd, *Honolulu, Sketches of Life*, 45.
38. *Historical Magazine*, 172.
39. Judiciary, First Circuit Court, Probate 1787, Hawaii State Archives.
40. Taylor, "Historical Notes," *Thirty-Eighth Annual Report*, 60.
41. Judd, "Minutes," 30.
42. Anderson, "Summary Report," 17.
43. Committee on Historic Sites, Sites—All Islands, List, n.d., 1958–1960, Hawaii State Archives, 201-1-16 [page 1 of list by Violet Hanson of Historical Sites on Hawaii Which Should Be Preserved," Feb. 1960].
44. "John Young Homestead Stabilization," https://www.argsf.com/portfolio/john-young-homestead/.
45. Twain, *Roughing It*, 495–496.
46. Arago, *Narrative*, 89–90.
47. "Freycinet's Voyage," 134.
48. Percy, *Mirror of Literature*, 66.
49. Committee on Historic Sites, Sites—All Islands, List, n.d., 1958–1960, Hawaii State Archives, 201-1-16 [page 1 of list by Violet Hanson of Historical Sites on Hawaii Which Should Be Preserved," Feb. 1960].
50. *A Cultural History of Three Traditional Hawaiian Sites on the West Coast of Hawai'i Island.* Chapter IX: "Pu'uhonua O Honaunau National Historical Park," http://www.cr.nps.gov/history/online_books/kona/history9w.htm
51. Clark, "Protection Sought," B5.
52. Hunt, *Past and Present*, 83.
53. Hunt, *Past and Present*, 83.
54. Alfred Tennyson, "Kapiolani," 864.
55. Stewart, *Visit*, 237.
56. Stewart, *Visit*, 237.
57. Barrot, *Unless Haste Is Made*, 27–28.
58. Judd, *Fragments II*, 122.
59. Hunt, *The Past and Present*, 82.
60. Paris, *Fragments*, 60.
61. Barrot, *Unless Haste Is Made*, 20–21.
62. Winne, *Kuakini and Hulihee*, 18.
63. Nellist, *The Story of Hawaii*, 613–614.
64. Lydgate "Hilo Fifty Years Ago," 103.
65. Land Court Award 7713.
66. "Government Officer," 1.
67. Ruth to Lot, September 14, 1860, Interior Department, Miscellaneous, Hawaii State Archives.
68. Isaac Young Davis to William Webster, Interior Department, Land, February 15, 1861, translated by E.H. Hart, Hawaii State Archives.
69. Kamehameha V to John Owen Dominis, Nov. 7, 1866, Emma Collection, M-45, NA-52.
70. Kamehameha V to John Owen Dominis, Nov. 7, 1866, Emma Collection, M-45, NA-52.
71. *Reports of Decisions*, 1887, 572.
72. R.C. Wyllie to Kamehameha IV, Sept. 17. 1859, Foreign Office and Executive, Local Officials, 1859, September, Hawaii State Archives.
73. Emma to Alex [Kamehameha IV], Jun. 27, 1861, Queen Emma Collection, M-45, Folder NA-1.
74. Emma to Alex [Kamehameha IV], Jun. 27, 1861, Queen Emma Collection, M-45, Folder NA-1.
75. "Every Inch a King," 306.
76. Emma to John Dominis, Dec. 18, 1867, Dec. 28, 1867, and Jan. 8, 1868, Queen Emma Collection, M-45, Folder AH05.
77. "An Ideal Volcano Trip," 2.
78. Samuel H. Davis to A.S. Cleghorn, Sept. 10, 1883, Education Department, General Correspondence, Records Relating to Land (Public Instruction) 1883, Hawaii State Archives.

Chapter 2

1. Pukui, trans., *Ōlelo No'eau*, 43.
2. Pukui, *Ōlelo No'eau*, 138.
3. *Native Register*, No. 384, trans. Frances Fraser, vol. 1, page 118–119.
4. Pukui, *Ōlelo No'eau*, 43.
5. Campbell, *Voyage Round the World*, 85–86.
6. Jacques Arago, *Narrative of a Voyage Round the World, in the Uranie and Physicienne Corvettes, Commanded by Captain Freycinet, Part II*, London: Treuttel and Wurtz, 1823, 65.
7. William Ellis, *Narrative of a Tour*, 55.
8. Macrae, *With Lord Byron*, 11.
9. *Missionary Reports, Sandwich Islands*, 200.
10. "Lahaina Palace," A-6.
11. "Lahaina Palace," A-6.
12. "Lahaina Palace," A-6.
13. "Lahaina Palace," A-6.
14. Fredericksen, *Report on the Archeological Excavation*, 1.
15. Fredericksen, *Report on the Archeological Excavation*, 11.
16. Fredericksen, *Report on the Archeological Excavation*, 14.
17. Fredericksen, *Report on the Archeological Excavation*, 14.
18. Stewart, *Journal of a Residence*, 192–193.
19. Richards, *Memoir of Keopuolani*, 22.
20. Hunt, *The Past and Present*, 76.
21. Richards, *Memoir of Keopuolani*, 36.
22. Claim 6325 by Kekauonohi, June 3, 1854, *Foreign Testimony*, vol. 16, 84–85.
23. Claim 6325 by Kekauonohi, June 3, 1854, *Foreign Testimony*, vol. 16, 84–85.
24. Memorandum, February 16, 1854, Interior Department, Miscellaneous, Box 143, February 1854, Hawaii State Archives.
25. Gorham D. Gilman, "Lahaina in Early Days," 171.
26. P. Nahaolelua to Aliiolani, Jan. 4, 1866, trans. E.H. Hart, Hawaii State Archives, Interior Dept., Land, Letters (Incoming) 1866, January.
27. Stewart, *Journal of a* Residence, 165.
28. Stewart, *Journal of a Residence*, 166.
29. *Reports of a Portion*, 119.
30. Hoapili to Liholiho, Sept. 13, 1824, Foreign

Office and Executive, Series 201, Box 2, Folder 16, Hawaii State Archives.

31. Order by Hoapili kane, Foreign and Executive, Series 402-79, October 21, 1837, Hawaii State Archives.

32. Hiram Bingham, *Residence*, 508.

33. Executive Order No. 52, Apr. 25, 1918, Series 265, vol. 1, Hawaii State Archives.

34. Minutes and Correspondence, Conservation Council for Hawaii, U-9, Hawaii State Archives. [Executive Minutes, Conservation Council for Hawaii, Feb. 9, 1966, 1.]

35. Taylor, "History of Iolani Palace," 3.

36. John Young (Keoni Ana), minister of the interior, to P. Namakeha, acting governor of Maui, dated Sep. 28, 1846, Interior Department Letters, Book 1, 289, Hawaii State Archives.

37. James Young to John Young, dated Jan. 13, 1848, Interior Department, Misc., January 1848, Hawaii State Archives, Translated by E.H. Hart.

38. J.Y. Kanehoa [James Young?] to John Young, dated Jan. 20, 1848, Interior Department, Misc., January 1848, Hawaii State Archives, Translated by E.H. Hart.

39. "Home Wallpaper Dictionary," http://www.designyourwall.com/store/dictionary.php.

40. Lot Kamehameha, minister of the interior, to R.A.S. Wood, superintendent of public works, dated Feb 13, 1859, Interior Department Letters, Book 7, 188.

41. "Address of the Hon. C.C. Harris," 5.

42. Kapena, "Hawaiian National Reminiscences," 75.

43. *Foreign Testimony*, vol. 7, 172, Hawaii State Archives.

44. Kekuanaoa to Kanaina, Apr. 1, 1840, Foreign Office and Executive, Series 402, Box 5, Folder 123, Hawaii State Archives.

45. *Native Register*, vol. 3, no. 8519b, Hawaii State Archives.

46. Fanny Young to Queen Emma, May 25, 1871, trans. Jason Achiu, M-45, NA-10, Hawaii State Archives.

47. Fanny Young to Queen Emma, July 7, 1871, trans. Jason Achiu, M-45, NA-10, Hawaii State Archives.

48. *Native Register*, testimony of Peke Akoni on Land Commission Award no. 5909, vol. 5, 177, trans. Frances Frazier, Hawaii State Archives.

49. *Native Testimony*, testimony of Z. Kaauwai on Land Commission Award no. 5909, vol. 3, 540, trans. Sarah Nakoa, Hawaii State Archives.

50. "Government Officer," 1.

51. *Native Register*, testimony of Peke Akoni on Land Commission Award no. 5909, vol. 5, 177, trans. Frances Frazier, Hawaii State Archives.

52. *Foreign Testimony*, vol. 15, 124, Hawaii State Archives.

53. Samuel G. Dwight to Minister of the Interior, Sep. 9, 1853, Department of the Interior, Box 68, Incoming Letters Sep. 1-15, 1853, Hawaii State Archives.

54. Interior Department, Book 15, 128, Hawaii State Archives.

55. "Court News," Local News, *Hawaiian Gazette*, July 31, 1867, 3.

56. "Court News," Local News, *Hawaiian Gazette*, Jan. 22, 1868, 3.

57. Vincent, *Through and Through the Tropics*, 61.

58. Holoholopinaau, "Touring Molokai," 23.

59. Anderson, "Sandwich Islands Leper Settlement," 173.

60. *Hawaiian Hansard*, 306.

61. Pukui, *Place Names of Hawaii*, 95.

62. Commission on Historical Sites Collection, M-201, Hawaii State Archives.

63. P.W. Kupa, et al, to F.W. Hutchinson, Nov. 6, 1871, Board of Health, Series 334, Box 4, Incoming Letters August–December, 1871, Hawaii State Archives.

64. *Roster, Legislatures of Hawaii*, 103.

65. *Roster, Legislatures of Hawaii*, 102.

66. Kekuaokalani [Peter Young Kaeo] to Queen Emma, Jul. 4, 1874, M-45, NA-16, Hawaii State Archives.

67. Kekuaokalani [Peter Young Kaeo] to Queen Emma, Jul. 4, 1874, M-45, NA-16, Hawaii State Archives, 2.

68. Kekuaokalani [Peter Young Kaeo] to Queen Emma, July 7, 1874, M-45, NA-16, Hawaii State Archives, 2.

69. Kekuaokalani [Peter Young Kaeo] to Queen Emma, July 9, 1874, M-45, NA-16, Hawaii State Archives, 2.

70. Minutes of the Meeting of the Board of Health, April 29, 1873, Board of Health, Series 259, vol. 2, folio, Hawaii State Archives.

71. Kekuaokalani [Peter Young Kaeo] to Queen Emma, July 23, 1873, M-45, NA-16, Hawaii State Archives, 2.

72. Kekuaokalani [Peter Young Kaeo] to Queen Emma, Sept. 30, 1873, M-45, NA-17, Hawaii State Archives, 1.

73. Kekuaokalani [Peter Young Kaeo] to Queen Emma, Oct. 11, 1873, M-45, NA-17, Hawaii State Archives, 1.

74. Bird, *The Hawaiian Archipelago*, 371.

75. "Leper Asylum of Molokai," 2.

76. Knighton, *Struggles for Life*, 186.

77. Parker, *Hygienic and Medical Reports*, 764.

78. Stevenson, *Robert Louis Stevenson*, 78–79.

79. Korn, *Letters from Molokai*, 207.

80. "A Visit to Kalawao," 3.

81. Minutes of the Board of Health, June 27, 1876, Series 259, vol. 2, 140–141, Hawaii State Archives.

82. Minutes of the Board of Health, Apr. 5, 1876, Series 259, vol. 2, 140–141, Hawaii State Archives.

83. London, *Cruise of the Snark*, 103.

Chapter 3

1. Pukui, *Ōlelo Noʻeau*, 190.
2. Ii, *Fragments*, 69.

3. Bates, *Sandwich Island Notes*, 1854, 93.
4. Liliuʻokalani, Notes in Liliʻuokalani's handwriting, traditions respecting Waikiki, n.d., M-93, Liliuokalani Collection, Hawaii State Archives.
5. Stone, "Royal Hawaiian Hotel," 9.
6. Andrews, *A Dictionary*, 144.
7. Malo, *Hawaiian Antiquities*, 85.
8. Damon, "The First Mission Settlement," 232.
9. Pukui, trans., *Ōlelo Noʻeau*, 190.
10. "Narrow Escape," 3.
11. "The King's Birthday," 3.
12. "The King's Birthday," 3.
13. "Daughters of Hawaii," 327–328.
14. Del Piano, *Na Lani Kaumaka*, 79–85.
15. Bureau of Conveyances, book 44, 219.
16. "Ainahau," *Paradise of the Pacific*, 12.
17. "Ainahau," *Paradise of the Pacific*, 12.
18. Pukui, *Place Names of Hawaii*, 7.
19. "Ainahau," *Paradise of the Pacific*, 12.
20. "Ainahau," *Paradise of the Pacific*, 10.
21. *Hawaiian Gazette*, Oct. 1, 1876, 3.
22. "A Drive to Waikiki," 3.
23. "A Drive to Waikiki," 3.
24. *Hawaiian Gazette*, October 17, 1877, 2.
25. *Daily Bulletin*, March 31, 1882, 1.
26. *Pacific Commercial Advertiser*, June 10, 1882, 2.
27. *Pacific Commercial Advertiser*, August 4, 1882, 2.
28. "Reception at Waikiki," supplement.
29. "Jottings About Town," 2.
30. "A Royal Birthday," 3.
31. "Ainahau," http://www.huapala.org/ah/Ainahau.html.
32. "Island Locals," February 1, 1887, 5.
33. "Death of Princess Likelike," 2.
34. "Royal Birthday," 1.
35. "Married," 4.
36. "James W. Robertson," second sec., 1.
37. "Princess Kaiulani," 3.
38. "Wedding Reception," 4.
39. "Wedding Reception," 4.
40. "Palace Square," 2.
41. "The Hawaiian Question," 3.
42. "Kaiulani's Birthday," 3.
43. "Local and General News," *Independent*, August 17, 1895, 3.
44. Kaʻiulani to Liliʻuokalani, February 5, 1892, Liliuokalani Collection, M-93, Box 5, 47a, 258, Hawaii State Archives.
45. "Entertainment at Ainahau," 3.
46. "Local and General News," *Independent*, October 17, 1898, 3.
47. "News in a Nutshell," *Hawaiian Star*, October 15, 1898, 8.
48. "Local and General News," *Independent*, October 31, 1898, 3.
49. "Local and General," *Evening Bulletin*, March 7, 1899, 5.
50. "The Place of Mourning," *Pacific Commercial Advertiser*, January 16, 1909, 11.
51. "At Ainahau," *Independent*, March 10, 1899, 3.
52. "At Ainahau," *Independent*, March 10, 1899, 3.
53. "Hawaiians Claim to Have Heard the Spirit of Princess Kaiulani," *The Call* (San Francisco), April 4, 1899, 1.
54. "Two Receptions for Shriners Yesterday," 2.
55. "Two Receptions for Shriners Yesterday," 2.
56. "United in Bonds of Holy Matrimony," 7.
57. "Ainahau Wedding," 2.
58. "Wores' Art," 6.
59. "Society Items," 6.
60. "Society Items," 6.
61. "Journalists Are Kept Busy," 6.
62. "Fair Guests Royally Received," 7.
63. "Many Fetes for Japan's Sailors," 1.
64. A.S. Cleghorn to Walter R. [*sic*] Frear, July 27, 1909, Walter Francis Frear, Frear—Miscellaneous (By Name), A-C, Box GOV3-11.
65. "Supervisors Held Session," 2.
66. Walter Francis Frear to A.S. Cleghorn, July 26, 1909, Walter Francis Frear, Frear—Miscellaneous (By Name-Unindexed), Ci-Con, Box GOV3-11.
67. "The Onlooker," 9.
68. "May Day Fete Saturday Event," 4.
69. "Society," *Evening Bulletin*, 16.
70. "Death Comes to A.S. Cleghorn," 2.
71. "Public Notice," 8.
72. "Legislature Spurns Gift," 1.
73. "Territory Loses Cleghorn Offer," 3.
74. J.M. McChesney to Governor Lucius Eugene Pinkham, Jan. 30, 1914, Gov 4, Box 9, Misc. (by subject) A-H.
75. Gov. Lucius Eugene Pinkham to J.M. McChesney, Gov 4, Box 10, Misc. (Unindexed) M, Hawaii State Archives.
76. Attorney General Opinion No. 358, Feb. 4, 1914, Hawaii State Archives.
77. Attorney General Opinion No. 358, Feb. 4, 1914, Hawaii State Archives.
78. "New Manager Will Come," 7.
79. "New Manager Will Come," 7.
80. "Ainahau Hotel Site Sought," 1.
81. "Ainahau Hotel Site Sought," 1.
82. "Ainahau Hotel Site Sought," 1.
83. "Ainahau Hotel Site Sought," 1.
84. "Ainahau Sold," 6.
85. "Beautiful Ainahau Is Opened," sec. 2, 2.
86. "Ainahau, Once Palace Burns," 1.
87. "Ainahau, Once Palace Burns," 2.
88. Gessler, "Honolulu Letter," 76.
89. "Noted Kaiulani Banyan," 7.
90. Land Court Application 350, Maps 20, 23 and 24, Bureau of Conveyances, State of Hawaii.
91. "Kaiulani's Ainahau Grass House," features sec., 1.
92. "Kaiulani's Ainahau Grass House," features sec., 1.
93. "Kaiulani's Ainahau Grass House," features sec., 1.
94. Krauss, "Stevenson's grass house," A3.
95. Krauss, "Stevenson's grass house," A3.
96. "Full Account of the Mutiny," 2.

97. "Full Account of the Mutiny," 2.
98. "Supreme Court," 5.
99. Korn, *News from Molokai*, 84.
100. Kaleleonalani to Lucy [K. Peabody], January 19, 1874, Copy, original in Henriques papers, Bishop Museum, M-45, Hawaii State Archives.
101. *Reports of Decisions*, 1900, 83.
102. *Reports of Decisions*, 1900, 83.
103. Queen Emma to Flora Jones, Oct. 9, 1883, Queen Emma Collection, M-45, FJ-3.
104. In the matter of the Will of the Late Majesty Emma Kaleleonalani deceased, June 16, 1885 First Circuit Court, Series 007, Box 27, 1787, Hawaii State Archives.
105. *Reports of Decisions Rendered*, 1887, 501–502.
106. In re. Estate of Emma Kaleleonalani deceased, Oct. 19, 1886, Probate 1787 (III), Judiciary, First Circuit Court, Hawaii State Archives.
107. Supreme Court Hawaiian Islands in Chambers, Dec. 24, 1892, Probate 1787 (III), Judiciary, First Circuit Court, Hawaii State Archives.
108. Whitney, *The Tourist's Guide*, 37.
109. In re. Estate of Emma Kaleleonalani deceased, Oct. 19, 1886, Probate 1787 (III), Judiciary, First Circuit Court, Hawaii State Archives.
110. Estate of Emma Kaleleonalani, 1903 Account of Bruce Cartwright Trustee under the Will, Probate 1787 (V), First Circuit Court, Judiciary, Hawaii State Archives.
111. In the Matters of the Estate of Emma Kaleleonalani Deceased, Masters Report, Probate 1787 (V), First Circuit Court, Judiciary, Hawaii State Archives.
112. State of Hawaii, Bureau of Conveyances, book 64, 127.
113. "Finance Committee's Report," 7.
114. "King Kalakaua Dead," 6.
115. "Local and General," *Evening Bulletin*, February 18, 1896, 5.
116. "Record of Events," 21.
117. "At Pualeilani," 3.
118. "Body in State," 3.
119. "Notice," *The Independent*, 2.
120. "Local and General News," *The Independent* Mar. 3, 1902: 3.
121. "Shadows of Coming Events," 3.
122. "Shadows of Coming Events," 3.
123. "Local and General News," *The Independent*, March 13, 1902, 3.
124. "Reception at Pualeilani," *The Independent*, 2.
125. "Reception at Pualeilani," *Hawaiian Star*, 7.
126. "Local and General News," *The Independent*, March 22, 1902, 3.
127. "Princess Will Receive," 8.
128. "Uluniu Estate," 2.
129. "Old Associations of Kailua Palace," 10.
130. *Honolulu Advertiser*, June 21, 1918, sec 2, 1.
131. Bureau of Conveyances, State of Hawaii, book 12, 26.
132. List of Lands of the King, Land Matters, Interior Department, Document No. 384, n.d., Hawaii State Archives.
133. Liliu'okalani, Notes in Lili'uokalani's handwriting, traditions respecting Waikiki, n.d., M-93, Liliuokalani Collection, Hawaii State Archives.
134. Bureau of Conveyances, State of Hawaii, book 24, 198.
135. *Daily Bulletin*, March 31, 1882, 1.
136. Hau, "Novelty of Railway Building," 228.
137. "A Pleasant Day," 3.
138. Lili'uokalani, *Hawaii's Story*, 95–96.
139. Liliuokalani to Henry C. Carter, September 15, 1905, Liliuokalani Trust Manuscript Collection, M-397, Box 8, Folder 22, Hawaii State Archives.
140. Liliuokalani to Henry C. Carter, September 15, 1905, Liliuokalani Trust Manuscript Collection, M-397, Box 8, Folder 22, Hawaii State Archives.
141. "Queen Lil's Will a Surprise," 13.
142. "Ka La Hanau o Liliu," *Kuokoa Home Rula*, Sept. 2, 1912.
143. "More on Liliuokalani's Birthday Celebration, 1912," http://nupepa-hawaii.com/2012/08/
144. "Over the Tea Cups," 7.
145. "Honolulu Vies with Maui," 8.
146. [Flyer] "Unveiling Ceremony," February 14, 1930, Miscellaneous, Cook Sesquicentennial Celebration, Hawaii State Archives.
147. "Kuhio Home Offered," 1.
148. "Kuhio Home Offered," 1.
149. "Urges City," 1.
150. "Board Divided on Purchase," 2.
151. "Board Divided on Purchase," 2.
152. "Fear Old Kuhio House," 1.
153. "Board Votes to Obtain," 8.
154. "City Obtains Kuhio Home," 1.
155. "City Obtains Kuhio Home," 1.
156. "Workers to Raze," 5.
157. [Caption] "Princes See a Bit of Old Hawaii," *Honolulu Advertiser*, June 17, 1935, 1.
158. He Buke Mele Hawaii, 1897, Hawaii State Archives, M-93, Box 14, 26.
159. "Good Concert," 6.
160. "The St. Andrew's Concert," 4.
161. Survey notes, Uluhaimalama, Pauoa, Jun. 23, 1891, M-93, Liliuokalani collection #57, Hawaii State Archives.
162. *Laws of the Territory of Hawaii, Passed by the Fourteenth Legislature, Regular Session*, 1927, Honolulu: Advertiser Publishing Co., 1927, 295.
163. Siddall, *Men of Hawaii*, 379.
164. Nellist, *Men of Hawaii*, 257.
165. Amendment of Lili'uokalani Deed of Trust, 1911.

Chapter 4

1. Pukui, *Ōlelo No'eau*, 157.
2. Kapena, "Hawaiian National Reminiscences," 75.

3. J.S. Hart to M. Kekuanaoa, Interior Department, Miscellaneous, May 15, 1844.
4. "Address of the Hon. C.C. Harris," 5.
5. *Report of the Minister of the Interior*, 9.
6. *Polynesian*, September 6, 1845, 67.
7. "Court Notes," *Polynesian*, 103.
8. "Court Notes," *Polynesian*, 103.
9. Privy Council Minutes, September 7, 1846, Hawaii State Archives, Series 421, vol. 2T, 38.
10. Journal of Levi Chamberlain, vol. 26, entry for Aug. 10, 1848, http://96.31.65.17:8282/greenstone/collect/levicham/index/assoc/HASH0894.dir/doc.pdf.
11. Baker, *Honolulu in 1853*, opposite 8.
12. Bates, *Sandwich Island Notes*, 36.
13. Bates, *Sandwich Island Notes*, 36.
14. Bates, *Sandwich Island Notes*, 36–37.
15. Gilman, "Streets of Honolulu in the Early Forties," 93.
16. Gorman D. Gilman, "Streets of Honolulu," 93–94.
17. "Miscellaneous Expenditures," 2.
18. Donne, *The Sandwich Islands*, 146–147.
19. Donne, *The Sandwich Islands*, 147.
20. Anderson, *Scenes in the Hawaiian Islands*, 72.
21. Donne, *The Sandwich Islands*, 150–151.
22. "Death of His Majesty Kamehameha IV," 2.
23. Privy Council Minutes, Dec. 7, 1863, Hawaii State Archives, Series 421, vol. 11T, 127.
24. Privy Council Minutes, Dec. 7, 1863, Hawaii State Archives, Series 421, vol. 11T, 129.
25. "Funeral of the Late King," 2.
26. "Audience at Iolani Palace," 2.
27. "Audience at Iolani Palace," 2.
28. "Audience at Iolani Palace," 2.
29. Vincent, *Through and Through the Tropics*, 58–59.
30. "By Authority," *Hawaiian Gazette*, 2.
31. Bird, *The Hawaiian Archipelago*, 261–262.
32. "Shall We Have a Public Park?" 2.
33. Korn, *Letters from Molokai*, 251.
34. Korn, *Letters from Molokai*, 286.
35. Liliʻuokalani, Diary, 1874–1875, Liliʻuokalani Collection, M-93, Box 16, Folder 129.
36. Interior Department, Book 13, 351, Hawaii State Archives.
37. Interior Department, Book 13, 391, Hawaii State Archives.
38. "Report of the Minister of Finance," 2.
39. Coote, *Wanderings, South and East*, 91–92.
40. Taylor, "History of Iolani Palace," 4.
41. "Prince Kunuiakea Joins Majority," 2.
42. Barrere, "The King's Mahele," 9.
43. Thrum, *Hawaiian Almanac and Annual for 1904*, 94.
44. Historical and Miscellaneous File, 1785–1842, Sept. 12, 1829, from Levi Chamberlain's Journal 1822–1849, Hawaii State Archives.
45. Warriner, *Cruise of the United States*, 226.
46. *Foreign Testimony*, vol. 2, part 1, 3, Hawaii State Archives.
47. *Native Testimony*, vol. 2, 287, Hawaii State Archives.
48. "The Marriage Ceremony of the King," *Ke Kumu Hawaii*, Feb. 1, 1837, U-187, Hawaii State Archives.
49. Ii, *Fragments*, 161.
50. Wilkes, *Narrative of the United States*, 384.
51. Wilkes, *Narrative of the United States*, 391.
52. Wilkes, *Narrative of the United States*, 392.
53. Wilkes, *Narrative of the United States*, 392.
54. Jarves, *Scenes and Scenery*, 29.
55. Jarves, *Scenes and Scenery*, 31.
56. "Address of the Hon. C.C. Harris," 5.
57. Judd, *Honolulu, Sketches of Life*, 127–128.
58. Foreign Office and Executive, Robert Wyllie to Foreign Representatives, Letter Book, page 80, Series 210, Box 2, vol. 8, Hawaii State Archives.
59. Taylor, "History of Iolani Palace," 4.
60. Registered Map 900, Land Survey Division, Department of Accounting and General Services.
61. Ii, *Fragments*, 91.
62. *Foreign Testimony*, Hawaii State Archives, No. 177, vol. 3, part 1, 30.
63. *Native Testimony*, Hawaii State Archives, vol. 3, 356.
64. "Address of the Hon. C.C. Harris," 5.
65. Taylor, "History of Iolani Palace," 4–5.
66. "Address of the Hon. C.C. Harris," 5.
67. "Address of the Hon. C.C. Harris," 5.
68. "Royalist Leader Dead," 1.
69. Interior Department File #73 1856 now Interior Department, Subject, Palace-Old Iolani, 1856–1876, Folder 4.
70. Subject Card Catalog, Palaces, Palace—Honolulu—New Residence for Kam IV, Near, Archives of Hawaii.
71. Bates, *Sandwich Island Notes*, 37.
72. "The Palace," 2.
73. "Address by His Excellency," 5.
74. "Miscellaneous Expenditures," 2.
75. Korn, *Letters from Molokai*, 86.
76. Korn, *Letters from Molokai*, 291.
77. Korn, *Letters from Molokai*, 301.
78. "Death of His Royal Highness," 2.
79. "Funeral of the late Prince," 2.
80. Pukui, *The Echo of Our Song*, 143.
81. Pukui, *The Echo of Our Song*, 149.
82. Ii, *Fragments*, 143.
83. *Native Register*, vol. 4, trans. Frances Frazier, Hawaii State Archives, 362.
84. *Native Register*, vol. 5, trans. Frances Frazier, Hawaii State Archives, 257.
85. *Bernice Pauahi Bishop Museum Polynesian Ethnology and Natural History*, vol. VI, Honolulu: Bishop Museum Press, 1919–1920, 253.
86. Privy Council Minutes, May 27, 1850, Hawaii State Archives, 657.
87. Privy Council Minutes, May 27, 1850, Hawaii State Archives, 657.
88. Gilman, "Streets of Honolulu," 83.
89. Sheldon, "Reminiscences of Honolulu—No 31," 1.
90. *Polynesian*, June 21, 1851, 22.

91. "By Authority," *Polynesian*, 27.
92. Copy of Will of M. Kekauonohi, 1st Circuit Court Probate Minutes book, Vol. 2, 1851–1858, page 2, trans. Jason Achiu, 1st Circuit Court, Probate 2081, Series 007, Box 4, Hawaii State Archives.
93. Marriage Records, Hawaii island, H-16, 72, H-14a, 29, Hawaii State Archives.
94. "Another Chief Dead," 2.
95. Inventory of the Personal property belonging to the Estate of the late Hon. Levi Haalelea, 1st Circuit Court, Probate 2415 (I), Series 007, Box 45, Hawaii State Archives.
96. Inventory of the Personal property belonging to the Estate of the late Hon. Levi Haalelea, 1st Circuit Court, Probate 2415 (I), Series 007, Box 45, Hawaii State Archives.
97. Bagot, *McKenney's Hawaiian Directory*, 201.
98. Taylor, "Haalelea Lawn," 1.
99. "A Week in Society," 6.
100. "A Week in Society," 7.
101. Dodge, *St. Nicholas*, 349.
102. "Local and General News," *Independent*, June 1, 1898, 3.
103. "Farewell Poi Supper," 2.
104. "Local and General," *Evening Bulletin*, August 15, 1899, 5.
105. *Evening Bulletin*, Feb. 2, 1899, 1.
106. "News of the Town," *Honolulu Republican*, Nov. 3, 1900, 7.
107. "Coney Stone Wall," 1.
108. "Reviving an Old Case," second ed., 8.
109. "A Memorial Tablet," 5.
110. "William H. Coney Passes Away," *Independent*, Mar. 25, 1904, 3.
111. "Orders Sale of University Club Corner," 1.
112. Bureau of Conveyances, Territory of Hawaii, Feb. 12, 1929, Book 992, 124–127.
113. Taylor, "Haalelea Lawn," 1.
114. Gorham Gilman, "Streets of Honolulu," 89.
115. *Native Register*, vol. 5, 257–258, trans. Frances Frazier, Hawaii State Archives.
116. Bureau of Conveyances, State of Hawaii, Book 10, 427.
117. "Died," *Polynesian*, Jan. 18, 1862, 2.
118. "Died," *Polynesian*, Jan. 18, 1862, 2.
119. "Notice," *Polynesian*, 3.
120. In the matter of the appointment of Guardian to Albert Kunuiakea a minor, June 16, 1858, First Circuit Court, Probate 2259 (I), Series 007, Box 31, Hawaii State Archives, trans. Jason Achiu.
121. In the matter of the appointment of Guardian to Albert Kunuiakea, June 30, 1858, First Circuit Court, Probate 2259 (I), Series 007, Box 31, Hawaii State Archives.
122. Bureau of Conveyances, State of Hawaii, Book 16, 282–283.
123. Inventory of the Real Estate of Albert Kunuiakea, Jan. 12, 1871, First Circuit Court, Probate 2259 (I), Series 007, Box 31, Hawaii State Archives.
124. In re. the Guardianship of Kunuiakea Kaeo, Nov. 11, 1872, First Circuit Court, Probate 2259 (I), Series 007, Box 31, Hawaii State Archives, trans. Jason Achiu.
125. In the matter of the appointment of a Guardian to the person and Estate of Albert Kunuiakea Kaeo, Nov. 11, 1872, First Circuit Court, Probate 2259 (I), Series 007, Box 31, Hawaii State Archives.
126. In the matter of the Guardianship of Albert Kunuiakea, Jan. 11, 1876, First Circuit Court, Probate 2259 (II), Series 007, Box 31, Hawaii State Archives.
127. In the matter of the Guardianship of Albert Kunuiakea, Jan. 13, 1876, First Circuit Court, Probate 2259 (II), Series 007, Box 31, Hawaii State Archives.
128. In the matter of the Guardianship of Albert Kunuiakea, Jan. 13, 1876, First Circuit Court, Probate 2259 (II), Series 007, Box 31, Hawaii State Archives.
129. In the matter of the Guardianship of Albert Kunuiakea, Jan. 13, 1876, First Circuit Court, Probate 2259 (II), Series 007, Box 31, Hawaii State Archives.
130. In the matter of the Guardianship of Albert Kunuiakea, Jan. 13, 1876, First Circuit Court, Probate 2259 (II), Series 007, Box 31, Hawaii State Archives.
131. In the matter of the Guardianship of Albert Kunuiakea, April 6, 1880, First Circuit Court, Probate 2259 (II), Series 007, Box 31, Hawaii State Archives.
132. *The Hawaiian Kingdom*, 83.
133. Albert K. Kunuiakea to Queen Emma, June 16, 1883, M-45, AH005, Hawaii State Archives.
134. Bagot, *McKenney's Hawaiian Directory*, 163.
135. E.G. Beckwith to Lili'uokalani, Foreign Office and Executive, Series 401, Box 1, Folder 17, Document #200, Hawaii State Archives.
136. "Na Wahi Pana," 5.
137. "Prince Kunuiakea Joins Majority," 2.
138. "At Rest," 2.
139. Bennett, *Honolulu Directory*, 92.
140. Bird, *The Hawaiian Archipelago*, 262.
141. Kaleleonalani to Lucy [K. Peabody], January 19, 1874, Copy, original in Henriques papers, Bishop Museum, M-45, Hawaii State Archives.
142. "Death of the King," 2.
143. Kaleleonalani to Lucy [K. Peabody], January 19, 1874, copy, original in Henriques papers, Bishop Museum, M-45, Hawaii State Archives.
144. "Notes of the Week," *Hawaiian Gazette*, 3.
145. "Administrator's Sale of Real Estate," 3.
146. "House for Sale," 3.
147. "House for Sale," 3.
148. "House for Sale," 3.
149. Court Notes, *Hawaiian Gazette*, 4.
150. "Independent Leaders Urge Steadfastness," 8.
151. "Mass Meeting," *Independent*, Apr. 26, 1901, 2.
152. Barrere, "The King's Mahele," 478.
153. Ii, *Fragments*, 169.

154. *Hawaiian Annual*, 1899, 102.
155. Phillips, *Report of the Minister of Finance*, 12.
156. Phillips, *Report of the Minister of Finance*, 27.
157. *Appendix to the Report*, 4.
158. C.N. Spencer to A.S. Cleghorn, May 21, 1892, Interior Department, Hawaii State Archives, 136.
159. Interior Department, Subject, Palace Proposed 1871, AH.
160. Interior Department, Subject, Palace Proposed 1871, AH.
161. Interior Department, Subject, Palace Proposed 1871, AH.
162. Interior Department, Subject, Palace Proposed 1871, AH.
163. Interior Department, Subject, Palace Proposed 1871, AH.
164. Fairfax, *Iolani Palace Restoration Architectural Report*, 27.
165. "The Inflation Calculator, available at http://www.westegg.com/inflation/infl.cgi, accessed May 7, 2013.
166. Fairfax, *Iolani Palace Restoration Architectural Report*, 27.
167. Fairfax, *Iolani Palace Restoration Architectural Report*, 27.
168. Fairfax, *Iolani Palace Restoration Architectural Report*, 27.
169. Fairfax, *Iolani Palace Restoration Architectural Report*, 27.
170. Fairfax, *Iolani Palace Restoration Architectural Report*, 98.
171. "Land of the Golden Fleece," 4.
172. Inventory of Iolani Palace, Healani House and Honuakaha, n.d., William Owen Smith Collection, M-133, Box 1–11, Hawaii State Archives.

Chapter 5

1. Pukui, *Ōlelo No‘eau*, 257.
2. Campbell, *Voyage Round the World*, 149.
3. Campbell, *Voyage Round the World*, 88.
4. "Chamisso's Account," 14.
5. Campbell, *Voyage Round the World*, 95.
6. Campbell, *Voyage Round the World*, 91.
7. Rockwood, "Honolulu in 1810."
8. Andrews, *A Dictionary of the Hawaiian Language*, 2003, 163.
9. *Punahou Jubilee Celebration*, 20.
10. *Honolulu in 1810: Explanation of Map*.
11. Campbell, *Voyage Round the World*, 87.
12. Rockwood, "Honolulu in 1810."
13. Von Kotzebue, *A New Voyage*, vol. II, 205.
14. Rockwood, "Honolulu in 1810."
15. Ii, *Fragments*, 82.
16. Mathison, *Narrative of a Visit*, 365.
17. Mathison, *Narrative of a Visit*, 366.
18. Stewart, *Journal of a Residence*, 68–69.
19. Stewart, *Journal of a Residence*, 73.
20. Stewart, *Journal of a Residence*, 73.
21. Stewart, *Journal of a Residence*, 73.
22. Stewart, *Journal of a Residence*, 73–74.
23. Registered Map 640, Land Survey Division, Department of Accounting and General Services.
24. "Supreme Court—In Equity, L. Keelikolani v. James Robinson," *Polynesian*, July 5, 1862, 4.
25. "Supreme Court—In Equity, L. Keelikolani v. James Robinson," *Polynesian*, July 5, 1862, 4.
26. *Polynesian*, Jan. 9, 1847, 138.
27. *Native Testimony*, trans. Sarah Nakoa, vol. 3, 596.
28. Barrere, *The Journal of John Young*, 6.
29. Barrere, *The Journal of John Young*, 6.
30. Ellis, *Narrative of a Tour*, 399.
31. Stewart, *Journal of a Residence*, 310.
32. Stewart, *Journal of a Residence*, 228.
33. Ii, *Fragments*, 143.
34. Bingham, *A Residence of Twenty-one Years*, 225–226.
35. Eveleth, *History of the Sandwich Islands*, 164.
36. Stewart, *Journal of a Residence*, 272.
37. Stewart, *Journal of a Residence*, 272.
38. *Missionary Reports, Sandwich Islands*, 315.
39. *Native Testimony*, vol. 3, 257–258, trans. Sarah Nakoa, Hawaii State Archives.
40. *Native Testimony*, vol. 2, 58, testimony by John Ii on Land Commission Award No. 278 to Laanui, trans. Sarah Nakoa, Hawaii State Archives.
41. Chamberlain Journal, June 7, 1826.
42. Jarves, *Scenes and Scenery*, 45–46.
43. Kekuanaoa to Haalilio, Feb. 28, 1844, Foreign Office and Executive, Series 402, Box 10, Folder 241, Hawaii State Archives.
44. Judd to Kekuanaoa, May 6, 1844, Foreign Office and Executive, Series 402, Box 10, Folder 254, Hawaii State Archives.
45. *Native Register*, vol. 2, 8.
46. Stewart, *Journal of a Residence*, 213.
47. "Notes of the Week," *Pacific Commercial Advertiser*, Apr. 9, 1864, 2.
48. Stewart, *Journal of a Residence*, 228.
49. Stewart, *Journal of a Residence*, 271.
50. Bloxam, *Diary of Andrew Bloxam*, 34–35.
51. Capt. Finch to Kaahumanu, Oct. 16, 1829, Foreign Office and Executive, Series 201, Box 3, Folder 26, Hawaii State Archives
52. Allen, "Kaahumanu," 185.
53. Ii, *Fragments*, 158.
54. "A Plan of the Harbour," G4382.O2:2H64 1825.M3.
55. Von Kotzebue, *A New Voyage*, vol. II, 245.
56. Von Kotzebue, *A New Voyage*, vol. II, 245.
57. *Foreign Testimony*, vol. 3, 373, Hawaii State Archives.
58. Ii, *Fragments*, 143.
59. Ii, *Fragments*, 153.
60. Stewart, *A Visit to the South Seas*, 226–227.
61. "Meyen's Voyage round the World," 18.
62. "Address of the Hon. C.C. Harris," 5.
63. Kapena, "Hawaiian National Reminiscences," 75.
64. Ii, *Fragments*, 153.

65. Silliman, "Hawaii (Owyhee), and Its Volcanic Regions," 246.
66. Silliman, "Hawaii (Owyhee), and Its Volcanic Regions," 246.
67. Silliman, "Hawaii (Owyhee), and Its Volcanic Regions," 246.
68. Silliman, "Hawaii (Owyhee), and Its Volcanic Regions," 246.
69. Silliman, "Hawaii (Owyhee), and Its Volcanic Regions," 246.
70. "Sandwich Islands," *London Illustrated News*, Apr. 1, 1843, 68.
71. "Meyen's Voyage Round the World," 17.
72. Reynolds, *Voyage of the United States*, 412–413.
73. Barrot, *Unless Haste Is Made*, 66.
74. Lili'uokalani, *Hawaii's Story*, 1.
75. Ii, *Fragments*, 145.
76. Stewart, *Journal of a Residence*, 260–261.
77. Stewart, *A Visit to the South Seas*, 143–144.
78. Ii, *Fragments*,, 158.
79. Judd, *Honolulu, Sketches of Life*, 47–48.
80. Judd, *Honolulu, Sketches of Life*, 48–49.
81. Twombly, *Hawaii and Its People*, 216.
82. Twombly, *Hawaii and Its People*, 216.
83. Francis Warriner, *Cruise of the United States Frigate Potomac Round the World During the Years 1831–34*, Boston: Crocker and Brewster, 223.
84. Samuel Parker, *Journal of an Exploring Tour Beyond the Rocky Mountains*, Ithaca, NY: Mack, Andrus and Woodruff, 1838, 346–347.
85. Land Patent Grant 473, Series 526, Box 6, Grant Survey Notes, No. 473, 474, Hawaii State Archives.
86. Privy Council Reports, Report of Committee on Missionary Lands and on the course to be pursued in regard to them, August 19, 1850 (3).
87. Privy Council August 19, 1850, Series 421, vol. 3B, typescript, Hawaii State Archives, 749.
88. Thomas G. Thrum, ed., *Hawaiian Almanac and Annual for 1891*, Honolulu: Press Publishing Company, 1890, 113.
89. Matiao Kekūanāo'a to John Young II, August 27, 1850, Department of the Interior, Land, Box 64, Hawaii State Archives.
90. Albert Pierce Taylor, *Under Hawaiian Skies*, Honolulu: Advertiser Publishing Company, 1922, 167.
91. "Home of Former Queen Is Visited by Daughters of Hawaii," *Honolulu Star-Bulletin*, June 18, 1932, sec. 2, 5.
92. Barbara Jane Del Piano, *Nā Lani Kaumaka, Daughters of Hawai'i, A Century of Historic Preservation*, Honolulu: Daughters of Hawaii, 2005, 181.
93. Home of Queen Kaahumanu in Manoa Valley, 1932, Land of Kahaumakaawe, Historical and Miscellaneous File, 1932, U-178, Hawaii State Archives.
94. Pukui, *Place Names of Hawaii*, 190.
95. Sterling, *Sites of Oahu*, 288.
96. Damon, "From Manoa to Punahou," 6.
97. Henry P. Judd, Report, Commission on Historical Sites, 201-1-12.
98. Hopkins, *Hawaii*, xi.
99. "Manoa Uplands," 12.
100. "Manoa Uplands," 12.
101. Pukui, *Place Names of Hawaii*, 53.
102. Stewart, *A Visit to the South Seas*, 143–144.
103. *Polynesian*, Jul 11, 1840, 18.
104. *Polynesian*, Jul. 11, 1840, 18.
105. *Stephen Reynolds Journal*, 49.
106. *Stephen Reynolds Journal*, 49–50.
107. Thrum, *Hawaii Almanac and Annual for 1892*, 114.
108. Kay, "Sandwich Islands," 104.
109. Reynolds, *Voyage of the United States*, 401.
110. Ruschenberger, *A Voyage Round the World*, 389.
111. Kamakau, *Ruling Chiefs of Hawaii*, 340.
112. Jarves, *History of the Hawaiian*, 393.
113. Jarves, *Scenes and Scenery*, 29.
114. Gilman, "Streets of Honolulu," 78.
115. *Polynesian*, Jan. 9, 1847, 138.
116. "Reminiscences of Honolulu LXI," 1.
117. "Old Government Building," 1.
118. Privy Council, March 8, 1852, vol. 6, 604, Hawaii State Archives.
119. "Old Government Building," 1.
120. "Old Government Building," 1, 4.
121. Bennett, *Honolulu Directory*, s.v. "Government House."
122. *The Hawaiian Kingdom Statistical and Commercial Directory and Tourists Guide*, 1880–1881, Honolulu: George Bowser, 1880, 81.
123. "Sudden Death of the Queen of the Sandwich Islands," *Sacramento Daily Record-Union*, May 9, 1885, 9.
124. Chauncey Bennett, *Honolulu Directory*, s.v. "Sisters of the Sacred Heart."
125. "Auction Sale of Valuable City Property," 6.
126. "Auction Sale of Valuable City Property," 6.
127. "Auction Sale of Valuable City Property," 6.
128. "Important Land Sale," 3.
129. "Important Land Sale," 3.
130. http://96.31.65.17:8282/greenstone/collect/levicham/index/assoc/HASH554d.dir/doc.pdf
131. Probate 2404, 1st. Circuit, John Young I, Hawaii State Archives.
132. "Sudden Death," 9.
133. T.C.B. Rooke to John Young, Feb. 11, 1848, Series 526, Grant Survey Notes no. 83, Hawaii State Archives.
134. "Died," Polynesian, January 26, 1850, 147.
135. *Polynesian*, October 4, 1851, 82.
136. R.C. Wyllie to Foreign Ministers, Oct. 2, 1851, Series 410, Foreign Office Letterbook, vol. 13A, Foreign Office and Executive, Hawaii State Archives, 1400.
137. "Good Queen Emma," 236.
138. Korn, *The Victorian Visitors*, 118.
139. "Priory Training at St. Andrew's," 3.
140. Nogelmeier, *He Lei no Emalani*, 125.
141. Bird, *The Hawaiian Archipelago*, 262–263.
142. Korn, *News from Molokai*, 75.
143. "Good Queen Emma," 236.
144. "Good Queen Emma," 236.

145. Gilman, "Streets of Honolulu," 78.
146. "Queen Emma Hall," *Daily Bulletin*, Mar. 2, 1887, 3.
147. "Queen Emma Hall," *Daily Bulletin*, Mar. 4, 1887, 3.
148. "Local and General News," *Daily Bulletin*, May 28, 1887, 3.
149. "Queen Emma Hall," *Hawaiian Gazette*, 9.
150. *Who's Who in New York City and State* 1188.
151. *Reports of Decisions*, 1900, 377.
152. *Reports of Decisions*, 1900, 408
153. "Auction Sale of Valuable City Property," 6.
154. "Important Land Sale," 3.
155. "To Let," 6.
156. "To Let," 6.
157. "Theft Was Not a Theft," 8.
158. "Queen Emma's Former Palace," 2.
159. "Queen Emma's Former Palace," 2.
160. "S. Yokomizo," *Evening Bulletin*, 2.
161. "S. Yokomizo," *Pacific Commercial Advertiser*, 8.
162. "Blazing Japanese Calls Out Engines," 5.
163. "Local and General," *Evening Bulletin*, Jul. 30, 1908, 2.
164. "The Theaters," *Hawaiian Star*, Feb. 22, 1912. 6.
165. Griffiss, *When You Go to Hawaii*, 151.
166. Barrot, *Unless Haste Is Made*, 51.
167. Barrot, *Unless Haste Is Made*, 54.
168. Kekauluohi to Mataio Kekūanāoʻa on March 13, 1840, Box 141, Interior Department, Miscellaneous, Hawaii State Archives.
169. Matiao Kekuanaoa to Puapua, May 7, 1842, Interior Department, Land, Letters (incoming), 1842, April–Sept.
170. Nye, *Journal of a Voyage*, 82.
171. Nye, *Journal of a Voyage*, 82.
172. Gorham Gilman manuscript, Gilman Collection, Hawaiian Historical Society, Honolulu, quoted in Lydia Rider Nye, *Journal of a Sea Captain's Wife, 1841–1845*, Spokane, WA: Arthur H. Clark Co., 2004, 221.
173. *The Friend*, March 2, 1844, 28–29.
174. Judd, *Honolulu*, 131.
175. M. Kekuanaoa to M. Auhea, n.d. Hawaiian Chiefs, Undated Documents, No. 31 (10) to 31 (20), No. 31 (13), trans. Jason Achiu, Hawaii State Archives.
176. *Report of the Minister of the Interior*, 9.
177. *Polynesian*, Sept. 6, 1845, 66.
178. "Restoration Day," 46.
179. "Restoration Day," 46.
180. "Restoration Day," 46.
181. "Restoration Day," 46.
182. Gilman, "Honolulu and its Suburbs," 123.
183. Baker, *Honolulu in 1853*, opposite 24.
184. Stoddard, *A Trip to Hawaii*, 22.
185. "Through Nuuanu," 35.
186. "Through Nuuanu," 35.
187. Report of the Committee on Site Conservation, Jan. 9, 1954. U-9 Minutes-Exec. Bd. Conservation Council—1950–1956, 14.
188. Report of the Committee on Site Conservation, Conservation Council for Hawaii, Fifth Annual Meeting, February 11, 1955. U-9 Minutes-Exec. Bd. Conservation Council—1950–1956 [14].
189. Report of the Committee on Site Conservation, Conservation Council for Hawaii, Sixth Annual Meeting, February 24, 1956. U-9 Minutes-Exec. Bd. Conservation Council—1950–1956 [14].
190. Eleanor S. Anderson, "Summary Report of Work by the Conservation Council of Hawaii," *The Proceedings of the Ninth Pacific Science Congress, 1957*, vol. 7, 1959, 17.
191. Kekahuna, "Our Ignored Gold Mine," 24.
192. Kekahuna, "Our Ignored Gold Mine," 24.
193. Kekahuna, "Our Ignored Gold Mine," 18.
194. Gilman, "Streets of Honolulu," 93.
195. *Polynesian*, May 22, 1847, 3.
196. "Death of Paki," *Friend*, Jun. 15, 1855, 45.
197. Paradise of the Pacific, Apr. 1892, 3.
198. "Liliuokalani's Childhood Home," 6.
199. Liliʻuokalani, *Hawaii's Story*, 110.
200. "Liliuokalani's Childhood Home," 6.
201. "Liliuokalani's Childhood Home," 6.
202. "Liliuokalani's Childhood Home," 6.
203. "Old Landmarks Gone," 85.
204. Mark Twain, "Scenes in Honolulu," 3.
205. "Government Officer," *Pacific Commercial Advertiser*, January 12, 1860, 1.
206. Ii, *Fragments*, 175.
207. *Hawaiian Almanac and Annual for 1902*, 144.
208. Ii, *Fragments*, 143.
209. Liliʻuokalani, *Hawaii's Story*, 32.
210. "Arrival of His Royal Highness," 69.
211. *Catalogue of Water-Colour Sketches*, 13.
212. Taylor, *Under Hawaiian Skies*, 422.
213. H.A. Widemann to Samuel. G. Wilder, Sept. 1879, Department of the Interior, Land, Box 85, Hawaii State Archives.
214. H.A. Widemann to Samuel. G. Wilder, Sept. 1879, Department of the Interior, Land, Box 85, Hawaii State Archives.
215. H.A. Widemann to Samuel. G. Wilder, Sept. 1879, Department of the Interior, Land, Box 85, Hawaii State Archives.
216. H.A. Widemann to Samuel. G. Wilder, Sept. 1879, Department of the Interior, Land, Box 85, Hawaii State Archives.
217. *The Evening Star* (Auckland, New Zealand), 2.
218. "Local & General News," *Daily Bulletin*, Aug. 10, 1889, 3.
219. "King's Palace Gives Way," 1.
220. "Royalist Leader Dead," 1.
221. Indenture of Lease Between M. Kekuanaoa and W.C. Parke, Nov. 25, 1852, Interior Department, Land, Letters (Incoming) 1852, November 11–30, Box 67, Hawaii State Archives.
222. Registered Map 1791, Land Survey Division, Department of Accounting and General Services.

223. Kapiolani-Namakaeha (k), Marriages: Oahu (1832–1910), O-32:122, Hawaii State Archives.
224. Last Will and Testament, Benita Namakeha, 1st Circuit Court, Probate 936.
225. Amendment to Last Will and Testament, Benita Namakeha, 1st Circuit Court, Probate 936.
226. "Death of Prince David Kawananakoa," 2.
227. Sarah Nakoa, trans., No. 1090, June 14, 1848, *Native Testimony*, vol. 3, 99–100, Hawaii State Archives.
228. Sarah Nakoa, trans., No. 1090, June 14, 1848, *Native Testimony*, vol. 3, 99–100, Hawaii State Archives.
229. Interior Department Land, July 21, 1842, English translation attached with Hawaiian language Deed, Hawaii State Archives, 1–3.
230. Bingham, *A Residence of Twenty-One Years*, 611.
231. Marriage Record, O-27:91, Hawaii State Archives.
232. "Ka make ana o Hon. J. Kapena," 2.
233. 1st Circuit Court, Probate no. 1840, Hawaii State Archives.
234. Bureau of Conveyances, State of Hawaii, book 35, 397.
235. Ruth Keʻelikolani to Kipine, Esq., Sept. 3, 1860., translated by E.H. Hart, Hawaii State Archives.
236. Ruth to Lot, September 14, 1860, Interior Department, Miscellaneous, Hawaii State Archives.
237. Ruth Keʻelikolani to S. Pine [S. Spencer], Sept. 21, 1860, translated by E.H. Hart, Interior Department, Miscellaneous, July-December, 1860, Box 147, Hawaii State Archives.
238. Ruth Keʻelikolani to C.P. Turner (Kale), July 15, 1861, Interior Department, Miscellaneous, July 1861, Hawaii State Archives. Translated by E.H. Hart.
239. Bennett, *Honolulu Directory*, 88.
240. Korn, *News from Molokai*, 136.
241. "Notes of the Week," *Pacific Commercial Advertiser*, Oct. 18, 1873, 3.
242. "Notes of the Week," *Pacific Commercial Advertiser*, Oct. 18, 1873, 3.
243. "Notes of the Week," *Pacific Commercial Advertiser*, Oct. 18, 1873, 3.
244. Minister of the Interior to Ruth Keʻelikolani, Aug. 17, 1874, Interior Department, Book 12, 533, Hawaii State Archives.
245. Bureau of Conveyances, State of Hawaii, Book 20, 415.
246. *Hawaiian Gazette*, February 3, 1869, 3.
247. Bennett, *Honolulu Directory*, 85.
248. Charles T. Gulick to A.S. Cleghorn, August 31, 1875, Interior Department, book 13, 67, Hawaii State Archives.
249. *The Hawaiian Kingdom Statistical and Commercial Directory and Tourists Guide*, 1880–1881, Honolulu: George Bowser, 1880, 58.
250. Bagot, *McKenney's Hawaiian Directory*, 103.
251. *Friend*, August 1, 1882, 85.
252. "Died," *Hawaiian Gazette*, 8.
253. "News in a Nutshell," *Hawaiian Star*, Mar. 2, 1896, 3.
254. "Death of Jas. Campbell," second ed., 1.
255. "Mrs. A. Campbell Marries," 1.
256. "Local and General," *Evening Bulletin*, January 11, 1902, 5.
257. "Great Doings When the Parker," 7.
258. "Reasons for Dole's Removal," 6.
259. "Parker Won't Accept," 3.
260. "Poi Luncheon," 2.
261. "No Clue to Thieves," 1.
262. "One of Mrs. Parker's Lost Rings," 1.
263. "Inflation Calculator," available at http://www.davemanuel.com/inflation-calculator.php?theyear=1903&amountmoney=80000
264. "The Parker Diamonds," 1.
265. Allen, "Mansion for the Governor," 9.
266. "Local and General News," *Independent*, Mar. 24, 1902, 3.
267. "News in a Nutshell," *Hawaiian Star*, Jan. 13, 1905, second ed., 8.
268. "Social Side of Life," 6.
269. "Social Side of Life," 6.
270. *Hawaiian Gazette*, June 9, 1905, 8.
271. "Social Side of Life," 6.
272. "Receipt for the Campbell Property," second ed., 5.
273. "Receipt for the Campbell Property," second ed., 5.
274. "Society," *Hawaiian Gazette*, May 12, 1908, 6.
275. "Death of Mrs. Campbell-Parker," 3.
276. "Mrs. Col. Parker Dies," 1.
277. "Death of Mrs. Campbell-Parker," 3.
278. "Mrs. Sam Parker's Funeral Wednesday," 2.
279. "Mrs. Parker's Funeral," 8.
280. "Impressive Are the Last Mortal Honors," 2.
281. "Mrs. Campbell-Parker's Estate," 1.
282. "Death of Mrs. Campbell-Parker," 3.
283. Robert W. Shingle-Ethel Muriel Campbell, Oahu Marriages, O-96:494, Hawaii State Archives.
284. "Child of Fortune," 1.
285. "Another Campbell Will Case," second ed., 1.
286. "Campbell-Beckley Wedding Brilliant," 1.
287. *Directory of Honolulu*, 1912, 199.
288. "Many Houses Going Up," 5.
289. "Oriental Art Exhibit," 8.
290. *Directory of Honolulu*, 1924, 160.
291. "Splendid Home," second ed., 1.
292. "Commercial Review," second ed., 7.
293. "Campbell House for Army Headquarters," 3.
294. *Directory of Honolulu*, 1924, 160.
295. *Directory of Honolulu*, 1924, 408.
296. Hyams, *Centennial Memoirs*, 84.
297. "Landmarks Going Down," 49.
298. "Notice No. 6," 54.
299. "Notice No. 6," 54.
300. "Japanese Buys House," 5.

301. "Notes of the Week, *Pacific Commercial Advertiser*, February 13, 1862, 3.
302. Bennett, *Honolulu Directory*, 91.
303. Bagot, *McKenney's Hawaiian Directory*, 169.
304. "Baseball Tourists!," 3.
305. "Unsuccessful Attempt at Revolution," *Daily Bulletin*, July 31, 1889, 3.
306. "Trial of Albert Loomens for Treason," *Daily Bulletin*, October 10, 1889, July 31, 1889, 3.
307. Local and General, *Pacific Commercial Advertiser*, Jul. 01, 1891, 3.
308. "Charity Luau," *Daily Bulletin*, Feb. 16, 1892, 2.
309. Inventory of Iolani Palace, Healani House and Holuakaha, n.d., William Owen Smith Collection, M-133, Box 1–11, Hawaii State Archives.
310. Inventory of Iolani Palace, Healani House and Holuakaha, n.d., William Owen Smith Collection, M-133, Box 1–11, Hawaii State Archives.
311. [Flyer] "Unveiling Ceremony," Feb. 14, 1930, Miscellaneous, Cook Sesquicentennial.
312. "Provision for Homeless," 7.
313. "Measures of Relief," 1.
314. "Topics of the Day," 2.
315. "Japanese Buys House," 5.
316. Notes Regarding Leilehua Ranch House, Liliʻuokalani Collection, M-93, Box 2, Folder 21, Item 125, Hawaii State Archives.
317. "Leilehua Ranch!" 2.
318. "Local and General," *Hawaiian Gazette*, Mar. 19, 1889, 7.
319. "Interest to Sportsmen," 3.
320. "Leilehua Ranch Lands," 1.
321. "Troopers of Fifth Cavalry," 3.
322. "Double Engagement," 8.
323. "Tropic Lightning Museum: Memoirs and Recollections," http://www.garrison.hawaii.army.mil/tlm/files/early-schofield-barracks.pdf
324. "Hunting Lodge of King Kalakaua," 3.
325. "Party at Schofield," 7.
326. *Infantry Journal*, 89.
327. Withington, *Hawaiian Tapestry*, 329.
328. Queen Emma to Flora Jones, Mar. 13, 1883, Queen Emma Collection, M-45, FJ-3, Hawaii State Archives.
329. Queen Emma to Flora Jones, Mar. 27, 1883, Queen Emma Collection, M-45, FJ-3, Hawaii State Archives
330. Queen Emma to Flora Jones, Apr. 3, 1883, Queen Emma Collection, M-45, FJ-3, Hawaii State Archives
331. Queen Emma to Flora Jones, Apr. 3, 1883, Queen Emma Collection, M-45, FJ-3, Hawaii State Archives
332. Queen Emma to Flora Jones, Jul. 10, 1883, Queen Emma Collection, M-45, FJ-3, Hawaii State Archives
333. Queen Emma to Flora Jones, Aug. 7, 1883, Queen Emma Collection, M-45, FJ-3, Hawaii State Archives
334. Queen Emma to Flora Jones, Oct. 9, 1883, Queen Emma Collection, M-45, FJ-3, Hawaii State Archives
335. Sands, *Mouth and Bar of Pearl River*.
336. *Pacific Islands*, vol. III, London: Hydrographic Office, Admiralty, 1885, 152.
337. Conyers, "An Analysis of Ground-Penetrating Radar's Ability," 66.
338. "Brief Mention," *Pacific Commercial Advertiser*, September 7, 1878: 3.
339. Registered Map 1382, Land Survey Division, Department of Accounting and General Services.
340. "Island Locals," *Hawaiian Gazette*, September 21, 1881, 3.
341. *Daily Bulletin*, April 10, 1882, 1.
342. *Daily Bulletin*, January 4, 1886, 3.
343. *Directory and Hand-Book of Honolulu*, 1892, 201.
344. "Local and General News," *Daily Bulletin*, February 24, 1893, 3.
345. "Treason and Conspiracy," 1.
346. "Jos. Nawahi's Remains," 4.
347. Sheldon, *Ka Puke Moʻolelo*, 167.
348. "Jos. Nawahi's Remains," 4.
349. "Jos. Nawahi's Remains," 4.
350. Emma Nawahi to Queen Liliʻuokalani dated January 28, 1897, Liliʻuokalani Collection, M-93, Box 2, Folder 19 (Hawaiian translated into English by Jason Achiu).
351. Emma Nawahi to Queen Liliʻuokalani dated March 9, 1897, Liliʻuokalani Collection, M-93, Box 2, Folder 19 (Hawaiian translated into English by Jason Achiu).
352. Emma Nawahi to Queen Liliʻuokalani, various dates, Liliʻuokalani Collection, M-93, Box 2, Folder 19.
353. Emma Nawahi to Queen Liliʻuokalani, n.d., Liliʻuokalani Collection, M-93, Box 2, Folder 19.
354. Mulholland, *Hawaii's Religions*, 194.
355. Oshita, "*Hawaii Conference—Conference History*," accessed Nov. 25, 2012, http://hwic.adventistfaith.org/conference-history. (Original timeline dated October 1961.)
356. Oshita, "*Hawaii Conference—Conference History*."
357. Howell, "Among the Chinese in Honolulu," 815.
358. Howell, "Among the Chinese in Honolulu," 815.
359. Howell, "Among the Chinese in Honolulu," 815.
360. Howell, "Among the Chinese in Honolulu," 816.
361. Howell, "Among the Chinese in Honolulu," 816.
362. Howell, "Among the Chinese in Honolulu," 816.
363. Howell, "Anglo-Chinese Academy," 103.
364. Howell, "Among the Chinese in Honolulu," 815.
365. Bishop Estate Map Registered No. 287. Endowment Group, Land Assets Division, Kamehameha Schools, Honolulu, Hawaii.
366. Allen, "Banyan Tree Is Center," *Honolulu Star-Bulletin*, sec. 2, 10.

367. "Estate B.P. Bishop, Receipts, Month of September 1901," [12], accessed Nov. 25, 2012, http://archives1.dags.hawaii.gov/gsdl/collect/judiciar/index-old/assoc/HASH288b.dir/doc.pdf

368. "Report, Financial and Statistical, Kamehameha Schools, Year Ending June 30, 1902," [216], accessed Nov. 25, 2012, http://archives1.dags.hawaii.gov/gsdl/collect/judiciar/index-old/assoc/HASH01f7.dir/doc.pdf.

369. "Report, Financial and Statistical, Kamehameha Schools, Year Ending June 30, 1902," [216], accessed Nov. 25, 2012, http://archives1.dags.hawaii.gov/gsdl/collect/judiciar/index-old/assoc/HASH01f7.dir/doc.pdf.

370. "Report, Financial and Statistical, Kamehameha Schools, Year Ending June 30, 1903," [266], accessed Nov. 25, 2012, http://archives1.dags.hawaii.gov/gsdl/collect/judiciar/index-old/assoc/HASHacfd.dir/doc.pdf.

371. "Democrats Attacked," 3.

372. Political Meetings," 2.

373. Bernice P. Bishop Estate, "Report, Financial and Statistical, Kamehameha Schools, Year Ending June 30, 1904," 243, accessed Nov. 25, 2012, http://archives1.dags.hawaii.gov/gsdl/collect/judiciar/index-old/assoc/HASH0103.dir/doc.pdf.

374. *Evening Bulletin,* June 3, 1904, 7.

375. Bernice P. Bishop Estate, "Real Estate Transactions, Trustees, Estate of B. P. Bishop, July 1, 1903-June 30, 1904," 199, accessed Nov. 25, 2012, http://archives1.dags.hawaii.gov/gsdl/collect/judiciar/index-old/assoc/HASH01f9.dir/doc.pdf.

376. *Hawaiian Gazette,* January 19, 1906, 7.

377. Bernice P. Bishop Estate, "Master's Report for Year Ending June 30, 1905, B.P. Bishop Estate," 278, accessed Nov. 25, 2012, http://archives1.dags.hawaii.gov/gsdl/collect/judiciar/index-old/assoc/HASH014f.dir/doc.pdf

378. *Pacific Commercial Advertiser,* May 8, 1910, 1.

379. Bernice P. Bishop Estate, "Report, Financial and Statistical, Kamehameha Schools, Year Ending June 30, 1909," 130, accessed Nov. 25, 2012, http://archives1.dags.hawaii.gov/gsdl/collect/judiciar/index-old/assoc/HASHacf8.dir/doc.pdf.

380. Bernice P. Bishop Estate, "Real Estate Transactions, Bernice P Bishop Estate, July 1, 1911–June 30, 1912," [344], accessed Nov. 25, 2012, http://archives1.dags.hawaii.gov/gsdl/collect/judiciar/index-old/assoc/HASH01e4.dir/doc.pdf.

381. Bernice P. Bishop Estate, "Report, Financial and Statistical, Kamehameha Schools, Year Ending June 30, 1912," [380], accessed Nov. 25, 2012, http://archives1.dags.hawaii.gov/gsdl/collect/judiciar/index-old/assoc/HASH01e4.dir/doc.pdf.

382. Lum, *Sun Yat-sen in Hawaii,* 82.

383. Allen, "Banyan Tree Is Center."

384. "For Sale," 6.

385. Nellist, *Men of Hawaii,* 257.

386. Nicholson, *From Sword to Share,* 69.

387. *Daily Bulletin,* February 4, 1882, 1.

388. Krout, *Memoirs of Bernice Pauahi Bishop,* 205.

389. *Daily Bulletin,* Mar. 31, 1882, 1.

390. *Daily Bulletin,* Mar. 31, 1882, 1.

391. "Death of Her Highness Princess Ruth Keelikolani," *Daily Bulletin,* May 28, 1883, 1.

392. "Local Items," *Daily Bulletin,* June 2, 1883, 1.

393. "By Authority," 2.

394. "Princess Ruth's Funeral," 2.

395. "Local & General News," *Daily Bulletin,* Oct. 15, 1883, 3.

396. "Local & General News," *Daily Bulletin,* March 14, 1884, 3.

397. "Lying in State," 3.

398. "Local & General News," *Daily Bulletin,* Apr. 07, 1886, 3.

399. "Bishop Furniture," 3.

400. *Laws of the Republic of Hawaii,* 43.

401. *Laws of the Republic of Hawaii,* 44.

402. "Financial Jugglery," 2.

403. "Financial Jugglery," 2.

404. "Dedication of the High School," 2.

405. "Report on Free Schools," 1.

406. "The Board of Education," 1.

407. "School Matters," 7.

408. "Sealed Tenders," 22.

409. "Fine New Building," 1.

410. "Appointments by Mayor Fern Today," 2.

411. *Report of the Superintendent of Public Instruction,* 13.

412. Minutes of Meeting, Commissioners of Public Instruction, April 25 to 29, 1927, 55, Series 235, vol. 12, 55. Hawaii State Archives.

413. "Local and General," *Pacific Commercial Advertiser,* Jan. 9, 1884, 2.

414. John E. Bush, Minister of the Interior, to Moses Kuaea, Minister of Finance, Sept. 3, 1880, Interior Department, Book 18, 60, Hawaii State Archives.

415. John E. Bush, Minister of the Interior, to Kekaulike, Oct. 26, 1882, Interior Department, Book 21, 381, Hawaii State Archives.

416. "Estate of James S. Lemon, Deceased," 2.

417. State of Hawaii, Bureau of Conveyances, Feb. 22, 1870, book 29, 345.

418. State of Hawaii, Bureau of Conveyances, Jan. 15, 1883, book 29, 200–201.

419. State of Hawaii, Bureau of Conveyances, Jan. 15, 1883, book 29, 200–201.

420. "Local and General," *Pacific Commercial Advertiser,* Jan. 9, 1884, 2.

421. "Order of Procession," 2.

422. "Funeral of H.R.H. Princess Kekaulike," 1.

423. "Na Make," 3.

424. Wilson, "Notes on the Music Collection of Queen Liliʻu-o-ka-lani," 2.

425. "Kapiolani Maternity Home," *Daily Bulletin,* 2.

426. "Kapiolani Maternity Home," *Hawaiian Gazette,* 4.

427. "Maternity Home," 5.

428. "Maternity Home Benefit," 3.

429. "Local and General News," *Independent,* Aug. 31, 1897, 3.

Notes—Chapter 5

430. Kapiolani to J.A. King, Sept. 8, 1897, Interior Department, Miscellaneous, June–December, 1897, trans. E.H. Hart, Hawaii State Archives.
431. Kapiolani from Jas. H. Boyd, Interior Department, Letterbook, Sept. 8, 1897, Book 88, 96, Hawaii State Archives.
432. Bureau of Conveyances, Territory of Hawaii, Book 514, 316.
433. Roster, Legislatures of Hawaii, 1841–1918, Honolulu: Hawaiian Gazette Co., 1918, 139.
434. Roster, Legislatures of Hawaii, 1841–1918, Honolulu: Hawaiian Gazette Co., 1918, 143.
435. "Island Locals," *Hawaiian Gazette*, December 1, 1880, 3.
436. Tayman, *The Colony*, 182.
437. Bagot, *McKenney's Hawaiian Directory*, 163.
438. Bureau of Conveyances, Kingdom of Hawaii, Book 130, 285–286.
439. U.S. Federal Census, 1900.
440. *Report of the Historical Commission of the Territory of Hawaii for the period ending December 31, 1922*. Honolulu: Honolulu Star-Bulletin, 1923, 12.
441. Allen, "Banyan Tree Is Center," section 2, 10.
442. "Death of Mrs. Kapena," 3.
443. "A Prince in the Toils," 7.
444. "The Prince Again," 3.
445. "Local and General News," *Independent*, Nov. 7, 1896, 3.
446. "Inflation Calculator 2013." Available at: http://www.davemanuel.com/inflation-calculator.php
447. "Island Locals," *Hawaiian Gazette*, September 21, 1881, 3.
448. "Sale of Valuable Real Estate," 9.
449. Liliʻuokalani, Diary, Feb. 6, 1885, Bishop Museum Archives.
450. Liliʻuokalani, Diary, Feb. 13, 1885, Bishop Museum Archives.
451. Liliʻuokalani, Diary, Feb. 17, 1885, Bishop Museum Archives.
452. Liliʻuokalani, Diary, Feb. 24, 1885, Bishop Museum Archives.
453. Liliʻuokalani, Diary, Mar. 8 1885, Bishop Museum Archives.
454. Liliʻuokalani, Diary, Mar. 12, 1885, Bishop Museum Archives.
455. Liliʻuokalani, Diary, Mar. 15, 1885, Bishop Museum Archives.
456. Liliʻuokalani, Diary, Mar. 21 1885, Bishop Museum Archives.
457. Liliʻuokalani, Diary, Mar 29, 1885, Bishop Museum Archives.
458. "He Inoa," 1.
459. Pukui, *Place Names of Hawaii*, 208.
460. Pukui, *Place Names of Hawaii*, 158.
461. Liliʻuokalani, *Queen's Songbook*, 253.
462. "Puʻuhonua Nani (Beautiful Refuge)," http://www.huapala.org/Puuhonua_Nani.html.
463. "Heavy Rain Storm," 3.
464. Stewart, *Journal of a Residence*, 286.
465. "Muʻolaulani," http://www.huapala.org/Mo/Muolaulani.html.
466. "Island Locals," *Hawaiian Gazette*, May 27, 1885, 4.
467. "Liliuokalani Educational Society," 3.
468. "Liliuokalani Educational Society," 3.
469. "Island Locals," *Hawaiian Gazette*, Aug. 17, 1886: 5.
470. "Birthday Festivities," 3.
471. "A Royal Anniversary," 3.
472. Liliʻuokalani, *Hawaii's Story*, 186.
473. Liliʻuokalani, *Hawaii's Story*, 116.
474. Liliʻuokalani, *Hawaii's Story*, 193.
475. Allen, *The Betrayal of Liliuokalani*, 217.
476. "Royal Jubilee Reception," 1.
477. "Local and General," *Hawaiian Gazette*, November 20, 1888, 7.
478. *Hawaiian Directory and Hand Book of the Kingdom of Hawaii* (San Francisco: McKenney Directory Co., 1888), 287.
479. Liliʻuokalani. *Hawaii's Story*, 194.
480. Liliʻuokalani. *Hawaii's Story*, 198.
481. Liliʻuokalani. *Hawaii's Story*, 198–199.
482. "After the Battle," 3.
483. "More Particulars of the Denouement," 2.
484. *Compilation of Reports of Committee on Foreign Relations, U.S. Senate, 1789–1901*, VI (1901): 800.
485. "More Particulars of the Denouement," 2.
486. "More Particulars of the Denouement: Incidents in the Aftermath: Residence of the Heir Apparent the Starting Point of the Rebel March," *Daily Bulletin*, Aug. 2, 1889: 2.
487. "He Mele no Wilikoki," 3.
488. Nakanaela, *Ka Buke Moolelo*, 1890, xv.
489. Liliʻuokalani, Lease, Oct. 10, 1890, Liliʻuokalani to Ernest Hutchinson. Manuscript Collection, Liliuokalani Trust, M-397, Land Records, Leases 1883–1899, box 6, folder 6, AH.
490. *Directory and Hand-Book of Honolulu and the Hawaiian Islands* (San Francisco: F.M. Husted, 1892) 155.
491. Liliʻuokalani. *Hawaii's Story*, 230.
492. "Draft of Constitution of January 14, 1893," Hawaii State Archives, Reference.
493. "Liliuokalani's Debts," 5.
494. "News in a Nutshell," *Hawaiian Star*, July 13, 1895: 3.
495. "Reception Last Night," 1.
496. Liliʻuokalani, Lease to A.G. Hawes, May 1896. Liliuokalani Collection, M-93 item 80, Hawaii State Archives.
497. "The Week in Society," *Hawaiian Gazette*, November 24, 1896, 7.
498. "Local and General News," *The Independent*, May 19, 1897, 4.
499. "A Beautiful Ball," 3.
500. *Husted's Directory and Hand-Book*, 100.
501. "The Dead Consul," 1.
502. "The Dead Consul," 1.
503. "Death of Capt. Hawes," 132.
504. *Husted's Directory and Hand-Book of Honolulu*, 1898, xlix.

Notes—Chapter 5

505. "Successor to Mr. Hawes," 1.
506. "Consul Selects a Home," 1.
507. *Husted's Directory and Hand-Book*, 1898, 152.
508. "Local and General News," *Independent*, January 28, 1898, 3.
509. "The Cricket Club," 1.
510. "Many Called," 2.
511. "Her Majesty the Queen," 1.
512. *Husted's Directory and Hand-Book*,1898, xlii.
513. "Foreign Consuls in Hawaii," 2.
514. "Lord Charles Arrives," 2.
515. "Are to Succeed," 2.
516. "Popular Cricket Patron," 6.
517. *Husted's Directory and Hand-Book of Honolulu*, 1900–1901, 226.
518. "Notes from Washington," *New York Times*, June 7, 1882, 1.
519. "Victoria Day Reception," 1.
520. Board of Trade, Wreck Report for "Dunreggan," Aug. 23, 1900, http://www.plimsoll.org/images/71157_tcm4-306609.pdf
521. "The Death of Her Britannic," 5.
522. Liliʻuokalani, Inventory of Palama Residence of Queen Liliʻuokalani, 8 July 1901. Liliʻuokalani Collection, M-93, item 75, Hawaii State Archives.
523. Liliʻuokalani Trust Collection, M-397, Hawaii State Archives.
524. "News of the Town," *The Honolulu Republican*, Aug. 20, 1901, 7.
525. "Entries Are Complete," 6.
526. "The Political Field," 3.
527. "Struggle for Supremacy," 3.
528. "Local and General News," *The Independent*, October 6, 1903, 3.
529. "Another Democratic Club Organized," 3.
530. "Political Meetings" *The Independent*, Oct. 12, 1904, 2.
531. "Political Meetings" *The Independent*, Oct. 15, 1904, 3.
532. "Liliuokalani gives $70,000 Mortgage," 3.
533. "Liliuokalani Obtains Big Loan," second ed., 1.
534. Codicil dated June 13, 1909, Liliuokalani Collection, M-93, Folder 29, Item 174, Hawaii State Archives.
535. "Liliuokalani Disposes of Estate," 8.
536. Territory of Hawaii Legislature, *Senate Journal*, 1911: 12.
537. Territory of Hawaii Legislature, *House Journal*, 1911: 1050–1051.
538. "Proposed Street Plan—Kapalama Section Nuuanu Street to Houghtailing," 1922, Hawaii State Archives.
539. *Foreign Testimony*, Hawaii State Archives, vol. 3, 424.
540. Survey of LCA 1926 to Nanauki, Liliuokalani Collection, Hawaii State Archives, M-93, Box 1, Folder 9, Item 72.
541. Letter from Liliʻuokalani to J.O. Carter, Jul. 20, 1900, M-397-8-82, Liliuokalani Trust, Hawaii State Archives.
542. Bureau of Conveyances, State of Hawaii, vol. 986, 98.
543. Thrum, *Hawaiian Almanac and Annual for 1892*, 115.
544. Liliʻuokalani to J.O. Carter, Sep. 19, 1904, M-397-8-87, Liliuokalani Trust, Hawaii State Archives.
545. Liliʻuokalani to J.O. Carter, Oct. 1, 1904, M-397-8-87, Liliuokalani Trust, Hawaii State Archives.
546. In the matter of the Claim of Lydia Kaloio et al. to 1.5 Acre of land at Manoa, M-397 Liliuolani Trust, Lands: Oahu Misc., Box 3, Hawaii State Archives.
547. Carrie A. Sabine to the Trustees of the Liliuokalani Estate, August 27, 1919, M-397 Liliuokalani Trust, Lands: Oahu Misc., Box 3, Folder 19, Hawaii State Archives.
548. Carrie A. Sabine to the Trustees of the Liliuokalani Estate, August 27, 1919, M-397 Liliuokalani Trust, Lands: Oahu Misc., Box 3, Folder 19, Hawaii State Archives.
549. Managing Trustee, Liliuokalani Trust, to Carrie A. Sabine, Sep. 23, 1919, M-397 Liliuokalani Trust, Lands: Oahu Misc., Box 3, Folder 19, Hawaii State Archives.
550. "Obituary Notice," *Independent*, March 13, 1902, 4.
551. "Obituary Notice," *Independent*, March 13, 1902, 4.
552. William O. Smith, Smith, Warren and Hemenway to C.P. Iaukea, May 27, 1910, M-397 Liluokalani Trust, Lands: Oahu Misc., Box 4, Hawaii State Archives.
553. Letter from William O. Smith, Smith, Warren and Hemenway to C.P. Iaukea, May 27, 1910, M-397 Liliuokalani Trust, Lands: Oahu Misc., Box 4, Hawaii State Archives.
554. Bureau of Conveyances, Kingdom of Hawaii, vol. 23, 378.
555. Bureau of Conveyances, Kingdom of Hawaii, vol. 26, 293.
556. Bureau of Conveyances, Kingdom of Hawaii, vol. 40, 207.
557. Liliʻuokalani. *Hawaii's Story*, 223.
558. Receipt, Apr. 4, 1892, Probate 2749, 1st Circuit Court, Hawaii State Archives.
559. "Society," *Pacific Commercial Advertiser*, May 29, 1904, 8.
560. Deed of Trust, Queen Liliuokalani Trust, http://www.onipaa.org/pages/her-deed-of-trust.
561. Articles of Agreement between Lot Kamehameha and W.C. Lane, Jan. 31, 1862. (Copy of Agreement Liber. 15, 20–21, Bureau of Conveyances.)
562. *Native Register*, Hawaii State Archives, vol. 4, 493.
563. *Native Register*, Hawaii State Archives, vol. 4, 493.
564. "Hotel at Waialua," *Pacific Commercial Advertiser*, Oct. 14, 1898,1.

565. "Waialua Hotel," 1.
566. Emerson, "Emersoniana," 58.
567. Emerson, "Anecdotes of Early Days," 108.

Chapter 6

1. Pukui, *Ōlelo No'eau*, 266.
2. Turnbull, *Voyages in the Pacific Ocean*, 213.
3. Turnbull, *Voyages in the Pacific Ocean*, 213.
4. *Hawaiian Club Papers*," 10–11.
5. Fornander, *An Account of the Polynesian Race*, London: Trübner and Co., 1880, 291.
6. Jarves, *History of the Hawaiian*, 244.
7. Hiram Bingham, *A Residence of Twenty-One Years*, 229–230.
8. Broeze, *A Merchant's Perspective*, 83.
9. Broeze, *A Merchant's Perspective*, 84.
10. Kamakau, *Ruling Chiefs of Hawaii*, 347.
11. *The Centennial Book*, 23.
12. Journal of Levi Chamberlain, vol. 19, Jan. 21, 1835, http://96.31.65.17:8282/greenstone/collect/levicham/index/assoc/HASHb636.dir/doc.pdf.
13. Townsend, *Sporting Excursions in the Rocky Mountains*, vol. 2, 63.
14. Townsend, *Sporting Excursions in the Rocky Mountains*, vol. 2, 61–62.
15. E. Keawamahi, Native Testimony, No. 2291, Dec. 24, 1846, vol. 3, 432–433.
16. E. Keawamahi, Native Testimony, No. 2291, Dec. 24, 1846, vol. 3, 433.
17. E. Keawamahi, Native Testimony, No. 3590, Jan. 10, 1848, vol. 9, 63–64.
18. "Koloa Kauai Sandwich Islands, No. 1," 40.
19. Griffin, "The Līhu'e Place Name," 67.
20. Kamakau, *Ruling Chiefs of Hawaii*, 346.
21. *The Missionary Herald*, 1840, 242.
22. Kamehameha III and Kekauluohi to Emili Keawamahi, Aug. 5, 1839, series 402, box 5, folder 105, Hawaii State Archives.
23. "Drippings from My Journal, No. 7," *Polynesian*, 83.
24. "Drippings from My Journal, No. 7," *Polynesian*, 83.
25. "Drippings from My Journal, No. 7," *Polynesian*, 83.
26. "Drippings from My Journal, No. 7," *Polynesian*, 83.
27. "Drippings from My Journal, No. 7," *Polynesian*, 83.
28. "Drippings from My Journal, No. 7," *Polynesian*, 83.
29. Privy Council Minutes, Nov. 6, 1850, Hawaii State Archives, vol. 6 A, 94.
30. Privy Council Minutes, Nov. 6, 1850, Hawaii State Archives, vol. 6 A, 94.
31. Edward P. Bond to the Minister of the Interior, Aug. 19, 1851, Interior Department, Misc., August 1851, Box 144, Hawaii State Archives.
32. "Government Officer," *Pacific Commercial Advertiser*, January 12, 1860, 1.
33. *Ka Hae Hawaii*, Mar. 7, 1860, 196.
34. "Governorship of Kauai," 3.
35. *Native Testimony*, Frances Frazier, trans., Hawaii State Archives, vol. 9, 12.
36. *Native Testimony*, Frances Frazier, trans., Hawaii State Archives, vol. 9, 12.
37. *Native Register*, Frances Frazier, trans., Hawaii State Archives, vol. 9, 55.
38. Bates, *Sandwich Island Notes*, 189.
39. Bates, *Sandwich Island Notes*, 237.
40. *Native Register*, Frances Frazier, trans., vol. 2, 535.
41. "Unveiling of Kuhio Monument," 11.
42. "Monument to Prince Kuhio Is Planned," 1.
43. Kauukualii to Keoni Ana, Nov. 18, 1852, Interior Department, Land, Letters (Incoming) 1852, November 11–30, Box 67, Hawaii State Archives.

Chapter 7

1. Pukui, *Ōlelo No'eau*, 46.
2. *Laws of the Republic of Hawaii*, 1898, 87–88.
3. Ralph S. Kuykendall, Papers Regarding Historical Sites 1924–1948, Commission on Historical Sites, 201-1-15.
4. Ralph S. Kuykendall, Papers regarding historical Sites 1924–1948, Commission on Historical Sites, 201-1-15, Hawaii State Archives.
5. *Laws of the Territory of Hawaii*, 1907, 323.
6. Ralph S. Kuykendall, Papers regarding historical Sites 1924–1948, Commission on Historical Sites, 201-1-15.
7. *Territory of Hawaii vs. William O. Smith, Curtis P. Iaukea and Alexander G.M. Robertson, Trustees under that certain Deed of Trust executed by Liliuokalani, May 11, 1921*, 3, GOV 5–8, McCarthy—Miscellaneous, Washington Place, Hawaii State Archives.
8. *Laws of the Territory of Hawaii*, 1921, 159.
9. *The Eleventh Legislature of the Territory of Hawaii in Regular Session, Journal of the Senate, 1921*, 40.
10. *The Eleventh Legislature of the Territory of Hawaii in Regular Session, Journal of the Senate, 1921*, 293.
11. *The Eleventh Legislature of the Territory of Hawaii in Regular Session, Journal of the Senate, 1921*, 657.
12. *Laws of the Territory of Hawaii Passed by the Eleventh Legislature, Regular Session 1921*, Honolulu: Advertiser Publishing Co., 1921, 160.
13. *The Eleventh Legislature of the Territory of Hawaii in Regular Session, Journal of the Senate, 1921*, 293.
14. *Laws of the Territory of Hawaii Passed by the Eleventh Legislature, Regular Session 1921*, Honolulu: Advertiser Publishing Co., 1921, 160.
15. Siddell, *Men of Hawaii*, vol. II, 81.
16. *Report of the Historical Commission of the Territory of Hawaii for the period ending December 31, 1922*. Honolulu: Honolulu Star-Bulletin, 1923, 6.
17. *Report of the Historical Commission of the*

Territory of Hawaii for the period ending December 31, 1922. Honolulu: Honolulu Star-Bulletin, 1923, 6.

18. *Report of the Historical Commission of the Territory of Hawaii for the period ending December 31, 1922*. Honolulu: Honolulu Star-Bulletin, 1923, 12.

19. *Senate Journal, The Twelfth Legislature of the Territory of Hawaii, Regular Session, 1923*, Honolulu: The New Freedom Press, 1923, 25.

20. *Laws of the Territory of Hawaii Passed by the Eleventh Legislature, Regular Session 1923*, Honolulu: Advertiser Publishing Co., 1923, 157.

21. *Journal of the House of Representatives of the Thirteenth Legislature of the Territory of Hawaii, Regular Session 1925*, Honolulu: Paradise of the Pacific, 1925, 28.

22. *Laws of the Territory of Hawaii Passed by the Thirteenth Legislature, Regular Session 1925*, Honolulu: Advertiser Publishing Co., 1925, 47–48.

23. *Laws of the Territory of Hawaii Passed by the Thirteenth Legislature, Regular Session 1925*, Honolulu: Advertiser Publishing Co., 1925, 48.

24. *Journal of the House of Representatives of the Fourteenth Legislature of the Territory of Hawaii, Regular Session 1927*, Honolulu: Paradise of the Pacific, 1927, 51.

25. Taylor, "150th Anniversary of the Discovery of Hawaii by Captain Cook," Cook Sesquicentennial Commission, COM-8, Box 4, Schedule for Captain Cook Sesquicentennial Celebration, 7.

26. Taylor, "150th Anniversary of the Discovery of Hawaii by Captain Cook," Cook Sesquicentennial Commission, COM-8, Box 4, Schedule for Captain Cook Sesquicentennial Celebration, 7.

27. *Journal of the House of Representatives of the Fifteenth Legislature of the Territory of Hawaii, Regular Session 1929*, Honolulu: New Freedom Press, 1929, 45.

28. Taylor, "Historical Notes," 13.

29. *Journal of the House of Representatives of the Seventeenth Legislature of the Territory of Hawaii, Regular Session 1931*, Honolulu: New Freedom Press, 1931, 34.

30. *Laws of the Territory of Hawaii Passed by the Sixteenth Legislature, Regular Session 1931*, Honolulu: Honolulu Star-Bulletin, 1931, 47.

31. "Objects to be Considered for Designation as Territorial Monuments by the Governor of Hawaii under Act 56, S.L. 1931," December 15, 1932, Commission on Historic Sites, Hawaii State Archives, 201-1-15.

32. Ralph S. Kuykendall, Memorandum of conference, September 21, 1942.

33. "Report of Henry P. Judd," August 1942, Commission on Historic Sites, Hawaii State Archives, 201-1-15.

34. *Revised Laws of Hawaii 1945*, chapter 86, section 4905.

35. *Revised Laws of Hawaii 1945*, chapter 86, section 4906.

36. L.J. Watson, "The Background and Organization of the Conservation Council for Hawaii, Presented at the Sixth Annual Meeting," UD-9.

37. "Report on Conservation in Hawaii" Pacific Science Council, Aug. 11, 1950, UD-9, 5.

38. *Laws of the Territory of Hawaii Passed by the Twenty-Sixth Legislature, Regular Session 1951*, Honolulu: Honolulu Star-Bulletin, 1951, 597–598.

39. Commission on Historical Sites, Conserve Council for Hawaii, Ann. Meeting—Minutes—1952, Hawaii State Archives, 201-1-1 (Annual Report—Committee on Sites, Conservation Council for Hawaii, Appendix III, Minutes of Second General Meeting, Feb. 25, 1952.)

40. Commission on Historical Sites, Sites—Attorney General, Corres—1951–1956, Hawaii State Archives, 201-1-1 (letter from John R. Canright to William O. Cogswell, Dec. 14, 1951).

41. Commission on Historical Sites, Sites—Attorney General, Corres—1951–1956, Hawaii State Archives, 201-1-1 (letter from John R. Canright to William O. Cogswell, Dec. 14, 1951).

42. Commission on Historical Sites, Sites—Attorney General, Corres—1951–1956, Hawaii State Archives, 201-1-1 (letter from Norito Kawakami to Alice Spalding Bowers [sic], Aug. 19, 1954).

43. L.J. Watson, "The Background and Organization of the Conservation Council for Hawaii," Histories, U-9, Hawaii State Archives, 8.

44. Alice Spalding Bowen to R.L. Cushing, Feb. 5, 1955, Blue Binder, Conservation Council for Hawaii, U-9, Hawaii State Archives.

45. Alice Spalding Bowen to R.L. Cushing, Feb. 5, 1955, Blue Binder, Conservation Council for Hawaii, U-9, Hawaii State Archives.

46. *Laws of the Territory of Hawaii Passed by the Twenty-Eighth Legislature, Regular Session 1955*, Honolulu: Tong Publishing Company, 1955, 60–61.

47. *Laws of the Territory of Hawaii Passed by the Twenty-Eighth Legislature, Regular Session 1955*, Honolulu: Tong Publishing Company, 1955, 61.

48. Commission on Historical Sites, Sites—Governor, Corres., Script, Budget Matl.—1953–1960, Hawaii State Archives, 201-1-1 (Alice Spalding Bowen to Gov. Samuel Wilder King, Feb. 3, 1955).

49. Commission on Historical Sites, Sites—Attorney General, Corres.—1951–1956, Hawaii State Archives, 201-1-1 (letter from Wadsworth Y.H. Yee to Alice Spalding Bowen, Apr. 17, 1956).

50. Commission on Historical Sites, Legislature, 1955–1959, Hawaii State Archives, 201-1-16 (letter from Alice Spalding Bowen to Committee on Tourist Development, January 27, 1957).

51. Commission on Historical Sites, Legislature, 1955–1959, Hawaii State Archives, 201-1-16 [(etter from Alice Spalding Bowen to Elmer F. Cravalho, Chairman House Finance Committee, February 25, 1957).

52. Eleanor S. Anderson, "Summary Report of Work by the Conservation Council of Hawaii," *The*

Proceedings of the Ninth Pacific Science Congress, 1957, vol. 7, 1959, 16.

53. Eleanor S. Anderson, "Summary Report of Work by the Conservation Council of Hawaii," *The Proceedings of the Ninth Pacific Science Congress, 1957*, vol. 7, 1959, 16.

54. Commission on Historical Sites, Sites—All Islands, List, n.d., 1958–1960, Hawaii State Archives, 201-1-16 (letter from Clarice B. Taylor to Mrs. Lloyd B. Osborne, Nov. 5, 1958).

55. Commission on Historical Sites, Sites—Governor, Corres, Script, Budget Matl—1953–1960, Hawaii State Archives, 201-1-1 (memorandum from Agnes C. Conrad to Gov. William F. Quinn, Dec. 12, 1958).

56. Commission on Historical Sites, Minutes (incomplete), 1951–1952; 1958–1959, Hawaii State Archives, 201-1-18 (Minutes, August 27, 1959).

57. Commission on Historical Sites, Minutes (incomplete), 1951–1952; 1958–1959, Hawaii State Archives, 201-1-18 [letter from Colin G. Lennox to Agnes C. Conrad, Sept. 3, 1959].

58. Commission on Historical Sites, Sites—Governor, Corres, Script, Budget Matl—1953–1960, Hawaii State Archives, 201-1-1 (letter from Agnes C. Conrad to Gov. William F. Quinn, January 26, 1960).

59. Commission on Historical Sites, Priv Agen & Individuals, Corres, Photos, Plque Text—1954–1960, Hawaii State Archives, 201-1-11 (letter from Agnes C. Conrad to Merle E. Severy, January 29, 1960).

60. *Session Laws of Hawaii Passed by the First State Legislature, Second Special Session 1959*, Honolulu: Honolulu Star-Bulletin, 1959, 597–598.

61. Department of Economic Development, "Marking Hawaii's Historical Sites: A Recommended Six-Year Program," January 1962, Hawaii State Archives [DU 624.3.H36 1962].

62. Alice C. Brown to Doak C. Cox, May 18, 1966, Annual Report, U-9, Hawaii State Archives.

63. Doak C. Cox to Yadao Yoshinaga, Feb. 21, 1966, Minutes & Correspondence, 1966–1967, Conservation Council for Hawaii, U-9, Hawaii State Archives.

64. Executive Minutes, Conservation Council for Hawaii, March 9, 1966, Minutes & Correspondence, 1966–1967, U-9, Hawaii State Archives.

65. Agnes C. Conrad to H. Thomas Kay, Jr., Jul. 27, 1966, President-1966/67—Correspondence, Conservation Council for Honolulu, U-9, Archive of Hawaii.

66. Executive Minutes, Conservation Council for Hawaii, Jan. 17, 1967, Minutes & Correspondence, 1966–1967, U-9, Hawaii State Archives.

67. Letter from Richard H. Cox to Dorothy Lindley, Mar. 20, 1967, President-1966/67—Correspondence, Conservation Council for Honolulu, U-9, Archive of Hawaii.

68. Nancy Bannick, "Mayor's Historic Buildings Task Force," Alphabetic Index to Historic Buildings Task Force Report, M-488-1-1, June 1966, Hawaii State Archives, 1.

69. Act 216, *Session Laws of Hawaii, Fifth State Legislature, Regular Session of 1969*, 405.

70. Arago, *Narrative of a Voyage*, 56.

Conclusion

1. Elbert, *Selections from Fornander's Hawaiian Antiquities*, 48.

2. *Report of the Historical Commission of the Territory of Hawaii for the period ending December 31, 1922*. Honolulu: Honolulu Star-Bulletin, 1923, 12.

3. *Report of the Historical Commission of the Territory of Hawaii for the period ending December 31, 1922*. Honolulu: Honolulu Star-Bulletin, 1923, 12.

4. House Concurrent Resolution, 2012 Regular Session, http://legiscan.com/HI/text/HCR51/id/631170.

Bibliography

Act 216, Session Laws of Hawaii, Fifth State Legislature, Regular Session of 1969, 405.
"Address by His Excellency John M. Kapena, Minister of Foreign Relations." *Pacific Commercial Advertiser*, January 3, 1880.
"Address of the Hon. C.C. Harris, Chief Justice & Chancellor." *Hawaiian Gazette*, January 14, 1880.
"Administrator's Sale of Real Estate." Advertisement. *Hawaiian Gazette*, March 3, 1880.
"Administrators' Sale of Real Estate on Emma Street." Advertisement. *Hawaiian Gazette*, February 3, 1869, 3.
"After the Battle." *Daily Bulletin*, July 31, 1889.
"Ainahau." http://www.huapala.org/ah/Ainahau.html.
"Ainahau." *Paradise of the Pacific*, March 1904.
"Ainahau Hotel Site Sought by Eastern People." *Honolulu Star Bulletin*, September 23, 1916.
"Ainahau, Once Palace Burns; Nearby Houses in Imminent Danger." *Honolulu Advertiser*, August 3, 1921.
"Ainahau Sold, to Be Building Lots." *Honolulu Advertiser*, January 20, 1917.
"Ainahau Wedding." *Hawaiian Star*, September 5, 1901.
Allen, Gwenfread. "Banyan Tree Is Center of Old District." *Honolulu Star-Bulletin*, October 6, 1934.
Allen, Gwenfread. "Kaahumanu." *Friend*, August 1925.
Allen, Gwenfread. "Mansion for the Governor Used by Club." *Honolulu Star-Bulletin*, February 10, 1934.
Allen, Helena G. *The Betrayal of Liliuokalani*. Glendale, CA: Arthur H. Clark, 1982.
Amendment of Lili'uokalani Deed of Trust, 1911.
Amendment to Last Will and Testament, Benita Namakeha, 1st Circuit Court, Probate 936, Hawaii State Archives.
Anderson, Carl. "Sandwich Islands Leper Settlement." *The Contributor: Representing the Young Men's and Young Ladies' Mutual Improvement Association of the Latter Day Saints*, vol. 1. Salt Lake City: Deseret Printing, 1880.
Anderson, Eleanor S. "Summary Report of Work by the Conservation Council of Hawaii." *The Proceedings of the Ninth Pacific Science Congress*, 1957, vol. 7, 1959, 16.
Anderson, Mary Evarts. *Scenes in the Hawaiian Islands and California*. Boston: Cornhill Press, 1869.
Andrews, Lorrin. *A Dictionary of the Hawaiian Language*. Honolulu: Henry M. Whitney, 1865.
Andrews, Lorrin. *A Dictionary of the Hawaiian Language*. Waipahu: Island Heritage Publishing, 2003.
"Annual Report—Committee on Sites, Conservation Council for Hawaii, Appendix III, Minutes of Second General Meeting, February 25, 1952," "Commission on Historical Sites, Conserv. Council for Hawaii, Ann. Meeting—Minutes—1952," Commission on Historical Sites Collection, M-201, 201-1-6, Hawaii State Archives.
"Another Campbell Will Case Was Decided This Morning." *Hawaiian Star*, July 29, 1911.
"Another Chief Dead." *Pacific Commercial Advertiser*, October 8, 1864.
"Another Democratic Club Organized." *Independent*, March 17, 1904.
Appendix to the Report of the Minister of Finance from the Interior Department, 1872, Hawaii State Archives.
"Appointments by Mayor Fern Today." *Honolulu Star Bulletin*, July 2, 1917.
Arago, Jacques. *Narrative of a Voyage Round the World, in the Uranie and Physicienne Corvettes, Commanded by Captain Freycinet*, Part II. London: Treuttel and Wurtz, 1823.
"Are to Succeed." *Hawaiian Gazette*, February 17, 1899.
"Arrival of His Royal Highness, the Duke of Edinburgh." *Pacific Commercial Advertiser*, July 24, 1869.
Articles of Agreement Between Lot Kamehameha and W.C. Lane, January 31, 1862. [Copy of Agreement Liber. 15, 20–21, Bureau of Conveyances.]
"At Ainahau." *Independent*, March 10, 1899.
"At Pualeilani." *Independent* June 28, 1899.
"At Rest." *Independent*, March 11, 1903.
"Attorney General Opinion No. 358." February 4, 1914, Hawaii State Archives.
"Auction Sale of Valuable City Property." Advertisement. *Pacific Commercial Advertiser*, February 15, 1901.
"Audience at Iolani Palace." *Hawaiian Gazette*, January 23, 1867.

Bagot, Frederick, ed. *McKenney's Hawaiian Directory*. San Francisco: L.M. McKenney and Co., 1884.

Baker, Ray Jerome. *Honolulu in 1853*. Honolulu: R.J. Baker, 1950.

Bannick, Nancy. "Mayor's Historic Buildings Task Force." Alphabetic Index to Historic Buildings Task Force Report, M-488-1-1, June 1966, Hawaii State Archives.

Barrere, Dorothy B. *The Journal of John Young with entries for the years 1808, 1809, 1821, 1825*. Honolulu: N.p., May 1994.

Barrere, Dorothy B. "The King's Mahele: The Awardees and Their Lands," 1994. Unpublished manuscript, Hawaii State Archives.

Barrot, Théodore-Adolphe. *Unless Haste Is Made*, translation of *Les Iles Sandwich*, which was originally pubished in *Revue des deux mondes*, August 1 and 15, 1839. Kailua: Pacifica Press, 1978.

"Baseball Tourists!" *Daily Bulletin*, November 27, 1888, Weekly Summary.

Bates, George Washington. *Sandwich Island Notes*. New York: Harper and Brothers, 1854.

"Beautiful Ainahau Is Opened for Homes on Fine Residence Lots: Historic Place at Waikiki Placed on Market as Subdivision, Next to Royal Grove, By Percy M. Pond and Guardian Trust Company." *Honolulu Advertiser*, May 1, 1919.

"A Beautiful Ball: Victoria's Representative Entertains the Elite of Honolulu." *Independent*, June 26, 1897.

Beckwith, E.G., to Liliʻuokalani, Foreign Office and Executive, Series 401, Box 1, Folder 17, Document #200, Hawaii State Archives.

Bennett, Chauncey C. *Honolulu Directory and Historical Sketch of the Hawaiian or Sandwich Islands*. Honolulu: C.C. Bennett, 1869.

Bernice P. Bishop Estate. "Master's Report for Year Ending June 30, 1905, B.P. Bishop Estate." [278], accessed November 25, 2012, http://archives1.dags.hawaii.gov/gsdl/collect/judiciar/index-old/assoc/HASH014f.dir/doc.pdf

Bernice P. Bishop Estate. "Real Estate Transactions, Bernice P. Bishop Estate, July 1, 1911–June 30, 1912" [344], accessed November 25, 2012, http://archives1.dags.hawaii.gov/gsdl/collect/judiciar/index-old/assoc/HASH01e4.dir/doc.pdf

Bernice P. Bishop Estate. "Real Estate Transactions, Trustees, Estate of B. P. Bishop, July 1, 1903–June 30, 1904" [199], accessed November 25, 2012, http://archives1.dags.hawaii.gov/gsdl/collect/judiciar/index-old/assoc/HASH01f9.dir/doc.pdf.

Bernice P. Bishop Estate. "Report, Financial and Statistical, Kamehameha Schools, Year Ending June 30, 1904" [243], accessed November 25, 2012, http://archives1.dags.hawaii.gov/gsdl/collect/judiciar/index-old/assoc/HASH0103.dir/doc.pdf.

Bernice P. Bishop Estate. "Report, Financial and Statistical, Kamehameha Schools, Year Ending June 30, 1909" [130], accessed November 25, 2012, http://archives1.dags.hawaii.gov/gsdl/collect/judiciar/index-old/assoc/HASHacf8.dir/doc.pdf.

Bernice P. Bishop Estate. "Report, Financial and Statistical, Kamehameha Schools, Year Ending June 30, 1912," [380], accessed November 25, 2012, http://archives1.dags.hawaii.gov/gsdl/collect/judiciar/index-old/assoc/HASH01e4.dir/doc.pdf.

Bernice Pauahi Bishop Museum Polynesian Ethnology and Natural History, vol. VI, Honolulu: Bishop Museum Press, 1919–1920.

Bingham, Hiram. *A Residence of Twenty-one Years in the Sandwich Islands*. Hartford, CT: Hezekiah Huntington, 1848.

Bird, Isabella L. *The Hawaiian Archipelago: Six Months Among the Palm Groves, Coral Reefs, & Volcanoes of the Sandwich Islands*. London: John Murray, 1875.

"Birthday Festivities." *Pacific Commercial Advertiser*, September 3, 1886.

Bishop Estate Map Registered No. 287. Endowment Group, Land Assets Division, Kamehameha Schools, Honolulu, Hawaii.

"Bishop Funiture." *Hawaiian Star*, March 11, 1895.

Black, Lydia T., trans. *The Round the World Voyage of Heiromonk Gideon, 1803–1809*. Kingston, Ontario, Canada: Limestone Press, 1989.

"Blazing Japanese Calls Out Engines." *Hawaiian Star*, March 14, 1907.

Bloxam, Andrew. *Diary of Andrew Bloxam, Naturalist of the "Blonde" on Her Trip from England to the Hawaiian Islands 1824–25*. Bernice P. Bishop Museum Special Publication Volume 10, Honolulu: Bernice P. Bishop Museum, 1925.

"Board Divided on Purchase of Kuhio Mansion." *Honolulu Advertiser*, March 20, 1935.

"The Board of Education." *Evening Bulletin*, Apr. 23, 1897.

Board of Trade. "Wreck Report for 'Dunreggan.'" August 23, 1900, http://www.plimsoll.org/images/71157_tcm4-306609.pdf

"Board Votes to Obtain Old Home of Kuhio." *Honolulu Star-Bulletin*, April 17, 1935.

"Body in State." *Hawaiian Gazette*, June 30, 1899.

Bond, Edward P., to the Minister of the Interior, August 19, 1851. Interior Department, Misc., August 1851, Box 144, Hawaii State Archives.

Bowen, Alice Spalding, to Committee on Tourist Development, January 27, 1957. Commission on Historical Sites, Legislature, 1955–1959, 201-1-16, Hawaii State Archives.

Bowen, Alice Spalding, to Elmer F. Cravalho, Chairman House Finance Committee, February 25, 1957. Commission on Historical Sites, Legislature, 1955–1959, 201-1-16, Hawaii State Archives.

Bowen, Alice Spalding, to R.L. Cushing, Feb. 5, 1955. Blue Binder, Conservation Council for Hawaii, U-9, Hawaii State Archives.

Bowen, Alice, to President and Directors, American Factors, Limited, Feb. 7, 1955. Blue Binder,

Conservation Council for Hawaii, U-9, Archive of Hawaii.
Boyd, Jas. H., to Kapiolani, Interior Department. Letterbook, September 8, 1897, Book 88, 96, Hawaii State Archives.
"Branching Out." *Pacific Commercial Advertiser*, May 15, 1893.
"Brief Mention." *Pacific Commercial Advertiser*, September 7, 1878.
Broeze, Frank J.A., trans. *A Merchant's Perspective: Captain Jacobus Boelen's Narrative of His Visit to Hawai'i in 1828.* Honolulu: The Hawaiian Historical Society, 1988.
Brown, Alice C., to Doak C. Cox, May 18, 1966. Annual Report, U-9, Hawaii State Archives.
Bureau of Conveyances, Book 44, 219.
Bureau of Conveyances, Kingdom of Hawaii, Book 130, 285–286.
Bureau of Conveyances, Kingdom of Hawaii, vol. 23, 378.
Bureau of Conveyances, Kingdom of Hawaii, vol. 26, 293.
Bureau of Conveyances, Kingdom of Hawaii, vol. 40, 207.
Bureau of Conveyances, State of Hawaii, Book 10, 427.
Bureau of Conveyances, State of Hawaii, book 12, 26.
Bureau of Conveyances, State of Hawaii, Book 16, 282–283.
Bureau of Conveyances, State of Hawaii, Book 20, 445.
Bureau of Conveyances, State of Hawaii, book 24, 198.
Bureau of Conveyances, State of Hawaii, book 35, 397.
Bureau of Conveyances, State of Hawaii, vol. 986, 98.
Bureau of Conveyances, Territory of Hawaii, Book 514, 316.
Bureau of Conveyances, Territory of Hawaii, February 12, 1929, Book 992, 124–127.
Bush, John E., Minister of the Interior, to Kekaulike, October 26, 1882, Interior Department, Book 21, 381, Hawaii State Archives.
Bush, John E., Minister of the Interior, to Moses Kuaea, Minister of Finance, Sept. 3, 1880. Interior Department, Book 18, 60, Hawaii State Archives.
"By Authority." *Daily Bulletin*, June 6, 1883.
"By Authority." *Hawaiian Gazette*, Dec. 11, 1872.
"By Authority." *Polynesian*, June 28, 1851.
Campbell, Archibald. *Voyage Round the World.* New York: Van Winkie, Wiley & Co., 1817, 91.
"Campbell House for Army Headquarters." *Hawaiian Gazette*, April 15, 1910.
"Campbell-Beckley Wedding Brilliant." *Hawaiian Star*, August 1, 1912.
Canright, John R., to William O. Cogswell, Dec. 14, 1951, Commission on Historical Sites. Sites—Attorney General, Corres. 1951–1956, 201-1-2, Hawaii State Archives.
Catalogue of Water-Colour Sketches and Drawings in Illustration of the Cruise Expressly Executed by Messrs. O.W. Brierly and N. Chevalier Together with Selections from the Objects of Science and Art, Collected by His Royal Highness and Lent for Exhibition in the South Kensington Museum. London: George E. Eyer and William Spottiswoode, 1872.
The Centennial Book: One Hundred Years of Christian Civilization in Hawaii. Honolulu: Central Committee of the Hawaiian Mission Centennial, 1920.
"Chamisso's Account of the Voyage Around the World on the Rurik, 1815–1818, Hawaiian Section," translated from the German, presented by Victor S.K. Houston. Transcript, Hawaii State Archives.
"Charity Luau." *Daily Bulletin*, February 16, 1892.
"Child of Fortune." *Hawaiian Star*, Apr. 21, 1910, second ed.
"City Obtains Kuhio Home." *Honolulu Advertiser*, May 16, 1935.
Claim 6325 by Kekauonohi, June 3, 1854. Foreign Testimony, vol. 16, Hawaii State Archives.
Clark, Hugh. "Protection sought for ancient village site." *Honolulu Advertiser*, March 19, 2001.
Cleghorn, A.S., to Walter R. [sic] Frear, July 27, 1909. Walter Francis Frear, Frear—Miscellaneous (by name), A-C, Box GOV3-11, Hawaii State Archives.
Codicil dated June 13, 1909, Liliuokalani Collection, M-93, Folder 29, Item 174, Hawaii State Archives.
"Commercial Review." *Hawaiian Star*, July 17, 1909.
Commission on Historical Sites, Sites—Attorney General, Corres. 1951–1956. Hawaii State Archives, 201-1-2, [letter from Norito Kawakami to Alice Spalding Bowers [sic], August 19, 1954].
Commission on Historical Sites. Sites—Attorney General, Corres. 1951–1956, Hawaii State Archives, 201-1-2 [letter from Wadsworth Y.H. Yee to Alice Spalding Bowen, Apr. 17, 1956].
Commission on Historical Sites. Sites—Governor, Corres. Script, Budget Matl.—1953–1960, Hawaii State Archives, 201-1-8 [letter from Agnes C. Conrad to Gov. William F. Quinn, January 26, 1960].
Commission on Historical Sites. Sites—Governor, Corres., Script, Budget Matl.—1953–1960, Hawaii State Archives, 201-1-8 [letter from Alice Spalding Bowen to Gov. Samuel Wilder King, February 3, 1955].
Commission on Historical Sites. Sites—Governor, Corres., Script, Budget Matl.—1953–1960, Hawaii State Archives, 201-1-8 [memorandum from Agnes C. Conrad to Gov. William F. Quinn, Dec. 12, 1958].
Commission on Historical Sites. Collection, M-201, Hawaii State Archives.
Committee on Historic Sites. Sites—All Islands, List, n.d., 1958–1960, Hawaii State Archives, 201-1-26 [page 1 of enclosure to letter from Clarice B. Taylor to Mrs. Lloyd B. Osborne, November 5, 1958].

Committee on Historic Sites. Sites—All Islands, List, n.d., 1958–1960, Hawaii State Archives, 201-1-26 [page 1 of list by Violet Hanson of "Historical Sites on Hawaii Which Should Be Preserved," February 1960].
Committee on Historic Sites. Sites—Kamakahonu (site), Kailua-Kona; Corres., Memo, Map—n.d., 1959, Hawaii State Archives, 201-1-26 [letter from Richard H. Howland to C. Hutton Smith, May 7, 1959].
Committee on Historic Sites. Sites—Kamakahonu (site), Kailua-Kona; Corres., Memo, Map—n.d., 1959, Hawaii State Archives, 201-1-26 [letter from Walter F. Dillingham to Commission on Historic Sites, May 22, 1959].
Compilation of Reports of Committee on Foreign Relations, U.S. Senate, 1789–1901, VI (1901): 800.
"Coney Stone Wall in Hotel Street Soon Will Be a Thing of the Past." *Pacific Commercial Advertiser*, Apr. 26, 1902.
Conrad, Agnes C. to H. Thomas Kay, Jr., July 27, 1966, President—1966/67—Correspondence, Conservation Council for Honolulu, U-9, Hawaii State Archives.
"Consul Selects a Home." *Evening Bulletin*, November 12, 1897.
Conyers, Lawrence B., and Samuel Connell. "An Analysis of Ground-Penetrating Radar's Ability to Discover and Map Buried Archaeological Sites in Hawai'i." *Hawaiian Archeology*, vol. 11 (2007).
Cook Sesquicentennial Celebration Commission. "Unveiling Ceremony." Honolulu: February 14, 1930.
Coote, Walter. *Wanderings, South and East*. London: Sampson, Low, Marston, Searle and Rivington, 1882. *Friend*, August 1, 1882.
Copy of Will of M. Kekauonohi, 1st Circuit Court Probate Minutes book, Vol. 2, 1851–1858, page 2. Trans. Jason Achiu, 1st Circuit Court, Probate 2081, Series 007, Box 4, Hawaii State Archives.
"Court News." *Hawaiian Gazette*, January 22, 1868.
"Court News." *Hawaiian Gazette*, July 31, 1867.
"Court Notes." *Hawaiian Gazette*, March 30, 1894.
"Court Notes." *Polynesian*, November 1, 1845.
"Courtyard King Kamehameha's Kona Beach Hotel," https://www.marriott.com/hotels/travel/koacy-courtyard-king-kamehamehas-kona-beach-hotel. Accessed June 30, 2021.
Cox, Doak C. to Yadao Yoshinaga, February 21, 1966, Minutes & Correspondence, 1966–1967, Conservation Council for Hawaii, U-9, Hawaii State Archives.
Cox, Richard H. to Dorothy Lindley, March 20, 1967, President—1966/67—Correspondence, Conservation Council for Honolulu, U-9, Hawaii State Archives.
"The Cricket Club." *Independent*, February 16, 1898.
A Cultural History of Three Traditional Hawaiian Sites on the West Coast of Hawai'i Island. Chapter IX: "Pu'uhonua O Honaunau National Historical Park." http://www.cr.nps.gov/history/online_books/kona/history9w.htm.

Daily Bulletin, April 10, 1882.
Daily Bulletin, February 4, 1882.
Daily Bulletin, March 31, 1882.
Damon, Ethel M. "The First Mission Settlement on Kauai." *The Friend*, October 1925.
Damon, Ethel M. "From Manoa to Punahou." *Forty-Ninth Annual Report of the Hawaiian Historical for the Year 1940*. Honolulu: Hawaii Company, 1941.
"Daughters of Hawaii." *Friend*, June 1934.
Davis, Isaac Young, to William Webster, Interior Department, Land, February 15, 1861, translated by E.H. Hart, Hawaii State Archives.
Davis, Samuel H., to A.S. Cleghorn, Sept. 10, 1883, Education Department, General Correspondence, Records Relating to Land (Public Instruction) 1883, Hawaii State Archives.
"The Dead Consul." *Hawaiian Gazette*, August 10, 1897.
"Death Comes to A.S. Cleghorn." *Evening Bulletin*, November 2, 1910.
"Death of Capt. Hawes." *Paradise of the Pacific*, September 1897.
"The Death of Her Britannic Majesty Queen Victoria." *Independent*, February 1, 1901.
"Death of Her Highness Princess Ruth Keelikolani." *Daily Bulletin*, May 28, 1883.
"Death of His Majesty Kamehameha IV." *Pacific Commercial Advertiser*, Dec. 3, 1863.
"Death of His Royal Highness William Pitt Leleiohoku." *Hawaiian Gazette*, April 11, 1877.
"Death of Jas. Campbell." *Evening Bulletin*, April 23, 1900.
"Death of Mrs. Campbell-Parker at the Hospital." *Hawaiian Gazette*, November 3, 1908.
"Death of Mrs. Kapena." *Daily Honolulu Press*, April 19, 1886.
"Death of Paki." *Friend*, June 15, 1855.
"Death of Prince David Kawananakoa Yesterday." *Hawaiian Gazette*, June 5, 1908.
"Death of Princess Likelike." *Daily Herald*, February 3, 1887.
"Death of the King." *Pacific Commercial Advertiser*, February 7, 1874.
Decisions Rendered by The Supreme Court of the Hawaiian Islands Admiralty Criminal Divorce Equity Law and Probate, July Term 1883 to October Term 1886 Inclusive, Hawaiian Reports, vol. V. Honolulu: Hawaiian Gazette, 1887.
"Dedication of the High School." *Independent*, October 31, 1895.
Deed of Trust, Queen Liliuokalani Trust, http://www.onipaa.org/pages/her-deed-of-trust.
Del Piano, Barbara Jane. *Nā Lani Kaumaka, Daughters of Hawai'i, A Century of Historic Preservation*. Honolulu: Daughters of Hawaii, 2005.
"Democrats attacked by Republicans on Dead Issues." *Independent* September 30, 1904.
Department of Economic Development. "Marking Hawaii's Historical Sites: A Recommended Six-Year Program." January 1962, Hawaii State Archives [DU 624.3.H36 1962]

Dibble, Sheldon. *History of the Sandwich Islands.* Lahainaluna: Press of the Mission Seminary, 1843.
"Died." *Hawaiian Gazette,* March 3, 1896.
"Died." *Polynesian,* January 18, 1862.
"Died." *Polynesian,* January 26, 1850.
Directory and Hand-Book of Honolulu and the Hawaiian Islands. San Francisco: F.M. Husted, 1892.
Directory of Honolulu and the Territory of Hawaii, 1912. Honolulu: Polk-Husted Directory Co., 1912, 199.
Directory of Honolulu and the Territory of Hawaii, 1924. Honolulu: Polk-Husted Directory Co., 1924.
Dodge, Mary Mapes, ed. *St. Nicholas: An Illustrated Magazine for Young Folks,* vol. 26 (1899).
Donne, M.A. Donne. *The Sandwich Islands and Their People.* London: Society for Promoting Christian Knowledge, 1866.
"Double Engagement Announced at Schofield; Will Be Followed in a Short Time by Double Wedding." *Honolulu Star-Bulletin,* February 1, 1913.
"Draft of Constitution of January 14, 1893." Reference. Hawaii State Archives.
"Drippings from My Journal, No. 7." *Polynesian,* August 14, 1841.
"A Drive to Waikiki, and Kapiolani Park, Near Honolulu, H.I." *Pacific Commercial Advertiser,* June 9, 1877.
Dwight, Samuel G., to Minister of the Interior, September 9, 1853, Department of the Interior, Box 68, Incoming Letters September 1–15, 1853, Hawaii State Archives.
The Eleventh Legislature of the Territory of Hawaii in Regular Session, Journal of the Senate, 1921.
Ellis, William. *Narrative of a Tour Through Hawaii, or, Owhyhee.* London: H. Fisher, Son, and P. Jackson, 1826.
Ellis, William. *Polynesian Researches: A Residence of Nearly Eight Years in the Society and Sandwich Islands,* vol. IV. New York: J & J Harper, 1833.
Emerson, J.S. "Anecdotes of Early Days." *Friend,* May 1925.
Emerson, Justin Edward. "Emersoniana." *Friend,* March 1, 1914.
"Entertainment at Ainahau in Honor of Prince David." *Hawaiian Gazette,* February 22, 1898.
"Entries are Complete for Regatta Day Races." *Evening Bulletin,* September 19, 1901.
"Estate B.P. Bishop, Receipts, Month of September 1901." [12], accessed November 25, 2012, http://archives1.dags.hawaii.gov/gsdl/collect/judiciar/index-old/assoc/HASH288b.dir/doc.pdf
Estate of Emma Kaleleonalani, 1903, Account of Bruce Cartwight Trustee under the Will, Probate 1787 (V), First Circuit Court, Judiciary, Hawaii State Archives.
"Estate of James S. Lemon, Deceased," Advertisement. *Daily Bulletin,* May 12, 1882.
Eveleth, Ephraim. *History of the Sandwich Islands.* Philadelphia: American Sunday-School League, 1829.

Evening Bulletin, February 2, 1899.
Evening Bulletin, June 3, 1904.
The Evening Star (Auckland, New Zealand), July 2, 1874.
"Every Inch a King." *Once a Week: An Illustrated Miscellany of Literature, Art, Science, & Popular Information,* March 5, 1864.
Executive Minutes, Conservation Council for Hawaii, January 17, 1967, Minutes & Correspondence, 1966–1967, U-9, Hawaii State Archives.
Executive Minutes, Conservation Council for Hawaii, March 9, 1966, Minutes & Correspondence, 1966–1967, U-9, Hawaii State Archives.
Executive Order No. 52, Apr. 25, 1918, Series 265, vol. 1, Hawaii State Archives.
"Fair Guests Royally Received at Ainahau." *Hawaiian Star,* March 19, 1907.
Fairfax, Geoffey W., AIA. *Iolani Palace Restoration Architectural Report.* Honolulu: N.p., 1972.
"Farewell Poi Supper." *Evening Bulletin,* July 8, 1898.
"Farewell Salutations of the Foreign Residents of Honolulu, to Rear-Admiral Thomas." *Friend,* March 2, 1844.
"Fear Old Kuhio House May Be Made Beer Hall." *Honolulu Star-Bulletin,* March 22, 1935.
"Finance Committee's Report to the Legislative Assembly of 1884." *Honolulu Star Bulletin* June 25, 1884.
"Financial Jugglery." *Independent.,* October 4, 1895.
Finch, Capt., to Kaahumanu, October 16, 1829, Foreign Office and Executive, Series 201, Box 3, Folder 26, Hawaii State Archives.
"Fine New Building at Central School Accepted by Board." *Honolulu Star-Bulletin,* August 11, 1916.
First Circuit Court, Probate no. 1840, Hawaii State Archives.
"For Sale." Advertisement. *Evening Bulletin,* September 25, 1905.
Forbes, David W. *Engraved at Lahainaluna.* Honolulu: Hawaiian Mission Children's Society, 2012.
"Foreign Consuls in Hawaii." *New York Times,* January 11, 1899.
Foreign Office and Executive, Chronological File, 1790–1849, 1801, Series 402-2-4 J17a, Hawaii State Archives.
Foreign Office and Executive, Letter from Robert Wyllie to Foreign Representatives, Letter Book, page 80, Series 210, Box 2, vol. 8, Hawaii State Archives.
Foreign Testimony, vol. 2. Hawaii State Archives.
Foreign Testimony, vol. 3. Hawaii State Archives.
Foreign Testimony, vol. 7. Hawaii State Archives.
Foreign Testimony, vol. 15. Hawaii State Archives.
Fornander, Abraham. *An Account of the Polynesian Race.* London: Trübner and Co., 1880.
Frear, Walter Francis, to A.S. Cleghorn, July 26, 1909, Walter Francis Frear, Frear—Miscellaneous (By Name-Unindexed), Ci-Con, Box GOV3-11.
Fredericksen, Walter, and Demaris Fredericksen. Report on the Archeological Excavation

of the "Brick Palace" of King Kamehameha I at Lahaina, Maui, Hawaii, March 31, 1965. Maui Historic Commission.

"Freycinet's Voyage Round the World." *Atheneum*, vol. XIII, April to October 1823.

"Full Account of the Mutiny at the Barracks." *Hawaiian Gazette*, September 17, 1873.

"Funeral of H.R.H. Princess Kekaulike." *Pacific Commercial Advertiser*, January 19, 1884.

"Funeral of the Late King." *Pacific Commercial Advertiser*, February 4, 1864.

"Funeral of the Late Prince William Pitt Leleiohoku." *Hawaiian Gazette*, May 2, 1877.

Gessler, Clifford F. "Honolulu Letter." *Step Ladder*, October 1921.

Gilman, Gorham D. "Honolulu and Its Suburbs in the Latter Forties." *Hawaiian Almanac and Annual for 1909*. Honolulu: Thomas Thrum, 1908, 123.

Gilman, Gorham D. "Lahaina in Early Days." *Hawaiian Almanac and Annual for 1907*. Honolulu: Thomas G. Thrum, 1906.

Gilman, Gorham D. "Streets of Honolulu in the Early Forties." *Hawaiian Almanac and Album for 1904*. Honolulu: Thomas Thrum, 1903.

Gilman, Gorham D., manuscript, Gilman Collection, Hawaiian Historical Society, Honolulu, quoted in Lydia Rider Nye. *Journal of a Sea Captain's Wife, 1841–1845*. Spokane, Washington: Arthur H. Clark Co., 2004.

"Good Concert." *Hawaiian Star*, November 2, 1896.

"Good Queen Emma." *The Banner of Faith*, August 1885.

"Government Officer." *Pacific Commercial Advertiser*, January 12, 1860.

"Governorship of Kauai." *Pacific Commercial Advertiser*, April 6, 1872.

"Great Doings When the Parker Party Returns." *Hawaiian Gazette*, February 18, 1902.

Griffin, Pat L. "The Līhuʻe Place Name on Kauaʻi." *Hawaiian Journal of History*, vol. 46 (2012).

Griffiss, Townsend. *When You Go to Hawaii You Will Need This Guide to the Islands*. Cambridge, MA: Riverside Press, 1930.

Gulick, Charles T., to A.S. Cleghorn, August 31, 1875, Interior Department, book 13, 67, Hawaii State Archives.

Haalelea, Levi. 1st Circuit Court, Probate 2415 (I), Series 007, Box 45, Hawaii State Archives.

"The Hamilton House." *Daily Bulletin*, February 21, 1890.

Hau, Alenui. "Novelty of Railway Building in Hawaii." *Engineering Magazine*, May 1891.

Hawaiian Annual, 1899. Boston: Abner A. Kingman, 1868, 10–11.

Hawaiian Directory and Hand Book of the Kingdom of Hawaii. Honolulu: N.p., 1888.

Hawaiian Gazette. January 19, 1906.

Hawaiian Gazette. June 9, 1905.

Hawaiian Gazette. October 1, 1876.

Hawaiian Gazette. October 17, 1877.

Hawaiian Hansard: A Complete Verbatim Report of the Proceedings and Speeches of the Hawaiian Legislative Assembly of 1886. Honolulu: Daily Bulletin, 1886.

The Hawaiian Kingdom Statistical and Commercial Directory and Tourists Guide, 1880–1881. Honolulu: George Bowser, 1880.

"Hawaiian National Reminiscences." *Hawaiian Almanac and Annual for 1906*. Honolulu: Thomas G. Thrum, 1905.

"The Hawaiian Question." *Daily Bulletin*, March 29, 1893.

"Hawaiians Claim to Have Heard the Spirit of Princess Kaiulani." *The Call* (San Francisco), April 4, 1899.

He Buke Mele Hawaii, 1897. Hawaii State Archives, M-93, Box 14.

"He Inoa No Ka Haku o Hawaii." *Ka Hoku o ka Pakipika*, November 21, 1861.

"He Mele no Wilikoki." *Ka Leo o ka Lahui*, September 17, 1889.

"Heavy Rain Storm." *Daily Bulletin*, May 11, 1885.

"Her Majesty the Queen." *Hawaiian Star*, May 24, 1898.

Historical and Miscellaneous File, 1785–1842, Sept. 12, 1829, from Levi Chamberlain's Journal 1822–1849, Hawaii State Archives.

The Historical Magazine, and Notes and Queries Concerning the Antiquities, History and Biography of America, vol. VIII, second series. Morrisania, NY: Henry B. Dawson, 1870.

"History of the Courtyard King Kamehameha's Kona Beach Hotel." http://www.konabeachhotel.com/historical.htm, Accessed March 17, 2013.

Hoapili to Liholiho, Sept. 13, 1824, Foreign Office and Executive, Series 201, Box 2, Folder 16, Hawaii State Archives.

Holoholopinaau, "Touring Molokai." *Ke Kumu Hawaiʻi*, June 8, 1870, quoted in Catherine C. Summers, *Sites of Molokai*, 1971, 23, trans. Mary Kawena Pukui.

"Home of Former Queen Is Visited By Daughters of Hawaii." *Honolulu Star-Bulletin*, June 18, 1932.

Home of Queen Kaahumanu in Manoa Valley, 1932, Land of Kahaumakaawe, Historical and Miscellaneous File, 1932, U-178, Hawaii State Archives.

"Home Wallpaper Dictionary." http://www.designyourwall.com/store/dictionary.php.

Honolulu Advertiser. June 21, 1918.

Honolulu in 1810: Explanation of Map. Honolulu: Hawaii: Bishop Museum Press, 1957.

"Honolulu Vies with Maui in Ovation to Delegate Baldwin." *Maui News*, April 7, 1922.

Hopkins, Manly. *Hawaii: The Past, Present, and Future of Its Island-Kingdom*. London: Longmans, Green, and Co., 1866.

"Hotel at Waialua." *Pacific Commercial Advertiser*, October 14, 1898.

House Concurrent Resolution, 2012 Regular Session, http://legiscan.com/HI/text/HCR51/id/631170.

"House for Sale." Advertisement. *Hawaiian Gazette*, July 27, 1881.

"House to Let or Lease." Advertisement. *Daily Bulletin*, January 4, 1886.
Howell, W.E. "Anglo-Chinese Academy." *Missionary Magazine*, March 1902, 103.http://96.31.65.17:8282/greenstone/collect/levicham/index/assoc/HASH554d.dir/doc.pdf
Howell, W.E. "Among the Chinese in Honolulu." *The Advent Review and Sabbath Herald*. September 21, 1897.
Hunt, Timothy Dwight. *The Past and Present of the Sandwich Islands*. San Francisco: Whitton, Towne & Co., 1853.
"Hunting Lodge of King Kalakaua to be a Club House." *Hawaiian Gazette*, August 10, 1915.
Husted's Directory and Hand-Book of Honolulu, 1898. Honolulu: Hawaiian Gazette Company, 1898.
Husted's Directory and Hand-Book of Honolulu, 1900–1901. Honolulu: Hawaiian Gazette Company, 1900.
Hyams, Ben. *Centennial Memoirs of the Pacific Club in Honolulu*. Honolulu: Pacific Club, 1951.
"An Ideal Volcano Trip, Notes and Narratives En Route." *Daily Honolulu Press*, April 28, 1886.
Ii, John Papa, Mary Kawena Pukui, trans. *Fragments of Hawaiian History: As recorded by John Papa Ii*. Dorothy B. Barrère, ed. Honolulu: Bishop Museum Press, 1959.
"Important Land Sale." *Independent*, March 16, 1901.
"Impressive Are the Last Mortal Honors." *Evening Bulletin*, November 5, 1908.
In re. Estate of Emma Kaleleonalani deceased, October 19, 1886, Probate 1787 (III), Judiciary, First Circuit Court, Hawaii State Archives.
In re. the Guardianship of Kunuiakea Kaeo, November 11, 1872, First Circuit Court, Probate 2259 (I), Series 007, Box 31, Hawaii State Archives, trans. Jason Achiu.
In the matter of the appointment of a Guardian to the person and Estate of Albert Kunuiakea Kaeo, November 11, 1872, First Circuit Court, Probate 2259 (I), Series 007, Box 31, Hawaii State Archives.
In the matter of the appointment of Guardian to Albert Kunuiakea, June 30, 1858, First Circuit Court, Probate 2259 (I), Series 007, Box 31, Hawaii State Archives.
In the matter of the appointment of Guardian to Albert Kunuiakea a minor, June 16, 1858, First Circuit Court, Probate 2259 (I), Series 007, Box 31, Hawaii State Archives, trans. Jason Achiu.
In the matter of the Clain of Lydia Kaloio et al to 1.5 Acre of land at Manoa, M-397 Liluokalani Trust, Lands: Oahu Misc, Box 3, Hawaii State Archives.
In the matter of the Guardianship of Albert Kunuiakea, April 6, 1880, First Circuit Court, Probate 2259 (II), Series 007, Box 31, Hawaii State Archives.
In the matter of the Will of the Late Majesty Emma Kaleleonalani deceased, June 16, 1885 First Circuit Court, Series 007, Box 27, 1787, Hawaii State Archives.
In the Matters of the Estate of Emma Kaleleonalani Deceased, Masters Report, Probate 1787 (V), First Circuit Court, Judiciary, Hawaii State Archives.Indenture of Lease between M. Kekuanaoa and W.C. Parke, November 25, 1852, Interior Department, Land, Letters (Incoming) 1852, November 11–30, Box 67, Hawaii State Archives.
Infantry Journal, United States Infantry Association, 1928, 89.
"Independent Leaders Urge Steadfastness." *Honolulu Republican*, Apr. 25, 1901.
"Interest to Sportsmen." *Hawaiian Gazette*, September 12, 1893.
Interior Department, Book 13, 351, Hawaii State Archives.
Interior Department, Book 15, 128, Hawaii State Archives.
Interior Department, Subject, Palace Proposed 1871, Hawaii State Archives.
Interior Department Index to Commissions, May 28, 1873, Series 415, Foreign and Executive, Hawaii State Archives, 70.
Interior Department Land, July 21, 1842, English translation attached with Hawaiian language Deed, Hawaii State Archives, 1–3.
Inventory of Iolani Palace, Healani House and Holuakaha, n.d, William Owen Smith Collection, M-133, Box 1–11, Hawaii State Archives.
Inventory of the Real Estate of Albert Kunuiakea, January 12, 1871, First Circuit Court, Probate 2259 (I), Series 007, Box 31, Hawaii State Archives.
Iolani Palace Restoration Architectural Report. Honolulu: Friends of Iolani Palace, 1970.
"Island Locals." *Hawaiian Gazette*, August 17, 1886.
"Island Locals." *Hawaiian Gazette*, February 1, 1887.
"Island Locals." *Hawaiian Gazette*, Dec. 1, 1880.
"Island Locals." *Hawaiian Gazette*, May 27, 1885.
"Island Locals." *Hawaiian Gazette*, September 21, 1881.
"James W. Robertson, Suddenly Stricken by Death, Will Be Laid to Rest This Afternoon." *Pacific Commercial Advertiser*, January 30, 1919.
Jarves, James Jackson. *History of the Hawaiian or Sandwich Islands*. Boston: Tappan and Dennet, 1843.
Jarves, James Jackson. *Scenes and Scenery in the Sandwich Islands*. Boston: James Munroe and Co., 1843.
"John Young Homestead Stabilization." https://www.argsf.com/portfolio/john-young-homestead/.
"Jos. Nawahi's Remains." *Hawaiian Gazette*, October 2, 1896.
"Jottings About Town." *Pacific Commercial Advertiser*, October 17, 1883.
Journal of Levi Chamberlain, vol. 19, January 21, 1835, http://96.31.65.17:8282/greenstone/collect/levicham/index/assoc/HASHb636.dir/doc.pdf.
Journal of Levi Chamberlain, vol. 26, entry for August 10, 1848, http://96.31.65.17:8282/greenstone/collect/levicham/index/assoc/HASH0894.dir/doc.pdf.

Journal of the House of Representatives of the Fifteenth Legislature of the Territory of Hawaii, Regular Session 1929. Honolulu: New Freedom Press, 1929, 45.

Journal of the House of Representatives of the Fourteenth Legislature of the Territory of Hawaii, Regular Session, 1927. Honolulu: Paradise of the Pacific, 1927, 51.

Journal of the House of Representatives of the Seventeenth Legislature of the Territory of Hawaii, Regular Session 1931. Honolulu: New Freedom Press, 1931, 34.

Journal of the House of Representatives of the Thirteenth Legislature of the Territory of Hawaii, Regular Session 1925. Honolulu: Paradise of the Pacific, 1925, 28.

"Journalists Are Kept Busy." *Hawaiian Gazette,* September 11, 1906.

Judd, Bernice. "Minutes of the 63rd Annual Meeting of the Hawaiian Historical Society." *Sixty-Third Annual Report of the Hawaiian Historical Society for the Year 1954.* Honolulu: N.p., 1955.

Judd, Gerrit Parmele. *Fragments II, The Letters of Dr. Gerrit P. Judd, 1827–1872.* Honolulu: Paradise of the Pacific, 1911.

Judd, Gerrit Parmele, to Kekuanaoa, May 6, 1844, Foreign Office and Executive, Series 402, Box 10, Folder 254, Hawaii State Archives.

Judd, Henry P. Report, Commission on Historical Sites, 201-1-12.

Judd, Laura Fish. *Honolulu Sketches of Life Social Political and Religious in the Hawaiian Islands from 1828 to 1861.* New York: Anson D.F. Randolph and Company, 1880.

Judiciary, First Circuit Court, Probate 1787, Hawaii State Archives.

Ka Hae Hawaii, March 7, 1860.

Ka Hoku o ka Pakipika, February 12, 1863.

"Ka La Hanau o Liliu I ke 74 o Kona Mau Makahiki." *Kuokoa Home Rula,* September 5, 1912.

"Ka Make Ana o Hon. J. Kapena." *Ka Nupepa Kuokoa,* March 14, 1868.

Ka Nupepa Kuoko. September 5, 1863.

Kailua Bay, Hawaii, 1883. Hawaii State Archives [G4382.H3:2K324.1883.H38.29].

Kaʻiulani to Liliʻuokalani, February 5, 1892, Liliuokalani Collection, M-93, Box 5, 47a, 258, Hawaii State Archives.

"Kaiulani's Ainahau Grass House Finds New Site in Manoa Valley." *Honolulu Star-Bulletin,* December 4, 1926.

"Kaiulani's Birthday." *Pacific Commerical Advertiser,* October 17, 1893.

"Kalakaua's Old Home Is Sold." *Pacific Commercial Advertiser,* January 4, 1901.

Kaleleonalani to Lucy [K. Peabody], January 19, 1874. Copy, original in Henriques papers, Bishop Museum, M-45, Hawaii State Archives.

Kamakau, Samuel M. *Ruling Chiefs of Hawaii.* Honolulu: Kamehameha Schools Press.

Kamehameha, Lot, minister of the interior, to R.A.S. Wood, superintendent of public works, February 13, 1859, Interior Department Letters, Book 7, 188.

Kamehameha III and Kekauluohi to Emili Keaweamahi, August 5, 1839, series 402, box 5, folder 105, Hawaii State Archives.

Kamehameha V to John Owen Dominis, November 7, 1866, Emma Collection, M-45, NA-52.

Kanehoa, J.Y. to John Young, January 20, 1848, Interior Department, Misc., January 1848, Hawaii State Archives, Translated by E.H. Hart.

Kapena, John M. "Hawaiian National Reminiscences." *Almanac and Annual for 1906.* Honolulu: Thomas G. Thrum, 1905.

"Kapiolani Maternity Home." *Daily Bulletin,* June 16, 1890.

"Kapiolani Maternity Home." *Hawaiian Gazette,* June 17, 1890.

Kapiolani to J.A. King, Sept. 8, 1897, Interior Department, Miscellaneous, June–December, 1897, trans. E.H. Hart, Hawaii State Archives.

Kapiolani-Namakaeha (k), Marriages: Oahu (1832–1910), O-32:122, Hawaii State Archives.

Kauukualii to Keoni Ana, November 18, 1852, Interior Department, Land, Letters (Incoming) 1852, November 11–30, Box 67, Hawaii State Archives.

Keawamahi, E. *Native Testimony,* No. 2291, December 24, 1846, vol. 3. Board of Commissioners to Quiet Land Titles.

Keawamahi, E. *Native Testimony,* No. 3590, January 10, 1848, vol. 9. Board of Commissioners to Quiet Land Titles.

Kekahuna, Henry Enoka Palenapa Kekahuna. "Ka-Maka-Honu, Cultural and Economic Gold Mine." Theodore Kelsey Manuscript Collection, M-86, Papers Relating to Identified Authors or Sources, 1.

Kekauluohi, to Mataio Kekūanāoʻa on March 13, 1840, Box 141, Interior Department, Miscellaneous, Hawaii State Archives.

Kekuanaoa, M., to M. Auhea, n.d. Hawaiian Chiefs, Undated Documents, No. 31 (10) to 31 (20), No. 31 (13), trans. Jason Achiu, Hawaii State Archives.

Kekuanaoa, Matiao, to Puapua, May 7, 1842, Interior Department, Land, Letters (incoming), 1842, April–Sept.

Kekūanāoʻa, Matiao, to John Young II, August 27, 1850, Department of the Interior, Land, Box 64, Hawaii State Archives.

Kekuanaoa to Haalilio, February 28, 1844, Foreign Office and Executive, Series 402, Box 10, Folder 241, Hawaii State Archives.

Kekuanaoa to Kanaina, Apr. 1, 1840, Foreign Office and Executive, Series 402, Box 5, Folder 123, Hawaii State Archives.

Kekuaokalani [Peter Young Kaeo] to Queen Emma, July 23, 1873, M-45, NA-16, Hawaii State Archives, 2.

Kekuaokalani [Peter Young Kaeo] to Queen Emma, July 4, 1874, M-45, NA-16, Hawaii State Archives, 2.

Kekuaokalani [Peter Young Kaeo] to Queen

Emma, July 4, 1874, M-45, NA-16, Hawaii State Archives.
Kekuaokalani [Peter Young Kaeo] to Queen Emma, July 7, 1874, M-45, NA-16, Hawaii State Archives, 2.
Kekuaokalani [Peter Young Kaeo] to Queen Emma, July 9, 1874, M-45, NA-16, Hawaii State Archives, 2.
Kekuaokalani [Peter Young Kaeo] to Queen Emma, October 11, 1873, M-45, NA-17, Hawaii State Archives, 1.
Kekuaokalani [Peter Young Kaeo] to Queen Emma, Sept. 30, 1873, M-45, NA-17, Hawaii State Archives, 1.
"King Kalakaua Dead." *Sacramento Daily-Record*, January 21, 1891.
"The King's Birthday." *Hawaiian Gazette*, December 15, 1869.
"King's Palace Gives Way for a Modern Feedstore." *Honolulu Republican*, December 28, 1900.
Knighton, William. *Struggles for Life*. London: Williams and Norgate, 1888.
"Koloa Kauai Sandwich Islands, No. 1." *Sabbath School Visiter* [sic], February 1838.
Korn, Alfons L. *The Victorian Visitors*. Honolulu: University of Hawaii Press, 1969.
Korn, Alfons L., ed. *News from Molokai*. Honolulu: University of Hawaii Press, 1976.
Kotzebue, Otto von. *A New Voyage Round the World, in the Years 1823, 24, 25, and 26*. London: Henry Colburn and Richard Bentley, 1830.
Krauss, Bob. "Stevenson's Grass House: Only the Spirit's Familiar." *Honolulu Advertiser*, May 14, 1983.
Krout, Mary Hannah. *Memoirs of Bernice Pauahi Bishop*. New York: The Knickerbocker Press, 1908.
"Kuhio Home Offered City for $30,000." *Honolulu Advertiser*, March 16, 1935.
Kunuiakea, Albert K., to Queen Emma, June 16, 1883, M-45, AH005, Hawaii State Archives.
Kupa, P.W., et al., to F.W. Hutchinson, November 6, 1871, Board of Health, Series 334, Box 4, Incoming Letters August–December, 1871, Hawaii State Archives.
Kuykendall, Ralph S. "Papers Regarding Historical Sites 1924–1948," Commission on Historical Sites, 201-1-15, Hawaii State Archives.
"Lahaina Palace to Be Restored." *Honolulu Advertiser*, November 12, 1963.
Land Court Application 350, Maps 20, 23 and 24, Bureau of Conveyances, State of Hawaii.
Land Patent Grant 473, Series 526, Box 6, Grant Survey Notes, No. 473, 474, Hawaii State Archives.
"Landmarks Going Down." *Honolulu Star Bulletin*," March 30, 1960.
Last Will and Testament, Benita Namakeha, 1st Circuit Court, Probate 936.
Laws of the Republic of Hawaii, Passed by the Legislative Assembly, Special Session 1895, Act 22. Honolulu: Robert Grieve Steam Book and Job Printer.
Laws of the Republic of Hawaii, passed by the Legislature at its Session, 1898. Honolulu: Hawaiian Gazette Company, 1898.
Laws of the Territory of Hawaii, Passed by the Eleventh Legislature, Regular Session 1921. Honolulu: Advertiser Publishing Co., 1921.
Laws of the Territory of Hawaii, Passed by the Eleventh Legislature, Regular Session 1923. Honolulu: Advertiser Publishing Co., 1923.
Laws of the Territory of Hawaii, Passed by the Fourteenth Legislature, Regular Session, 1927. Honolulu: Advertiser Publishing Co., 1927.
Laws of the Territory of Hawaii, Passed by the Legislature at Its Regular Session 1907. Honolulu: The Bulletin Publishing Co., 1907.
Laws of the Territory of Hawaii, Passed by the Sixteenth Legislature, Regular Session 1931. Honolulu: Honolulu Star-Bulletin, 1931.
Laws of the Territory of Hawaii, Passed by the Thirteenth Legislature, Regular Session 1925. Honolulu: Advertiser Publishing Co., 1925.
Laws of the Territory of Hawaii, Passed by the Twenty-Eighth Legislature, Regular Session 1955. Honolulu: Tong Publishing Company, 1955.
Laws of the Territory of Hawaii Passed by the Twenty-Sixth Legislature, Regular Session 1951. Honolulu: Honolulu Star-Bulletin, 1951.
"Legislature Spurns Gift of Ainahau as Park." *Honolulu Advertiser*, April 2, 1911.
"Leilehua Ranch Lands Are to Be Opened for Use." *Hawaiian Gazette*, January 31, 1908.
"Leilehua Ranch! For Sale at Auction." Advertisement. *Daily Bulletin*, March 8, 1889.
Lennox, Colin G., to Agnes C. Conrad, Sept. 3, 1959, Commission on Historical Sites, Minutes (incomplete), 1951–1952; 1958–1959, 201-1-18,
"Leper Asylum of Molokai." *Pacific Commercial Advertiser*, April 18, 1874.
Liliʻuokalani, Diary, February 13, 1885, Bishop Museum Archives. Liliʻuokalani, Diary, February 17, 1885, Bishop Museum Archives.
Liliʻuokalani, Diary, February 24, 1885, Bishop Museum Archives. Liliʻuokalani, Diary, February 6, 1885, Bishop Museum Archives.
Liliʻuokalani, Diary, Mar 29, 1885, Bishop Museum Archives.
Liliʻuokalani, Diary, March 8, 1885, Bishop Museum Archives.
Liliʻuokalani, Diary, March 15, 1885, Bishop Museum Archives.
Liliʻuokalani, Diary, March 12, 1885, Bishop Museum Archives.
Liliʻuokalani, Diary, March 21, 1885, Bishop Museum Archives.
"Liliuokalani Disposes of Estate." *Hawaiian Gazette*, December 3, 1909.
Liliʻuokalani, Dorothy K. Gillett, and Barbara Barnard Smith. *Queen's Songbook*. Honolulu: Hui Hanai, 1999.
"Liliuokalani Educational Society." *Daily Bulletin*, August 4, 1886.
"Liliuokalani gives $70,000 Mortgage." *Hawaiian Gazette*, November 13, 1908.

Liliʻuokalani. *Hawaii's Story by Hawaii's Queen.* Boston: Lothrop, Lee and Shepard, 1898.
Liliʻuokalani, Inventory of Palama Residence of Queen Liliʻuokalani, 8 July 1901. Liliʻuokalani Collection, M-93, item 75, Hawaii State Archives.
Liliʻuokalani, Lease, July 8, 1901, Liliʻuokalani to Nakata, Liliʻuokalani Trust Collection, M-397, Hawaii State Archives.
Liliʻuokalani, Lease, May 1896, Liliʻuokalani to A.G. Hawes, May 1896. Liliuokalani Collection, M-93, item 80, Hawaii State Archives.
Liliʻuokalani, Lease, October 10, 1890, Liliʻuokalani to Ernest Hutchinson. Manuscript Collection, Liliuokalani Trust, M-397, Land Records, Leases 1883–1899, box 6, folder 6, Hawaii State Archives.
Liliuʻokalani, Notes in Liliʻuokalani's handwriting, traditions respecting Waikiki, n.d., M-93, Liliuokalani Collection, Hawaii State Archives.
"Liliuokalani Obtains Big Loan at Low Rate." *Hawaiian Star,* November 11, 1908.
Liliʻuokalani to Henry C. Carter, September 15, 1905, Liliuokalani Trust Manuscript Collection, M-397, Box 8, Folder 22, Hawaii State Archives.
Liliʻuokalani to J.O. Carter, July 20, 1900, Liliuokalani Trust Manuscript Collection, M-397, Box 8, Folder 12, Liliuokalani Trust, Hawaii State Archives.
Liliʻuokalani to J.O. Carter, October 1, 1904, Liliuokalani Trust Manuscript Collection, M-397, Box 8, Folder 17, Liliuokalani Trust, Hawaii State Archives.
Liliʻuokalani to J.O. Carter, September 19, 1904, Liliuokalani Trust Manuscript Collection, M-397, Box 8, Folder 17, Hawaii State Archives.
"Liliuokalani's Childhood Home to Go Under the Hammer Today." *Pacific Commercial Advertiser,* September 6, 1900.
"Liliuokalani's Debts." *Hawaiian Star,* November 23, 1893.
Lisiansky, Urey. *A Voyage Round the World in the Years 1803, 4, 5, & 6.* London: S. Hamilton, 1814.
List of Lands of the King, Land Matters, Interior Department, Document No. 384, n.d., Hawaii State Archives.
"Local and General." *Evening Bulletin,* August 15, 1899.
"Local and General." *Evening Bulletin,* February 18, 1896.
"Local and General." *Evening Bulletin,* January 11, 1902.
"Local and General." *Evening Bulletin,* July 30, 1908.
"Local and General." *Evening Bulletin,* March 7, 1899.
"Local and General." *Hawaiian Gazette,* March 19, 1889.
"Local and General." *Hawaiian Gazette,* November 20, 1888.
"Local and General." *Pacific Commercial Advertiser,* January 9, 1884.
"Local and General." *Pacific Commercial Advertiser,* July 1, 1891.
"Local and General News." *Daily Bulletin,* Apr. 7, 1886.
"Local and General News," *Daily Bulletin,* August 10, 1889.
"Local and General News." *Daily Bulletin,* February 24, 1893.
"Local and General News." *Daily Bulletin,* March 14, 1884.
"Local and General News." *Daily Bulletin,* May 28, 1887.
"Local and General News." *Daily Bulletin,* October 15, 1883.
"Local and General News." *Independent* March 3, 1902.
"Local and General News." *Independent,* August 17, 1895.
"Local and General News." *Independent,* August 31, 1897.
"Local and General News." *Independent,* January 28, 1898.
"Local and General News." *Independent,* June 1, 1898.
"Local and General News." *Independent,* March 13, 1902.
"Local and General News." *Independent,* March 22, 1902.
"Local and General News." *Independent,* March 24, 1902.
"Local and General News." *Independent,* May 19, 1897.
"Local and General News." *Independent,* November 7, 1896.
"Local and General News." *Independent,* October 17, 1898.
"Local and General News." *Independent,* October 31, 1898.
"Local and General News." *Independent,* October 6, 1903.
"Local Items." *Daily Bulletin,* June 2, 1883.
London, Jack. *Cruise of the Snark.* New York: Macmillan, 1911, 103.
"Lord Charles Arrives." *Independent.* February 3, 1899.
Lum, Yansheng Ma, and Raymond Mun Kong Lum. *Sun Yat-sen in Hawaii: Activities and Supporters.* Honolulu: University of Hawaiʻi Press, 1999.
Lydgate, J.M. "Hilo Fifty Years Ago." *Hawaiian Almanac and Annual for 1923.* Honolulu: Black & Auld, Printers, 1922.
"Lying in State." *Hawaiian Gazette,* October 22, 1884.
Macrae, James, and William Frederick Wilson, ed. *With Lord Byron at the Sandwich Islands in 1825: Being Extracts from the MS Diary of James Macrae, Scottish Botanist.* Honolulu: 1922.
Malo, David. *Hawaiian Antiquities,* trans. N.B. Emerson, 1898. Honolulu: Hawaiian Gazette Co., 1903.
Managing Trustee, Liliuokalani Trust, to Carrie A. Sabine, September 23, 1919, M-397 Liliuokalani Trust, Lands: Oahu Misc, Box 3, Folder 19, Hawaii State Archives.

"Manoa Uplands Is Scene of Realty Development." *Honolulu Advertiser,* February 20, 1950.

"Many Called." *Hawaiian Gazette,* May 27, 1898.

"Many Fetes for Japan's Sailors." *Evening Bulletin,* June 26, 1909.

"Many Houses Going Up." *Honolulu Star-Bulletin,* April 29, 1912.

"The Marriage Ceremony of the King." *Ke Kumu Hawaii,* February 1, 1837, U-187, Hawaii State Archives.

Marriage Records, Hawaii island, H-16, 72, H-14a, 29, Hawaii State Archives.

Marriage Records, Oahu, O-27: 91, Hawaii State Archives.

"Married." *Daily Bulletin,* August 21, 1888.

"Mass Meeting." *Independent,* April 26, 1901.

"Maternity Home." *Hawaiian Gazette,* Sept. 3, 1897.

"Maternity Home Benefit." *Daily Bulletin,* March 7, 1892.

Mathison, Gilbert Farquhar. *Narrative of a Visit to Brazil, Chile, Peru and the Sandwich Islands.* London: Charles Knight, 1825.

"May Day Fete Saturday Event." *Evening Bulletin,* Apr. 29, 1910.

McChesney, J.M., to Governor Lucius Eugene Pinkham, January 30, 1914, Gov 4, Box 9, Misc. (by subject) A–H.

"Measures of Relief." *Evening Bulletin,* January 21, 1900.

Memorandum, February 16, 1854, Interior Department, Miscellaneous, Box 143, February 1854, Hawaii State Archives.

"A Memorial Tablet in Kawaiahao Church." *Hawaiian Gazette,* October 8, 1907.

"Meyen's Voyage Round the World." *The Foreign Quarterly Review,* March 1835, 17.

Minister of the Interior to Ruth Keʻelikolani, August 17, 1874, Interior Department, Book 12, 533, Hawaii State Archives.

Minutes and Correspondence, Conservation Council for Hawaii, U-9, Hawaii State Archives, February 9, 1966.

"Minutes, August 27, 1959." Commission on Historical Sites, Minutes (incomplete), 1951–1952; 1958–1959, 201-1-18, Hawaii State Archives.

Minutes of Meeting, Commissioners of Public Instruction, April 25 to 29, 1927, Series 235, vol. 12, 55. Hawaii State Archives.

Minutes of the Board of Health, Apr. 5, 1876, Series 259, vol. 2, 140–141, Hawaii State Archives.

Minutes of the Board of Health, June 27, 1876, Series 259, vol. 2, 140–141, Hawaii State Archives.

Minutes of the Meeting of the Board of Health, April 29, 1873, Board of Health, Series 259, vol. 2, folio, Hawaii State Archives.

"Miscellaneous Expenditures." *Pacific Commercial Advertiser,* March 20, 1862.

Missionary Album. Honolulu: Hawaiian Mission Children's Society, 1969.

The Missionary Herald. Boston: Crocker and Brewster, 1840.

Missionary Reports, Sandwich Islands. London: Religious Tract Society, 1839.

"Monument to Prince Kuhio Is Planned." *Honolulu Advertiser,* May 10, 1924.

"More on Liliuokalani's Birthday Celebration, 1912." http://nupepa-hawaii.com/2012/08/

"More Particulars of the Denoument: Incidents in the Aftermath: Residence of the Heir Apparent the Starting Point of the Rebel March." *Daily Bulletin,* August 2, 1889.

Mortimer, George. *Observations and Remarks Made During a Voyage to the Island of Teneriffe, Amsterdam, Maria's Islands Near Van Diemen's land; Otaheite, Sandwich Islands; Owhyhee, the Fox Islands on the North West Coast of America, Tinian, and from thence to Canton, in the Brig Mercury Commanded by John Henry Cox, Esq.* London: N.p., 1791.

"Mrs. A. Campbell Marries Col. Parker." *Evening Bulletin.* January 10, 1902.

"Mrs. Campbell-Parker's Estate as Inventoried." *Hawaiian Star,* January 14, 1909.

"Mrs. Col. Parker Dies at Hospital." *Evening Bulletin,* October 31, 1908.

"Mrs. Parker's Funeral." *Hawaiian Star,* November 3, 1908.

"Mrs. Sam Parker's Funeral Wednesday." *Evening Bulletin,* November 2, 1908.

Mulholland, John Field. *Hawaii's Religions.* Rutland, VT: Charles E. Tuttle Publishing, 1970.

"Muʻolaulani." http://www.huapala.org/Mo/Muolaulani.html.

"Na Make." *Ka Nupepa Kuokoa,* January 12, 1884.

"Na Wahi Pana A Kaulana o Honolulu, Oahu Nei, I Uhiia I ka Lepo a Nalowale Loa Hoi I Kei Au Hou." *Ke Aloha Aina,* September 26, 1896.

Nahaolelua, P., to Aliiolani, January 4, 1866, trans. E.H. Hart, Hawaii State Archives, Interior Dept., Land, Letters (Incoming) 1866, January.

Nakanaela, Thomas K. *Ka Buke Moolelo O Hon. Robert William Wilikoki.* Honolulu: Lake and Nakanaela, 1890.

"Narrow Escape of His Majesty." *Hawaiian Gazette,* April 21, 1869.

National Register of Historic Places Inventory—Nomination Form, http://pdfhost.focus.nps.gov/docs/NRHP/Text/78001018.pdf.

Native Register, vol. 1, trans. Frances Fraser. Honolulu: Hawaii State Archives, 1976.

Native Register, vol. 2, trans. Frances Frazier. Honolulu: Hawaii State Archives, 1976.

Native Register, vol. 3, trans. Frances Frazier. Honolulu: Hawaii State Archives, 1976.

Native Register, vol. 4, trans. Frances Frazier. Honolulu: Hawaii State Archives, 1976.

Native Register, vol. 5, trans. Frances Frazier. Honolulu: Hawaii State Archives, 1976.

Native Register, vol. 9. Trans. Frances Frazier. Honolulu: Hawaii State Archives, 1976.

Native Testimony, 1844–1854. Hawaii Department of Land and Natural Resources. Hawaii State Archives.

Nawahi, Emma, to Queen Liliʻuokalani, n.d., Liliʻuokalani Collection, M-93, Box 2, Folder 19.

Nawahi, Emma to Queen Liliʻuokalani, various

dates, Liliʻuokalani Collection, M-93, Box 2, Folder 19.
Nawahi, Emma, to Queen Liliʻuokalani dated January 28, 1897, Liliʻuokalani Collection, M-93, Box 2, Folder 19 [Hawaiian translated into English by Jason Achiu].
Nellist, George F., ed. *Men of Hawaii.* Honolulu: Honolulu Star-Bulletin, 1930.
Nellist, George F., ed. *The Story of Hawaii and Its Builders.* Honolulu: Honolulu Star-Bulletin, 1925.
"New Manager Will Come from Coast to Take Ainahou [sic] Hotel." *Honolulu Star-Bulletin*, July 11, 1916.
"The New Palace." *Pacific Commercial Advertiser*, January 3, 1879.
"New Palace." *Pacific Commercial Advertiser*, September 24, 1881.
"News in a Nutshell." *Hawaiian Star*, January 13, 1905.
"News in a Nutshell." *Hawaiian Star*, July 13, 1895.
"News in a Nutshell." *Hawaiian Star*, March 2, 1896.
"News in a Nutshell." *Hawaiian Star*, October 15, 1898.
"News of the Town." *Honolulu Republican*, August 20, 1901.
"News of the Town." *Honolulu Republican*, November 3, 1900.
Nicholson, Henry Whalley. *From Sword to Share: Or a Fortune in Five Years at Hawaii.* London: W. H. Allen & Co., 1881.
"No Clue to Thieves." *Evening Bulletin*, August 3, 1903.
Nogelmeier, M. Puakea, ed. *He Lei no Emalani: Chants for Queen Emma Kaleleonalani.* Honolulu: Bishop Museum Press, 2001.
"Noted Kaiulani Banyan Enjoyed by R.L. Stevenson Will Be Marked by Tablet." *Honolulu Advertiser*, February 18, 1925.
"Notes from Washington." *New York Times*, June 7, 1882.
"Notes of the Week." *Hawaiian Gazette*, March 18, 1874.
"Notes of the Week." *Pacific Commercial Advertiser*, Apr. 9, 1864.
"Notes of the Week." *Pacific Commercial Advertiser*, February 13, 1862.
"Notes of the Week." *Pacific Commercial Advertiser*, October 18, 1873.
Notes Regarding Leilehua Ranch House, Liliʻuokalani Collection, M-93, Box 2, Folder 21, Item 125, Hawaii State Archives.
"Notice." Advertisement. *Independent* February 26, 1902.
"Notice." Advertisement. *Polynesian*, January 25, 1862.
"Notice No. 6." *Polynesian*, August 13, 1853
Nye, Lydia Rider. *Journal of a Voyage from the United States to the Sandwich Islands, 1842* and *Dairy of Life in Honolulu, 1842–1843, Kept by the Wife of Capt. Gorham Nye.* Spokane, WA: Arthur H. Clarke, 2004.

"Obituary Notice." *Independent*, March 13, 1902.
"Objects to Be Considered for Designation as Territorial Monuments by the Governor of Hawaii under Act 56, S.L. 1931," December 15, 1932, Commission on Historic Sites, 201-1-15. Hawaii State Archives.
Of Decisions Rendered by the Supreme Court of the Hawaiian Islands Admiralty Criminal Divorce Equity Law and Probate July Term 1883 to October Term 1886 Inclusive, Hawaiian Reports, vol. V. Honolulu: Hawaiian Gazette Co., 1887.
"Old Associations of Kailua Palace," *Honolulu Star-Bulletin*, March 8, 1913.
"Old Government Building About to Be Demolished." *Hawaiian Star*, March 9, 1912.
"Old Landmarks Gone." *Friend*, October 1900.
"One of Mrs. Parker's Lost Rings Was Worth $4500." *Evening Bulletin*, August 3, 1903.
"The Onlooker." *Hawaiian Star*, February 4, 1911.
Order by Hoapili kane, Foreign and Executive, Series 402-79, October 21, 1837. Hawaii State Archives.
"Order of Procession." *Pacific Commercial Advertiser*, January 12, 1884.
"Orders Sale of University Club Corner." *Honolulu Advertiser*, July 10, 1928.
"Oriental Art Exhibit at the Colonial." *Honolulu Star-Bulletin*, September 25, 1915.
Oshita, Hideo. "Hawaii Conference—Conference History." accessed November 25, 2012, http://hwic.adventistfaith.org/conference-history. [Original timeline dated October 1961.]
"Over the Tea Cups." *Hawaiian Gazette*, October 13, 1896.
Pacific Commercial Advertiser, August 4, 1882, 2.
Pacific Commercial Advertiser, June 10, 1882, 2.
Pacific Commercial Advertiser, May 8, 1910.
Pacific Islands, vol. III. London: Hydrographic Office, Admiralty, 1885.
"The Palace." *Pacific Commercial Advertiser*, July 2, 1856.
"Palace Square." *Pacific Commercial Advertiser*, March 24, 1893.
Paris, John D. *Fragments of Real Missionary Life.* Honolulu: The Friend, 1926.
Parker, Joseph B. *United States Navy Dept., Bureau of Medicine and Surgery, Hygienic and Medical Reports.* Washington, D.C.: Government Printing Office, 1879.
Parker, Samuel. *Journal of an Exploring Tour Beyond the Rocky Mountains.* Ithaca, NY: Mack, Andrus and Woodruff, 1838.
"The Parker Diamonds." *Hawaiian Star*, October 20, 1903.
"Parker Won't Accept." *Hilo Tribune*, August 1, 1902.
"Party at Schofield." *Honolulu Star-Bulletin*, December 5, 1917.
Percy, Reuben, John Timbs, and John Limbird, eds. *The Mirror of Literature, Amusement, and Instruction.* London: John Limbird, vol. 4, no. 5 (July 24, 1824).
Pinkham, Lucius Eugene to J.M. McChesney, Gov

4, Box 10, Misc (Unindexed) M, Hawaii State Archives.
"The Place of Mourning." *Pacific Commercial Advertiser*, January 16, 1909.
"A Plan of the Harbour of Honoruru, in the Island of Oahu." Hawaii State Archives.
"A Pleasant Day with H.R.H. Liliuokalani." *Pacific Commercial Advertiser*, March 26, 1890.
"Poi Luncheon." *Evening Bulletin*, September 13, 1902.
"The Political Field." *Independent*, October 28, 1902.
"Political Meetings." *Independent*, October 12, 1904.
"Political Meetings." *Independent*, October 15, 1904.
Polynesian, January 9, 1847.
Polynesian, July 11, 1840.
Polynesian, June 21, 1851.
Polynesian, May 22, 1847.
Polynesian, October 4, 1851.
Polynesian, September 6, 1845.
"Popular Cricket Patron." *Evening Bulletin*, March 1, 1899.
"The Prince Again." *Daily Bulletin*, March 28, 1892.
"A Prince in the Toils: An Immersionist Saved by a Miracle." *Hawaiian Gazette*, November 3, 1891.
"Princes See a Bit of Old Hawaii." *Honolulu Advertiser*, June 17, 1935.
"Princess Kaiulani." *Hawaiian Gazette*, May 20, 1890.
"Princess Ruth's Funeral." *Hawaiian Gazette*, June 20, 1883.
"Princess Will Receive." *Hawaiian Star*, July 11, 1904.
"Priory Training at St. Andrew's." *Hawaiian Gazette*, December 25, 1914.
Privy Council, August 19, 1850, Series 421, vol. 3B, typescript, Hawaii State Archives, 749.
Privy Council, March 8, 1852, vol. 6, 604, Hawaii State Archives.
Privy Council Minutes, December 7, 1863, Hawaii State Archives, Series 421, vol. 11T, 127.
Privy Council Minutes, December 7, 1863, Hawaii State Archives, Series 421, vol. 11T, 129.
Privy Council Minutes, May 27, 1850, Hawaii State Archives, 657.
Privy Council Minutes, November 6, 1850, Hawaii State Archives, vol 6 A, 94.
Privy Council Minutes, September 7, 1846, Hawaii State Archives, Series 421, vol. 2T, 38.
Privy Council Reports, Report of Committee on Missionary Lands and on the course to be pursued in regard to them, August 19, 1850, Hawaii State Archives.
Probate 2404, 1st. Circuit, John Young I, Hawaii State Archives.
Proposed Street Plan—Kapalama Section Nuuanu Street to Houghtailing, 1922. Hawaii State Archives.
"Provision for Homeless." *Hawaiian Star*, January 11, 1900.
"Public Notice." Advertisement. *Hawaiian Star*, July 22, 1897.

Pukui, Mary Kawena, and Alfons L. Korn. *The Echo of Our Song: Chants an Poems of the Hawaiians*. Honolulu: University of Hawaii Press, 1973.
Pukui, Mary Kawena, and Samuel H. Elbert. *Hawaiian Dictionary*. Honolulu: University Press of Hawaii, 1971.
Pukui, Mary Kawena, Samuel H. Elbert, and Esther Mookini. *Place Names of Hawaii*. Honolulu: University of Hawaii Press, 1974.
Pukui, Mary Kawena, trans. *Ōlelo Noʻeau: Hawaiian Proverbs & Poetical Sayings*. Honolulu: Bishop Museum Press, 1983.
Punahou Jubilee Celebration, June 25–26, 1891. Honolulu: Hawaiian Gazette Co, 1891.
"Puʻuhonua Nani (Beautiful Refuge)," http://www.huapala.org/Puuhonua_Nani.html.
"Queen Emma Hall." *Daily Bulletin*, March 2, 1887.
"Queen Emma Hall." *Daily Bulletin*, March 4, 1887.
"Queen Emma Hall." *Hawaiian Gazette*, January 24, 1888.
Queen Emma to Alex [Kamehameha IV], June 27, 1861, Queen Emma Collection, M-45, Folder NA-1, Hawaii State Archives.
Queen Emma to Flora Jones, Apr. 3, 1883, Queen Emma Collection, M-45, FJ-3, Hawaii State Archives.
Queen Emma to Flora Jones, August 7, 1883, Queen Emma Collection, M-45, FJ-3, Hawaii State Archives.
Queen Emma to Flora Jones, July 10, 1883, Queen Emma Collection, M-45, FJ-3, Hawaii State Archives.
Queen Emma to Flora Jones, March 13, 1883, Queen Emma Collection, M-45, FJ-3, Hawaii State Archives.
Queen Emma to Flora Jones, March 27, 1883, Queen Emma Collection, M-45, FJ-3, Hawaii State Archives.
Queen Emma to Flora Jones, October 9, 1883, Queen Emma Collection, M-45, FJ-3, Hawaii State Archives.
Queen Emma to John Dominis, Dec. 18, 1867, Dec. 28, 1867, and January 8, 1868, Queen Emma Collection, M-45, Folder AH05, Hawaii State Archives.
"Queen Emma's Former Palace." *Pacific Commercial Advertiser*, June 8, 1904.
"Queen Lil's Will a Surprise." *Washington Times*, Dec. 16, 1909.
"Reasons for Dole's Removal Are Told in Washington and New York Papers." *Evening Bulletin*, February 11, 1902.
Receipt, Apr. 4, 1892, Probate 2749, 1st Circuit Court, Hawaii State Archives.
"Receipt for the Campbell Property." *Hawaiian Star*, July 28, 1905.
"Reception at Pualeilani." *Hawaiian Star*, March 19, 1902.
"Reception at Pualeilani." *Independent*, March 19, 1902.
"Reception at Waikiki." *Hawaiian Gazette*, January 17, 1883.

"Reception Last Night." *Hawaiian Gazette*, December 24, 1895.
"Record of Events." *Friend*, March 1898.
Registered Map 900, Land Survey Division, Department of Accounting and General Services.
Registered Map 1791, Land Survey Division, Department of Accounting and General Services.
Registered Map 1382, Land Survey Division, Department of Accounting and General Services.
Registered Map 1323, Land Survey Division, Department of Accounting and General Services.
"Reminiscences of Honolulu LXI." *Saturday Press*, Apr. 14, 1883.
"Report, Financial and Statistical, Kamehameha Schools, Year Ending June 30, 1902," accessed November 25, 2012, http://archives1.dags.hawaii.gov/gsdl/collect/judiciar/index-old/assoc/HASH01f7.dir/doc.pdf.
"Report, Financial and Statistical, Kamehameha Schools, Year Ending June 30, 1903," accessed November 25, 2012, http://archives1.dags.hawaii.gov/gsdl/collect/judiciar/index-old/assoc/HASHacfd.dir/doc.pdf.
"Report of Henry P. Judd." August 1942, Commission on Historic Sites, 201-1-15, Hawaii State Archives.
Report of the Committee on Site Conservation, Conservation Council for Hawaii, Fifth Annual Meeting, February 11, 1955. U-9 Minutes-Exec. Bd. Conservation Council-1950–1956, 14.
Report of the Committee on Site Conservation, Conservation Council for Hawaii, Sixth Annual Meeting, February 24, 1955. U-9 Minutes-Exec. Bd. Conservation Council—1950–1956, 10.
Report of the Committee on Site Conservation, Conservation Council for Hawaii, Sixth Annual Meeting, February 24, 1956. U-9 Minutes-Exec. Bd. Conservation Council—1950–1956, 14.
Report of the Committee on Site Conservation, January 9, 1954. U-9 Minutes-Exec. Bd. Conservation Council—1950–1956, 14.
Report of the Historical Commission of the Territory of Hawaii for the period ending December 31, 1922. Honolulu: Honolulu Star-Bulletin, 1923, 12.
Report of the Historical Commission of the Territory of Hawaii for the period ending December 31, 1922. Honolulu: Honolulu Star-Bulletin, 1923, 6.
"Report of the Minister of Finance." *Hawaiian Gazette*, May 24, 1876.
Report of the Minister of the Interior, By Order of His Majesty, King Kamehameha III, Read Before His Majesty, to the Hawaiian Legislature, On Wednesday, May 21st., 1845. Honolulu: Polynesian Press, 1845.
Report of the Superintendent of Public Instruction to the Governor for the Biennium Ending December 31, 1918, Honolulu: New Freedom Press, 1919.
"Report on Conservation in Hawaii." *Pacific Science Council*, August 11, 1950, UD-9, 5.
"Report on Free Schools." *Hawaiian Star*, June 3, 1899.

Reports of a Portion of the Decisions Rendered by the Supreme Court of the Hawaiian Islands. Honolulu: Government Press, 1866.
Reports of Decisions Rendered by the Supreme Court of the Hawaiian Islands in Law Equity Admiralty and Probate, 1877–1883. Honolulu: Pacific Commercial Advertiser Company, 1883.
Reports of Decisions Rendered by the Supreme Court of the Republic of Hawaii. Honolulu: Hawaiian Gazette Company, 1900.
"Restoration Day." *Polynesian*, August 7, 1847.
Revised Laws of Hawaii 1945, chapter 86, section 4905. Honolulu: Honolulu Star-Bulletin, 1945.
"Reviving an Old Case." *Hawaiian Star*, August 23, 1904.
Reynolds, Jeremiah N. *Voyage of the United States Frigate Potomac Under the Command of Commodore John Downes, During the Circumnavigation of the Globe in the Years 1831, 1832, 1833, and 1834*. New York: Harper and Brothers, 1835.
Reynolds, Stephen. "Stephen Reynolds Journal: November 27, 1823, to November 29, 1849." Typescript. Hawaiian Mission Children's Society Library, Honolulu, Hawaii.
Richards, William. *Memoir of Keopuolani, Late Queen of the Sandwich Islands*. Boston: Crocker and Brewster, 1825.
Robert W. Shingle–Ethel Muriel Campbell, Oahu Marriages, O-96:494, Hawaii State Archives.
Rockwood, Paul, and Dorothy Barerre. *Honolulu in 1810*. Honolulu: Bishop Museum Press, 1957.
Rooke, T.C.B., to John Young, February 11, 1848, Series 526, Grant Survey Notes no. 83, Hawaii State Archives.
Roster, Legislatures of Hawaii, 1841–1918. Honolulu: Hawaiian Gazette Co., 1918.
"A Royal Anniversary." *Daily Bulletin*, September 2, 1886.
"Royal Birthday." *Hawaiian Gazette*, October 16, 1888.
"A Royal Birthday." *Pacific Commercial Advertiser*, October 18, 1886.
"Royal Jubilee Reception." *Hawaiian Gazette*, September 11, 1888.
"Royalist Leader Dead." *Times* (Richmond, Virginia), January 10, 1901.
Ruschenberger, W.S.W. [William Samuel Waithman]. *A Voyage Round the World: Including an Embassy to Muscat and Siam in 1835, 1836, and 1837*. Philadelphia: Carey, Lea & Blanchard, 1838.
Ruth Keʻelikolani to C.P. Turner (Kale), July 15, 1861, Interior Department, Miscellaneous, July 1861, Hawaii State Archives. Translated by E.H. Hart.
Ruth Keʻelikolani to Kipine, Esq., September 3, 1860, translated by E.H. Hart, Interior Department, Miscellaneous, Hawaii State Archives.
Ruth Keʻelikolani to S. Pine [S. Spencer], September 21, 1860, translated by E.H. Hart, Interior Department, Miscellaneous, July–December, 1860, Box 147, Hawaii State Archives.
Ruth to Lot, September 14, 1860, Interior Department, Miscellaneous, Hawaii State Archives.

"S. Yokomizo." *Evening Bulletin*, September 6, 1904.
"S. Yokomizo." Advertisement. *Pacific Commercial Advertiser*, April 13, 1905.
Sabine, Carrie A. to the Trustees of the Liliuokalani Estate, August 27, 1919, M-397 Liluokalani Trust, Lands: Oahu Misc., Box 3, Folder 19, Hawaii State Archives.
"The St. Andrew's Concert." *Evening Bulletin*, November 30, 1897.
Sala, George Augustus. "Land of the Golden Fleece." *Sydney Morning Herald*, July 8, 1885.
"Sale of Valuable Real Estate." Advertisement. *Hawaii Gazette*, November 12, 1884.
Sands, J.H., R.M. Cutts, and D.L. Wilson, surveyors. *Mouth and Bar of Pearl River, Island of Oahu, Hawaiian Islands*. 1873. Map. https://www.loc.gov/item/2010592867/.
"Sandwich Islands." *London Illustrated News*, April 1, 1843.
"School Matters." *Hawaiian Gazette*, May 14, 1897.
"Sealed Tenders." Advertisement. *Honolulu Star-Bulletin*, April 22, 1916.
Senate Journal, The Twelfth Legislature of the Territory of Hawaii, Regular Session, 1923. Honolulu: The New Freedom Press, 1923.
Session Laws of Hawaii Passed by the First State Legislature, Second Special Session 1959. Honolulu: Honolulu Star-Bulletin, 1959, 597–598.
"Shadows of Coming Events." *Independent* March 11, 1902.
"Shall We Have a Public Park?" *Hawaiian Gazette*, June 3, 1874.
Sheldon, H.L. "Reminiscences of Honolulu—No 31." *Saturday Press*
Sheldon, J.G.M., E.L. Like, and J.K. Prendergast. *Ka Puke Moʻolelo O Hon. Iosepa K. Nāwahī* (1908; rpt. Hilo, HI: Hale Kuamoʻo, Ka Haka ʻUla o Keʻelikōlani, 1996) 167.
Siddell, John William, ed. *Men of Hawaii*, vol. II. Honolulu: Honolulu Star-Bulletin, Limited, 1921.
Silliman, Benjamin, ed. "Hawaii (Owyhee,) and Its Volcanic Regions and Productions; with Notices of Its Inhabitants, and Those of Oahu." *American Journal of Science*, vol. 20 (July 1831).
Smith, William O., et al., to C.P. Iaukea, May 27, 1910, M-397 Liliuokalani Trust, Lands: Oahu Misc, Box 4, Hawaii State Archives.
"Social Side of Life." *Evening Bulletin*, January 21, 1905.
"Social Side of Life." *Evening Bulletin*, June 24, 1905.
"Society." *Evening Bulletin*, Apr. 30, 1910.
"Society." *Hawaiian Gazette*, May 12, 1908.
"Society." *Pacific Commercial Advertiser*, May 29, 1904.
"Society Items." *Evening Bulletin*, January 27, 1906.
"Society Items." *Evening Bulletin*, March 17, 1906.
"Splendid Home for the University Club." *Hawaiian Star*, July 14, 1909.
State of Hawaii, Bureau of Conveyances, February 22, 1870, book 29, 345.
State of Hawaii, Bureau of Conveyances, January 15, 1883, book 29, 200–201.
State of Hawaii, Bureau of Conveyances, n.d., book 64, 127.
Sterling, Elspeth P., and Catherine C. Summers. *Sites of Oahu*. Honolulu: Bernice Pauahi Bishop Museum, 1978, 288.
Stevenson, Robert Louis. *Robert Louis Stevenson: His Best Pacific Writings*. St. Lucia, Queensland, Australia: University of Queensland Press, 2004.
Stewart, C.S. *Journal of a Residence in the Sandwich Islands During the Years 1823, 1824, and 1825*. New York: John P. Haven, 1828.
Stewart, C.S. *A Visit to the South Seas, in the U.S. Ship Vincennes, During the Years 1829 and 1830*. New York: John P. Haven, 1831.
Stoddard, Charles Warren. *A Trip to Hawaii*. San Francisco: Oceanic Steamship Co. 1885.
Stone, John F. "Royal Hawaiian Hotel Stands on Temple Site." *Aloha*, Matson Navigation Co., vol. 7, no. 8 (October 1926).
"Struggle for Supremacy: Martial Torchlight Procession and Many Meetings Held." *Independent*, November 3, 1902.
"Successor to Mr. Hawes." *Evening Bulletin*, November 8, 1897.
"Sudden Death of the Queen of the Sandwich Islands." *Sacramento Daily Record-Union*, May 9, 1885.
"Supervisors Held Session." *Hawaiian Gazette*, July 21, 1905.
Supreme Court Hawaiian Islands in Chambers, Dec. 24, 1892, Probate 1787 (III), Judiciary, First Circuit Court, Hawaii State Archives.
"Supreme Court of the Hawaiian Islands." *Hawaiian Gazette*, February 20, 1878.
"Supreme Court—In Equity, L. Keelikolani v. James Robinson." *Polynesian*, July 5, 1862.
Survey notes, Uluhaimalama, Pauoa, June 23, 1891, M-93, Liliuokalani collection #57, Hawaii State Archives.
Survey of LCA 1926 to Nanauki, Liliuokalani Collection, Hawaii State Archives, M-93, Box 1, Folder 9, Item 72.
Taylor, Albert P. "Haalelea Lawn, Honolulu." Albert P. Taylor Collection, M-141, File 17, Paper # 56, Hawaii State Archives, n.d.
Taylor, Albert P. "Historical Notes." Papers of the Hawaiian Historical Society, no. 17, Honolulu: The Printshop Co., 1930, 13.
Taylor, Albert P. "Historical Notes." *Thirty-Eighth Annual Report of the Hawaiian Historical Society for the Year 1929*. Honolulu: Honolulu Star-Bulletin, 1930.
Taylor, Albert P. "History of Iolani Palace, Honolulu, Hawaiian Islands." Albert P. Taylor Collection, M-141, File 20, Paper # 82, Hawaii State Archives, n.d.
Taylor, Albert Pierce. "150th Anniversary of the Discovery of Hawaii by Captain Cook, Cook Sesquicentennial Commission." COM-8, Box 4, Schedule for Captain Cook Sesquicentennial Celebration, 7.

Taylor, Albert Pierce. *Under Hawaiian Skies.* Honolulu: Advertiser Publishing Company, 1922.

Taylor, Clarice B., to Mrs. Lloyd B. Osborne, November 5, 1958, Commission on Historical Sites, Sites—All Islands, List, n.d., 1958–1960, 201-1-26, Hawaii State Archives.

Tayman, John. *The Colony: The Harrowing True Story of the Exiles of Molokai.* New York: Scribner's, 2010.

Tennyson, Alfred Lord. "Kapiolani." In *Works of Alfred Lord Tennyson.* New York: Macmillan, 1911.

"Territory Loses Cleghorn Offer." *Honolulu Star-Bulletin,* April 22, 1913.

Territory of Hawaii Legislature, Senate Journal, 1911.

Territory of Hawaii vs William O. Smith, Curtis P. Iaukea and Alexander G.M. Robertson, Trustees under that certain Deed of Trust executed by Liliuokalani, May 11, 1921, 3, GOV 5-8, McCarthy—Miscellaneous, Washington Place, Hawaii State Archives.

"The Theaters." *Hawaiian Star,* February 22, 1912.

"Theft Was Not a Theft." *Hawaiian Star,* June 4, 1903.

"Through Nuuanu." *Paradise of the Pacific,* December 1903.

Thrum, Thomas G., ed. *Almanac and Annual for 1904,* Honolulu: Thomas G. Thrum, 1903.

Thrum, Thomas G, ed. *Hawaiian Almanac and Annual for 1902.* Honolulu: Thomas G. Thrum, 1901.

Thrum, Thomas G., ed. *Hawaiian Alamanac and Annual for 1892.* Honolulu: Press Publishing, 1891.

Thrum, Thomas G., ed. *Hawaiian Almanac and Annual for 1891.* Honolulu: Press Publishing Company, 1890.

"To Let." Advertisement. *Evening Bulletin,* March 3, 1904.

"To Let." Advertisement. *Evening Bulletin,* March 4, 1903.

"Topics of the Day." *Independent,* January 11, 1900.

Townsend, John Kirk. *Sporting Excursions in the Rocky Mountains: Including a Journey to the Columbia River and a Visit to the Sandwich Islands, Chili &c.* London: Henry Colburn, 1840.

"Treason and Conspiracy: The Government Does Not Wait for Overt Acts." *Daily Bulletin,* December 10, 1894.

"Trial of Albert Loomens for Treason." *Daily Bulletin,* October 10, 1889, July 31, 1889.

"Troopers of Fifth Cavalry Settle Down in Their New Post." *Hawaiian Gazette,* January 19, 1909.

"Tropic Lightning Museum: Memoirs and Recollections," http://www.garrison.hawaii.army.mil/tlm/files/early-schofield-barracks.pdf

Turnbull, John. *Voyages in the Pacific Ocean.* London: W. McDowall, 1805, 203.

Twain, Mark. *Roughing It.* Hartford, CT: American Publishing, 1872.

Twain, Mark. "Scenes in Honolulu—No. 13." *Sacramento Daily Union,* July 16, 1866.

"Two Receptions for Shriners Yesterday." *Honolulu Republican,* October 24, 1900.

Twombly, Alexander Stevenson. *Hawaii and Its People: The Land of Rainbow and Palm.* New York: Silver Burdett and Company, 1900.

"Uluniu Estate to Be Put on Market." *Hawaiian Gazette,* September 15, 1910.

"United in Bonds of Holy Matrimony." *Evening Bulletin,* February 25, 1901.

"Unsuccessful Attempt at Revolution." *Daily Bulletin,* July 31, 1889.

"Unveiling of Kuhio Monument Seen by Thousands at Koloa." *Honolulu Advertiser,* June 22, 1928.

"Urges City to Buy Home of Kuhio." *Honolulu Star-Bulletin,* March 18, 1935.

U.S. Federal Census, 1900.

"Victoria Day Reception." *Evening Bulletin,* May 24, 1900.

Vincent, Frank, Jr. *Through and Through the Tropics: 30,000 Miles of Travel in Polynesia, Australasia and India,* Second Edition. New York: Harper & Brothers, 1882.

"A Visit to Kalawao." *Hawaiian Gazette,* June 28, 1876.

"Waialua Hotel." *Pacific Commercial Advertiser,* August 5, 1899.

Warriner, Francis. *Cruise of the United States Frigate Potomac Round the World During the Years 1831–34.* Boston: Crocker and Brewster, 1835.

"Wedding Reception." *Daily Bulletin,* December 22, 1890.

"A Week in Society." *Hawaiian Gazette,* February 11, 1896.

"A Week in Society." *Hawaiian Gazette,* March 17, 1896.

"The Week in Society." *Hawaiian Gazette,* November 24, 1896.

Whitney, Henry M., ed. *The Tourist's Guide Through the Hawaiian Islands Descriptive of Their Scenes and Scenery.* Honolulu: Hawaiian Gazette, 1895.

Who's Who in New York City and State, vol. 4. New York: Hamersly and Company, 1909.

Widemann, H.A., to Samuel. G. Wilder, Sept. 1879, Department of the Interior, Land, Box 85, Hawaii State Archives.

Wilkes, Charles. *Narrative of the United States Exploring Expedition, During the Years 1838, 1839, 1840, 1941, 1842,* vol III. London: Wiley and Putnam, 1845.

"William H. Coney Passes Away After Short Illness." *Independent,* March 25, 1904.

Wilson, Jennie K. "Notes on the Music Collection of Queen Lili'u-o-ka-lani," typewritten pages inserted at end of *He Buke Mele,* 1897, M-93, Lili'uokalani Collection, Box 14, 2, Hawaii State Archives.

Winne, Jane Lathrop. *Kuakini and Hulihee: The Story of the Kailua Palace, Kona, Hawaii.* Honolullu: N.p., 1928.

Withington, Antoinette. *Hawaiian Tapestry.* New York: Harper & Brothers, 1937.

"Wores' Art Receives Favorable Attention." *Evening Bulletin,* December 4, 1902.

"Workers to Raze Old Kuhio Home." *Honolulu Advertiser,* June 15, 1935.

Wyllie, R.C., to Foreign Ministers, October 2, 1851, Series 410, Foreign Office Letterbook, vol. 13A, Foreign Office and Executive, Hawaii State Archives, 1400.

Wyllie, R.C., to Kamehameha IV, Sept. 17. 1859, Foreign Office and Executive, Local Officials, 1859, September, Hawaii State Archives.

Young, Fanny, to Queen Emma, July 7, 1871, trans. Jason Achiu, M-45, NA-10, Hawaii State Archives.

Young, Fanny to Queen Emma, May 25, 1871, trans. Jason Achiu, M-45, NA-10, Hawaii State Archives.

Young, James to John Young, dated January 13, 1848, Interior Department, Misc., January 1848, Hawaii State Archives, Translated by E.H. Hart.

Young, John (Keoni Ana), minister of the interior, to P. Namakeha, acting governor of Maui, September 28, 1846, Interior Department Letters, Book 1, 289, Hawaii State Archives.

Index

Numbers in *bold italics* indicate pages with illustrations

adobe 19, 132, 148
Aea, Joseph Kaiponohea 84, 214
'aha'aina 54
Ahu'ena 16, *17*, 238
ahupua'a 20, 29, 42, 45, 186, 227, 229, 245
Aikake *see* Davis, Isaac
Aikanaka 59, 82, 179
'Āinahau 1, 58, 59, 60, *61*, 62, 63, 64, *65*, *66*, *67*, *68*, 69, 70, 71, *72*, 73, 74, 76, 77, 81, 82, 240, 245; destroyed by fire 73
Ainahau Gardens 75
Akoni, Peke *see* Davis, Peke
Ala Wai Canal 73
Albert Edward Kauikeaouli Leiopapa A Kamehameha, Prince 29, 95, 171
Aldrich, W.F. 72, 73
Alebada *see* Ka'eo, Keli'imaika'i
Alexander Young Hotel 167, 177
ali'i 3, 7, 19, 32, 52, 54, 112, 158, 173, 225, 229, 230
ali'i nui 32
Ali'iolani Hale 117, 239
America (ship) 93
American Board of Commissioners for Foreign Missions 192
Ana, Keoni 41, 42, 45, 99, 103, 112, 143, 152, 230
Anahulu 217
Anderson, Mary Evarts 96
Anglo-Chinese School 191
Antonio, Peke *see* Davis, Peke
Apuakehau Stream 56, 73, 82
Arago, Jacques 14, 18, 19, 22, 33, 122, 241
Architectural Resources Group/Conservation Services 21
Ariyoshi, George 237
Arlington Hotel 165, 166, 167, 244
Arnemann, George 162, 180
Auanakeo *27*
'Au'aukai 58
Auld, Lily 73
Auwae 35

Baldwin, Henry Alexander 85
Bannick, Nancy 240, 241

banyan tree 1, *60*, 61, 63, 65, 66, 72, 73, 74, 106, 190, 192, 193, 246
Barrot, Théodore-Adolphe 7, 25, 26, 138, 158
Bates, George Washington 40, 52, 93, 94, 106, 228, 229
Bayer, Walter 162
Beckley, Emma Kaili Metcalf Beckley Nakuina 195
Beckley, George C. 178, 180
Beckley, Mary Beatrice Campbell *see* Campbell, Mary Beatrice
Beckley, William C. 16
Beckwith, Edward Griffin 113
Beechey, F.W. 136
Benicia (ship) 170
Beretania (residence) 133–134
Berger, Henry 62
Bergstrom, James 73
Bernice Pauahi Bishop Estate 56, 220
Bernice Pauahi Bishop Museum 198, 232
Bingham, Hiram 100, 127, 131, 133, 141, 142, 146, 173, 234
Bird, Isabella Lucy 49, 98, 118, 153
Bishop, Bernice Pauahi, Princess 29, 55–57, *165*, 167, 188, 193, 195, 198, 217, 220, 244
Bishop, Charles Reed 29, 113, 165, 195, 232
Bishop, Keolaokalani Paki 165
Bishop Museum *see* Bernice Pauahi Bishop Museum
Bishop of Oxford 145
Blaisdell, Neil S. 241
Blakesley, Thomas 134
Blonde (ship) 33, 101, 123, 126, 128, 130, 132
Blossom (ship) 136
Bloxam, Andrew 132–133
Boki 59, 122, 123, *133*, 134–135, 140, 158, 215
Bonite (ship) 7, 25–26, 138, 158
Bowen, Alice Spalding 16, 236–237
Brick Palace 33–34, 240
Bright, Abigail Kuaihelani Mapinepine *see* Campbell, Abigail Kuaihelani Mapinepine Bright
British Club 242; *see also* Pacific Club
The Bungalow *see* Hale 'Ākala
Byron, George Anson 7, 33, 128, 234

Campbell, Abbie Margaret 175
Campbell, Abigail (daughter of Campbell, Abigail Kuaihelani Mapinepine Bright) *see* Kawānanakoa, Abigail W., Princess
Campbell, Abigail Kuaihelani Mapinepine Bright 175, 188
Campbell, Alice 80–81
Campbell, Archibald 5, 33, 121–123
Campbell, Ethel Muriel 178
Campbell, James 175–176
Campbell, Mary Beatrice 178
Campbell, Royalist Maddire Laakapu 176
Captain Cook Monument *31*
Carter, George Robert 177, 233
Carter, Henry A.P. 233
Carter, Joseph Oliver 215
Carter, Sybil Augusta Judd (wife of Henry A.P. Carter) 233
Carter, William Giles Harding 185
Cartwright, Alexander Joy 76, 113, 180, 184
Cartwright, Bruce 90, 151
Castle, Ethelinda Shaefer 66
Cathedral Church of St. Andrew 70, 84, 139, 211
Central Grammar School 196–197
Chamberlain, Levi 93, 225
Chamisso, Adelbert von 18, 121
Champion (ship) 62
Chevalier, Nicholas 169
Chiefess Kapi'olani: residence 24
Chiefess Kekela House Site 23–24
Chiefs' Children's School 133
Choris, Louis 7–8, 15, 125
civilization 7, 137

Index

C.K.C Rooke v. Queen's Hospital 156
Cleghorn, Archibald Scott 30, 59, 61–66, 68–72, 74, 76, 82, 111, 118, 170, 175–177, 179, 212; residence at Emma Street, Honolulu 175, **176**, 177–179
Cleghorn, Rose 63
Cleveland, Grover 64
Coan, Titus 109
Colonial Hotel 178–179
Commission on Historic Sites 23, 236–230
Commission on Historical Sites 17
Community Planning, Inc. 30
Coney, John Harvey 109
Coney, Laura Ena 109
Coney, William H. 111
Confederate States of America 29
Conrad, Agnes 16, 17, 38, 238, 240
Conservation Council for Hawaii 16
Conyers, Lawrence B. 187
Cook, James 6, 11, 14, 25, 30–31, 85–86, 90; Cook Sesquicentennial 90
Cooke, Amos Starr 102
Cooke, Charles Montague 182
Cooke, Juliette Montague 102
Cooke, Pat 17
Cooper, J. Fenimore 127
Cooperstown, New York 132
Coote, Walter 99
corrugated iron 9, 32, 49
Council of Hawaiian Civic Clubs 17
Country Residence of Boki and Liliha 134–135
Courtyard King Kamehameha's Kona Beach Hotel 17
Cox, Richard H. 240
Cracroft, Sophia 152
Crowningberg, Eliza 69
Cummins, John A. 180, **188**

Daughters and Sons of Hawaiian Warriors 17
Daughters of Hawai'i 13, 23, 236, 242
Davis, Elizabeth "Betty" *see* Davis, Peke
Davis, Isaac 43, 44, 122, 223–224; residence at Honolulu 122
Davis, Isaac Young (grandson of Isaac Davis) 28
Davis, Kale 229
Davis, Peke 43–45, 223–224; residence at Kapewakua, Lahaina **43**, 44; residence at Kūpeke, Moloka'i 45; residence at Wahiawa, Kaua'i 223–224
Davis, Samuel H. 30
Davis, Sarah *see* Davis, Kale
Del Piano, Barbara Jane 58, 144
Dibble, Sheldon 14
Dillingham, Benjamin Franklin 220

Dillingham, Walter F. 17
Dole, Sanford Ballard 79, 177, 196, 201, 231
Dominis, John Owen 6, 29, 47, 96, 113, 166, 169–170, 186, 207, 217–218; residence at Waialua 217–218
Doubleday, Abner 180
Duke of Edinburgh 168–170
Duke of Wellington 97
Duncan, R.M. 191
Duperrey, Louis Isidore 18

Eleanora (ship) 20, 99
Ellis, William 7, 33, 126–127, 129, 204
Emma, Queen 3, 5, 10, 18, 20, 23–24, 29–30, 42–43, 48–50, 74–77, 96–98, 106–108, 113, 115, 139, 150–152, **153**, 154, **155**, 156–158, 171–172, 175–176, 185–187, 193, 200, 202, 229, 232, 236, 238–239, 241; birth site 150
Emma Square 71, 175
Emmert, Paul 5, 93–94, 100, 103, 116, 159, 162.
Emory, Kenneth P. 17, 24, 238
Ena, J. 180
Eveleth, Ephraim 6, 14, 127

Farrington High School 57
Federal Emergency Relief Administration 87
Finch, W.B. 128, 132, 136
Fort Kamehameha 185
Frame House of Ka'ahumanu, Honolulu 132
Franklin, Jane, Lady 96
Franklin Court, Philadelphia 245
Frear, Walter F. 69–70, 90
Freycinet, Louis de 14, 122, 128
Friends of 'Iolani Palace 241, 245
Friends of Washington Place 245

Galatea (ship) 169
Gear, Albert V. 181
Gideon, Heiromonk 18
Gilman, Gorham Dummer 37, 95, 109, 112, 149, 156, 160–161, 164
Great Mahele 10, 116. 126, 227
Greek Revival 3–6, 92, 94, 101, 151, 154, 156, 164–165
Greenway, Francis J. 131

Ha'alelea, Amoe Ena 111, 177
Ha'alelea, Levi 109–112, 130, 171, 174
Haalelea Lawn 110–111, 114
Ha'alilio, Hana 131, 147
Ha'alilio, Timoteo 111, 127, 130, **131**, 132, 146–147; residence 130–131
Ha'imoeipo 114–116, 168
Hakaleleponi *see* Kalama, Queen
Hale 'Ākala 95, 99, 105, **119**, 120

Hale Ali'i 5, 9, 29, 92, **93**, **94**, 95–96, 98–100, 104, 106–107, 114, 116, 150, 152–153, 244
Hale Keōua *see* Keōua Hale
Hale Lā'au 132
Hale Lama 54–55, **56**, 57, **58**
Hale O Na Alii 17
hale pili 4–7, **8**, 9, 11–12, 19, 21, 24–28, 31–32, 36, 54–56, 61–62, 72–74, 92, 101, 124–125, 128–129, 131–132, 137–138, 147–148, 152, 156, 158–159, 165, 174, 186, 194, 223–229, 243
Hale Piula 9, **40**, 41, 106, 240
Haleakalā 164–167, 168, 244
Halehui 123–124
Halehuki, Honolulu 171
Halehuki, Lahaina *see* Hale Piula
Halekamani 9, 35–37
Halekauwila 109, 148, **149**, 243
Haleopeope 53–54
Haleuluhe 62, 134, 135, **136**, 137–139, 140, 149, 243
Hāli'imaile 102, **103**, **104**, 105
Hall, Edwin Oscar 160
Hamilton House 165, **166**, 167, 244; role in the overthrow 167
Hamohamo 59, 77, 82–84, 87, 90
Hānaiakamalama 3, **5**, 57–58, 76, 162, 185, 232, 238–239, 241, 244
Hanson, Violet 12, 16, 21, 23
Harris, Charles Coffin 76, 92, 103, 105, 135
Hart, J.S. 92
Hawaii State Archives 4–6, 8, 12–13, 15, 17, 19, 20–22, 26–28, 31, 34, 36, 44, 48, 53–61, 65–68, 75, 78–80, 85–87, 89, 93, 99, 102–104, 106, 110, 114, 116–117, 119, 122–123, 125, 128–129, 131, 133, 143, 149, 151, 153, 159, 165–167, 172, 176, 182, 188, 194, 196, 198. 201, 207, 210, 218–221, 230, 234
Hawaii Visitors' Bureau 236
Hawaiian Ballasting Company 191
Hawaiian Folklore Commission 233
Hawaiian Mission Academy 190, 244
Hawaiian Mission Children's Society 233, 240
Hawaiian Relief Society 181
Hawaii's Story by Hawaii's Queen 5, 83, 166, 207, 217
Hawes, Albert George Sidney **210**, 211
Healani Boat House 119, 120, 182, **183**, 184
heiau 15–19, 90, 124, 146, 231, 234–240
Helumoa 55, 56, 77, 245
Hewahewa 21
His Majesty v Mr. Samuel Parker 195
Historic Building Task Force 164, 240–241

Index

Historic Hawaiʻi Foundation 245
Historical Commission 90, 232–235
Historical Marker Program 239–240
Historical Sites Commission 16, 163, 240
Hitchcock, H.R. 191
Hoapili 37–39, 122, 133, 225; residence at Lahaina 38, *39*; residence at Punahou 122–123
Hoapiliwahine 38; residence at Lahaina 38, *39*
Hoihoikea 29, 104, 105, 107
Hōlani *104*, 108–109, **110**, 111–12, 116, 130, 177, 227
Honokaʻupu 99, 100, 101
Honolulu High School 106, 244
Honolulu Historical Center 240
Honolulu House, Kalawao, Molokaʻi 47, **48**, 49–51
Honolulu Rifles 56
Honuakaha 123, 179, **180**, 181–182, 200
Hookuku 14, 123
Hooper, Hana 130
Hopkins, Manly 5, 145
Horschler, Walter 238
Howell, Hugh, Jr. 112
Hui Kaahumanu 178
Huliheʻe 3, **4**, 24, 26, 27, 236
Humehume **223**, 224, 228; residence at Wahiawa, Kauaʻi 223–224
Hunt, Timothy Dwight 25, 35
Hutchinson, Ernest 209
Hutchinson, Ferdinand William 47, 118

Ihikapukalani/Kauluhinano 105, **106**, 107, 108, 152; fire at 108
ʻĪʻī, John Papa 14, 52, 101, 102, 108, 116, 123, 124, 127, 133, 135, 140, 141, 168, 169
ʻili 28, 29, 59, 76, 82, 187, 218
ʻili kupono 29
Inter-Island Steam Navigation Company 241
ʻIolani Barracks 74, 97, 239
ʻIolani Palace 3, **4**, 5, 9, 40, 41, 45, 66, 74, 78, 85, 92, 96–99, 101–103, 105–108, 118–120, 130, 135, 169, 173, 180, 193, 197, 204–205, 209–210, 237–238, 241, 243–245
Isbell, Virginia 24

Jaeger, James F. 69
James Robinson & Co. 126
Jarves, James Jackson 14–15, 101, 130, 149
John Young Residence 18, 19, 20, **21**
Johnson, Hamilton 165
Johnson, Mary 178
Judd, Albert Francis 76, 156, 209
Judd, Charles H. 47, 119, 184
Judd, Gerrit P., 90, 92, 101, 131, 141, 171

Judd, Henry P., 145
Judd, Laura Fish 19, 101, 141, 160
Judd, Lawrence M., 20, 90, 235

Ka Haku o Hawaiʻi 107
Kaʻahumanu, Queen 12–14, 25, 33, 36, 52, **53**, 59, 99, **123**, 124–125, 132–133, 140–146, 219, 223, 225, 228, 234, 244–245; residence at Pohukaina 132–133
Kaʻahumanu II (Kuhina Nui) *see* Kīnaʻu
Kaʻahumanu III (Kuhina Nui), *see* Kekāuluohi
Kaʻahumanu IV (Kuhina Nui), *see* Victoria Kamāmalu
Kaakopua 173–174, 187, 196–197
Kaauwai 126
Kaʻawaloa, Hawaiʻi 24–25, **26**, 30
Kaeo, Asa 41
Kaʻeo, Jane Lahilahi Young *see* Young, Jane Lahilahi
Kaʻeo, Joshua 173, 227, 229
Kaʻeo, Keliʻimaikaʻi 229
Kaʻeo, Peter Young 47, 48, 49, 50, 51, 75, 98, 107, 154, 175, 200, 201; residence on Emma Street 200–201
Kahalaopuna 140
Kahanamoku, Duke 169
Kahanu, Elizabeth 84, **85**, **219**, 220
Kahaumakaawe 143–144
Kaheiheimālie *see* Hoapiliwahine
Kahekili 40, 225
Kahekili, King 33
Kahoalii, Grace Kamaikui Wahineikaili 77
Kahoiwai 140, 144
kahuna 54, 123
Kai, Peggy 20
Kaikioʻewa 34–35, 38, 223–227, 229; residence at Kōloa, Kauaʻi 226–228; residence at Lahaina, Maui 34–35; residence at Waimea, Kauaʻi 224–226
Kailua, Hawaiʻi 16
Kaʻiulani, Princess 1, 30, 58–60, **61**, 62–64, 66, **67**, 68–69, 76, 111
Kaʻiulani Park 71
Kalahoʻolewa, William Pitt Leleiohoku *see* Leleiohoku, William Pitt, II, Prince
Kalaikini 32, 173
Kalaimoku *see* Kalanimoku
Kalākaua, David, King 9, 24, 28, 47, 62, 64, 69, 73–74, 77, 78, 81–83, 86–87, 92, 96, 98–99, 105, 107–108, 115, 118–120, 130, 135, 139, 171–174, 177, 179–181, **182**, 183–185, 187, 193–194, 198, 206, 210, 217, 223, 228, 233, 238, 243
Kalākua *see* Hoapiliwahine
Kalama, Queen 99–100, 107–116, 149, 163, 201, 237
Kalanianaʻole, Jonah Kūhiō, Prince 78, 80–81, 83–84, **85**,

86–87, 90, 177, 181, 198, 200, 219, 220, **230**, 232–233
Kalanimoku 5, 15, 27, 32, 36, 38, 108, 125–127, **128**, 129–130, 133–134, 140, 169, 225, 245; residence at Honolulu 126
Kalaukumuole 32
Kalaupapa, Molokaʻi 44, 47–51, 113, 239
Kalawao, Molokaʻi 47–49, 51, 200
Kaleleonalani *see* Emma, Queen
kalo 52, 76, 216, 218, 227
Kaluaʻaha, Molokaʻi 29
Kaluakau 74
Kaluaokiha, Luaʻehu, Lahaina, Maui 35
Kamaikui *see* Young, Grace Kamaikui
Kamakahonu 5, 9, 13–14, **15**, 16, **17**, 18, 31, 90, 123, 164, 238, 240, 241, 247, 268
Kamakahonu National Historic Landmark 17–18
Kamakau, E.S. 160
Kamakau, Samuel 135, 148
Kamakau, W.P. 55
Kamāmalu, Queen 22–23, 127, 132, 134, 137
Kamanele 130, 149; residence at Honolulu 130
Kamaukoli 59
Kamehameha I 3, 7, 9, 11, **12**, 13–16, 18, 20–21, 31, 33–35, 37–38, 40, 43–44, 47, 52–53, 92, 97, 99, 108–109, 121, **122**, 123–124, 140, 144, 150, 169, 172–173, 199, 219, 222–224, 229, 241, 270; residence at Honolulu 121–122; residence at Kealakekua 11
Kamehameha II 5, 14, 18, 21, **22**, 23–25, 37–38, 94, 109, 123, 126, 127, 130, 132, 134, 137–138, 146, 169, 173, 220, 223, 227; residence 21, 22, **23**; residence at Honolulu 126
Kamehameha III 9, 12, **13**, 23, 24, 29, 31–32, 34–35, 37–40, 54–55, 92–94, 97, 99,-100, 102, 105–108, 111–112, 114, 134–137, 139–140, 148–149, 158, 160, 162–163, 168, 171, 201, 226, 228–229, 232, 237, 240–241; birthplace *see* Lokomaikaʻi, birthplace of Kamehameha III; residence at Helumoa, Waikīkī 54, 55; royal residential complex *see* Mokuʻula
Kamehameha IV 5, 18, 24, 29–30, 37, 44, 47, 92, 94–95, 97, 103, 105–107, 139, 143, 150, 152, 157, 171, 173, 187, 205, 226, 238
Kamehameha V 29, 37, 41, 43–45, 47, 54–56. **57**, 58, 82, 92, 97–98, 102, 104–105, 107, 117, 118, 143, 168–169, 171, 205, 217, 226, 232, 239, 241, 243
Kamehameha House 33, 240
Kamehameha, Lot *see* Kamehameha V

Index

Kamehameha Schools 13, 189
Kamehameha the Great *see* Kamehameha I
Kanahele, George 145
Kanaʻina, Charles 37, 41, 44, 75, 100, 107, 109, 115, 130, 146, 149, 173, 215
kane 19
Kanehoa, James Young 41, 152, 173, 228–229, 249; residence at Kōloa, Kauaʻi 229
Kaniakapūpū 9, 135, 158, *159*, 160, 161, 162, *163*, *164*, 237, 241
Kaʻōanāʻeha 18, 150, 152
Kapālama, Oʻahu 1, 5 29, 57, 113, 187–190, 192–193, 196, 201, 202, 204–207, 210, 213–215, 227, 243–246
Kapapoko 14
Kapena, Iona 172–173; residence 172–173
Kapena, John M. 41, 107, 135
"Kapiolani" (poem) 24
Kapiʻolani, Chiefess 9, 24, *25*, 26, 31
Kapiʻolani, Princess *see* Kawananakoa, Kapiʻolani
Kapiolani, Queen 69, 77–78, *79*, 81–82, 84, 105, 119, 171–172, 179, 181, 198, 200, 206, 244; residence at Kaʻalaʻa, Pauoa, Honolulu 171, *172*
Kapiolani Maternity Home 199–200
Kapoli 116
kapu 9, 12, 13, 14, 16, 124, 145
Kapule, Debora 228–229; residence at Pohoula, Wailua, Puna, Kauaʻi 228–229; residence at Waimea, Kauaʻi 229
Karaimoku *see* Kalanimoku
Kaʻu, Hawaiʻi 24–25, 88
Kauaʻi 3, 9, 10, 24, 26, 35, 37, 38, 47, 54, 64, 69, 73–74, 77, 78, 81–83, 87, 90, 96, 109, 121–122, 137. 172–174, 198, 208, 222–230, 234, 239
Kaʻuaʻumokuokamanele *see* Kamanele
kauhale 7, 9, 11, 121, 129, 136, 139
Kauikeaouli *see* Kamehameha III
Kauluhinano *see* Ihikapukalani/Kauluhinano
Kaumualiʻi 10, 37, 53, 109, 124, 132, 174, 222–224, 227, 228–229, 230; residence at Waimea, Kauaʻi 222–223
Kaumualiʻi, George *see* Humehume
Kaunakakai, Molokaʻi 45–47
Kauukualii 230
Kawaihaʻo Church 3, 68, 100, 102, 111, 130, 136, 145, 173, 176, 179, 194; deed of 173
Kawaihaʻo Female Seminary 83
Kawaihae, HawaiʻI 18–23, 31, 234

Kawaihoolana 141
Kawānanakoa, Abigail W., Princess 176
Kawānanakoa, David, Prince 78, 81, 176, 198, 200, 213, 229, 230
Kawānanakoa, Kapiʻolani 178
Kawapopo 146
Kea, William C. 17
Kealakekua, Kona 11, 14, 20, 31, 137
Kealiʻiahonui 109
Kealohilani, Hamohamo, Waikīkī *83*, 84, 87, 88, 91
Keauhou, Hawaii 9, 12–13, 228
Keaweamahi 34–35, 224–227, 229; residence at Lahaina, Maui 34–35; residence at Waimea, Kauaʻi 224–226
Keʻelikōlani, Princess 1, 4, 9, 26–27, *28*, 29, 31, 55–56, 59, 69, 78, 126, 165, 173–174, 186–187, *188*, 189, 191–198, 201–202, 205, 211, 214, 217, 227, 244–245; residence at Piopio 27–29; residence on Emma Street, Kaakopua, Honolulu 173–175
Keelikolani School 196–197
Keelikolani *v*. James Robinson 126
Kekahuna, Henry E.P. 17, 164
Kekaulike, Princess 81, 171, *198*, 199–200, 229; residence at Hoʻai, Kōloa, Kauaʻi 229–230
Kekāuluohi 37, 73, 100–101, *102*, 139, 152, 158, 160, 173, 223, 226, 228, 244
Kekauʻōnohi 35–37, 104, 108–112, 116, 130
Kekauōnohi 36, 37, 104, 108–109, 111, 112, 116, 130, 171, 173, 227; residence at Lahaina 37–38
Kekela, Chiefess *see* Young, Fanny Kekelaokalani
Kekelaokalani *see* Young, Fanny Kekelaokalani
Kekuaiwa, Moses 226–227
Kekūanāoʻa 7, 28, 41, 44, 59, 82, 92–93, 101–102, *103*, 116, 131, 133, 139–140, 143, 146, 158–160, 168–171, 237
Keliʻiahonui, Aarona 37, 111, 173–174, 227
Keliʻiahonui, Edward Abnel 82, 198, 229, *230*
Keliʻimaikaʻi 18, 150, 229
Kendrick, John 20
Kenny, W.J. 211–212
Keohokālole, Ane 82, 87
Keomailani, Stella 154, 172
Keōpūolani, Queen 12–14, 33, 35–37, 114; residence at Kaluaokiha, Luaʻehu, Lahaina 35, *36*
Keōua 20
Keōua (wife of Kuakini) 19
Keōua Hale 9, 173, 186, 193, *194*, 195, *196*, 197–198, 204, 243–244
Kiʻilae 23–24

Kilauea (crater) 28, 73
Kilauea (residence) 140
Kilauea (ship) 50
Kilohana Art League 66
Kīnaʻu, John William Pitt (son of Keʻelikōlani and William Pitt Leleiohoku) 126, 174
Kīnaʻu, Queen 13, 25, 99, 102
Kīnaʻu Hale 99, *100*
King of Denmark 94
King of Prussia 137–138
King's Wharf 126
Kinimaka 182
Knight of the Order of Kamehameha I 169
Knighton, William 49
Kohala, Hawaiʻi 18, 21, 23, 199
Komoawaa 143
Kōnia 41, 165; residence at Pakala, Lahaina 41–42
konohiki 59, 226
Korean Boarding School for Boys 245
Korean National Association Headquarters Site 245–246
Kotzebue, Otto von 11, 14, *15*, 124, 133
Kuaihelani 108, 112–113, *114*, 116, 201
Kuakini 4, 10, 26–27, 32, 130, 149; residence 26–27
Kualalua 14
Kuhina Nui 30, 99, 101–103, 139–140, 147–148, 152, 158, 160, 169, 223, 226, 230
Kuloloi 124
Kūnuiākea, Albert, Prince 1, 20, 78, 112, *201*, 202–203; residence at Kapālama 201–202, *203*, 204
"Kuʻu Pua I Paoakalani – My flower at Paoakalani" (song) 88, *89*
Kuykendall, Ralph S. 202, 231, 233, 235, 244–245

Laʻanui, Gideon 130, 218–221; residence at Waialua, Oʻahu 218–221
Lahaina, Maui 3, 9, 29, 32–38, 40–44, 54, 92, 128, 135, 158, 232, 240
Lahaina Palace 33
Lahaina Restoration Project 38, 240
Lahainaluna School 239
Lalani Hawaiian Village *87*
Leilehua Ranch 119, 184–185
Lele, Maui 32, 40
Leleiohoku, William Pitt, I 126, 131, 152
Leleiohoku, William Pitt, II, Prince 108, 170, 174–175
Lewers and Cooke 181, 242
Lewis, E.H. 71
Liholiho *see* Kamehameha II
Likelike (wife of Kalanimoku) 126
Likelike, Miriam, Princess 9, 26,

30–31, 58, *59*, 61–64, 66, 73, 130, 179, 198, 241–242
Liliha 122, *133*, 134–135
Lilikalani, Edward K. 81, 179
Liliʻuokalani, Queen 1, 3, *5*, 6, 13, 26, 52, 59, 62, 64, 69, 73, 77, 82–84, 86–88, 90–91, 98, 112–113, 120, 139, 164, 165–167, 169–170, 174, 177, 190–191, 196, 199, 204–206, *207*, 208–211, 213–216, 217–218, 220, 220, 232, 242, 245, 246; residence at Kahala 217; residence at Hamohamo, Waikīkī 82–91; residence at Mānoa 215–217
Liliʻuokalani Church 220
Lilly Bird (ship) 121
Lindley, Dorothy 240
Lisiansky, Urey 11
Lokomaikaʻi, Birthplace of Kamehameha III 12–13
Lono 18
Louis Philippe, King of the French 94
Luahine, Iolani 17
Lunalilo, William Charles, King 3, 44, 47, 62, 74, *75*, 76, 92, 98, 100–102, 107, 114–115, 149, 215, 217, 239
Lunalilo Mausoleum 3
Lydgate, John Mortimer 28

Macfarlane, Alice Kamokila (wife of Walter Macfarlane) *see* Campbell, Alice Kamokila
Macfarlane, Henry 170
Macfarlane, Walter 177
Malama House 45, *46*
Malamanui 184–185
Malden, C.R. 125, 130, 133
Malo, David 53, 173
Manoa Japanese Language 216
Manoa Uplands 146, 244
Mansfield, G. Allen 118
Margaret (ship) 7
Marin, Francisco de Paula 149
Marine Residence, Kaluakau, Waikīkī 74–76, *77*, 186
Marine Residence of Kailua *see* Huliheʻe
Mason, George 239
Massee, E.K. 111
Mathison, Gilbert Farquhar 124, 128
Mauna ʻAla *see* Royal Mausoleum
Mauna Kamala 29, 177, 187, 189–192, 202, 227, 244, 246
Mauna Kea 19
Mauna Loa 19
Mayor's Historic Building Task Force 184, 240
McChesney, J.M. 71
McCrae, James 33
Mercury (ship) 11
Meyen, Franz Julius Ferdinand 134, 137–138
Mililani *116*, 117

Mission Houses Historic Site and Archives 244
Moana Hotel 73, 220
Moanalua Gardens Foundation 245
Moehonua, William L. 98, 175
Mokuʻula 38–40
Montano, Mary Jane Fayerweather 16, 144
Montreal (ship) 131
Morgan, Edward 162
Morgan, James F. 151, 182
Morris, Ray 33–34, 74
Mortimer, George 11, 158
Muʻolaulani 62, 80, 177, 191, 196, 204–213, *214*, 215, 246; site of meetings to discuss a proposed new constitution 209–210; site of the fiftieth birthday of Liliʻuokalani 207; site of the planning for the Wilcox Rebellion of 1889 184

Naʻea, George 18, 171
Nahaolelua, Paul 37, *44*, 75, 113; residence 44
Nāhiʻenaʻena, Princess 12, 35, *36*, 37, 128, 148
Naihe 24, 100
Nakamakaweuweu 171
Nakuina, Emma Kaili Metcalf Beckley *see* Beckley, Emma Kaili Metcalf
Nāmāhana, Queen 100, 124, 133, *218*; residence 124
Namakeha, Benjamin 41
Namakeha, Bennet 171–173, 227
Namauu, Nueku 116, 173, 227
Napela, Kiti Richardson 48–49
National Historic Landmark 18, 241
National Park Service 18, 24, 51
National Register of Historic Places 13, 40, 164, 241, 244
National Trust for Historic Preservation 17
Nāwahī, Joseph 29, 177, *189*, 190–191, 243, 246
Neilson, Henry A. 29
Neva (ship) 11
Nicholson, Henry Whalley 193
"Nohea I Muʻolaulani" (song) 205–206
Norton, Tillie 17
Norwood, William 17
Nye, Lydia Rider 152, 159

Oahu College *see* Punahou School
Ophelia (ship) 150
Order of Kamehameha 20, 230
Osborne, Joan 17, 237–238, 247

Pa Pelekane 139
Pacific Club 111–112, 176, 179, 242
Pākākā 124–126
Pakala, Lahaina, Maui 41–42
Pākī, Abner 37, 41, 42, 75, 103, 133, 164–165, 173; residence at Pakala, Lahaina 41–42
Palace of Kalanimoku 126–130
Pālama Chinese School 190–191
Paoakalani, Hamohamo, Waikīkī 62, 87–88, *89*
Papa 14, 123
Papakanene 114, *168*, 169–170
Paris, John D. 25–26
Parke, William Cooper 113, 171
Parke Chapel 112
Parker, Abigail K. *see* Campbell, Abigail Kuaihelani Mapinepine Bright
Parker, Samuel 142, 176–177, 180, *188*, 195
Payne, R. 73
Pele 24, 26
Pelekane 133, 135–136, 138–139
Peterson, Charles E. 240
Phillips, Stephen 98
Physicienne (ship) 128, 248
Pihanakalani 107–108, 114, 116, 168
Piʻikoi, David 171–172, 220
Pinkham, Lucius E. 38, 71
Piopio, Hilo, Hawaiʻi 27–29, 31
Plan of Honolulu 102, *104*, 105
Poepoe, Joseph 129
Pohukaina 92, 99, 101–102, 107–108, 127, 130, 133
Pond, Percy M. 72, 82
Potomoc (ship) 138
Pratt, Elizabeth K. 150
Pratt, James W. 72
Princess Louise (ship) 137
Proposed Palace of 1871 118–119
Puaʻaliʻiliʻi 53
Pualeilani 77, *78*, 79, *80*, 81–82
Pualeilani II 84, *85*, *86*, 87
Pukaʻōmaʻomaʻo 140, *141*, 142, *143*, 144, *145*, 146, 235, 244
Pukui, Mary Kawena 54, 60, 108, 144
Punahou 122, 123
Punahou Preparatory School 234
Punahou School 123
Puʻuhonua O Hōnaunau 24, 205, 244
Puʻukohola 234
Puʻuloa, Queen Emma 185–187; birth site of 150–151; residence at ʻEwa 185–187
Puuonioni 171

Queen Emma Hall *see* Rooke House
Queen Emma Summer Palace *see* Hānaiakamalama
Queen's Medical Center 77
Quinn, William F. 238–239
Quixote (ship) 226

Republicans 192
Restoration Day 159–160, 163
Reynolds, John N. 138, 146, 148
Richards, William 35, 49
Rives, Jean Baptiste 220

Index

Rives, Owana 219
Robertson, Archibald Scott Pauli 69, 71
Robertson, Elsie Mae 68
Robertson, James William 63, 180
Robinson, James 126, 217
Rodby, Carita 184
Rooke, Charles Keane Creswell 157
Rooke, Grace Kamaikui *see* Young, Grace Kamaikui
Rooke, Thomas Charles Byde 20, 112–113, 134, 150–152, **153**, 154, 156; residence on Union Street 150, **151**
Rooke House 10, 20, 151–158, 185–186
Rooke *v.* Queen's Hospital 156–157
Rose, William 30
Rowe, Thomas 118
Royal Hawaiian Band 62, 66, 208, 212
Royal Hawaiian Hotel 53, **54**, 56
Royal Mausoleum 3, 71, 96, 133, 194, 228, 239
Royal Residences of Niʻihau 230
Rurik (ship) 14, 18, 121, 125
Ruth, Princess *see* Keʻelikōlani, Princess

St. Alexander Palace 96
St. Andrew's Cathedral *see* Cathedral Church of St. Andrew
St. Andrew's Priory 76, 138–139, 153, 186
St. Peter's Episcopal Church 138–139, 197
Salvation Army 72–74, 216–217
Savage, Beatrice 39, 239
Schofield, John McAllister 184
Schofield Barracks 185
Shingle, Ethel Muriel *see* Campbell, Ethel Muriel
Shingle, Robert W. 177–178
Silva, Louise Akeo 17
Smith, William Owen 120, 181
South Kona, Hawaiʻi 24–26, 30
Spalding, Albert Goodwill 180
Spencer, Charles Nicholas 117–118

State Historic Preservation Division 245
Sterling, Robert 98
Stevenson, Robert Louis 50, 63, 72–73, **182**, 184, 242
Stewart, Charles S. 5, 7, 25, 35, 37, 124–125, 127, 128, 132–134, 136–140, 145–146, 205, 223
Stoddard, Charles Warren 162
Stone House 112, 114, 235
Strauch, Fanny 192
Strauch, Paul Ernst Richard 73, 192–193, 202
Summer Residence of Princess Likelike 30

Taylor, Albert Pierce 16, 20, 26, 40, 90, 88, 102, 105–106, 108–109, 143, 169, 178, 221, 234
Taylor, Clarice B. 238
Taylor, Emma Ahuena Davison 233
Tennyson, Alfred Lord 24
Thomas, Richard Darton, Rear Admiral 98, 105, 131, 160, 162, 164
Thurston, Lorrin A. 90, 110, 231–232
"To Kaiulani" (poem) 63
Turnbull, John 6, 7, 14, 222
Twain, Mark 21, 168
Twombly, Alexander Stevenson 142

Uluhaimālama 88, 90
uluhe 135–136
ʻUlulani 198, **199**, 200; also known as Kēhaulani 199
Ulumāheihei *see* Hoapili
Uluniu 77–78, 81–82, 245
Union Feed Company 170
University Club 111, 179
Uranie (ship) 14, 128, 248

Vancouver, George 7, 14
Venus (ship) 149
Victoria, Queen 95, 97, 155, 206–207, 210–213
Victoria Kamāmalu, Princess 28, 92, 99, 101–102, **103**, 114, 143, 168–169
Vincennes (ship) 132, 140
Vincent, Frank 45
Vos, Hubert 110–111

Wahiawa, Kauaʻi 223–224
Wahiawā, Oʻahu 184
Waiakea 29
Waikīkī 9, 33, 52–87, 89, 91, 96, 102, 103, 107, 109, 130, 143, 149, 176, 182, 185–187, 190, 202, 215, 220, 230, 245
Waikiki Townhouse 74
Waiola Cemetery 3, 28, 239
Waioli Mission 239
Waioli Tea Room 74, 145
Warriner, Francis 100, 142
Washington (ship) 20
Washington Place 3, **6**, 59, 84, 88, 112–114, 166, 204, 207, 209, 216, 232, 239, 243, 245
Webster, A.S. 118
Widemann, Emma 170
Widemann, H.A. 170
Wilcox, Elsie 236
Wilcox, Robert 80, 116, 120, 180–182, 184, 190, 207, 209, 213, 245
Wilcox Revolution of 1889 120, 181–182
Wilder, James "Kimo" A. 90
Wilder, Samuel Gardner 169, 184
Wilhemina & Maria (ship) 224
Wilkes, Charles 97, 101
Wilson, Eveline Townsend 88
Wilson, Jennie K. 88, 90
Windsor Castle 7
Withington, Antoinette 185
Wodehouse, James Hay 30, 62, 64, 96, 97, 154, 169
Wolters, W. 151
Woods, James Frank 85
Wyllie, Robert Crichton 29, 30, 143, 152

Ye Liberty Theatre 158
Young, Alexander 167
Young, Fanny Kekelaokalani 9, 18, **23**, 42, 43, 112, 113, 151, 154, 229; residence at Pakala, Lahaina, Maui **42**, 43
Young, Grace Kamaikui 20, 112, 150, **153**
Young, Jane Lahilahi 8, 108, 112, 116, 122, 126, 201, 229
Young, John 9, 18, **19**, 20, 21, 42, 152, 157; will of 151
Young, John II *see* Ana, Keoni
Young Men's Christian Association 156